Reading and Writing for Success Senior

JANICE ADAMS   CATHY COSTELLO   STEVE NAYLOR

 Harcourt
Canada

Harcourt Canada

Toronto Orlando San Diego London Sydney

Canadian Cataloguing in Publication Data

Adams, Janice Lynn Oberg, 1948 –
Reading and writing for success senior
For use in grades 11 & 12.
Includes Index.

ISBN 0-7747-1490-5

1. English language — Rhetoric.   2. readers (Secondary).   I. Naylor, Stephen.   II. Costello, Cathy.   III. Title.

PE1408.A34   2001   808'.0427   C00-932954-4

AUTHORS

Janice Adams teaches in St. John's, Newfoundland. Although she began her career teaching elementary language arts and science, she has spent the last decade teaching English and Science in grades 7–12. She has served on a number of provincial and school board curriculum committees. Janice has in-serviced teachers and presented workshops on fostering interpretive skills with poetry.

Cathy Costello is the Curriculum Consultant for literacy issues for York Region District School Board in Ontario. She has developed numerous resources at the elementary and secondary levels to support teachers in developing the reading and writing skills of their students. Cathy is an active member of the English Language Arts Network of Ontario and of the Ontario Secondary School Teachers Federation. She is a frequent presenter at conferences.

Steve Naylor teaches secondary English in Salmon Arm, British Columbia. He is an executive member of the British Columbia Teachers of English Language Arts and has been President of that organization. Steve is a frequent presenter at conferences and workshops in British Columbia and other provinces.

REVIEWERS

Nancy Browne
English Program Facilitator
Pinetree Secondary School
Coquitlam, British Columbia

Mary Lou Smitheram
Curriculum Consultant and
Special Assignment Teacher
Upper Canada District School Board
Prescott, Ontario

Tom St. Amand
English Teacher
St. Christopher Secondary School
Sarnia, Ontario

Noeline Laccetti
English Teacher
St. Martin Secondary School
Mississauga, Ontario

Mary Dannigan
English Teacher
Austin O'Brien High School
Edmonton, Alberta

Bryan J. Smith
English Teacher
College Avenue Secondary School
Woodstock, Ontario

Bob Bright
Program/Team Leader
Communications
George S. Henry Academy
Don Mills, Ontario

Sheila Bacon
English Teacher
Colonel Bray High School
Charlottetown, Prince Edward
Island

Project Manager: Deborah Davidson
Lead Writer and Developmental Editor: Heather McWhinney
Writer and Developmental Editor: Donna Flynn Porter
Contributing Editors: Joanne Buckley, Joanne Sanche
Editor: Brett Savory
Production Editor: Laurie Thomas
Copy Editor: James Leahy

Production Coordinator: Jon Pressick
Permissions Coordinator: Mary Rose MacLachlan
Permissions Editor: Cindy Howard
Cover and Interior Design: Renata Chubb, Mighty Design Inc.
Page Composition: Carolyn Hutchings Sebestyen
Cover Illustration: Lyse-Anne Roy
Printing and Binding: Transcontinental Printing Inc.

∞ This book was printed in Canada on acid-free paper.

1 2 3 4 5   05 04 03 02 01

Table of Contents

249 Section Four: Power Tools

A Note About the Icons

You will notice the following icons in the margin throughout the book:

 identifies activities that emphasize critical reading

 identifies activities that emphasize writing

 suggests methods for generating ideas

 reminds you of special editing or proofreading requirements

 reminds you to consider your audience and purpose when you write

 identifies activities that emphasize research and independent study

 highlights opportunities for partner/group collaboration

 identifies a useful tip for when you are working on a computer

Dear Student,

Welcome to *Reading and Writing for Success Senior*.

This book can help you strengthen your essential reading and writing skills at the senior high school level. In this tutorial-based approach to numerous genres, clear explanations and examples demonstrate relationships among forms, audience, and purpose. The Power Tools section will support your development by providing advanced reading strategies, senior writing techniques, and oral and visual communication skills across many disciplines. Within this cross-curricular framework, *Reading and Writing for Success Senior* supports the development of your literacy skills as it opens up opportunities in your personal life, in school, and in your postsecondary educational or career goals.

Using This Book

Reading and Writing for Success Senior is divided into four sections:

- Narrating and Describing
- Explaining and Reporting
- Persuading
- Power Tools

The first three sections of the text contain readings and tutorials that focus on reading and creating specific types of writing. The final section contains a reference guide with specific and detailed strategies for reading, writing, listening, speaking, and analyzing and interpreting media works.

Readings

This book contains a wide variety of reading selections from different time periods and from different cultures. The readings are placed in chapters and sections that illustrate specific forms of writing:

- The readings in Narrating and Describing explore expressive writing in the form of fiction, poems, personal essays, and memoirs.

- The readings in Explaining and Reporting explore writing for informational purposes in the form of essays, procedures, graphics, summaries, and reports.

- The readings in Persuading explore writing intended to persuade, such as editorials, essays, advertisements, and letters.

Each chapter begins with a brief introduction to the form of writing, which is followed by the reading itself. You will notice that the readings have notes written in the margins. Notice how your own responses to the readings compare with the marginal notes.

Tutorials

Following the reading selections are two tutorials for you to work through, either with a partner, in a group, or on your own. The tutorials have three objectives:

- to develop your reading skills by showing you strategies for analyzing and interpreting a range of literary, informational, persuasive, and media texts

- to hone your writing skills by writing letters, explanations, essays, stories, dialogues, reports, and by creating media works

- to develop your speaking and listening skills by working in groups, with partners, and independently

Most tutorials have a blend of activities that include listening, reading, writing, and speaking.

As you complete the tutorials, consult the checklist that appears on the last page of each tutorial to make sure you have understood the concept.

Power Tools

As you work on the tutorials, consult the Power Tools in the final section of the book. These tools provide a handy reference guide to reading, writing, listening, and speaking. The Power Tools include

- Reading Power Tools
- Writing Power Tools
- Oral Communication Power Tools
- Media Power Tools

Further Explorations

Additional reading selections are included at the end of the first three sections of the book. These are followed by activities that encourage you to make thematic links and connections among the selections from the various sections of the book.

Reading Strategies

Below are some strategies you can use as you read the selections in this book.

Before you read the selection

- Read the introduction to the genre that precedes the reading.

- Predict what the selection is about based on the title, the author's name, and its format.
- Read any headings, and examine any graphics, captions, and labels.
- Recall what you already know about the subject.

When you first read the selection

- Read the selection through once.
- Just enjoy what you are reading, without worrying about the meaning of unfamiliar words.

When you reread the selection

- Read the section aloud, either to yourself or to others.
- Take notes, and create diagrams, charts, or webs to help you organize the information.
- Use strategies to decipher the meaning of unfamiliar words. (Throughout this book, you will develop reading strategies.)
- Keep a Reader Response Journal.
- Read the notes in the margin, and compare your responses to the selection with the responses of the students who wrote the margin notes.

After you read the selection

- Think about and reflect on your reading, and write your reflections, your analysis, and your interpretation in your journal.
- Ask questions, and discuss your response and your interpretation with a partner or in a group.
- Complete the tutorials that follow the readings, using the final section of the book—Power Tools—as a reference.

SECTION 1: NARRATING AND DESCRIBING

Narration is, quite simply, the telling of a story. Storytellers use description to paint vivid and evocative word pictures that help their narratives come alive for their readers. We read and listen to stories so that we may learn about the lives of others, enter new worlds, and gain insight into what it means to be human.

This section of the book explores narration in many of its forms. Some of these forms—such as short stories and novels—are fictional, and some—such as biographies and personal essays—are based on real experiences. Whatever form these narratives take, all are examples of expressive writing. The writers in this section seek to entertain, sensitize, or move their readers through the expression of their views about life as well as their deepest feelings.

We all respond to literature differently. A story that profoundly moves one reader may make little impression on another. We also respond to literature differently at different times. A story that makes us laugh one day may leave us puzzled the next time we read it. How you respond to literature depends on the details of the story, your own life experiences, and how you are feeling.

This unit offers strategies to help you enjoy, appreciate, and interpret narrative literature, and the tutorials provide you with opportunities to tell your own stories.

Chapter 1: The Descriptive Essay

What Is Description?

Description provides a verbal picture of a person, animal, event, object, process, place, or experience. We use descriptive language every day: you might describe to a friend an intriguing person you met at a party, a city you just visited, or the flavour of a new ice cream you have just tried. Descriptive language is used by different writers for different purposes. Writers of technical reports, summaries, and instructions use description to explain or re-create precise events, scenes, objects, or procedures. Writers of persuasive essays, editorials, and advertising use description to convince their readers to change their minds about something, to do something, or to buy something. Writers of fiction, poetry, drama, and essays use description to help their readers imagine ideas more vividly and feel emotions more intensely. A descriptive essay is a short, non-fiction piece of prose that uses sensory images to create a dominant impression in the mind of the reader.

Elements of Description

A good descriptive passage conveys a sense of something seen, heard, touched, tasted, or felt. Instead of telling us what to think or feel, it communicates an impression through vivid and evocative images. A story without description is like a pencil sketch without detail and colour; the basic outline is there, but we need details in order to engage our imagination. Consider the following examples. In the first example, we are told what to think; in the second, we use details the writer provides to create a mental image of Bob.

> Bob sat down in the chair opposite the interviewer. He was nervous.

> Bob's hands were shaking as he lowered himself into the chair opposite the interviewer, a serious, dark-haired woman of about 35. He fidgeted with his tie, and cleared his throat.

Sensory Images

Evocative descriptive passages use sensory images that appeal to one or more of our senses of sight, hearing, smell, taste, and touch, making it possible for us to imagine what a writer is describing. Consider the two sentences below. The first uses sensory details; the second uses no sensory details.

> A warm wind filtered through the prairie like gentle fingers through soft hair.

> A wind blew on the prairie.

To form a mental image, you may wish to use specific sensory details that convey the appearance, texture, weight, volume, or other quality of the thing or experience being described. The word *wind* by itself conveys very little. However, the phrase "a warm wind filtered through the prairie like gentle fingers through soft hair" gives the reader a vivid picture of the wind.

Writers use adjectives, nouns, and action verbs to create their sensory images. The first example uses the adjective *warm* to describe the wind and the action verb *filtered* to describe how the wind blew across the prairie. The second example is weak because it lacks adjectives and a strong action verb.

Dominant Impression

A dominant impression is the overall feeling created by a description. Each sensory detail forms part of a picture that becomes clear when you finish the passage. A description of a place might leave you with a dominant impression of elegance or dreariness or clutter. A description of a person might leave you with a dominant impression of someone shy or outgoing or kind.

Longer essays may leave you with more than one dominant impression. A first paragraph, for example, may create an impression of happiness, and a final paragraph may leave you with an impression of sadness or bitterness.

How to Read a Descriptive Essay

Here are some strategies you can use to get the most from reading a descriptive essay:

- Think about the essay before you read it. Look at the title. What do you think the essay might be about? If you know anything about the author, how might this affect your reading of the essay?

- Read the first paragraph. What images did you form in your mind? Did they give you a dominant impression or an overall feeling?

- Read the essay in its entirety. Did the essay leave you with a different dominant impression than the one you felt in the first paragraph?

- Read the essay aloud, or ask a partner to read it aloud. As you listen to the words, what images come to mind? What tastes, sounds, feelings, and smells can you imagine?

- What are the most powerful sensory passages, phrases, and words in the essay? Why are they powerful? Are there similar images that recur?

- Start a Reader Response Journal to record your impressions and feelings as you read. See Writing Power Tools for more details.

Refer to these strategies as you read "The Skier," the descriptive essay on page 6. "The Skier" won a national essay contest the year its author, Nancy Dorey, was in her first year of college. Dorey says that once she starts writing, she has difficulty stopping, but she finds that she needs to write about four drafts before she is satisfied with her work.

The Skier

Nancy Dorey

1 Why use the word fetal *with* warmth?

Under the fetal warmth of a heavy quilt, muscles stretch and groan, sore from yesterday's turns and spills. *1* The room is dark; outside it's snowing. Sweaty ski clothes are waiting to be put on again. An early morning breakfast is eaten in haste. Stiff boots must once again encase sore feet before you can venture out into the astounding silence of falling snow. You wade through it, shin deep, boots crunching, skis on shoulder; the whole world is white.

The lift is silent and snow covered. You are early. And so, with cold feet and impatience, you share the falling snow with a few others, all waiting while stomping their feet to keep warm.

The lift operator arrives and is soon sweeping snow off the lift with an over-worked broom. White fluff scatters in clouds to reveal dark, greasy metal. A cough, a hum, gears clank, and the chairs lurch into motion, beginning their daily, repetitive journey. The operator nods and you slide *2* into place; the chair comes and you glide upward into the still descending snow.

2 Slide and glide—*these words give you the sense of smooth motion.*

3 The colours here are so vivid.

The silent spruce are black against the sombre sky. Suddenly, there's a hint of blue *3* and the falling snow is thinner now. You watch as a single crystal fairy dances down from the sky; another taps you on the nose.

The sky is blue now, the distant peaks etched silver against it. Three more towers and you are in the sun. The ramp arrives and your skis cut through the ridges as you slide off the chair, down into two feet of sparkling virgin snow. You struggle through the drift, then begin working your skis through the wind-packed snow toward the mountain's lip. Looking down, you see the quick, easy runs below, and above, the more remote slopes still lost in the tattered patch of a cloud that remains in the lee of the mountain. You start creeping upward. The track is long gone; you must guess a line and begin the long journey to the top.

4 What a struggle!

Morning creaks, groans, and grunts abound. The sky is a dazzling blue; the snow sparkles. You go slowly, picking up one ski at a time, *4* stomping down a place for it, then shifting upward one step. Progress is slow, and in places it seems nonexistent.

Struggling still; the lower slopes are distant now; the top still hides. Sweat, sunglare, and aching muscles—what a way to start the day—but on you go, *5* thrashing upward.

The top draws near—edging slowly, so slowly, closer. Sweat has collected around your waist; clothing half on, half off, goggles up one minute and down the next, eyes squinting into the glare and distance. The final few feet take forever: finally you collapse, panting, exhausted, in the snow.

On the ridge the wind is cutting and stray snow sandpapers *6* your face. Beneath your feet the mountain drops away. Amid the silver minarets of the Canadian Rockies you whisper a chant and contemplate your first turn: that first soft sifting of snow, mind, and body. On the very edge you hesitate, lost in the mountains, snow, and sky. Finally goggles come down; bindings are checked. No words are spoken.

Softly you are away. You turn gently, slowly, then turn again. Turns, more turns, each one like a waltz. *7* You watch the slow arc of arm and pole, feel the flex, turn, and twist of muscles and tendons as you come down the mountain. Your skis are free, arcing around and down into the snow again, creating a fine wave that washes up and over you.

One final steep pitch and you land in an explosion of snow. *8* This time the snow is very deep and you are seconds emerging from it. The surface of the snow is fluid. Whiteness surrounds you again—where is up? Where is the mountaintop? Where is down? Where are you going? Will you survive?

Down and down, through the last few remaining turns to the bottom. The last turn, you carve it wide and slow, coming around to look back up the mountain.

Soon others arrive and walk across the flat ground and into the crowd. There in the middle of the mechanical madness of a bigtime ski resort you stop, skis on your shoulder, and lose yourself in the wonder of skiing.

5   *I am amazed that you could keep going.*

6   *Sandpapers—an effective verb to describe how your face would feel.*

7   *Softly, gently, waltz—the words signal a change in tone— the struggle is over!*

8   *How can snow explode?*

Tutorial 1: Revising a Descriptive Passage

Learning Expectations

You will learn

- to identify sensory images and vague, overused words
- to revise a passage that lacks sensory images and uses vague words

Understanding the Task

All good writers paint vivid pictures with words that enable their readers to imagine what they are describing. In this tutorial, using examples from "The Skier," you will explore how writers use sensory language to create a dominant impression. Then you will revise a passage that lacks sensory images and discuss your revision with a partner. Finally, you will create an action plan for improving your descriptive writing.

Getting Ready

Identifying Sensory Images

Reread the first paragraph of "The Skier." What pictures form in your mind? Make a chart like the one below. In the left-hand column make a list of specific sensory images you found in the paragraph. Then indicate to

which of your senses the images appeal. The first example is done for you.

Creating an Image Web

On a piece of paper or in your journal draw a diagram like the one below.

In each of the circles, write down the most powerful images from "The Skier." Then, in the centre circle, write the dominant impression you formed of the essay.

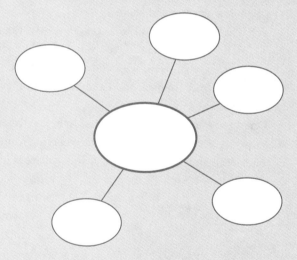

Revising Vague Words

Some words have become so overused that they create only a vague, imprecise impression. Following is a list of some of these words:

IMAGE	APPEALS TO SIGHT	APPEALS TO HEARING	APPEALS TO SMELL	APPEALS TO TOUCH	APPEALS TO TASTE
Fetal Warmth	✔			✔	

- good, fine, OK
- fun
- nice
- cute
- normal, typical, mediocre
- interesting
- important
- beautiful

Good writers avoid using words from the list above because these words do not convey enough details to their readers. With a partner, make a list of five other words that are overused. If none come to mind immediately, try recalling recent conversations you have had with friends or family. Are there words that you find yourself using frequently that, perhaps, could be considered tired and overused?

Revising a Descriptive Passage

The following passage demonstrates the kind of bland, imageless writing that can result from using vague and overused words:

Yesterday was a typical day on the ski slopes. The weather was nice, and the snow was beautiful. The skiing was mediocre, but I met an interesting person on the chairlift. We had fun.

Notice that all the details in the passage are vague. The writer has failed to convey any sensory detail that would enable us to re-create her experience on the ski slopes. Nor has she given us an overall impression of her day. The reader is left with questions like these:

- What exactly was the weather like?
- What is mediocre skiing?
- Was the person the writer met male or female? What does he or she look like?
- What made the person interesting?
- What is the writer's idea of fun?

Rewrite the previous passage. Replace the tired, imageless words with vivid, meaningful words that allow your readers to imagine your experience. Keep a dominant impression in mind as you rewrite the paragraph. Read pages 304 to 306 in Writing Power Tools on revising your work with a partner. Also refer to the questions in the checklist below. Exchange passages with a partner. Read both passages, first silently, and then aloud, in the presence of your partner. Then listen while your partner reads both passages. What dominant impression does your partner's passage convey? Discuss ways in which both passages could be improved, remembering to look closely at the verbs, adjectives, and adverbs. Discuss the images in your passages, and select those that you both agree are the most powerful. Then revise your passage again based on your partner's feedback. Edit and proofread your work for correctness.

Checklist: Revising a Descriptive Passage

- ○ Did I think of a dominant impression?
- ○ Did I include sensory details that appeal to at least three of the five senses?
- ○ Did I include sufficient detail so that my readers will be able to create word pictures?
- ○ Did I avoid tired, overused words?
- ○ Did I use precise action verbs and specific adjectives and adverbs?
- ○ Did I edit and proofread my work?

Tutorial 2: Writing a Descriptive Paragraph About a Place

Learning Expectations

You will learn
- the elements of a good descriptive paragraph
- to compose a well-structured paragraph

Understanding the Task

As you probably already know, a paragraph is a series of related sentences that develops one main idea. A good paragraph should have the following:

- a stated or implied topic sentence that tells the reader what the paragraph is about

- a unified structure that focuses on one main idea

- transition words that make the paragraph flow

- supporting details presented in an order that makes sense to the reader

- a concluding sentence that makes it clear that the paragraph is finished or that provides a link to the next paragraph

In this tutorial, you will write a descriptive paragraph about a place that demonstrates the above elements and that contains strong sensory images.

Getting Ready

Finding Something to Write About
If you are having difficulty finding a place to write about or finding anything to say about your topic, try one of the following methods:

- **Make a list of places that you know.** These could be rooms in your home, your workplace, or the school. Or they might be a park, a beach, a hilltop with a view, a lake, a barn, a restaurant, a coffee shop, a store, and so on.

- **Draw a word association web.** In the centre of a blank piece of paper write a word related to one of the places on your list. Around the word in the centre, jot down the first things that come to your mind. Then make a list of potential topics and subtopics. Suppose you select your neighbourhood coffee shop. Your word association web might look like the one below.

For more information on word association webs and other brainstorming techniques, see Writing Power Tools, pages 277 to 279.

Thinking of a Dominant Impression

Once you have decided on a topic for your descriptive paragraph, you need to think of the dominant impression you want to make. Use your word association web to choose a dominant impression you want to convey to your readers. For example, if you have chosen your neighbourhood coffee shop as your topic, the dominant impression could be "warmth" or "comfort."

Writing a Topic Sentence

A topic sentence identifies the main idea of a paragraph. The other sentences in a paragraph typically describe, explain, or support the topic sentence by providing specific details and examples. Read the following paragraph from "The Skier," and see if you can identify the topic sentence:

One final steep pitch and you land in an explosion of snow. This time the snow is very deep and you are seconds emerging from it. The surface of the snow is fluid. Whiteness surrounds you again—where is up? Where is the mountaintop? Where is down? Where are you going? Will you survive?

The topic sentence occurs at the beginning of the paragraph: "One final steep pitch and you land in an explosion of snow." Notice that this is the most general sentence in the paragraph and that all the other sentences describe the snow and the experience of landing in the drift. Now see if you can identify the topic sentence in another paragraph from "The Skier":

Morning creaks, groans and grunts abound. The sky is a dazzling blue; the snow sparkles. You go slowly, picking up one ski at a time, stomping down a place for it, then shifting upward one step. Progress is slow, and in places it seems nonexistent.

The topic sentence is the last, most general sentence of the paragraph; the other sentences build up to it.

Some paragraphs in descriptive and narrative essays contain no stated topic sentence; their main idea is implied. Successful descriptions and narrations often depend on an element of intrigue or surprise; to state the point of the paragraph overtly could, in some cases, ruin the whole effect of the passage.

Writing a Topic Sentence With a Dominant Impression

A topic sentence for a descriptive paragraph should establish the dominant impression. Suppose you have chosen warmth as your dominant impression in your paragraph on the neighbourhood coffee shop. Your topic sentence could emphasize the warmth of the place compared with the cold outside:

The coffee shop is a warm, welcoming place, especially on those frigid January mornings when it almost hurts to breathe.

Supporting Your Topic Sentence With Specific Details

Once you have written your topic sentence, you are ready to support your ideas with details. Supporting details will make your paragraph convincing. It is not enough to tell your readers that the coffee shop is a warm, inviting place; you need to show them that this is true.

Use your word association web to think of words and images that convey your dominant impression. For the paragraph about the coffee shop, you might come up with the following details to support your topic sentence:

- warm air contrasts with cold outside
- aroma of fresh coffee
- bagels warm from oven

 Putting Your Supporting Details in Order

Now that you have gathered your supporting details, you need to decide the order in which you are going to present them. The two common methods for arranging supporting details in a descriptive paragraph are by space and time:

1. **Space order** means that details are put in an order related to the physical environment—for example, left to right, near to far, top to bottom, and so on. Space order is most often used in descriptive essays and paragraphs. If you are describing a room, for example, you might start at the left and move to the right, or start at the front and move to the back.

2. **Time order** means that time is used as an organizing principle for your paragraph. If you use chronologic order, you arrange your supporting details in the order in which they happen or happened. Chronologic order is most commonly used when you are telling a story, relating an experience, or explaining how to make or do something. The writer of "The Skier" has arranged her story in chronologic order.

Note that many descriptive paragraphs use a combination of time order and space order.

Making Sure Your Paragraph Is Coherent

For your paragraph to be coherent, your ideas should flow and the reader should be able to follow your train of thought easily. The simplest way to ensure that your paragraph will flow is to use signal words or phrases that lead your reader through the paragraph. The signal words you use will vary, depending on whether you use time or space as an organizing principle for your paragraph (see box below).

Making Sure Your Paragraph Is Unified

When a paragraph is unified, all the sentences support, describe, or explain the topic, and the paragraph contains no irrelevant information. When you write your paragraphs, make sure they are unified; each sentence should relate to the topic sentence. In the following paragraph about the neighbourhood coffee shop, how well do the sentences relate to the topic sentence?

My neighbourhood coffee shop is a warm, welcoming place, especially on those frigid January mornings when it almost hurts to breathe. As I open the door, I inhale the aroma of freshly brewed coffee, hear the welcoming hiss of the cappuccino machine, and feel the warmth begin to seep into my fingertips. Along the left wall are oak tables and chairs occupied by people enjoying their first coffee of the morning. To the right of the tables is a gleaming white counter behind which sit racks

EXAMPLES OF SIGNAL WORDS AND PHRASES FOR "SPACE ORDER" PARAGRAPHS	EXAMPLES OF SIGNAL WORDS FOR "TIME ORDER" PARAGRAPHS
at the front / to the front / in the front / toward the front / in the front corner	next / then / after
at the back / at the far end / at the other end	first, second, third, etc.
to the left / right / in the centre / middle	to begin with / to start with
at the top / bottom / on top / at the bottom	at the same time / by the time / when / while
above / below	now / later
near / beside / adjacent / to the side	at last / finally / eventually / in the end

brimming with fresh doughnuts and muffins. Stacked on top of the counter are trays full of bagels still warm from the oven. As I sink into a chair with a steaming cup of coffee, I can almost forget I must leave this circle of warmth for the cold, sharp reality of a winter's day.

Writing Your Paragraph

Review the steps above. Then decide on a topic and a dominant impression for your paragraph. Next write your topic sentence and select your supporting details. Begin to write your paragraph. When you have written a draft with which you are satisfied, exchange paragraphs with a partner. Read each other's paragraphs. Then examine each paragraph using the checklist below to guide your discussion. Read pages 304 to 306 of Writing Power Tools for ideas about peer revision and editing.

When you have finished discussing your paragraphs, create an action plan for revising your descriptive passage. Then revise your paragraph, making sure that you follow your action plan and that you edit and proofread the paragraph carefully based on your partner's feedback. Use the checklist below as a guide. Ask your partner to edit and proofread your final draft.

Checklist: Proofreading a Descriptive Paragraph

○ Is my paragraph unified? Do all the sentences describe or support the topic sentence?

○ Does my topic sentence reinforce a dominant impression?

○ Do my supporting details appeal to at least three of five senses?

○ Have I organized my paragraph according to time or space, or a combination of the two?

○ Have I used effective signal words to ensure that my paragraph is coherent?

○ Have I followed my action plan in the revision of my paragraph?

○ Have I edited and proofread my paragraph?

Chapter 2: The Narrative Essay

What Is Narration?

As you learned in the introduction to this section, narration is the telling of a story. People have been listening to and telling stories since ancient times. We listen to stories to share in the lives and worlds of others. We tell stories to inform and to entertain, to give structure and drama to our lives, and to communicate and connect with others. Most of us tell stories naturally, without being aware of what we are doing. We tell stories when we describe something that happened, when we relate a sequence of events, when we gossip about a friend, and when we tell a joke. In each case, we plan what we are going to say, choose the important points, and leave out irrelevant details. We might even exaggerate some points to make the story more interesting.

Narration takes many forms: novels, short stories, essays, biographies, feature movies, documentaries, situation comedies, and soap operas, to name just a few examples. A narrative essay is a short prose composition that tells a story, often based on the writer's personal experience.

Elements of a Narrative Essay

Most narrative essays have the following elements or characteristics:

- **Sensory details.** Writers of good narrative essays do not simply tell their readers what happened. They show them what happened so that their readers feel as if they were actually there. They use sensory details that appeal to all five senses: sight, smell, hearing, touch, and taste.

- **Time order.** Narrative essays use time as an organizing principle. Most are organized in chronologic order: they tell what happened first, what happened second, what happened third, and so on. An event could take place in less than an hour or over a period of many years. Some narrative essays use flashbacks to tell stories: they begin in the present, then relate events that happened in the past. Other essays begin in the middle of a story, then move both forward and backward in time.

- **Thesis statement.** An essay's main idea is called a thesis. This controlling idea is a point that the author wants to make. In some narrative essays, the thesis is stated explicitly; in others, it is implied. Thesis statements are explored in further detail in the tutorials that follow the reading "Growing Up Native."

 ## How to Read a Narrative Essay

On the following page are some strategies that you may find useful as you read a narrative essay. Reading

Power Tools, pages 260 to 270, elaborates further on these strategies.

- Think about the essay before you read it. Look at the title. What do you think the essay might be about? Does knowing about the author suggest what might be discussed?

- Read the first paragraph. What images did you form in your mind as you read the first paragraph?

- From whose point of view is the essay written?

- Read the essay in its entirety. Is the essay told in chronologic order or some other time order?

- Does the essay remind you of a similar experience you or someone you know has had?

- Is there an explicit thesis statement or is the thesis implied? If there is an explicit thesis statement, identify it. If the thesis is implied, what do you think it is?

- Start a Reader Response Journal to record your impressions and feelings as you read. See page 277 of Writing Power Tools for more details.

The reading that follows is a narrative essay called "Growing Up Native" by Carol Geddes. Geddes, a member of the Tlingit Nation, first published this essay in *Homemaker's* magazine in 1990. Geddes is a filmmaker whose film *Doctor, Lawyer, Indian Chief* portrays the struggle of Native women.

As you read "Growing Up Native," ask yourself some of the questions from the list above. After you have finished reading the story, try doing the tutorials that follow.

Growing Up Native ₁

Carol Geddes

I remember it was cold. We were walking through a swamp near our home in the Yukon bush. Maybe it was fall and moose-hunting season. I don't know. I think I was about four years old at the time. The muskeg 2 was too springy to walk on, so people were taking turns carrying me—passing me from one set of arms to another. The details about where we were are vague, but the memory of those arms and the feeling of acceptance I had is one of the most vivid memories of my childhood. 3 It didn't matter who was carrying me—there was security in every pair of arms. That response to children is typical of the native community. It's the first thing I think of when I cast my mind back to the Yukon bush, where I was born and lived with my family.

I was six years old when we moved out of the bush, first to Teslin, where I had a hint of the problems native people face, then to Whitehorse, where there was unimaginable racism. Eventually I moved to Ottawa and Montreal, where I further discovered that to grow up native in Canada is to feel the sting of humiliation and the boot of discrimination. But it is also to experience the enviable security of an extended family and to learn to appreciate the richness of the heritage and traditions of a culture most North Americans have never been lucky enough to know. As a film-maker, I have tried to explore these contradictions, and our triumph over them, for the half-million aboriginals who are part of the tide of swelling independence of the First Nations today.

But I'm getting ahead of myself. If I'm to tell the story of what it's like to grow up native in northern Canada, I have to go back to the bush where I was born, because there's more to my story than the hurtful stereotyping that depicts Indian people as drunken welfare cases. Our area was known as 12-mile (it was 12 miles from another tiny village). There were about 40 people living there—including 25 kids, eight of them my brothers and sisters—in a sort of family compound. Each family had its own timber plank house for sleeping, and there was one large common kitchen area with gravel on the ground and a tent frame over it. Everybody would go there and cook meals together. In summer, my grandmother always had a smudge fire going to smoke fish and tan moose hides. I can remember the cosy warmth of the fire, the smell of good food, and always having someone to talk to. We kids had built-in playmates and would spend hours running in the bush, picking berries, building rafts on the lake and playing in abandoned mink cages. 4

4 *A different picture from the "hurtful stereotype"— the narrator's childhood sounds fun.*

One of the people in my village tells a story about the day the old lifestyle began to change. He had been away hunting in the bush for about a month. On his way back, he heard a strange sound coming from far away. He ran up the crest of a hill, looked over the top of it and saw a bulldozer. He had never seen or heard of such a thing before and he couldn't imagine what it was. We didn't have magazines or newspapers in our village, and the people didn't know that the Alaska Highway was being built as a defence against a presumed Japanese invasion during the Second World War. That was the beginning of the end of the Teslin Tlingit people's way of life. From that moment on, nothing turned back to the way it was. Although there were employment opportunities for my father and uncles, who were young men at the time, the speed and force with which the Alaska Highway was rammed through the wilderness caused tremendous upheaval for Yukon native people.

It wasn't as though we'd never experienced change before. The Tlingit Nation, which I belong to, arrived in the Yukon from the Alaskan coast around the turn of the century. They were the middlemen and women between the Russian traders and the Yukon inland Indians. The Tlingit gained power and prestige by trading European products such as metal goods and cloth for the rich and varied furs so much in fashion in Europe. The Tlingit controlled Yukon trading because they controlled the trading routes through the high mountain passes. When trading ceased to be an effective means of survival, my grandparents began raising wild mink in cages. Mink prices were really high before and during the war, but afterwards the prices went plunging down. So, although the mink pens were still there when I was a little girl, my father mainly worked on highway construction and hunted in the bush. The Yukon was then, and still is in some ways, in a transitional period—from living off the land to getting into a European wage-based economy.

As a young child, I didn't see the full extent of the upheaval. I remember a lot of togetherness, a lot of happiness while we lived in the bush. There's a very strong sense of family in the native community, 5 and a fondness for children, especially young children. Even today, it's like a special form of entertainment if someone brings a baby to visit. That sense of family is the one thing that has survived all the incredible difficulties native people have had. Throughout a time of tremendous problems, the extended family system has somehow lasted, providing a strong circle for people to survive in. When parents were struggling with alcoholism or had to go away to find work, when one of the many epidemics swept through the community, or when a marriage broke up and one parent left, aunts, uncles, and grandparents would try to fill those roles. It's been very important to me in terms of emotional support to be able to rely on my extended family. There are still times when such support keeps me going.

5   The narrator has a strong
    belief in family.

Life was much simpler when we lived in the bush. Although we were poor and wore the same clothes all year, we were warm enough and had plenty to eat. But even as a youngster, I began to be aware of some of the problems we would face later on. Travelling missionaries would come and impose themselves on us, for example. They'd sit at our campfire and read the bible to us and lecture us about how we had to live a Christian life. I remember being very frightened by stories we heard about parents sending their kids away to live with white people who didn't have any children. We thought those people were mean and that if we were bad, we'd be sent away, too. Of course, that was when social workers were scooping up native children and adopting them out to white families in the south. The consequences were usually disastrous for the children who were taken away—alienation, alcoholism and suicide, among other things. I knew some of those kids. The survivors are still struggling to recover.

The residential schools were another source of misery for the kids. Although I didn't have to go, my brothers and sisters were there. They told stories about having their hair cut off in case they were carrying head lice, and of being forced to do hard chores without enough food to eat. They were told that the Indian culture was evil, that Indian people were bad, that their only hope was to be Christian. They had to stand up and say things like "I've found the Lord," when a teacher told them to speak. Sexual abuse was rampant in the residential school system.

By the time we moved to Whitehorse, I was excited about the idea of living in what I thought of as a big town. I'd had a taste of the outside world from books at school in Teslin (a town of 250 people), and I was tremendously curious about what life was like. I was hungry for experiences such as going to the circus. In fact, for a while, I was obsessed with stories and pictures about the circus, but then when I was 12 and saw my first one, I was put off by the condition and treatment of the animals.

Going to school in Whitehorse was a shock. The clash of native and white values was confusing and frightening. Let me tell you a story. The older boys in our community were already accomplished hunters and fishermen, but since they had to trap beaver in the spring and hunt moose in the fall, and go out trapping in the winter as well, they missed a lot of school. We were all in one classroom and some of my very large teenage cousins had to sit squeezed into little desks. These guys couldn't read very well. We girls had been in school all along, so, of course, we were better readers. One day the teacher was trying to get one of the older boys to read. She was typical of the teachers at that time, insensitive and ignorant of cultural complexities. In an increasingly loud voice, she kept commanding him to "Read it, read it." He couldn't. He sat there completely still, but I could see that he was breaking into a sweat. The teacher then said, "Look, she can read it," and she pointed to me, indicating that I should stand up and read. For a young child to try to show up an older boy is wrong and totally contrary to native cultural values, so I refused. She told me to stand up and I did. My hands were trembling as I held my reader. She yelled at me to read and when I didn't she smashed her pointing stick on the desk to frighten me. In terror, I wet my pants. As I stood there fighting my tears of shame, she said I was disgusting and sent me home. I remember feeling this tremendous confusion, on top of my humiliation. *6* We were always told the white teachers knew best, and so we had to do whatever they said at school. And yet I had a really strong sense of receiving mixed messages about what I was supposed to do in the community and what I was supposed to do at school.

Pretty soon I hated school. Moving to a predominantly white high school was even worse. We weren't allowed to join anything the white kids started. We were the butt of jokes because of our secondhand clothes and moose meat sandwiches. We were constantly being rejected. The prevailing attitude was that Indians were stupid. When it was time to make course choices in class—between typing and science, for example—they didn't even ask the native kids, they just put us all in typing. You get a really bad image of yourself in a situation like that. I bought into it. I thought we were awful. The whole experience was terribly undermining. Once, my grandmother gave me a pretty little pencil box. I walked into the classroom one day to find the word "squaw" carved on it. That night I burned it in the wood stove. I joined the tough crowd and by the time I was 15 years old, I was more likely to be leaning against the school smoking a cigarette than trying to join in. I was burned out from trying to join the system. The principal told my father there was no point in sending me back to school so, with a Grade 9 education, I started to work at a series of menial jobs. *7*

Seven years later something happened to me that would change my life forever. I had moved to Ottawa with a man and was working as a waitress in a restaurant. One day, a friend invited me to her place for coffee. While I was there, she told me she was going to university in the fall and showed me her reading list. I'll never forget the minutes that followed. I was feeling vaguely envious of her and once again, inferior. I remember taking the paper in my hand, seeing the books on it and realizing, Oh, my God, I've read these books! It hit me like a thunderclap. I was stunned that books I had read were being read in university. University was for white kids, not native kids. We were too stupid, we didn't have the kind of mind it took to do those things. My eyes moved down the list, and my heart started beating faster and faster as I suddenly realized I could go to university, too! *8*

My partner at the time was a loving supportive man who helped me in every way. I applied to the university immediately as a mature student but when I had to

6 This story made me feel angry and sad—no one deserves to be treated badly.

7 Menial must be the kind of job you get without an education.

8 The narrator realizes that she is not inferior.

write Grade 9 on the application, I was sure they'd turn me down. They didn't. I graduated five years later, earning a bachelor of arts in English and philosophy (with distinction). *9* ...

Today, there's a glimmer of hope that more of us native people will overcome the obstacles that have tripped us up ever since we began sharing this land. Some say our cultures are going through a renaissance. Maybe that's true. Certainly there's a renewed interest in native dancing, acting and singing, and in other cultural traditions. Even indigenous *10* forms of government are becoming strong again. But we can't forget that the majority of native people live in urban areas and continue to suffer from alcohol and drug abuse and the plagues of a people who have lost their culture and have become lost themselves. And the welfare system is the insidious glue that holds together the machine of oppression of native people. *11*

Too many non-native people have refused to try to understand the issues behind our land claims. They make complacent pronouncements such as "Go back to your bows and arrows and fish with spears if you want aboriginal rights. If not, give it up and assimilate into white Canadian culture." I don't agree with that. We need our culture, but there's no reason why we can't preserve it and have an automatic washing machine and a holiday in Mexico, as well.

The time has come for native people to make our own decisions. We need to have self-government. I have no illusions that it will be smooth sailing—there will be trial and error and further struggle. *12* And if that means crawling before we can stand up and walk, so be it. We'll have to learn through experience.

While we're learning, we have a lot to teach and give to the world—a holistic *13* philosophy, a way of living with the earth, not disposing of it. It is critical that we all learn from the elders that an individual is not more important than a forest; we know that we're here to live on and with the earth, not to subdue it.

The wheels are in motion for a revival, for change in the way native people are taking their place in Canada. I can see that we're equipped, we have the tools to do the work. We have an enormous number of smart, talented, moral Indian people. It's thrilling to be a part of this movement. *14*

Someday, when I'm an elder, I'll tell the children the stories: about the bush, about the hard times, about the renaissance, and especially about the importance of knowing your place in your nation.

9 The power of reading!

10 Indigenous. *What does that mean? Look it up.*

11 How does the welfare system oppress?

12 The narrator knows that progress and change will be difficult.

13 Holistic. *From the sentence, I think this means that we should respect nature and the earth. Check in dictionary.*

14 The narrator is proud of "growing up native."

Tutorial 3: Understanding Time Order in a Narrative Essay

Learning Expectations

You will
- learn how to find an author's thesis
- analyze how the order in which events are presented helps communicate the writer's thesis

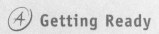 **Getting Ready**

Finding an Essay's Thesis

As you learned in the introduction to this section, an essay's thesis is its main idea. A thesis statement tells you both the topic of the essay and the writer's opinion of the topic. Think of a thesis as the writer's viewpoint. When you read an essay, look for the writer's thesis to provide you with a key for understanding the essay.

Be careful not to confuse a writer's thesis with an essay's title. A title usually tells you the subject of the essay, but it does not tell you the author's viewpoint on the subject. The title "Growing Up Native" gives you the subject of the essay, but it does not tell you the writer's views on growing up Native. Similarly, the title of the descriptive essay "The Skier" (page 6) tells you that skiing is the subject of the essay, but it does not tell you the author's views on skiing.

A thesis statement can appear anywhere in an essay. In some essays, the thesis statement appears at the end of the first paragraph, or at the end of a series of introductory paragraphs. These essays often open with a broad statement or anecdote that leads to a thesis statement. In other essays, the thesis statement appears in one of the middle paragraphs or in the last paragraph. In still other essays, the thesis is implied:

the writer does not actually tell you the thesis, leaving you to figure it out for yourself. See pages 25 to 26 of Tutorial 4 for more details about a writer's thesis.

What is the writer's thesis of "Growing Up Native"? Did you locate an actual thesis statement, or is the thesis implied?

Recognizing How the Order of Ideas Reinforces Meaning

"Growing Up Native" is told mainly in chronologic order. The writer starts with a description of her earliest memory, and she ends the essay with a prediction that she will become an elder. (An elder is a man or woman from a Native band respected for his or her wisdom.) The writer inserts one flashback into the straight chronology that takes the reader back in time. In this case, she takes us back to a time before she was born, to the beginning of the twentieth century when her ancestors arrived in the Yukon from Alaska. Why do you think the writer inserted this flashback into the narrative? How does it enhance our knowledge of the Tlingit Nation?

In addition to revealing details about her ancestors, the writer interrupts her own chronology to tell us things about the future. Look at paragraph 2. Why do you think the author tells us early in the essay that as an adult she moved to Ottawa and Montreal? Why do you think she reveals that she became a film-maker? How would the essay's effect have been different if she had not interrupted the narrative to tell the reader these details about her future life?

The writer of "Growing Up Native" uses the chronology of her life to explore the struggle of all Native people in Canada, shifting from personal stories to statements about the Native community in

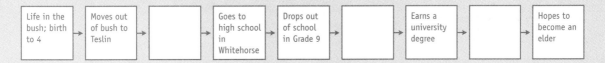

| Life in the bush; birth to 4 | → | Moves out of bush to Teslin | → | | → | Goes to high school in Whitehorse | → | Drops out of school in Grade 9 | → | | → | Earns a university degree | → | | → | Hopes to become an elder |

general. There are examples of this technique in paragraphs 1 and 7. Roughly draw the chart below in your journal or on a piece of paper. Then reread these paragraphs, and complete the chart.

SPECIFIC MEMORY	COMMENTARY ON THE NATIVE COMMUNITY
As an infant, the writer felt secure in the arms of many different adults.	
As a child, the writer was frightened by stories about children being sent away to live with white people.	

At the end of the essay, the writer finishes her own personal chronology and explains her views on the current situation and future of Native people in Canada. If the author had written an essay about her views without telling us her life story, how would the essay's effect have been different? Why does knowing the author's own story make her views more convincing?

 ## Connecting Chronology and Social Views

In groups of three, discuss "Growing Up Native," and decide on the main events of the writer's life, as they are revealed in the essay. Then, look above at the diagram A Chronology of the Writer's Life. Redraw the chronology on a large piece of paper, leaving lots of white space around the boxes. Then fill in the empty boxes with the main events from the writer's life. Above the boxes, record the specific memories that the writer recalls, and below the boxes, record the commentary that she makes about the Native community. Use different colours to highlight or distinguish between main life events, specific memories, and general comments. The completed chart should show you how the author skillfully moves from her own story to experiences of the Native community. Keep the following checklist in mind as you work.

Checklist: Understanding Time Order in a Narrative Essay

○ Have we identified the main events of the author's life?

○ Have we read the essay carefully to find examples of anecdotes told from memory and generalized comments on the experience of Native Canadians?

○ Have we identified the number of the paragraph where we found the example so we can go back and look at it again?

Tutorial 4: Writing and Revising a Narrative Essay

Learning Expectations

You will learn

- to choose a topic, an audience, and a purpose for a narrative essay
- to write a thesis statement
- to draft, edit, and revise your narrative essay

Understanding the Task

A good narrative essay is unified. Writing without a common thread or a point leaves the reader asking, "So what? What is the point of you telling me these things?" Good narration helps the reader to understand why experiences were memorable, humorous, traumatic, or enjoyable. The events you relate should contain a unified thread so your reader will say, "I understand" or "No wonder you felt that way" or "Yes, I can see why you remembered that."

You will write a brief narrative essay based on an event or events from your childhood or a recent experience. The essay should re-create the events or the experience for others and show why they were significant.

Getting Ready

An essay is a more formal kind of writing than the less structured kind of writing you probably do when you write in a journal. When you write in your journal, you may start writing without reflection, jotting

down the first thing that comes into your mind. When you write an essay, you need to spend as much time planning your essay as you do writing it.

Finding Something to Write About

If you cannot think of a topic, here are several methods that may help:

- **Freewriting.** On a fresh sheet of paper, start writing about anything that comes to mind. If you are still having trouble, think about incidents involving school, your brothers and sisters, your friends, and so on.

- **Recent experiences.** Make a list of experiences you have had recently. Think of work, school, your friends, family, places you have been, and people you have met, times of frustration, enjoyment, or satisfaction.

See page 10 for more ways to find something to write about.

Making Your Topic Specific

Once you have a general idea for a topic, you need to make sure it is a suitable topic for an essay. Your essay should be specific. Although skillful writers, like the author of "Growing Up Native," can write well on a broad topic, this is not an easy task. With a broad topic, you may be tempted to mention too many events, which may lead to a tendency to tell rather than show your readers what happened. With a specific topic, you have more scope to include the sensory images and specific details that your essay needs to engage its readers. For this reason, it may be preferable to write about one or two events rather than a whole series of events. In the chart below are examples of student essay topics. Those on the left are too broad; those on the right are more focused.

BROAD TOPICS	REVISED TOPICS
My job at Burgers Galore	My first day at Burgers Galore
My family's move to Canada	Finding a place to live in Vancouver
Growing up in a small town	Going to high school in a small town

 Considering Your Audience

Essays are easier to write if they are written for a specific audience. Knowing your audience will help you choose the appropriate level of detail. When you are writing a personal essay, it usually helps to think of your audience as a good friend. Here are three questions to ask yourself about your audience:

1. What does my audience know about the subject?

2. What will interest my audience?

3. How would I talk to this audience in person?

Considering Your Purpose

Your purpose in writing a personal essay can vary. Depending on what you have chosen to write about, your purpose might be to entertain, to amuse, or to surprise or sensitize your audience. Your purpose determines your tone and attitude toward your subject and audience. You may, for example, choose a tone that is joyful, sad, or serious.

See pages 280 to 287 in Writing Power Tools for more information on audience, purpose, and tone.

Writing a Thesis

As you learned in Tutorial 3 on page 22, the key to an essay's organization is its thesis. The thesis is the foundation upon which you construct your essay. A thesis is different from a topic. Your topic is the subject you have chosen to write about; your thesis should express your opinion of the topic, or your reason for writing the essay. A strong thesis gives your essay unity.

A thesis should be specific. A vague thesis results in a vague essay. A clear thesis provides focus for your essay. The table below illustrates some examples of weak thesis statements, states reasons why they are weak, and demonstrates revised and improved thesis

WEAK THESIS STATEMENT	WHY IT IS WEAK	REVISED THESIS STATEMENT
In this essay I will discuss my family's move to Canada.	• Not an opinion • Not specific	My family's move to Canada was a distressing experience from which I learned that not all Canadians are hospitable, and to survive in this country, you have to stand up for yourself.
The birth of my brother, Mark.	• Not a complete sentence • Not an opinion • Not specific	The birth of my brother, Mark, brought joy and renewed energy to our household.
My first part-time job.	• Not a complete sentence • Not an opinion • Not specific	My first part-time job convinced me that I needed to develop communication and people skills.
Listening to music.	•	
Hockey is an exciting sport.	•	
My last camping experience.	•	

statements. The last three boxes contain weak thesis statements that are not revised. Write these thesis statements on a piece of paper and record the reasons why they are weak. Then revise them, using your imagination to supply details.

As mentioned on page 22 of Tutorial 3, theses can be either stated or implied. Implying your thesis rather than stating it directly takes considerable skill and experience. Therefore, in most school essays, you will be expected to state your thesis directly as a complete sentence at the end of your introductory paragraph. However, if your essay depends on surprise, you may not want to give your thesis away in the first paragraph. In this case, you may want to place your thesis statement at the end of the essay.

Organizing Your Supporting Details

As mentioned in Tutorials 1 and 2, some writers like to use word association webs to help them select and organize supporting details. See pages 278 and 292 of Writing Power Tools for an example. Preparing a rough outline of your essay can also help you sort through your ideas and order them in a logical way. When creating an outline, it is a good idea to write your thesis statement at the top of the page, and then jot down in point form what you plan to say in each paragraph. See pages 290 to 291 in Writing Power Tools for more information on how to use an outline to help you plan your narrative essay.

As mentioned in Tutorial 3, most narrative essays are organized according to time; they are either told in chronologic order, or they move backward and forward in time through the use of flashbacks. Decide whether you will narrate your essay in strict chronologic order, or whether you will include flashbacks.

Writing a Narrative Essay

For your first draft, concentrate on getting your ideas down on paper without concerning yourself too much with structure and spelling. You will have plenty of time to revise your work. Do, however, keep your audience, purpose, and tone in mind. Double-space your draft to allow for revision and editing later.

Revising and Editing Your First Draft

Once you have a first draft on paper, read the essay through once silently, then once aloud. Try to imagine you are reading someone else's essay. Reading aloud gives you the opportunity to listen to the rhythm and flow of your sentences. Sometimes we are unaware that a sentence sounds awkward or that an expression is vague or trite, until we read it aloud. As you read, ask yourself the following questions. Record revision ideas on your essay.

- Is my essay a narration? Does it focus on events or experiences rather than a general situation?

- What is my thesis? Have I stated it clearly? Will my readers understand the point of my essay?

- Have I put the details in a particular time order? Have I used connecting words that show the time sequence?

- Have I included sensory details that will enable the reader to imagine what happened?

- Does the tone of the essay reflect my purpose?

- Is any part of the story missing? Should I include more details?

- Is my essay unified? Have I included irrelevant details that would be better left out?

- Can I think of a better way to begin or end my essay?

- Have I used vivid words and sensory details? Have I used any tired words or expressions?

Can I substitute some better nouns or verbs, or add modifiers to help my reader picture what happened?

- Does the draft follow essay form? Does it have an introduction, three to five body paragraphs, and a conclusion?

After you have finished reading, ask a partner to read your essay to you. The advantage of having someone else read your essay is that you can put all your energy into listening. Then, using the above questions as a guide, ask your partner to offer advice for revising your essay. Record these ideas on your essay.

Use the notes you have made on your essay to make an action plan for revising your first draft. Keep in mind that you are free to add details, drop others, and rearrange the order of ideas. Word processing makes it easy to move text around without rewriting a whole essay. As you revise, look at each paragraph beginning with your introduction. Pages 303 to 315 of Writing Power Tools contain further information on creating action plans, strategies for revising and editing, and tips for revising with a partner. See pages 293 to 295 of Writing Power Tools for an example of a student's essay as it evolves from a rough draft to the final draft.

Revising the Introduction

Your introduction should be so inviting that it makes your reader want to keep reading. There are many ways to write engaging introductions to narrative essays, and you may find one of the following strategies helpful:

- Establish the context for the essay. Provide your reader with some background; introduce the scene, the event, or the people.

- Begin with a specific anecdote, and leave the context for the essay until the second paragraph.

- Begin with a general subject that can be narrowed down to the specific topic and thesis of your essay.

Revising the Body Paragraphs

When you revise your body paragraphs, look closely at the paragraphs themselves, the order in which they are presented, and the flow from paragraph to paragraph. Each paragraph should have the following:

- a topic sentence that unifies the paragraph

- enough supporting details to help the reader visualize the scene or the event

- linking words that connect sentences and ideas

- a link to either the previous paragraph or the next paragraph

- paragraph breaks in appropriate places

Revising the Conclusion

A concluding paragraph to a narrative essay should give your readers a sense of satisfaction. They should feel that the story is complete, loose ends are tied up, and that there is nothing more for the writer to say. Avoid making a new point or starting a new story. You might use one of these strategies in a concluding paragraph:

- Come full circle. Return to the material in your introduction. This strategy gives your essay a sense of unity and completion.

- Summarize the lesson you learned from the experience.

- Remind your readers of your thesis by stating it in different words.

- Consider placing your thesis statement in the concluding paragraph. As noted earlier, sometimes putting it in the first paragraph of a narrative essay can spoil any suspense or surprise created by the story.

See pages 290 to 297 in Writing Power Tools for more tips on writing and revising paragraphs.

Editing Sentences

Check the sentences in your paragraphs. If they all sound alike, your essay may be boring to read. Keep the following suggestions in mind as you revise your sentences:

- **Vary your sentence structure.** Do too many of your sentences begin with the word *I*? You can avoid overuse of the word *I* in a narrative essay by adding a subordinate clause that helps set the scene. Instead of "I tentatively pushed the door open," try, "When nobody answered my knock, I tentatively pushed the door open."

- **Vary your sentence length.** Are too many of your sentences the same length? Try combining some of your sentences into one longer sentence. Instead of "I could tell my boss was angry. He pursed his lips and frowned," try, "I could tell my boss was angry because he frowned and pursed his lips." If too many sentences seem overly long, check to make sure they are punctuated properly. See Writing Power Tools, page 309, for more details.

Editing Words

Vivid language will help your reader imagine the experience you are describing. Check your nouns, verbs, and modifiers to make sure that they are colourful and descriptive. See Writing Power Tools, pages 308 to 309, for more details on editing words.

 ## Proofreading Your Essay

After you are satisfied with everything else about your essay, you need to proofread it to correct errors in grammar, punctuation, and spelling. Read each sentence slowly, from beginning to end, one word at a time. Have your partner read it one more time, this time asking him or her to look for errors in grammar, punctuation, and spelling. A fresh pair of eyes may detect something you have missed.

 ## Technological Tip

Most word processing programs have spell check and grammar check programs to help you proofread your work. In the more recent programs, words that are incorrectly spelled and some incorrect grammar constructions are underlined in different colours. However, do not depend entirely on the computer to check for errors in your essay. The spell checks do not catch correctly spelled words that are used incorrectly, and the grammar checks are only able to pick up some grammatical errors.

Checklist: Writing and Revising a Narrative Essay

❍ Is my thesis clear? Should I restate it or move it to another place in the essay?

❍ Does my introduction invite my reader to read on?

❍ Do my paragraphs flow? Have I used time order effectively?

❍ Are the body paragraphs unified? Do they contain unnecessary information? Do they contain enough detail?

❍ Does each event contribute to the point I am making? Is there a common thread in all that I have presented?

❍ Are my sentences varied?

❍ Have I used sensory detail and colourful, vivid words?

❍ Does my conclusion leave my readers satisfied and convinced?

❍ Have I read my essay aloud, and have I listened to a partner read it?

❍ Has a partner read my essay silently and offered suggestions for revision?

❍ Have I created an action plan for improving my essay and used it as a guide to revising my essay?

❍ Have I edited and proofread my essay for correctness?

Chapter 3: Biography

Learning Expectations

You will learn
- what makes a good biography or autobiography
- how to use keyword and context clues to find the meanings of unfamiliar words
- how to use anecdotes to reveal character
- how to write a brief biographical sketch

What Is a Biography?

A biography is an account of a person's life written by someone else. Biography differs from fiction in that it is based on a real-life story rather than on an imagined event. In a sense, good biographers try to get under the skin of the people they write about, spending time in the places where these people lived, reading their letters and diaries, and interviewing friends, family members, acquaintances, or descendants. Out of this meticulous research, which sometimes includes reading volumes of books and masses of papers, a good biographer reconstructs a person's life and selects those details that best convey that life to the reader.

Since many biographers have strong views on their subjects, it is quite possible to read two biographies of the same person in completely different lights. For example, some of the biographers of the late Diana, Princess of Wales, portray her as a selfless saint, while others portray her as a paranoid manipulator. Authors who have not already made up their minds before they embark on their research usually write the most honest, unbiased biographies.

An autobiography is a personal account of one's own life, generally covering an entire life span, from birth through to the point of writing. If you write about your feelings and thoughts in a diary, most likely you want to keep that diary private. In contrast, writers of published autobiographies want others to read about their lives. They write about themselves in order to entertain or to amuse their readers, or to share lessons about life that they have learned. Autobiographies do not present an objective, balanced point of view because the writer is far too involved in the story to present an impartial perspective.

A memoir is different from an autobiography because it generally limits what it includes. It may, for example, focus on a particular period in a person's life. Frank McCourt's *Angela's Ashes* depicts the author's life as a child in Limerick, Ireland. A coming-of-age memoir, which is generally restricted to retelling childhood stories, has now become a distinct literary genre. An example is Maya Angelou's *I Know Why the Caged Bird Sings*. A memoir, then, can be limited by anything the author chooses; these limits provide a distinct frame or organizational pattern for the story.

Elements of a Biography

Good biographies and autobiographies do more than tell you what happened in someone's life; they re-create that life so that you can imagine what it was like to be that person. They use the following elements to reveal the essence of the person's character and the events of the person's life.

Descriptive Language

Like other writers, biographers use rich, descriptive language to create sensory impressions, skillfully conveying concrete details that allow the reader to form images in his or her mind. These images may appeal to all five senses; they enable the reader to see, hear, feel, smell, and even taste the world as it was experienced by the person in the biography. Good biographers use language to convey not only the events in a life, but also the person's character, values, and feelings.

Language That Reveals

Good biographers avoid telling you directly what they think of a person. Instead, they use the recollections of others and anecdotes to reveal a person's character. For example, instead of telling you that they think a person is selfish and conceited, they relate an incident that reveals these qualities.

Selection of Details

If the details of someone's entire life were recorded, they would fill many volumes. Biographers have to select details that best convey a person's experiences, personality, values, and feelings. The details they select depend on the subject of the biography. A biographer of Canada's former prime minister Pierre Elliott Trudeau probably would not mention Trudeau's favourite breakfast food, but a biographer of the famous chef Julia Child would consider her breakfast preferences essential.

Order of Events

Biographers organize the details they have selected so that crucial aspects of a person's life are revealed. Many biographers tell the story of a life in chronologic order, beginning with birth and ending with death (if the person has died). However, this may not necessarily be the best order of presentation. Some biographers prefer to begin by describing what a person is like in middle or old age and then tell the story of his or her life in a series of flashbacks. Even biographers who choose to relate events in chronologic order usually have to use flashbacks to add background detail. Many biographers also use foreshadowing, in which they introduce details that hint at important events that occur later.

 ## How to Read a Biography

When you read biographies, autobiographies, or memoirs, try to imagine what life was like for the people you are reading about. Try some of these strategies to help you read biographies and autobiographies:

- Read the title and any information that is provided about the author. Can you tell if this is a biography, autobiography, or a memoir? Is it about a famous person?

- Do you think you will have anything in common with this author or the subject of the biography? Might you have had similar experiences?

- Put yourself in the shoes of the people you are reading about. Form opinions about them.

- Write about the people in your Reader Response Journal. How did they make you feel? Did you find their story amusing or entertaining? Did it inspire you to make any changes in your own life?

The excerpt that follows is from "Roy," a chapter in a memoir by Catherine Gildiner called *Too Close to the Falls*. Gildiner, who lives in Toronto, was nominated for a Trillium Book Award for these memoirs about growing up in Lewiston, New York.

Roy

Catherine Gildiner

Over half a century ago I grew up in Lewiston, a small town in western New York, a few miles south of Niagara Falls on the Canadian border. As the Falls can be seen from the Canadian and American sides from different perspectives, so can Lewiston. It is a sleepy town, protected from the rest of the world geographically, nestled at the bottom of the steep shale Niagara Escarpment on one side and the Niagara River on the other. The river's appearance, however, is deceptive. While it seems calm, rarely making waves, it has deadly whirlpools swirling on its surface which can suck anything into their vortices in seconds.

My father, a pharmacist, owned a drugstore in the nearby honeymoon capital of Niagara Falls. My mother, a math teacher by training rather than inclination, was an active participant in the historical society. Lewiston actually had a few historical claims to fame, which my mother eagerly hyped. The word *cocktail* was invented there, Charles Dickens stayed overnight at the Frontier House, the local inn, and Lafayette gave a speech from a balcony on the main street. Our home, which had thirteen trees in the yard that were planted when there were thirteen states, was used to billet soldiers in the War of 1812. It was called into action by history yet again for the Underground Railroad to smuggle slaves across the Niagara River to freedom in Canada.

My parents longed for a child for many years; however, when they were not blessed, they gracefully settled into an orderly life of community service. Then I unexpectedly arrived, the only child of suddenly bewildered older, conservative, devoutly Catholic parents.

I seem to have been "born eccentric"—a phrase my mother uttered frequently as a way of absolving herself of responsibility. By today's standards I would have been labelled with attention deficit disorder, a hyperactive child born with some adrenal problem that made her more prone to rough-and-tumble play than was normal for a girl. Fortunately I was born fifty years ago and simply called "busy" and "bossy," the possessor of an Irish temper.

I was at the hub of the town because I worked in my father's drugstore from the age of four. This was not exploitive 1 child labour but rather what the town pediatrician prescribed. When my mother explained to him that I had gone over the top of the playground swings making a 360-degree loop and had been knocked unconscious twice, had to be removed from a cherry tree the previous summer by the fire department, done Ed Sullivan imitations for money at Helm's Dry Goods Store, all before I'd hit kindergarten, Dr. Laughton dutifully wrote down all this information, laid down his clipboard with certainy, and said that I had worms and needed Fletcher's Castoria. His fallback position (in case when I was dewormed no hyperactive worms crept from any orifice) was for me to burn off my energy by working at manual labour in my father's store. He explained that we all had metronomes inside our bodies and mine was simply ticking faster than most; I had to do more work than others to burn it off.

Being in the full-time workforce at four gave me a unique perspective on life, and I was exposed to situations I later realized were unusual for a child. For over

1 Exploitive—*Other possible words:* unfair, illegal.

ten years I never once had a meal at home, and that included Christmas. I worked and went to restaurants and delivered everything from band-aids to morphine in the Niagara Frontier. I had to tell people whether makeup looked good or bad, point out what cough medicines had sedatives, count and bottle pills. *2* I also had to sound as though I knew what I was talking about in order to pull it off. I was surrounded by adults, and my peer group became my co-workers at the store.

2   Wow—that is a lot of work to do at such a young age.

My father worked behind a counter which had a glass separating it from the rest of the store. He and the other pharmacists wore starched white shirts which buttoned on the side with "McCLURE'S DRUGS" monogrammed in red above the pocket. The rest of us wore plastic ink guards in our breast pockets which had printed in script letters "McClure's has free delivery." (The word *delivery* had wheels and a forward slant.) I worked there full-time when I was four and five and I suspected that when I went to school next year I would work a split shift from 6:00 to 9:00 A.M. and then again after school until closing time at 10:00 P.M. Of course I would always work full-time on Saturday and Sunday when my mother did her important work with the historical board. I restocked the candy and makeup counters, loaded the newspaper racks, and replenished the supplies of magazines and comics. I read the comics aloud in different voices, jumped out of the pay-phone booth as Superman and acted out Brenda Starr "in her ruthless search for truth," and every morning at 6:00 A.M. I equipped the outdoor newsstand of blue wood with its tiered layers with the *Niagara Falls Gazette*.

My parents were removed from the hurly-burly of my everyday existence. My father was my employer, and I called him "boss," which is what everyone else called him. My mother provided no rules nor did she ever make a meal, nor did I have brothers or sisters to offer me any normal childlike role models. While other four-year-olds spent their time behind fences at home with their moms and dads, stuck in their own backyards making pretend cakes in hot metal sandboxes or going to stagnant events like girls' birthday parties where you sat motionless as the birthday girl opened *her* presents and then you waited in line to stick a pin into a wall while blindfolded, hoping it would hit the rear end of a jackass, I was out doing really exciting work. I spent my time in the workforce delivering prescriptions with Roy, *3* my co-worker.

3   Finally, Roy is introduced!

One thing about a drugstore: it's a great leveller. Everyone from the rich to the poor needs prescriptions and it was my job to deliver them. Roy, the driver, and I, the assistant who read the road maps and prescription labels, were dogged as we plowed through snowstorms and ice jams to make our deliveries. The job took us into mansions on the Niagara Escarpment, to the home of Dupont, who invented nylon, to deliver hypodermic needles to a new doctor on the block, Dr. Jonas Salk, an upstart who thought he had a cure for polio, to Marilyn Monroe on the set of *Niagara*, to the poor Indians on the Tuscarora reservation, and to Warty, who lived in a refrigerator box in the town dump. The people we delivered to felt like my "family," and my soulmate in this experience was Roy.

He was different from my father, the other pharmacists, and Irene, the salmon-frocked cosmetician. He was always in a good mood and laughed at all the things I found funny and never told me to "calm down." He made chestnuts into jewels, bottle tops into art, music into part of our joy together, and he always saw the comedy in tragedy.

He never put off a good time, yet he always got his work done. To me that was amazing, a stunning high-wire act done without a net. *4* He effortlessly jumped into the skin of whomever he was addressing. He made each life we entered, no matter where it was pinned on the social hierarchy, seem not only plausible, but inevitable, even enviable.

Every town has its elaborate social hierarchy and cast of characters. Maybe all children are fascinated by the idiosyncratic, *5* those who have difficulty walking the tightrope of acceptable behaviour in a small town where the social stratification is so explicit and the rules feel so inviolable. Those who opt out of the social order are as terrifying as they are enviable. Maybe I identified with these people because I was trying, even at four, to work out how and why *I* was different. Whatever the reasons, my interest in whatever it took to be different, or to be the same, began early and has persisted. They say architects always played with Lego. Well, I'm a psychologist who was always interested in what the social psychologists refer to as "individual differences," or the statisticians refer to as "the extremes of the bell curve," or what we colloquially refer to as "the edge."

Roy and I made up complicated systems for working together efficiently. He threw magazines to me. I printed "Return" on them if they were past a certain date, threw them on the bright red upright dolly, *6* and we whipped out to pile them on the return truck when it beeped. I always rode on top of the magazines and Roy pushed the dolly, tearing around corners of the store. (We set an egg timer and always tried to beat our last time.)

Roy loved to bet, and after I got the hang of it from him, I found it gave life just that bit of edge it needed. Our days were packed with exciting wagers. *7* For example, we never just rolled the dolly back from the truck; instead we played a game called "dolly-trust." Roy would drop the dolly backwards with me standing upright on it and then he would grab it one tiny second before it hit the cement. I felt my stomach dropping and my knees would go weak but I *had* to trust him. If I twitched or stiffened one muscle, I lost the bet and had to line up all the new

4 Roy balanced work and fun—definitely like walking a "tightrope."

5 Idiosyncratic—*Looking at what goes before this word and after it, maybe it means* strange *or* unusual.

6 Dolly—*Possible words:* wagon *or* cart *to haul things.*

7 Wagers—*This paragraph is about betting, so* wagers *must be another word for* bets.

8   Equidistant—*Must be like equal + distance.*

magazines and he got to be boss. If I never made a peep, I got to be boss and he had to do the job. The winner was merciless in extracting obeisance from the other. The magazines had to be arranged exactly as the "boss" suggested. If one was not equidistant *8* from the next or, God forbid, hidden behind another, the "assistant" had to pile them up and start all over again.

At precisely 10:30 A.M. each Saturday all the employees had a break. We sat around the large red Coke cooler where the ice had melted and we fished out our Cokes. I had to stand on a wooden bottle crate to reach inside. Roy had a game, of course, to make it more interesting. Each twisted green Coke bottle had the name of a city on the bottom indicating which bottling plant it had come from. Roy would yell out a city and whoever had the bottle with the closest city had to pay for all seven of the Cokes. Roy knew every city and what cities were closest to it. Whenever anyone challenged him and we looked at the map of the U.S. in the toy section, he was right. Once I lost my whole salary when he yelled out "Tulsa" and I had Wichita and Irene had Oklahoma City.

When I was in grade one Sister Timothy, my teacher, told my mother that she had never met a child who knew more about geography than I did and that one of the advantages of having an only child is you can give her so much in terms of travel. My mother was perplexed since I had never been more than thirty miles from Lewiston. Roy said people learn best when the stakes are high. . . .

Roy was my best friend for a number of years. We went through rough times on the Tuscarora reservation, dined with millionaires when they visited the Falls, had lunch with Joseph Cotten, witnessed birth and death together, and helped each other out of scrapes—although now I realize he helped me out of more. Finally one day in grade six I went to work and Roy didn't show up. No one ever saw him again. Irene said that a few men had been looking for him the day before. She said they didn't seem any too pleasant and she was sure gambling was involved. My father suggested to Irene that it was uncharitable to gossip about Roy's departure and told me if Roy could have said goodbye he would have. It was not like him to be rude and he must have had a good reason. When Irene "started up on him"—as Roy used to refer to her bossiness—my father said we would only remember Roy at his best. To me Roy was always at his best. *9*

9   *The child enjoys Roy's perspective on life.*

Tutorial 5: Strategies for Understanding Unfamiliar Words

Learning Expectation

You will learn various strategies to decipher the meaning of unfamiliar words.

 ## Understanding the Task

The more widely you read, the more you will come across unfamiliar words. Unfamiliar words can be irritating because they slow down your reading and create barriers to immediate understanding. However, they can also create an opportunity for you to expand your vocabulary, and go beyond what initially were hindrances. Enrichment of your vocabulary can permit new experiences and impressions about the world.

 ## Getting Ready

You will learn five strategies for understanding the meaning of unfamiliar words in "Roy." Three of the word strategies involve looking for clues in the *context*—the words, sentences, and paragraphs that surround the unfamiliar word. The fourth strategy involves looking for clues to its meaning in the word itself. The remaining strategy is the one with which you are probably most familiar: using a dictionary to find the meaning of the unfamiliar word.

Strategy 1: Defining Words by Their Immediate Context

Sometimes words are defined in the sentence in which they are used or in the surrounding sentences. Here is an example of this kind of context clue from "Roy":

By today's standards I would have been labelled with attention deficit disorder, a hyperactive child born with some adrenal problem that made her more prone to rough-and-tumble play than was normal for a girl.

The definition of *attention deficit disorder* is provided in the context. The author's description of herself as a child should give you a strong clue to the meaning of attention deficit disorder.

Strategy 2: Defining Words by Contrast

Writers sometimes give you clues to words by contrasting them with other words that mean something completely different. You can then guess the meaning of a word you do not know by saying "if it doesn't mean this then it must mean that." Here is an example from "Roy":

My mother, a math teacher by training rather than inclination, was an active participant in the historical society.

Suppose you do not know the meaning of *inclination*. You might guess at the correct meaning by going through the following thought process: "The mother has trained to be a math teacher, but she works at the historical society. "Training rather than inclination" suggests that *inclination* means something different from *training*. The mother obviously enjoys her work with the historical society because the author says she is an active participant. Therefore, the word *inclination* must mean *like* or *wish*. Oh, I see, it is a noun, so perhaps it means *preference*."

Strategy 3: Defining Words by the Wider Context

Sometimes you need to look beyond the words surrounding the word you do not know for clues. In the following example from "Roy," let us assume that you know what the term *hierarchy* means, but that you do not know what *stratification* means. You can use clues given in the paragraph to make an educated guess at the meaning of *stratification*.

Every town has its elaborate social hierarchy and cast of characters. Maybe all children are fascinated by the idiosyncratic, those who have difficulty walking the tightrope of acceptable behaviour in a small town where the social stratification is so explicit and the rules feel so inviolable. Those who opt out of the social order are as terrifying as they are enviable.

A hierarchy is a system in which things are ranked one above the other. A social hierarchy is a system of people who are ranked one above the other. By knowing what *social hierarchy* means and knowing what *social order* means, you can guess that *social stratification* means something similar to hierarchy and order.

Strategy 4: Looking for Clues in the Word Itself

As you may already know, words are made up of parts called *roots*, *prefixes*, and *suffixes*. The base of a word is called its root. Roots can appear anywhere in a word—at the beginning, in the middle, or at the end. Prefixes are letters that are attached to the beginning of the root, and suffixes are letters that are attached to the end of the root. If you understand the meaning of various roots, suffixes, and prefixes, you can guess at the meaning of an unfamiliar word. Take the word *autobiography* as an example. Its root is the word element *bio*, which means *life*; its suffix is the word element *-graphy*, which means *record* or *write*; and its prefix is the word element *auto-*, which means *self*.

If you do not know the meaning of a word or the meaning of its root, suffix, or prefix, try thinking of a word that you know that has similar elements. For example, suppose you do not know the meaning of the word *anachronism*, but you know that *chronologic* means "events unfolding according to time of occurrence"; you might guess that *anachronism* has something to do with time. If you know that the prefix *an-* can mean *not*, then you have practically figured out the meaning of the word.

In the tables on page 39 are meanings of some common roots, prefixes, and suffixes, with examples provided of each. Roughly sketch the columns in your Reader Response Journal or on a piece of paper. Then provide examples of your own words in the blank column. Note that some of these word elements have more than one meaning. For example, the prefix *in-* can mean *not* and *into*. As well, some word elements have the same meaning. For example, the prefixes *a-*, *an-*, *dis-*, *im-*, *in-*, and *un-* all mean *not*, and the word elements *com*, *con*, *col*, and *cor* all mean *together* or *with*.

Select a word from "Roy" that you do not understand. Copy the charts on page 39 onto a separate piece of paper. Look up the word's parts. Then, see if you can figure out its meaning. If you cannot find the meaning of a word element, select another word.

Strategy 5: Looking Up the Word in a Dictionary

A dictionary is the obvious place to look up the meaning of a word, but it may not always be the most convenient method to use. Stopping to look up every

PREFIX	MEANING OF PREFIX IN EXAMPLE	EXAMPLE	YOUR EXAMPLE USING THE SAME PREFIX
con-	together, with	congenial	connect
de-	down, from	decline	
dis-	not	disengage	
inter-	between	intercept	
pre-	before	prehistoric	

ROOT	MEANING OF ROOT IN EXAMPLE	EXAMPLE	YOUR WORD USING THE SAME ROOT
bene	good, well	benevolent	beneficial
cred	believe	incredulous	
dict	say	dictation	
phone	sound	telephone	
sol	alone	solitude	

SUFFIX	MEANING OF SUFFIX IN EXAMPLE	EXAMPLE	YOUR WORD USING THE SAME SUFFIX
-able	capable of	agreeable	sociable
-ness	state of	sadness	
-ology	study of	zoology	
-ous	having nature of	marvellous	
-tion	state of	combustion	

unfamiliar word can disrupt the flow of your reading and interfere with your understanding. By all means keep a dictionary at hand when you read, but try some other strategies first. You will be surprised at how much you can learn without consulting a dictionary. If you do not need to consult a dictionary, remember that words often have multiple meanings. You must be careful to choose the meaning that fits the context of what you are reading.

Understanding Unfamiliar Words

The chart on page 40 contains some challenging words from "Roy." Copy the chart onto a separate piece of paper. In groups of four or five, discuss each word, using the following strategies to find its meaning:

- Strategy 1: Defining words by their immediate context

- Strategy 2: Defining words by contrast
- Strategy 3: Defining words by the wider context
- Strategy 4: Looking for clues in the word itself

You may need to use all four strategies to decipher some of the more challenging words. Transfer the chart into your notebook and use the questions in the checklist below to guide you in the activity. Then look up the meaning of the words in a dictionary. How close were you?

UNFAMILIAR WORD	STRATEGY OR STRATEGIES YOU USED	THE MEANING THE CLUES GAVE YOU	THE ACTUAL DICTIONARY DEFINITION OF THE WORD
monogrammed			
hurly-burly			
idiosyncratic			
bell curve			
wagers			
obeisance			
inviolable			
replenish			
equidistant			

Checklist: Strategies for Understanding Unfamiliar Words

- ◯ Can any of us think of similar words whose meaning we know?

- ◯ Can we find the meaning of the word in the surrounding words?

- ◯ Is there a clue to the meaning of the word in a contrasting word?

- ◯ Can we find any clues in the paragraph that contains the word?

- ◯ Can we find any clues in the rest of the memoir?

- ◯ Have we tried breaking down the word into its root, prefix, and suffix?

- ◯ Were we careful to pick the meaning from the dictionary that fit the way the word was used?

Tutorial 6: Writing and Speaking About a Person

Learning Expectation

You will learn how to write a brief biographic sketch.

Understanding the Task

Writing and speaking about another person can be a challenge. How do you capture in words the essence of that person? How do you convince your audience that the person you are writing about is worthy of attention? In this tutorial, you will learn the answers to these questions as you write a biographic sketch about someone you admire, someone you consider a mentor, or someone who has had a positive influence on your life. When you have written your sketch you will deliver it to the class. As a subject you might choose a sibling, a parent, a friend, a teacher, or a co-worker. If you cannot think of anyone to write about, try some of the brainstorming techniques on pages 277 to 279 of Writing Power Tools.

Getting Ready

As you learned in the introduction on pages 30 to 31, good biographers do more than simply tell you about people's lives. They use concrete details and anecdotes to show you how people live or have lived. Had Catherine Gildiner chosen merely to tell her readers about Roy, she might have written a paragraph such as this:

Roy drove the delivery truck for the pharmacy. I used to accompany him on his delivery route. He was a kind man who liked children. He was a hard worker, but he liked games, and he didn't take himself too seriously.

Which are you likely to remember: this brief, dull account that tells the reader what Roy was like, or Catherine Gildiner's lively details and *anecdotes*—brief, personal narratives—that show us what he was like?

The anecdotes about Roy say something about his personality and his values, and they also reveal details about Catherine Gildiner's childhood and the impact Roy had on her developing personality. Think of three words to describe Roy's *qualities*—his personality, values, feelings, and attitudes—and find three details or anecdotes that reveal these qualities. Then do the same for Catherine.

Brainstorming About the Person

One way to develop a message is to brainstorm about your person's character. Think about what that person is like. In your Reader Response Journal or on a piece of paper, write down the first words about the person that enter your mind. See the example on the next page of a student's brainstorming notes about her cousin.

If you think you understand the person, but cannot think of any details or anecdotes that illustrate his or her character, try brainstorming to remember stories about him or her. Recollect the times you have spent together and try to recall specific details. Jot down your recollections. Do any of your recollections reveal anything about the person's character?

Creating a Dominant Impression

Once you have an understanding of your person's character and a collection of anecdotes, you need to

My Cousin Laurie

- *Generous, loving, and giving. Loves children—adopted baby Nicholas because he needed a home. Tell story of Nicholas's adoption—winter; not much room in Laurie's house. She made room for Nicholas.*

- *Positive attitude. Always cheerful, smiling.*

- *Influenced me. Because of her, started doing volunteer work.*

- *Always puts others first: gets up at 5:00 a.m. to do chores, so not to take time away from Nicholas. Delivers meals on wheels. Incredible at balancing work and family.*

select the details that best capture your dominant impression of the person. You may recall from the tutorial on descriptive writing in Chapter 1 that the dominant impression is the overall feeling created by a piece of writing. As you learned in that tutorial, a strong, dominant impression gives a biographic sketch unity, a sense that every detail contributes to the whole picture.

If you try to include details or anecdotes about all of a person's character traits, your readers may find that your sketch lacks unity. It is best to choose one trait that best represents the person and make this the focus of your sketch. You can still bring in some of the other traits, but not as the main focus.

Think about the people in "Roy." What is your dominant impression of Roy? of Catherine? of her father? of her mother?

Selecting Significant Details

Select only those details that say something significant about a person. You might have noticed that in the excerpt from "Roy," we are given no hints about Roy's appearance, his age, or his personal life, but we still have a very strong impression of his character. If you do choose to describe your person's appearance, try to connect it to his or her character.

Using Fresh Images and Vivid Language

People and events come alive for readers when memorable and evocative images appeal to their senses. When you write your sketch, carefully observe the picture you have in your own mind in order to capture it for your readers. If you are relating an anecdote, imagine that you are where it took place. What do you see? Is it light or dark? Do you see colours? What can you touch? What can you smell? Does the smell remind you of anything? What can you hear? Is it noisy, quiet, peaceful, or silent? Try to distinguish the sounds that you hear. Can you taste anything?

Now imagine the person you are writing about in the picture you have just created. What does the person look like? What was the person wearing that day? Close your eyes and imagine the person talking to you. Can you remember what was said? Can you remember the tone of his or her voice?

Putting Ideas and Details in Order

There is no particular order in which you need to present your ideas and details in a character sketch. You might begin your sketch by explaining to your readers why you have chosen to write about a particular person and by providing some background to your relationship. You might begin with a description of the person and use examples and anecdotes to illustrate your points. Or you might open with an anecdote that illustrates a character trait you want to emphasize.

Writing and Speaking About a Person

Before you begin your character sketch, read the biographic sketch that follows. It is the moving eulogy that Justin Trudeau gave for his father, Pierre Elliott Trudeau, at his funeral on October 3, 2000. A eulogy is a speech or piece of writing written in praise of a person, usually given after the person has died. Why do you think Justin chose to begin his eulogy with the anecdote about Santa Claus? What vivid details

does he relate that make this anecdote memorable? Why do you think he relates the second anecdote about the encounter in the parliamentary restaurant? What impression of Pierre Trudeau are you left with after reading the eulogy?

Now write your character sketch, keeping in mind the points you have learned in this tutorial. After you have completed your sketch, review it using the checklist at the end of this chapter.

When you have finished a first draft, exchange character sketches with a partner, and suggest revisions to each other's work.

Once you are satisfied with your sketch and you feel comfortable reading it aloud, take the main points of your sketch and transcribe them onto speech cards. Rehearse in front of your partner at least once more. If possible, deliver your speech to the class.

Text of the Eulogy Given by Justin Trudeau for His Father, the Rt. Hon. Pierre Elliott Trudeau

Friends, Romans, countrymen . . .

I was about six years old when I went on my first official trip. I was going with my father and my grandpa Sinclair up to the North Pole.

It was a very glamorous destination. But the best thing about it is that I was going to be spending lots of time with my dad because in Ottawa he just worked so hard.

One day, we were in Alert, Canada's northernmost point, a scientific military installation that seemed to consist entirely of low shed-like buildings and warehouses.

Let's be honest. I was six. There were no brothers around to play with and I was getting a little bored because dad still somehow had a lot of work to do.

I remember a frozen, windswept Arctic afternoon when I was bundled up into a Jeep and hustled out on a special top-secret mission. I figured I was finally going to be let in on the reason of this high-security Arctic base.

I was exactly right.

We drove slowly through and past the buildings, all of them very grey and windy. We rounded a corner and came upon a red one. We stopped. I got out of the Jeep and started to crunch across towards the front door. I was told, no, to the window.

So I clambered over the snowbank, was boosted up to the window, rubbed my sleeve against the frosty glass to see inside and as my eyes adjusted to the gloom, I saw a figure, hunched over one of many work tables that seemed very cluttered. He was wearing a red suit with that furry white trim.

And that's when I understood just how powerful and wonderful my father was.

Pierre Elliott Trudeau. The very words convey so many things to so many people. Statesman, intellectual, professor, adversary, outdoorsman, lawyer, journalist, author, prime minister.

But more than anything, to me, he was Dad.

And what a dad. He loved us with the passion and the devotion that encompassed his life. He taught us to believe in ourselves, to stand up for ourselves, to know ourselves and to accept responsibility for ourselves.

We knew we were the luckiest kids in the world. And we had done nothing to actually deserve it.

It was instead something that we would have to spend the rest of our lives to work very hard to live up to.

He gave us a lot of tools. We were taught to take nothing for granted. He doted on us but didn't indulge.

Many people say he didn't suffer fools gladly, but I'll have you know he had infinite patience with us.

He encouraged us to push ourselves, to test limits, to challenge anyone and anything.

There were certain basic principles that could never be compromised.

As I guess it is for most kids, in Grade 3, it was always a real treat to visit my dad at work.

As on previous visits, this particular occasion included a lunch at the parliamentary restaurant which always seemed to be terribly important and full of serious people that I didn't recognize.

But at eight, I was becoming politically aware. And I recognized one whom I knew to be one of my father's chief rivals.

Thinking of pleasing my father, I told a joke about him—a generic, silly little grade school thing.

My father looked at me sternly, with that look I would learn to know so well, and said: "Justin, never attack the individual. We can be in total disagreement with someone without denigrating them as a consequence."

Saying that, he stood up and took me by the hand and brought me over to introduce me to this man. He was a nice man who was eating there with his daughter, a nice-looking blond girl a little younger than I was.

He spoke to me in a friendly manner for a bit, and it was at that point that I understood that having opinions that are different from those of another does not preclude one being deserving of respect as an individual.

This simple tolerance and [recognition of] the real and profound dimensions of each human being, regardless of beliefs, origins, or values—that's what he expected of his children and that's what he expected of our country.

He demanded this with love, love of his sons, love of his country, and it's for this that we so love the letters, the flowers, the dignity of the crowds, and we say to him, farewell.

All that to thank him for having loved us so much.

My father's fundamental belief never came from a textbook. It stemmed from his deep love for and faith in all Canadians. And over the past few days, with every card, every rose, every tear, every wave and every pirouette, you returned his love.

It means the world to Sacha and me.

Thank you.

We have gathered from coast to coast to coast, from one ocean to another, united in our grief, to say goodbye.

But this is not the end. He left politics in '84. But he came back for Meech. He came back for Charlottetown. He came back to remind us of who we are and what we're all capable of.

But he won't be coming back any more. It's all up to us, all of us, now.

The woods are lovely, dark and deep. He has kept his promises and earned his sleep.

I love you, Papa.

Checklist: Writing and Speaking About a Person

○ Have I created a dominant impression?

○ Have I chosen details and anecdotes that reinforce the dominant impression?

○ Have I used fresh images and vivid language?

○ Have I chosen details that make the person's life seem remarkable, memorable, or moving?

○ Will my audience understand why I chose to write about this person?

○ Have I incorporated my partner's suggestions into my revised drafts?

○ Have I edited and proofread my work?

○ Have I practised delivering my speech aloud, and have I listened attentively to my partner's suggestions for improvement?

Chapter 4: The Short Story

What Is a Short Story?

A short story is a brief account of fictional events and characters. Skillful storytellers do more than merely narrate a series of events. They use words to create an imaginary world that you can picture in your mind.

Elements of a Short Story

Most short stories contain standard elements. You may already be familiar with some of these—characters, setting, plot, point of view, theme, and tone.

Characters

Short stories generally focus on one or two main characters. The main character is called a *protagonist*. Most protagonists encounter conflict with *antagonists*. The antagonist can be another character, the natural world, or the protagonist's own inner self. In the course of a story, protagonists are typically presented with opportunities to gain insight into themselves or others, to grow or change. In other stories, the characters may miss opportunities to learn about themselves and fail to grow. Characters are revealed by what they think and say about themselves and others and by how they act. They are also revealed by what the narrator and other characters say about them.

Setting

The setting is the time and place in which the story takes place. Settings help you to visualize events. Settings can be linked to the theme of a story. They can also contribute to the atmosphere or mood, and they can tell you something about the characters. For example, a violent storm raging in the background of a story may help create a dark mood and reflect the inner turmoil of its characters or foreshadow an evil happening.

Plot

Authors organize events into a sequence that is called the plot. Many plots follow a similar pattern. The author first establishes the setting, the characters, and the initial conflict, or the *situation*. Details and complications are added as events continue to build. This escalation is called the *rising action*. The rising action eventually reaches a *climax*, or the turning point of a story. After the climax, the conflict is usually resolved in the *denouement*. Plots do not always unfold in chronologic order, the order in which events happen. Sometimes authors use flashbacks to introduce earlier events that help you to understand the present situation.

Narrative Point of View

Writers create narrators to tell their stories. In some stories, the narrator tells the story in the first person. In others, the narrator uses the third person but tells you everything from the point of view of only one of the characters. In still other stories, the narrator is an unnamed person who knows and sees everything. You should not always accept the narrator's version of events or point of view. Authors often deliberately create unreliable narrators whose attitudes colour the events they report.

Theme

The theme is the main idea in a story; it generally reflects the writer's purpose for writing the story. While different readers may identify different themes in the same story, most themes are observations about life and human nature. Here is an example that illustrates the difference between a topic and a theme:

Topic: *childhood friendships*
Theme: *Childhood friendships are the best and clearest of friendships because they are simple.* A story like this might focus on a memorable incident that shows what the author believes to be a "true" friendship.

Tone

Tone is the writer's or narrator's attitude toward the story and the audience. Authors create tone through their choice of words, details, imagery, and style. In some short stories, the tone remains constant. In others, it may shift, for example, from a melancholy tone to a mocking tone, and, finally, to a poignant tone.

How to Read a Short Story

To understand a short story, you need to read it critically, and more than once. Pages 250 to 261 of Reading Power Tools describe some useful strategies for reading a story.

- Before you read a story, read the title. How does it help you predict what might happen in the story?

- Make notes in your Reader Response Journal. Draw diagrams and webs to help you understand plot details, timelines, and relationships.

- Think about the author. Have you read anything else by this author? When was the story published?

- Ask questions about the characters. Who is the protagonist? Does he or she learn and grow? How are the characters revealed to you?

- Ask questions about the plot. Can you spot the initial conflict? What events contribute to the rising action? Do events unfold in chronologic order or does the author use flashbacks? How does the order of events contribute to the meaning of the story?

- Ask questions about the theme. Why do you think the author chose to write about this theme?

The story that follows is "Long, Long After School" by Ernest Buckler, a Canadian writer from Nova Scotia who lived from 1908 to 1984. "Long, Long After School" appeared in the *Atlantic Advocate* in 1959.

Long, Long After School [1]

Ernest Buckler

1 Does this mean hours, days, or years?

I ran into Wes Holman the very day I was collecting for Miss Tretheway's flowers. But it never came into my head to ask him for a contribution.

Miss Tretheway had taught Grade Three in our town for exactly fifty years. She had died the night before in her sleep. As chairman of the school board I had thought it would be fitting if all the Grade Three alumni who were still around made up enough money to get a really handsome "piece." She had no relatives. If I'd given it an instant's consideration, I'd have known that Wes himself must have been in Grade Three some time or other; but I didn't.

Wes was just coming through the cemetery gate as I was going in. Wes "looks after" the cemetery, and I sometimes take a short cut through it on my way to work. I should say that Wes is our local "character." His tiny house up behind the ball park is furnished with almost nothing but books, and he can quote anyone from Seneca to Henry James. But that's his job: caretaker-about-town.

When I spoke to him about Miss Tretheway, a curious change came into his face. You couldn't say that he turned pale, but his stillness was quite different from the conventional one on such occasions. I had expected him to come out with some quote or other, but he didn't say a word. [2]

2 The narrator seems puzzled by Wes' reactions.

He didn't go to her funeral. But he sent her flowers of his own. Or brought them, rather. The following day, when I took the short cut again, I surprised him on his knees placing them.

His little bunch of flowers was the most incongruous thing you could imagine. It was a corsage. A corsage of simple flowers, such as a young boy sends his girl for her first formal dance. And more incongruous than its presence in the circumstance of death was its connection with Miss Tretheway herself. I'm quite sure that Miss Tretheway never once had a beau send her flowers, that she'd never been to a dance in her whole life.

I suppose it would never have occurred to me to question anyone but Wes about his motive for doing a thing like that. But I asked Wes about it with no thought of rudeness whatever. Wes's privacy seemed to be everyone's property. There was probably a little self-conscious democracy in the gesture when we talked to him at all. *3*

"She was so beautiful," he answered me, as if no other explanation was needed.

That was plainly ridiculous. That Miss Tretheway was a fine person for having spent a lifetime in small, unheralded services could not be disputed—but obviously she hadn't *ever* been beautiful. Her sturdy plainness was never transfigured,

3 *Why does Wes not seem to have the respect of the people in the town?*

4   The narrator seems to
    think that beauty is
    primarily physical.

not even for an instant, by the echo of anything winsomer which had faded. Her eyes had never been very blue, her skin very pink, or her hair very brown. She wasn't very anything. 4 Her heart might have been headlong (I think now that it was), but there was always that curious precision and economy in her face which lacks altogether the grain of helter-skelter necessary to any kind of charm. In short, even when she'd been a girl, she'd been the sort of girl whose slightest eagerness, more than if she were ugly or old, a young man automatically shies away from.

"But, Wes," I said, half-joking, "she wasn't beautiful. What made you say that?"

His story went something like this. He told it with a kind of dogged, confessional earnestness. I guess he'd come to figure that whenever we asked him a personal question he might as well satisfy our curiosity completely, first as last.

"Perhaps you remember how the kids used to tease me at school," he said. (I didn't. I guess those things stick in your mind according to which end of the teasing you happen to be on.) "If the boys would be telling some joke with words in it to giggle over, they'd look at me and say, 'Shhh . . . Wes is blushing.' Or if we were all climbing up the ladder to the big beam in Hogan's stable, they'd say, "Look at Wes. He's so scared he's turning pale.' Do you remember that night you steered your sled into mine, going down Parker Hill?"

"No," I said. "Did I do it on purpose?"

"I don't know," Wes said. "Maybe you didn't. I thought you did."

Maybe I did. I don't remember.

"I was taking Mrs. Banks's wash home on my sled, and you were coasting down the hill. The basket upset and all the things fell out on the snow. Don't you remember . . . Miss Tretheway came along and you all ran. She helped me pick up the stuff and shake the snow off it. She went with me right to Mrs. Banks's door and told her what had happened. I could never have made Mrs. Banks believe *I* didn't upset the stuff myself." 5

5   Miss Tretheway seemed to
    know that people would
    not believe Wes.

"I'm sorry," I said. I probably *had* done it on purpose.

"That's all right," he said. "I didn't mind the boys so much. It was the girls. You can't hit a girl. There just wasn't anything I could do about the girls. One day Miss Tretheway was showing us a new game in the school yard. I don't remember exactly how it went, but that one where we all made a big circle and someone stood in the centre. I put my hand out to close up the ring with the biggest Banks girl, but she wouldn't take it. She said, 'Your hands are dirty.' Miss Tretheway made us both hold out our hands. She said, 'Why, Marilyn, Wes's hands are much cleaner than yours. Maybe Wes doesn't like to get *his* hands dirty, did you ever think about that?' She took Marilyn's place herself. Her hand felt safe and warm, I remember . . . and I guess that's the first day I thought she was beautiful."

"I see," I said.

I did, and yet I didn't. The Wes I remembered would hate anything with the suggestion of teacher's pet about it. The only Wes I could seem to remember was the Wes of adolescence: the tough guy with the chip on his shoulder. *6*

He was coming to that. But he stuck in an odd parenthesis first.

"Did you ever notice Miss Tretheway," he said, "when . . . well, when the other teachers would be talking in the hall about the dances they'd been to over the weekend? Or when she'd be telling some kid a story after school and the kid would run off right in the middle of a sentence when she saw her mother coming to pick her up?"

"No," I said. "Why? What about it?"

"Oh, nothing, I guess." He drew a deep breath. "Anyway, I decided I'd be stronger and I'd study harder than anyone. And I was, wasn't I? I did. Do you remember the year they voted me the best all-round student in High School?" *7* (I didn't. It must have been after I'd graduated.) "I guess I just can't remember how happy I was about that. I guess I was so happy I could believe anything. That must have been why I let the boys coax me into going to the closing dance." He smiled. "I thought since they'd voted for me . . . but you can't legislate against a girl's glance."

Those were his exact words. Maybe he'd read them somewhere. Maybe they were his own. I don't know. But it was the kind of remark which had built up his quaint reputation as the town philosopher.

"I didn't want to go out on the dance floor," he said. "I'd never danced a foxtrot or anything. The girls all had on their evening dresses, and somehow they looked different altogether. They looked as if they wouldn't recognize *themselves* in their day clothes. Anyway, the boys grabbed hold of me and made me get into a Paul Jones.* I was next to Toby Wenford in the big ring. Jane Evans was right opposite me when the music stopped, but she danced with Toby instead—and the girl next *to* Jane just glanced at me and then went and sat down. I guess it was a pretty foolish thing to do, but I went down in the basement and drove my fist through a window."

"Is that the scar?" I said. I couldn't think of anything else to say.

"Oh, it was a lot worse than that," he said. He pulled up his sleeve and traced the faint sickle of the scar way up his arm. "You can hardly see it now. But I almost bled to death right there. I guess I might have, if it hadn't been for Miss Tretheway."

"Oh?" I said. "How's that?"

---

*In this type of dance, there are two circles; one inside the other.

6 The narrator only remembers Wes as being angry, not sensitive.

7 Finally . . . something positive happened in Wes' life!

"You see, they didn't have any plasma around in bottles then," he said, "and in those days no one felt too comfortable about having his blood siphoned off. I guess no one felt like taking any chances for me, anyway. Mother said I could have hers, but hers wasn't right. Mine's that odd type—A negative, isn't it? Miss Tretheway's was A negative, too . . . and that's funny, because only seven per cent of people have it. She gave me a whole quart, just as soon as she found out that hers would match." *8*

"I see," I said. So that was it. And yet I had a feeling that that *wasn't* it—not quite.

"She used to come see me every day," he said. "She used to bring me books. Did you know that books . . . well, that for anyone like me that's the only way you can . . .?" He hesitated, and I knew that that wasn't quite it either.

Not until he spoke again, when he spoke so differently, was I sure that only now was he coming to the real thing.

"Do you know what Miss Tretheway said when I thanked her for the transfusion?" he said. "She made a joke of it. She said: 'I didn't know whether an old maid's blood would be any good to a fine young specimen like you, Wes, or not.' The thing I always remember, I knew that was the first time she'd ever called herself an old maid to anyone, and really felt like laughing. And I remember what *I* said. I said: 'Miss Tretheway, you're making me blush.' And do you know, that was the first time I'd ever been able to say *that*, and laugh, myself."

There was quite a long silence.

"She was beautiful," he added softly. "She was a real lady."

The cemetery is right next to the river. I looked down the river where the cold December water lapped at the jagged ice thrown up on the banks, and I thought about a boy the colour of whose skin was such that he could never blush, and I thought about a girl who had never been asked to dance. I thought about the corsage. My curiosity was quite satisfied. But somehow I myself had never felt less beautiful, or less of a gentleman. *9*

8 No one cared but Miss Tretheway.

9 This encounter has made the narrator think about himself and his own behaviour.

Tutorial 7: Analyzing Point of View in a Short Story

Learning Expectation

You will learn
- to recognize point of view
- to determine how point of view, irony, and tone connect in a short story
- to write a short story in a different point of view

Understanding the Task

People read stories for pleasure, for excitement, and for the opportunity to gain insight into human nature. When we read primarily for pleasure and excitement, we often read quickly, eagerly turning the pages to see what happens next. But if we read for a deeper understanding, we need to read more slowly and critically. We need to consider how a writer has used elements such as plot, character, and setting. We also need to look closely at literary techniques such as point of view, irony, tone, and unity. Close, deep, critical reading of a work can make possible new experiences, insights, and impressions.

Getting Ready

This tutorial focuses on point of view. We also discuss irony and tone because they are closely related to point of view. You will analyze the point of view in "Long, Long After School" and its influence on the meaning of the story. Learning how to analyze point of view, recognize irony, and identify tone will help you hone your skills as a critical reader. You will then write a version of "Long, Long After School" from another point of view.

Focusing on Point of View

Authors tell their stories from the point of view that best enables them to reveal their theme. Examining the point of view of a story will help you understand the meaning. To determine point of view, you need to ask yourself the following questions:

- Who is telling the story?
- Does the person telling the story know the thoughts and feelings of some or all of the characters?

Stories are told from four basic points of view:

1. **Omniscient.** This is a third-person point of view. An omniscient narrator knows and records the thoughts and feelings of the characters, but is not identified as a character in the story. In some stories, the omniscient narrator has infinite knowledge of all the characters. In other stories, the omniscient narrator has infinite knowledge of only two or three characters.

2. **Limited omniscient.** This is a third-person point of view in which the narrator has complete knowledge of one character in the story. Through this narrator, the reader can enter the mind of the character and know his or her thoughts and feelings. Other characters' thoughts and feelings may or may not be revealed. The identity of the narrator also may not be revealed.

3. **Objective.** This is a third-person point of view in which only details that can be seen or heard are

recorded. Readers become spectators as they would of a film or a play. There is no narrator to interpret events or analyze a character's motivation. You must draw your own inferences.

4. **First person.** A character, major or minor, tells the story from his or her point of view. This character is the *I* of the story. The reader must determine the credibility of this character as a narrator. He or she may be attentive and reliable. On the other hand, the narrator may be unreliable.

In your journal, write down what point of view is used in "Long, Long After School" and list the reasons for your choice.

Understanding the Personality of the Narrator

"Long, Long After School" is told in time order, using flashbacks to the narrator's school days. Therefore, we see the narrator as a child and as an adolescent; we see him as an adult, someone who, as a "pillar of the community," is probably in early middle age; and we see him at some unspecified later time when he is telling the story about his encounters with Wes.

The narrator's personality is revealed to us by what he says, by his thoughts about Wes and Miss Tretheway, and by Wes' stories about their school days. Think about the following comments and incidents and what they reveal about the narrator. For each point, record your thoughts in your journal.

- The narrator tells us that "Wes is our local 'character,' " and that his job is "caretaker-about-town."

- The narrator collects flowers for Miss Tretheway because he thinks this is the proper and "fitting" thing to do.

- The narrator does not understand how Wes could describe Miss Tretheway as beautiful.

- The narrator did not notice that Wes was teased at school.

If you look at the list of words you used to describe the narrator, you might have words such as unfeeling, insensitive, patronizing, and selfish. But there is another side to the narrator's personality revealed in some of his other comments. What do comments such as the following tell us about the narrator? Record your thoughts in your journal.

If I'd given it an instant's consideration, I'd have known that Wes himself must have been in Grade Three some time or other; but I didn't.

I thought about a boy the colour of whose skin was such that he could never blush, and I thought about a girl who had never been asked to dance. I thought about the corsage. My curiosity was quite satisfied. But somehow I myself had never felt less beautiful, or less of a gentleman.

Comments such as these tell us that the narrator has changed as a result of his encounter with Wes in the cemetery. How do you think he has changed? Does he finally recognize that Wes and Miss Tretheway are his equals? Can we trust the narrator? What does the title "Long, Long After School" tell you about the narrator's attitude toward his story?

Focusing on Tone

Tone is the author's attitude toward the events and characters in the story. Tone is conveyed by point of view, as well as by the words and images the author uses. The dominant tone of "Long, Long After School" is regret. As we have just seen, the narrator's words reveal his superior attitude toward Wes and Miss Tretheway, but they also convey a tone of regret. This tone helps us to realize that the narrator has changed.

Focusing on Irony

Irony is the difference between what seems to be happening and what actually is happening. Irony is one of the most frequently used literary techniques in stories. Authors use it to help make their meaning clear to readers. The first-person point of view is often ironic. There are three types of irony. Dramatic irony occurs when readers understand situations more clearly than the characters in the story. Verbal irony occurs when a character says one thing but actually means something else. Situational irony occurs when there is a difference between what the characters (or readers) expect to happen and what actually happens. "Long, Long After School" contains all three types of irony. The table gives examples of the three types. With a partner, find one other example of each type, and explain why the example is ironic.

TYPE OF IRONY	EXAMPLE
Dramatic irony	Although the narrator has regrets about his treatment of Wes, he seems unaware of his continuing superior attitude. However, the reader detects it.
Verbal irony	When Miss Tretheway tells the Banks girl that her hands are dirty, she is really saying that the girl's behaviour toward Wes is discriminatory and cruel.
Situational irony	Wes was the top student in his class. But instead of finding a good job and becoming a respected member of his community, he has become a caretaker. The people of the community do not consider Wes their equal.

Rewriting a Story from a Different Point of View

Rewrite one scene from "Long, Long After School" from another point of view. When you are satisfied with a draft, exchange stories with a partner. Read both stories, first silently, and then aloud, in the presence of your partner. Then listen while your partner reads both passages.

After you have discussed the two stories, form an action plan for making revisions to your own version based on your discussion. After you have made these revisions, exchange stories again. This time read each other's work for correctness. Finally, edit and proofread your own work.

Checklist: Analyzing Point of View in a Short Story

○ Is my story's point of view completely consistent?

○ Have I successfully conveyed the tone I intended to convey through my use of words and images and through my writing style?

○ Have I used examples of irony?

○ Have I used evocative images and vivid language?

○ Have I incorporated useful suggestions from my partner into an action plan?

○ Have I used the action plan to help me revise my work?

○ Have I edited and proofread my work?

Tutorial 8: Planning a Literary Essay on a Short Story

Learning Expectations

You will learn
- to find a topic and formulate a thesis statement
- to make a mind-map and prepare an outline

Understanding the Task

A literary essay is a more formal kind of writing than the informal, unstructured kind of writing you do in your Reader Response Journal. When you write in your journal, you probably start writing without reflection, jotting down the first thing that comes to mind. When you write a literary essay, you need to spend as much time planning it as you do writing it. This tutorial outlines strategies you can use in planning your essay on a short story. The same strategies would apply if you were writing an essay on a poem, novel, or play. Most of the strategies can be used in any order, though we suggest that you start with reading the story carefully. Each of the strategies can be adapted to suit your own purposes. Use them in the tutorial to plan your own essay on "Long, Long After School." Remember that you are conveying points about the literary works to your audience.

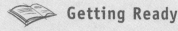 Getting Ready

Reading the Work Carefully

To write a good essay, you need to read the story at least twice. You might want to start by reading it quickly and forming your first impressions. As you read, record your impressions in your journal. Now read the story again. This time think about more than your impressions. Read the story more critically, taking note of the elements: setting, characters, point of view, plot, theme, and so on. What do you think the story means? Do you think the author is successful in conveying his meaning? Can you detect any irony? You may need to read the story a third time before you can answer these questions. Here are two extracts from a student's journal on "Long, Long After School." The first was written after a first reading of the story, the second after she had read the story three times:

Journal Entry One

I don't like the narrator. He is arrogant. I feel sorry for Wes. Sounds like nobody in the town treats him well. I wonder why? Poor Miss Tretheway. She was lonely too. She must have been a kind woman. The last paragraph makes me think that the narrator realizes he has been a jerk.

Journal Entry Two

Now I see why the writer chose to let Wes tell his own story using flashbacks. They help the writer to show how Wes' life has been ruined. They also help the author show how hearing the stories about Wes' youth (and Miss Tretheway) has changed the narrator. He finally sees the part he played in the tragedy of Wes' life. The narrator makes this clear in the last paragraph when he says, "I myself had never felt less beautiful, or less of a gentleman." I think he feels guilty for the way he talked to Wes in the cemetery because all the way through the story he keeps implying that he could have behaved better with Wes.

In the second journal entry, the student writes observations about the plot, the narrator, and the author's meaning that she didn't notice the first time she read the story. She records direct evidence from the story to back up her ideas.

Choosing Your Topic

You may choose your own topic, or your teacher may choose one for you. The key to choosing a topic is to find something that works for you. To see if a topic works, try answering the following questions:

- Am I interested in this topic?

- Is it an important aspect of the story?

- Is it specific enough to be covered well in a short essay?

- Can I find evidence in the story to support this topic?

You will find the essay easier to write if you are interested in the topic, so choose something you want to write about. Your topic should be on an important aspect of the story, but it should also be specific. Given a choice between a broad topic and a narrow topic, choose the narrow one. You will find it easier to control. With a narrow topic, you will avoid the temptation of writing down everything you know about the story. Here are examples of two essay topics:

Too Broad: *plot, setting, and character development in "Long, Long After School"*

Better: *the characterization of the narrator in "Long, Long After School"*

 Identifying Your Audience

Your teacher or classmates are obviously the audience for your literary essay, but you will write with more confidence if you forget this for a moment. Imagine that your audience has read the story two or three times but that you are better informed about your topic. Remember to avoid boring your audience with

details about the plot. A literary essay requires a slightly more formal tone than a personal essay. If you think of your audience as someone you do not know very well, you should find this easier to achieve.

 Identifying Your Purpose

A literary essay is usually written to explain a particular aspect of a work. You may wish to interpret the meaning of a work or evaluate how successful the author is in conveying his or her meaning. Finally, you may wish to discuss your personal response to the work. No matter what the purpose of a literary essay, you should always refer to examples from the story in the body of your essay.

Forming a Thesis Statement

You need to formulate a thesis statement. This should be a single idea that grows out of your exploration of your topic. The simplest way to form a thesis statement is to ask questions about your topic. The answers to these questions should provide you with a list of possible thesis statements. Use your knowledge of elements in a short story to make a list of questions, then try to answer the questions. In the table on the next page is a partial list of questions and answers about "Long, Long After School" based on the topic of the characterization of the narrator. With a partner, discuss other questions you might ask about the characters of the narrator and Wes.

For more on how to write thesis statements, see Tutorial 4 in Chapter 2.

 Identifying Supporting Details Using Organizers

Once you have a main idea for your essay, you need to find details from the story that support the idea. This can be done at any time during the planning process. A good method for identifying supporting details is to draw a mind-map, which is similar to the word association web that you learned about in

QUESTION	ANSWER (POSSIBLE THESIS STATEMENT)
What is the narrator like?	The narrator is insensitive, patronizing, and self-important, but his encounter with Wes in the cemetery gives him sudden insight into his own character flaws.
What are the effects of the narrator's insensitivity and racist attitudes?	The narrator's insensitivity contributes to Wes' and Miss Tretheway's loneliness and alienation from the community.
How are Wes and Miss Tretheway alike?	Wes and Miss Tretheway are kindred spirits: both are lonely, marginalized, and alienated from the community.

Chapter 1. Place a word or phrase representing your main idea in the middle of a blank page. Read the story again, looking for evidence to support your main idea. Scatter ideas for supporting details around the main idea. Circle any ideas that seem to go together, and connect them with lines. These ideas will become the points you will make in your essay. Let us assume that we have selected the question "What is the narrator like?" A mind-map for this topic might look like the one below:

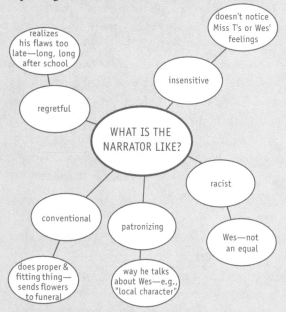

Choose one of the other main ideas about Wes' character and draw your own mind-map.

Preparing an Outline

Some writers like to use an outline as an organizer before they begin drafting their essay. Others prefer to use their mind-map to organize their ideas. If you use your mind-map to group ideas and details, try colour-coding those that go together. Alternatively, you could use a numbering system, or use the editing feature of a word processor to position words and phrases in order.

If you choose to prepare an outline, write down the main points you wish to make in your essay. Underneath each point, list the supporting details from the story. An outline is like a table of contents for your essay.

Here is an incomplete outline for an essay on the narrator's character. In your journal, record the details that fit III A and B.

Introduction

Main Idea: Narrator insensitive, patronizing, and self-important, but his encounter with Wes gives him sudden insight into his own character flaws.

I   Narrator is insensitive
   A. Does not show any feelings for Miss Tretheway
      1. Expresses no regret or sorrow at Miss Tretheway's death

2. Concerned only with doing something "fitting"

3. Did not notice her reaction when other teachers talked about dances

B. Does not detect Wes' feelings about Miss Tretheway

1. Does not understand the meaning of the corsage

2. Does not understand Wes' use of the word "beautiful"

C. Does not notice how Wes felt at school

1. Does not remember sled incident

2. Not aware of racial slurs suffered by Wes

II Narrator is patronizing and self-important

A. Treats Wes like a child or an object

1. Does not think of asking Wes for a contribution

2. Asks Wes personal questions with "no thought of rudeness"

3. Instead of admiring Wes for his knowledge, sees him as inferior. Patronizing language used to describe Wes—"our local character," "town philosopher," "quaint reputation." Feels himself superior to Wes: He is "chairman of the school board." Wes is merely "caretaker-about-town."

III But narrator recognizes his own character flaws

A. Hints at his shame all the way through story

1.

2.

3.

B. Last line reveals sudden insight

1.

Planning a Literary Essay on a Short Story

Using the strategies that work best for you, plan an essay on "Long, Long After School." When you have planned your essay, use the checklist below to decide whether you are ready to start writing. For information about drafting a literary essay, read pages 84 to 85.

Checklist: Planning a Literary Essay on a Short Story

○ Have I taken the time to read the work carefully and critically?

○ Have I identified my audience and purpose?

○ Have I narrowed down my topic into a workable thesis statement?

○ Have I found at least two or three main ideas to support my thesis?

○ Have I found enough details to support my main points?

○ Have I included sufficient detail in my outline?

Chapter 5: The Novel

What Is a Novel?

A novel is a story about characters and events. Novels are longer and more complex than short stories, but they share many of the same elements: they contain characters that engage in actions and dialogue in a specific place or places; they are told from a specific point of view in a particular tone; and they explore themes about life.

Elements of a Novel

The novel is a freer and more fluid form of fiction than the short story. The novel form ranges from brief narratives of 50 pages to epic novels such as *War and Peace* with more than 2000 pages. In spite of this great variety within the form, there are certain conventions that all novels observe. In this section of the book, we will look at how novels use these conventions—or literary elements—differently than do short stories.

Characters

Without characters, the novel would not exist. To capture the readers' attention, characters must be real enough for readers to suspend disbelief and interesting enough for them to keep turning the pages. Characterization in the novel is more complete and varied than it is in the short story. Because of space restrictions, short story writers typically portray their characters on a particular day, or over the course of a few days. We may receive glimpses of the characters as they were in flashbacks and dialogue, but we rarely watch them evolve over a number of years. Novelists, on the other hand, are not constricted by space; they can write about a particular incident in their characters' lives or they can write about the whole of a character's life, from birth to death. Whereas short story writers have room for only a handful of characters, novelists can—and very often do—introduce their readers to a large and varied cast of characters.

Setting

Just as the characters in a novel are more varied than in a short story, so is the setting. Some novels are situated in only one time and place; others take place over the course of many years—even generations—in a wide variety of places. In some novels, the setting is little more than a backdrop for the action. In others, the setting figures prominently, contributing to the mood of the story and reflecting the feelings of the characters.

Point of View

Point of view is just as important to the novelist as it is to the short story writer. Novelists can choose to narrate their story from one of four points of view: omniscient, limited omniscient, objective, and first person (see pages 53 to 54 for a definition of these terms). The omniscient point of view is the choice of many novelists because it allows them to freely explore the thoughts of all their characters. Other novelists use the limited omniscient point of view because it allows them to tell their story primarily from one character's perspective but still shift to another perspective when they need to. Not as many novelists use the first-person point of view, since it is difficult to maintain through the course of a long novel.

Plot

Without a plot, a novel would be a series of unconnected events and characters, one event no more important than another. In the creation of plot, authors select and organize events, emphasizing some more than others. As you learned in the chapter on short stories, conflict is the key to advancing a plot. Most novels present conflict of more than one type as their protagonists struggle to define themselves through their conflict with others. Unlike short stories, which usually have just one main plot, novels often have several plots going on at once. The smaller plots are known as *subplots*. The novels of Charles Dickens, for example, are well known for subplots that eventually have a bearing on the main plot (e.g., *A Tale of Two Cities*). Like short stories, novels are not always told in chronologic order, but authors of novels generally make more use of flashbacks than short story writers.

Theme

A theme—or main idea—is one of the key elements in every literary novel. It is the central message or insight of the novel for the reader. If you finish a novel and find yourself asking, "What was the point?" you may not have grasped the theme, but if you finish it and say, "Yes, I can see the point; I understand why the author wrote this book," then you have probably understood the theme. While a short story typically has no more than one or two themes, a novel often has several closely related themes.

How to Read a Novel

- Before you begin to read, take some time to think about the author and title. What do you know about the author? When was the novel written? Have you read anything else by the author? From the title, can you make predictions about what the novel will be about?

- Skim through the book. How many chapters does it have? Are the chapters short enough to read at one sitting?

- If this is a novel that you have been assigned for school, set a schedule for reading it based on how long you think it will take.

- Now read the first few pages and ask yourself where and when the novel is set. Do any of the characters remind you of someone you know?

- As you read the whole novel, think about which characters you identify with most. For which characters do you feel empathy?

- What is the central conflict of the novel?

- How does the setting contribute to the atmosphere or mood of the novel?

- From whose point of view is the story told? Who is the narrator?

- What tone or tones are used in the novel?

- What views of life or themes do you detect in the novel?

Keep some of these questions in mind as you read the passage that follows. The passage that follows is the first few pages of Mordecai Richler's novel, *The Apprenticeship of Duddy Kravitz*. Richler was born in Montreal in 1931 and grew up in the Jewish neighbourhood of St. Urbain Street. *The Apprenticeship of Duddy Kravitz* was published in 1959 to immediate acclaim. Richler is well known and respected not only for his novels, but also for his essays, short stories, film and television scripts, newspaper columns, anthologies, and children's books. He has received numerous awards, including the Governor General's Award for Fiction for two of his novels.

The Apprenticeship of Duddy Kravitz 1

Mordecai Richler

1   The main character must be Duddy Kravitz. I think apprentice means "learning a trade." So, this must mean that Duddy learns something.

2   Sounds like they only have male teachers at this school.

3   "Ode to the West Wind" must be a poem.

4   Cold-water flats? Must be apartments with no hot water.

5   Must be a boys' school.

What with his wife so ill these past few weeks and the prospect of three more days of teaching before the weekend break, Mr. MacPherson felt unusually glum. He trudged along St. Dominique Street to within sight of the school. Because it was early and he wanted to avoid the Masters' Room, 2 he paused for an instant in the snow. When he had first seen that building, some twenty years ago, he had shut his eyes and asked that his work as a school master be blessed with charity and achievement. He had day-dreamed about the potential heritage of his later years, former students—now lawyers or doctors or M.P.s—gathering in his parlour on Sunday evenings to lament the lost hockey games of twenty years ago. But for some time now Mr. MacPherson had felt nothing about the building. He couldn't describe it or tell you how to get there any more than he could forget that Shelley's 'Ode to the West Wind' 3 was on page eighty-nine of *Highroads to Reading*, the central idea being the poet's dedication to a free and natural spirit.

Since he had first come to the school in 1927—a tight-lipped young Scot with a red fussy face—many of Mr. MacPherson's earliest students had, indeed, gone on to make their reputations in medicine, politics, and business, but there were no nostalgic gatherings at his home. The sons of his first students would not attend Fletcher's Field High School, either. For making their way in the world his first students had also graduated from the streets of cold-water flats 4 that surrounded FFHS to buy their own duplexes in the tree-lined streets of Outremont. In fact, that morning as Mr. MacPherson hesitated on a scalp of glittering white ice, there were already three gentiles in the school (that is to say, Anglo-Saxons; for Ukrainians, Poles, and Yugoslavs, with funny names and customs of their own, did not count as true gentiles), and ten years hence FFHS would no longer be *the* Jewish high school. At the time, however, most Jewish boys 5 in Montreal who had been to high school had gone to FFHS and, consequently, had studied history out of *The World's*

Progress (Revised) with John Alexander MacPherson; and every old graduate had an anecdote to tell about him.

Mr. MacPherson's most celebrated former student—Jerry Dingleman, the Boy Wonder—liked to tell the one about the merit cards.

Once Mr. MacPherson tried giving out merit cards to his students for such virtues as exceptionally high examination results, good behavior, and neat writing. Each month he collected the cards and gave the boy who had earned the most of them the afternoon off from school. But at the end of the third month it was Jerry Dingleman who stood up to claim and, on demand, produce, a suspiciously high stack of soiled merit cards. Now Mr. MacPherson knew that he had never awarded Dingleman, a most inattentive and badly-behaved boy, one single card. On the threat of a week's expulsion from school Dingleman confessed that he had won all the cards playing nearest-to-the-wall with the other boys in the toilet, *6* and so the system ended.

Many of the other anecdotes, especially the more recent (and vastly exaggerated) ones had to do with Mr. MacPherson's drinking habits. It was true that by 1947 he was a heavy drinker, though he was certainly not, as they say, a problem. He was still much slimmer than his first students, but his face seemed more bitingly angry *7* and the curly black hair had greyed. Mr. MacPherson was more inclined to stoop, but, as on his first day at FFHS, he still wore the brim of his battered little grey fedora turned down, rain or shine, spoke with a thick Scots accent, and had yet to strap a boy.

If Mr. MacPherson had altered somewhat with the years the school building had remained exactly the same.

Fletcher's Field High School was five storeys high, like the Style-Kraft building that flanked it on one side and the tenement on the other. Across the street at Stein's the bare-chested bakers worked with the door open even during the winter and, at school recess-time, were fond of winking at the boys outside and wiping the sweat from under their armpits with an unbaked kimel bread before tossing it into the oven. *8* Except for the cracked asphalt courtyard to the right of the school, separating it from the tenement, there was little to distinguish this building from the others.

There were, of course, the students.

At that moment several of the older boys leaned against Felder's frosted window. The biggest sign in Felder's tiny tenement store, DON'T BUY FROM THE GOYISHE *9* CHIP MAN—FELDER IS YOUR FRIEND FOR LIFE, was no longer needed. The last time the chip man, an intrepid French-Canadian, had passed with his horse and wagon the boys, led by Duddy Kravitz, had run him off the street.

6   The tone is quite humorous here.

7   Mr. MacPherson sounds like an angry, disappointed man.

8   Yuk! What an image! Humour again.

9   What does Goyishe mean? The context suggests it might mean someone who is not Jewish.

Duddy Kravitz was a small, narrow-chested boy of fifteen with a thin face. His black eyes were ringed with dark circles and his pale, bony cheeks were criss-crossed with scratches as he shaved twice daily in his attempt to encourage a beard. Duddy was president of room forty-one. *10*

"Hey, guess what," Samuels shouted, running up to the boys. "Mr. Horner's not coming back. He's got triple pneumonia or something. So we're getting a new class master. Mac, of all people."

"Mac'll be a breeze," Duddy said, lighting a cigarette. "He never straps or nothing. Mac believes in *per*-suasion."

Only Hersh failed to laugh. *11* "We're lucky to get Mac," he said, "so let's not take advantage like."

Mr. MacPherson didn't want to cross the street in order to chastise the smokers, but the boys had clearly seen him.

"Weasel! Can the cigs. Here comes Mac himself."

"I should care," Duddy said.

"Kravitz! Put out that cigarette immediately."

"My father is aware that I smoke, Sir."

"Then he's not fit to bring up a boy."

"He's my father, Sir."

"Would you like to stay on in this school, Kravitz?"

"Yes, Sir. But he's my father, Sir."

"Then let's not have any more of your cheekiness. Put out that cigarette immediately."

"Yes, Sir."

No sooner had Mr. MacPherson turned his back on them than Duddy began to hum *Coming Through the Rye*. *12* But, turning sharply into the boys' side of the courtyard, Mr. MacPherson guessed that he was far enough away to pretend that he hadn't heard.

"Boy, are you ever lucky," Hersh said. "Horner would've strapped you ten on each."

Mr. MacPherson began to climb the icy concrete steps that led into the school. When he was on the last step a high-pitched shriek rose among the students. He felt a plunk on the back of his neck as the snowball smashed to smithereens just above his coat collar. Particles of snow began to trace a chilling pattern down his back. Mr. MacPherson whirled about and turned on the students, knitting his eyebrows in an attempt at ferocity. An innocent bustle filled the courtyard. Nobody looked at him. Mr. MacPherson fled into the dark stuffy school building. *13* His horn-rimmed glasses fogged immediately. Ripping them off, he prepared to be vile in class all day.

10 Duddy Kravitz does not sound like a happy person. Sounds like he wants to be admired.

11 Hersh seems like a decent person.

12 I wonder if Coming Through the Rye *is a drinking song?*

13 I do not know whether to laugh or to feel sorry for Mr. MacPherson.

Duddy Kravitz bobbed up in the middle of a group of boys. "How's that for pitching?" he asked.

"Oh, big hero. You didn't mean to hit him. You meant to hit me," Hersh said.

"Mighty neat, anyway," Samuels said.

The bell rang.

"Nobody gets away with insulting my old man," Duddy said. *14*

14 *Duddy has it in for Mr. MacPherson.*

Tutorial 9: Analyzing Characters in a Novel

Learning Expectations

You will learn
- how writers make their characters come alive for their readers
- to analyze the character of Mr. MacPherson
- to write a character sketch of Duddy Kravitz

Understanding the Task

Characters are at the heart of all fiction. The characters that we remember are as real to us as our best friends. In fact, we may even know the characters in novels better than we know our best friends. Think of how well you know the main characters in novels you have read. You may know everything about them—their innermost feelings, opinions, values, hopes, dreams, disappointments, and regrets.

What makes characters real? First, do you believe in them? Do they talk like real people talk? Do they remind you of people you know? Second, ask yourself if they are interesting. Do you want to find out what happens to the characters? Do you care about them? Are they people you would like to meet in real life? Third, do the characters stay in character? Do they behave consistently, without seeming dull? If they change, does the change seem real? If a cold, selfish, and mean character becomes loving, kind, and giving, is the change realistic? Has the change occurred gradually, as a result of the character's experiences and interactions with other people? Or has it come about suddenly and unexpectedly for no apparent reason?

Getting Ready

How do authors turn fictional characters into living, breathing human beings? They use three main techniques to reveal character:

1. They manipulate point of view so that you may hear the characters' thoughts and feelings, and they use a narrator to comment on those thoughts and feelings.

2. They use images that let you see how characters look and move.

3. They use dialogue that lets you hear their characters speak.

In using these techniques, authors pay careful attention to detail, and they write in strong, vivid, colourful language.

Revealing Character Through Point of View

In most novels, everything you read about a character is filtered through the eyes of a narrator. As you have learned, the narrator may be the *I* in the story, an all-knowing presence, or a presence who knows the thoughts and feelings of some, but not all, of the characters. What kind of narrator has Mordecai Richler used in *The Apprenticeship of Duddy Kravitz*?

Telling

An author uses a narrator to tell you about a character's thoughts, feelings, and personality traits. Since omniscient narrators are usually trustworthy and reliable judges of character, we typically believe what they tell us. In this excerpt from *The Apprenticeship of Duddy Kravitz*, the narrator tells us the following facts about Mr. MacPherson: his wife is ill; the thought of teaching for three days before the weekend is making him feel glum; and he had asked "that his work as a school master be blessed with charity and achievement." In relating these facts about Mr. MacPherson, the narrator implies that Mr. MacPherson's hopes for his teaching career remain unfulfilled.

Showing

An author also uses a narrator to show us what a character is like through incidents and anecdotes. As you learned in the tutorial on writing biography, anecdotes are short, personal narratives. The narrator of *The Apprenticeship of Duddy Kravitz* tells us that every old graduate of Fletcher's Field High School has a story to tell about Mr. MacPherson, but chooses to relate only one. What does this anecdote tell you about Mr. MacPherson? How does the incident with the snowball add to your knowledge of the school teacher?

Describing Characters

Like other writers, novelists paint word pictures that allow their readers to visualize their characters. They select concrete details about their characters' physical appearance and movements, and they convey these details using evocative images and strong verbs.

Describing Physical Appearance

Good writers seldom describe the way their characters look without revealing something about their habits, their personality traits, and their feelings. Mordecai Richler describes Mr. MacPherson when he first came to Fletcher's Field High School as "a tight-lipped young Scot with a red fussy face." Imagine, for a moment, that Richler had described Mr. MacPherson instead as a "handsome young Scot with curly black hair." What do you learn about Mr. MacPherson's personality from Richler's original description that you don't learn in the second description?

Here is Richler's description of Mr. MacPherson as he is in the novel, 20 years after he first came to the school:

He was still much slimmer than his first students, but his face seemed more bitingly angry and the curly black hair had greyed. Mr. MacPherson was more inclined to stoop, but, as on his first day at FFHS, he still wore the brim of his battered little grey fedora turned down, rain or shine, spoke with a thick Scots accent, and had yet to strap a boy.

Now read this rewritten description of Mr. MacPherson in middle age. What is the main difference between the two passages?

He was still much slimmer than his first students, but his face had become lined, and the curly black hair had greyed. Mr. MacPherson was no longer as straight as he once was, but he still wore the brim of his battered little grey fedora turned down, rain or shine, and spoke with a thick Scots accent.

Describing Movements

Authors use the physical movements of their characters to reveal personality, feelings, and state of mind. They avoid weak verbs and verb forms such as *went* and *walked*, in favour of strong, precise verbs that

VERB USED TO DESCRIBE MR. MACPHERSON	WHAT THE VERB TELLS YOU ABOUT MR. MACPHERSON'S STATE OF MIND, FEELINGS, OR PERSONALITY
He *trudged* along St. Dominique Street . . .	
. . . Mr. MacPherson *hesitated* on a scalp of glittering white ice . . .	
Mr. MacPherson *fled* into the dark, stuffy school building.	

convey more meaning. In the chart on page 67 are the verbs that Richler uses to describe Mr. MacPherson's movements. Transfer this chart into your journal and record what these verbs tell you about Mr. MacPherson's state of mind.

Revealing Character Through Dialogue

Almost all novels use dialogue to reveal character. Through dialogue we learn directly the thoughts and feelings of a novel's characters. We also infer a good deal about their personality by what they say about themselves and other people, and by how they conduct themselves in conversation. When reading dialogue, remember that people do not always say what they mean.

Not only does dialogue reveal character, it also reveals relationships among characters. It is often the main way in which novelists portray characters in conflict. What do we learn about Mr. MacPherson, Duddy Kravitz, and Hersh in the dialogue on pages 64 and 65?

Creating a Character Sketch of Duddy Kravitz

Using what you have learned from reading the passage from *The Apprenticeship of Duddy Kravitz*, write a character sketch of Duddy Kravitz. Before writing your sketch, you may find it helpful to make a web. Each line should lead to a character trait that can be supported by details from the excerpt. Use the checklist below to guide you as you write your sketch. When you have finished, exchange sketches with a partner, and offer suggestions for revision. Make an action plan based on your partner's comments and your own ideas. Then use the action plan as a basis for your revision of the sketch. As you write and revise your sketch, keep the following checklist in mind.

Checklist: Analyzing Characters in a Novel

○ What does the narrator tell us about Duddy Kravitz?

○ How does the narrator describe Duddy? What does Duddy's physical appearance reveal about his character?

○ What does the narrator say about the boys who attend Fletcher's Field High School? Does this tell us anything about Duddy?

○ What do Duddy's actions and words tell us about his character?

○ Have I shared my character sketch with a partner, and made revisions to my work based on my partner's response as well as my own?

○ Have I edited and proofread my work?

Tutorial 10: Writing a Scene From a Novel

Learning Expectations

You will learn
- to write a creative passage
- to integrate description, anecdote, and dialogue in writing a scene from *The Apprenticeship of Duddy Kravitz*

Understanding the Task

The passage that you read from *The Apprenticeship of Duddy Kravitz* ends with the bell ringing to indicate the start of the school day. Duddy and his friends' first class is history with Mr. MacPherson. This class has a reputation for being the toughest in the school and, as you will recall from the passage you read, Mr. MacPherson is filling in for a teacher who has pneumonia. The boys enter the classroom before Mr. MacPherson and talk among themselves as they wait for him. Your task in this tutorial is to write the next scene of the novel.

Getting Ready

Before you write your scene, consider its purpose. What do you want to reveal about the characters? How do you want the scene to advance the plot? Now close your eyes and let the scene unfold before you. Are there any hints provided in the passage you read about the physical appearance of the school? How do you visualize the classroom? Is it warm or cold on this winter day? What are the predominant colours you see? How are the desks arranged? What do the desks feel like? On a piece of paper or in your journal, write down the details that you can hear, see, smell, feel, and taste.

Setting

Use your list of details to select those that help give the scene a dominant impression. (See Chapter 1, pages 5 and 13 for more about creating a dominant impression.) All the details about the setting should contribute to the dominant impression, or the mood of the scene. If you are trying to create an oppressive mood, rather than referring to the light streaming through the windows, you could mention the tiny windows and the poor light coming from a single bulb.

Plot

As you have learned, authors use conflict to advance their plot. Typically, in a novel, conflicts escalate in what is called *rising action*, until they reach a climax. Think about how you will use the next scene to build on the conflict of the last scene. Obviously, a quiet, uneventful history class would not advance the plot.

Character

So far in the novel, the character of Mr. MacPherson has been fairly well established, but there are still many things that we do not know about Duddy. How can you reveal further details about him? Perhaps there are other things that you want to reveal about Mr. MacPherson. Are there other minor characters you want to develop in your scene?

In your depiction of the characters, try to be consistent with the personality traits that have already been established. For instance, it would not be consistent with what we already know about Mr. MacPherson to suddenly reveal that he has a good sense of humour.

Using what you learned in the last tutorial, develop your characters with details that the narrator tells the readers. Use description, anecdotes, incidents, and dialogue.

Dialogue

Before you write any of your own dialogue, study the speech patterns and sentence structure in the existing dialogue. Good novelists write dialogue that convinces us that their characters are real. To do this, characters must speak in a way the reader expects. A well-educated schoolteacher like Mr. MacPherson uses better grammar and syntax than do his students, and the boys from the neighbourhood talk less formally among themselves than they do to their teacher.

Use dialogue both to advance the plot and to reveal character, keeping in mind that people do not always say what they mean. Your dialogue should reinforce and add details to the impression your readers already have of the characters.

Tone

The tone of the passage that you read from *The Apprenticeship of Duddy Kravitz* is straightforward and matter-of-fact, but there are also moments of comedy, such as the story of Jerry Dingleman and the merit cards, the description of the bare-chested bakers, and even the slightly absurd picture of Mr. MacPherson gingerly mounting the icy steps of the school only to be hit by a snowball. In your passage, try to maintain the same matter-of-fact tone with the occasional humorous moment.

Language

Use vivid language, fresh images, and strong verbs to describe the setting, characters, and events. Describe how Mr. MacPherson looks when he enters the classroom. Instead of saying "Mr. MacPherson entered the room," describe how he entered the room. For example, if you want to show that Mr. MacPherson fears facing the students, you could say, "Mr. MacPherson sidled into the room, his eyes on the floor and his shoulders drooping more than usual." If you want to show that he has recovered from the snowball incident, you could say, "Mr. MacPherson strode purposefully into the room."

For some examples of vivid language, fresh images, and strong verbs, study the box below. The box also features passages that use dull language, conventional, or tired images, and weak verbs. On the left are examples from the book. Which version is more interesting to read?

EXAMPLES FROM *THE APPRENTICESHIP OF DUDDY KRAVITZ*	EXAMPLES FOR COMPARISON
Across the street at Stein's the bare-chested bakers worked with the door open even during the winter and, at school recess-time, were fond of winking at the boys outside and wiping the sweat from under their armpits with an unbaked kimel bread before tossing it into the oven.	Across the street at Stein's, the bakers worked with the door open even during the winter. At school recess-time, they were fond of winking at the boys outside as they kneaded the dough and put it in the oven to make kimel bread.
He felt a plunk on the back of his neck as the snowball smashed to smithereens just above his coat collar. Particles of snow began to trace a chilling pattern down his back. Mr. MacPherson whirled about and turned on the students, knitting his eyebrows in an attempt at ferocity.	The snowball landed on the back of his neck, and he felt particles of snow trickling down his back. Frowning, Mr. MacPherson turned around to face the students.

In the original passage about the snowball incident, notice the power of the verbs and adjectives. The snowball did not just land, "it smashed to smithereens." The modifier "chilling" reflects not only the way Mr. MacPherson feels physically, but also his emotional shock. The last sentence gives us another detail about Mr. MacPherson's personality: being really ferocious is beyond him.

Writing Your Creative Passage

Write a first draft of your creative passage. Then go back and compare it with the excerpt from the novel. Are you satisfied with the way you have portrayed the characters? Have you escalated the conflict between Duddy and Mr. MacPherson? What does your dialogue reveal about your characters? To test the authenticity of your dialogue, try reading it aloud. Exchange creative passages with a partner. Read both passages, first silently and then aloud. Then listen while your partner reads the passages aloud. As you listen, pay particular attention to how the dialogue sounds. Does it capture the flavour of the dialogue in the original passage? Listen as well to the tone of each passage. How well does it capture the tone of the original novel? Based on your partner's feedback and your own critical response, devise an action plan for revising your passage. Then make the appropriate revisions to your passage, using the following checklist.

Checklist: Writing a Scene From a Novel

○ Have I included details that help establish the mood and create a dominant impression?

○ Does my passage advance the plot of the novel?

○ Is my dialogue realistic? Does it reflect the way readers expect these characters to talk?

○ Have I established a matter-of-fact tone, with some comic moments?

○ Have I used vivid language, strong verbs, and fresh images to describe events, people, and the setting?

○ Have I revised my passage according to my action plan?

○ Have I edited and proofread my passage?

Chapter 6: Poetry

Learning Expectations

You will learn
- to read a poem
- to recognize the elements of poetry
- to plan and write a comparison and contrast essay

What Is a Poem?

There are three types of poems: lyric, narrative, and dramatic. You may have seen a lyric poem in the form of a sonnet or an ode, a narrative poem in the form of an epic, or a dramatic poem in the form of one of Shakespeare's monologues.

A lyric poem is an arrangement of words that captures an experience. The experience may be real or imagined. It may be an emotion, an observation, or a thought. Poets write poems because they wish to communicate anything from their deepest feelings to their most superficial annoyances. To feel the power of poetry, read the following selections. The first is a definition of a tiger found in *The Canadian Oxford Paperback Dictionary*. The second is the first verse of a poem called "The Tyger" by William Blake. (*Tyger* is an Old English spelling; "symmetry" means balance or proportion.)

A tiger is a large, carnivorous feline, tawny yellow in colour with blackish transverse stripes and a white belly, found in several places in parts of Africa.

Tyger Tyger, burning bright,
In the forests of the night;
What immortal hand or eye,
Could frame thy fearful symmetry?

After you have read both selections, close your eyes. Visualize the tiger in the dictionary definition. You are probably imagining a still picture of a large animal. Now visualize the tiger in the poem. You might be imagining a powerful beast, eyes flaming and muscles rippling as it bounds through a dark forest. The dictionary provides a factual definition, but the poem captures the tiger's essence.

Elements of a Poem

The basic elements of a poem are images, sounds, and word structures.

Images
As you have learned, most good writers create images that appeal to our five senses, but poetic images are typically more vivid than those you encounter in other writing. Poets often create fresh images by using words in unexpected or even startling ways. In "The Tyger," the poet brings together the words *fearful* and *symmetry* to create a particularly powerful image of the tiger.

Sounds
Sound is an important element of poetry because it contributes to meaning. Poems should be read aloud. As you read, notice if any words rhyme. Is there a rhythm that you can tap with your foot?

Listen for words that sound like other words and for words and sounds that are repeated. Repetition may emphasize important ideas. Read the verse from "The Tyger" again and notice the sound and the rhythm of the verse.

Structures

The way a poem looks on the page is different from the way a story looks. Stories are organized into sentences and paragraphs. Poems are organized into lines and verses or stanzas. The arrangement of the words on the page may give you a clue to a poem's meaning. How do the words look on the page? Are the lines short or long? Are they regular or irregular? How would the verse from "The Tyger" have been different if the poet had used two long lines instead of four short ones?

 ## How to Read a Poem

The key to reading a poem is to become an active participant in the poem. Ask yourself questions, and think about your responses to what you are reading. Use your Reader Response Journal (see page 277 of Writing Power Tools) to record your impressions and thoughts. Here are some points to think about when you approach a poem for the first time.

- Before you read a poem, look at its structure and shape. What is the meaning of the title? Scan the poem for words that catch your eye.

- Read the poem straight through to get a feel for it. Do not worry about what it means. How does it make you feel? What do you see and hear?

- Read the poem again, paying attention to the punctuation. Pause only when you see punctuation marks. Do not stop at the end of a line unless there is a punctuation mark.

- Read the poem out loud. Listen for the rhythm and the rhyme. Listen to the sound of the words. Are any words or sounds repeated?

- Focus on any images that come to mind.

- Focus on the meaning of the poem.

Use these strategies as you read the poems that follow. The first poem is "A November Landscape" by E.J. Pratt (1882–1964), one of Canada's best-known poets of the twentieth century. Born in Newfoundland, Pratt received the Governor General's Award for Literature for two of his poetry collections. He wrote "A November Landscape" in 1932. The second poem is "Winter" by Dorothy Livesay. A contemporary of Pratt's, Dorothy Livesay (1909–1996) was born in Winnipeg and started writing poetry at a young age. She wrote "Winter" in 1928 when she was just 19. Dorothy Livesay twice received the Governor General's Award for Literature.

Keep your own notes as you read these two poems. The notes in the margins represent one person's response to the poems. How do these notes compare with your own notes? When you have read the poems at least four times, work through the tutorials that follow.

A November Landscape

E.J. Pratt

November came today and seized the whole 1
Of the autumnal store of reds, and left
But drabs and yellows on a land bereft 2
Of bird and leaf, of body and of soul.

Outside my window now rain-winds patrol
The earth; last August elms and birches seem
Like half-remembered legends in a dream;
Melodious myths—the Thrush and Oriole— 3

Such strange delusions when November weaves
The sense of desolation and regret
Through clay and stubble, through dead ferns and leaves 4
As here lie sodden 5 on the ground; and yet

This was the story told six months ago,
When April lured the crocus through the snow. 6

1 This makes November seem like a person.
2 Bereft—look this up.
3 Thrush and Oriole—these are birds.
4 A bleak picture.
5 Sodden—look up.
6 This image is a hopeful one.

Winter

Dorothy Livesay

Winter, by whom our stumbling feet were caught,
Who held us long in iron chains of cold, *1*
Winter has turned reluctantly at last, *2*
Unfastened the sharp snares and soberly
Moved like a dream up slopes and over hills,
Breathing a last cool sigh *3* before he went.
Winter has gone. The marsh-hawk and the crow
Follow relentlessly his backward step.

Now you *4* would think that spring must take his place,
Heal up the wounds, breathe freedom on the earth,
Throw all her singing on the barren air.
I tell you, no: we must be captives still *5*
Who watch each other with the winter's look, *6*
Touch with his hand, speak with his bitter breath.

1   This makes winter sound
    hard and unforgiving.
2   Why is it a reluctant
    change?

3   Winter breathes a last
    cool sigh—you can feel
    this.

4   It is as though the narra-
    tor is speaking directly to
    me.
5   The narrator is not pleased;
    we are still captives.
6   People show the charac-
    teristics of winter as they
    watch, touch, and speak
    with each other.

Tutorial 11: Interpreting or Understanding a Poem

Learning Expectations

You will learn
- to read a poem aloud
- to listen to different readings of the same poem
- to identify the use of poetic elements
- to interpret a poem collaboratively

Understanding the Task

To interpret or understand a poem you must become a critical, active reader. This may mean reading a poem four or five times before you grasp its meaning. Critical reading also requires an understanding of the elements that poets use in their poems. Remember that nothing in a poem is there by accident. The author has deliberately placed every line, every word, and every punctuation mark on the page to highlight the meaning of the poem.

Getting Ready

We have already discussed how poems are different from stories in their emphasis on images, sound, and shape. Below, we explore how poets use these elements and other devices to create and enhance their meaning.

The Speaker

Most poems have a voice that is called the *speaker*. The speaker establishes the tone and the point of view. See pages 53 to 54 for more detail about point of view in literature. Like a story, a poem may be written in the first person or the third person. Sometimes the first-person *I* in the poem is the poet, and sometimes it is a character created by the poet. When you read a poem, ask yourself who could be speaking: is it the poet or is it someone else? Who might the speakers in "A November Landscape" and "Winter" be?

Tone

Tone is the writer's or speaker's attitude toward the subject and the audience. Just as someone's tone of voice may be angry, sad, sarcastic, or playful, so may the tone of a poem. Because you cannot hear the speaker's voice, tone can be difficult to detect. Details, word choice, imagery, sound, and structure all contribute to a poem's tone.

Many poems shift from one tone to another. Each shift in tone demonstrates the poet's or speaker's change of attitude. Look for clues to tonal shifts in the following:

- signal or transition words (e.g., *but, yet, still, however, although*)
- punctuation (e.g., periods, colons, dashes, commas)
- repeated words
- changes in line or stanza length
- changes in the shape of the poem or in stanza divisions

The best way to detect a poem's tone is to read it aloud or to ask a classmate to read it aloud. Look closely at "A November Landscape" and "Winter" for clues of tonal shifts. Then find a partner and read both poems out loud in a tone or tones that you think are appropriate. After you have finished, ask your partner what tone or tones he or she detected. Then reverse roles: your partner reads the poem while you listen. How was the tone you used different from your partner's? How did this activity change your interpretation of the poems?

Imagery

As you know, images are vivid pictures that we form in our imagination and that appeal to our senses. Select three images each from "A November Landscape" and "Winter." To which of your senses do these images appeal?

Poets often juxtapose images for a startling or dramatic effect. Juxtaposition is a poetic and rhetorical device in which normally associated ideas, words, or phrases are placed side by side, creating a surprising, shocking, or witty effect.

Figurative Language

We use figurative language, sometimes known as *figures of speech*, every day. The opposite of figurative language is literal language. If you say "I am soaked," you are speaking literally; whereas if you say "I'm a drowned rat," you are speaking figuratively. When we speak figuratively, we say one thing but mean more. Poets use figurative language to evoke unique and memorable images and to create emotional intensity.

Similes and Metaphors

Poets use similes and metaphors to compare things that are actually unlike. You can recognize similes easily because they use the words *like*, *as*, or *seems*. An example of a simile is "her lover's heart is *like* stone." Metaphors compare unlike things without using the words *like*, *as*, or *seems*. An example of a metaphor is "her lover's heart *is* stone." Metaphors are more diffi-

cult to recognize than similes because many of them are implied. There is an implied metaphor in "The Tyger" on page 72. The poet implies that the tiger is fire, but he does not state this directly. Instead, he says the tiger is burning bright. Can you find any similes or metaphors in "A November Landscape" and "Winter"?

Personification

Personification is the description of an object, animal, or concept as if it had human qualities. In both "A November Landscape" and "Winter," the seasons are given human qualities. For example, in "Winter" we read that winter "held" us.

Apostrophe

Apostrophe is a form of personification in which the absent, dead, or nonhuman are addressed directly, giving the impression that they could reply to the speaker. Can you find any examples of apostrophe in "A November Landscape," "Winter," or the verse from "The Tyger"?

Hyperbole

Hyperbole is a deliberate exaggeration used to illustrate a truth or to emphasize a point. "A November Landscape" opens "November came today and seized the whole / Of the autumnal store of reds. . . . " Of course, it is unlikely that every possible shade of red was represented, but the power of the idea—that every bit of autumn colour has been taken by November—comes across better with this exaggeration. Can you identify any hyperbole in "A November Landscape" or "Winter"?

Understatement

The opposite of hyperbole is understatement—saying less than what you mean. Understatement is often used for ironic or comic effect. A classic example of comic understatement occurs in Shakespeare's

A Midsummer Night's Dream, in which Bottom, the weaver, is changed into a donkey while he is sleeping. The first person to see him after he awakes exclaims, "O, Bottom, thou art changed."

Paradox and Oxymoron

A paradox is an apparent contradiction that at some level is true. An example of a paradox occurs in *Hamlet* when Hamlet tells his mother, "I must be cruel only to be kind."

Oxymoron is a form of paradox in which contrary terms are placed side by side in a single phrase, as in "sweet sorrow," "wise fool," and "darkness visible." In bringing together apparently contradictory words and images, poets extend or underscore their meaning.

Can you find any examples of paradox and oxymoron in "A November Landscape," "Winter," or the verse from "The Tyger"?

Irony

Irony is a frequently used literary device in fiction, poetry, and drama. As discussed in Chapter 4 on the short story, irony results when words say one thing but imply the opposite, and when there is discrepancy between the surface meaning and the implied meaning. Irony is a powerful poetic device that enables poets to suggest meanings without stating them. Irony is often integral to the theme of a poem. Poets and other writers often create irony by giving their works titles that are opposite in meaning to the work itself.

Read the following poem, "Birth" by Cécile Cloutier. How does the poet use irony to convey her theme?

Perfect from the start
That small cell
Contains
Already

The wrinkles and death
Of an old man

Sarcasm

Sarcasm is a type of irony in which the speaker makes a positive comment that turns out to be negative. In speech, sarcasm is often conveyed by tone of voice. For example, the words "thanks for your help" could convey appreciation or annoyance depending on the tone the speaker uses. Poets sometimes create sarcasm through a sudden, jarring change of tone.

Pun

A pun is a play on words that are identical or similar in sound but have diverse meanings. Puns are often used for comic effect. Can you detect the pun in the following example (by Laurence Perrine)?

Two brothers devised what at sight
Seemed a bicycle crossed with a kite.
    They predicted—rash pair!
    It would fly through the air!
And what do you know? They were Wright!

Puns can also have a serious intent. When Mercutio lies dying in *Romeo and Juliet*, he says to his friends, "Ask for me tomorrow, and you shall find me a grave man."

Allusion

An allusion is a reference to something in previous literary works or in history. Many literary allusions refer to the Bible or to Greek mythology. Poets and other writers use allusions to suggest more than the surface meaning of the words. Through the use of allusions, they can intensify emotion, extend ideas, and reinforce meaning.

Symbol

A symbol is an object, action, person, animal, or plant that represents something else. Image, metaphor, and symbol are sometimes difficult to distinguish from one another. The writer Laurence Perrine uses the examples in the box below to help students distinguish between images, metaphors, and symbols.

Poets and other writers use symbols to express ideas and emotions and to add depth to their writing. Symbols can provide writers with a succinct way of expressing an idea or emotion that is difficult to put into words. In some poems, the symbolic meaning of a poem is imprecise, complex, and ambiguous. In others, it is clearly defined. Read "Stopping by Woods on a Snowy Evening" on page 112. Is the use of the word "sleep" literal, symbolic, or metaphoric? Now look again at "A November Landscape" and "Winter." Are any of those poems' images used symbolically?

Sound Devices

Poets use sound devices to emphasize certain sounds. These sound devices often contribute to a poem's meaning. Below, we look at several important sound devices.

Rhythm and Rhyme

Rhythm is a wavelike repetition of sound. Rhyme occurs when identical or similar-sounding words are used at the ends of lines. Many poems written before the twentieth century rhyme and have a regular rhythm, while many modern poems are written in free verse. Free verse has no rhyme, so poems written in free verse often sound like regular speech. "The Tyger" has a regular rhythm and a musical lilt to its lines, most of which rhyme. "Winter" is an example of free verse. Read "A November Landscape" again. Does it have a regular rhyme or is it written in free verse?

Even poems that rhyme sometimes contain lines that don't rhyme or that half rhyme. Look again at "The Tyger" and notice that the word "symmetry" does not rhyme with the word "eye." Poets often alter the regularity of a rhyme to create a sense of the unexpected and to add force to a particular word or words.

Alliteration

Alliteration is the repetition of consonants at the beginning of words. Poets use alliteration to give certain words and phrases extra power and emphasis. In "The Tyger," the poet uses the *b* sound in "burning bright" to add force to his metaphor of the tiger as fire. Look for examples of alliteration in "A November Landscape" and "Winter." Did you notice the alliteration in the last line of "Winter"? To test the power of "bitter breath," try substituting the word *sour* for *bitter*. With this change in wording, the last line loses some of its impact.

Onomatopoeia

Onomatopoeia generally refers to the use of words that imitate the sounds the words refer to—for

Image	"A shaggy brown dog was rubbing its back against a white picket fence."	In this sentence the shaggy brown dog is an image, and nothing more.
Image as metaphor	"Some dirty dog stole my wallet at a party."	This sentence is not about a dog at all; the dog is representing something else and is therefore a metaphor.
Image as symbol	"You can't teach an old dog new tricks."	This sentence is about a dog, but it is also about living creatures of any species. The old dog is therefore a symbol.

example, *whiz* or *clang*. This term, however, has been expanded to refer to any word whose sound is suggestive of its meaning.

Read aloud the verse from "The Tyger," "A November Landscape," and "Winter." Can you find any examples of onomatopoeia?

Assonance and Consonance

Assonance refers to the repetition of vowel sounds in a series of words, for example, *cry* and *tide*. Notice the repetition of the long *i* sound in the first line of "The Tyger."

Consonance is the repetition of a consonant sound within or at the end of words. Notice the consonance in the repeated *t* sound in the following line of "Meeting at Night" on page 113: "And blue spurt of a lighted match." Can you find any examples of assonance and consonance in "A November Landscape" and "Winter"?

Number of Syllables

The number of syllables in a word can affect meaning. Poets deliberately choose short, one-syllable words with long vowels to slow down the pace and emphasize certain words. Notice how the word "no" in the last stanza of "Winter" slows down the pace of the line. Why do you think the poet chose to draw attention to this word?

Punctuation

Poets also use punctuation to emphasize certain words. Punctuation slows your reading down. When there is no punctuation, the pace is usually much faster. You do not stop reading or pause at the end of a line if there is no punctuation. The term *enjambment* refers to the continuation of a sentence without pause, from one line or couplet to the next. On the other hand, the term *end-stopped line* marks a full pause at the end of a line of poetry, usually marked by a punctuation mark. Punctuation used in the middle of a line can draw particular attention to a word or group of words. Look at the word "no" in the last stanza of "Winter" again. Notice the effect of the comma and colon that surround it. How does the use of the word "no" affect the tone of the poem?

 ## Responding to a Poem

Read the poem "Blow, Blow, Thou Winter Wind" on page 81. Then form groups of three. Review the strategies for reading a poem on page 73. As a group, take turns reading the poem aloud, while the others listen attentively. As you listen to each reading of the poem, close your eyes and listen specifically for the following:

- specific images that enter your mind as the poem is read aloud

- the tone or tones that you detect in the speaker's voice

Every time the poem is read aloud, notice the particular images that you visualize and to which of your senses they appeal. Notice, as well, the tone or tones that are used. After each reading, the listeners should describe the images they visualized and the tones they heard. Are these different, depending on who is reading the poem? If so, how? Then use the elements we have reviewed in this chapter as a guide to interpreting and discussing the poem. Before you begin, read the tips about effective listening and effective discussions on pages 321 to 322 of Oral Communication Power Tools. The checklist on page 81 might also be useful as a guide to your discussion.

Blow, Blow, Thou Winter Wind (from *As You Like It*)

William Shakespeare

Blow, blow, thou winter wind,
Thou art not so unkind
　　As man's ingratitude;
Thy tooth is not so keen,
Because thou art not seen,
　　Although thy breath be rude.
Heigh-ho! sing, heigh-ho! unto the green holly:
Most friendship is feigning, most loving mere folly:
　　Then, heigh-ho, the holly!
　　This life is most jolly.

Freeze, freeze, thou bitter sky,
That dost not bite so nigh
　　As benefits forgot:
Though thou the waters warp,
Thy sting is not so sharp
　　As friends remember'd not.
Heigh-ho! sing, heigh ho! unto the green holly:
Most friendship is feigning, most loving mere folly:
　　Then, heigh-ho, the holly!
　　This life is most jolly.

Checklist: Interpreting or Understanding a Poem

○ What are our different impressions of the poem?

○ How did our different interpretations affect how we read the poem?

○ Is the speaker the poet, or is it someone else?

○ Are there any examples of similes, metaphors, or personification? If so, what are they? How or what do these images add to the poem?

○ How do the rhyme and rhythm affect our interpretation of the poem?

○ Are there any examples of alliteration or other sound devices? How do they contribute to our interpretation of the poem?

○ What forms of figurative language can you identify in the poem? How do these forms enhance or deepen the meaning of the poems?

Tutorial 12: Planning and Writing a Comparison and Contrast Essay

Learning Expectation

You will learn to plan and write a comparison and contrast literary essay.

Understanding Comparison and Contrast

You might be expected to write an essay that compares and contrasts two literary works. This might be an essay on two poems or two stories or, perhaps, a story and a film. Comparison deals with similarities, while contrast deals with differences. You compare and contrast two works when you point out both similarities and differences. Considering how two writers handle similar subjects can deepen your understanding of both works.

Comparison and contrast come naturally to us. Every day we make choices that involve considering similarities and differences. When we ask ourselves whether we want a hamburger or a salad for lunch, we make a mental comparison of the two items. When we choose between going to a movie or seeing a hockey game, we compare and contrast the two activities in our minds. In writing a comparison and contrast essay, you ask yourself some of the same questions you ask yourself every day:

1. What are the main similarities between item one and item two?

2. What are the main differences between item one and item two?

Choosing a Topic

Before you begin to write a comparison and contrast essay, you need to choose a topic. Your topic should not be too large and inclusive. Comparing one or two elements of a literary work is easier than comparing every element of each work. If you choose to write an essay on "Winter" and "A November Landscape," select one or two elements to write about. You could compare and contrast the use of imagery in the poems, the mood, the speaker's tone, the use of sound, personification, the theme, and so forth.

After you have chosen your topic, you need to consider why you are writing the essay and for whom you are writing it. Read page 25 for suggestions on audience and purpose.

Organizing Your Comparison and Contrast Essay

A Venn diagram can help you organize your ideas for a comparison and contrast essay. Suppose you have chosen to write about the tone of "Winter" and "A November Landscape." To sketch a Venn diagram, draw two intersecting circles. In the part where the circles intersect, jot down any similarities in the tones of the two poems. Write down the differences in the individual circles. On page 83 is a Venn diagram comparing and contrasting the tone of "Winter" and "A November Landscape."

Your Venn diagram should give you some ideas for the details you will include in your essay. Your next step is to narrow your topic down into a thesis statement.

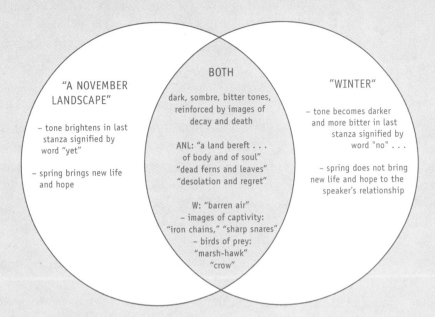

For ideas on how to transform your topic into a thesis statement, see pages 25 to 26. Let us assume that our thesis statement for an essay on tone is "Although the tone of both poems is bleak, the tone of 'A November Landscape' brightens at the end, while the tone of 'Winter' grows even more bleak."

Preparing an Outline

Once they have thought of a thesis and sketched a Venn diagram, some writers feel ready to work on a first draft. Others tinker with their diagram to colour-code, circle, or number central ideas. Still others make an outline for their essay. The key is to try various strategies until you find what works best for you. To prepare an outline for a comparison and contrast essay, organize your ideas into main points, and compare and contrast the two subjects under each point. An outline for an essay on tone in "A November Landscape" and "Winter" might look like this:

Paragraph 1   Introduction and thesis statement

Paragraph 2   The tone in both poems is bleak
  a. Images of death and decay
    - In "A November Landscape": "land bereft" and "dead ferns"
    - In "Winter": "iron chains," "sharp snares," "birds of prey"
  b. Sombre words
    - In "A November Landscape": "desolation" and "regret"
    - In "Winter": "soberly" and "relentlessly"

Paragraph 3   Tone in both poems changes in the last stanza
  a. The tone in "A November Landscape" brightens
    - Signified by word "yet" in third stanza
    - Images of spring ("crocus" and "April") bring new life and hope

   b. Tone in "Winter" appears to brighten, then grows bleak again
     – Vision of spring shut down by speaker
     – Phrase "bitter breath" ends poem on note of despair

Paragraph 4   Conclusion summarizing the similarities and differences

Strategies for Writing Your Essay

Use your Venn diagram or your outline as a guide when you write a draft of your essay. Make sure you observe the following conventions for writing a literary essay. (These conventions apply to any kind of literary essay, not just an essay on poetry.)

- Identify the title and author of the poems in your introductory paragraph.

- Use the present tense to write about the poems.

- Use quotations from the poems to support your points.

Integrating Quotations in Your Literary Essay

The best evidence for your thesis is an actual quotation from the work itself. If, for example, you say that the tone of a poem is sombre, you should quote words or lines from the poem that support your point. Here are some details about the use of quotations in a literary essay:

- Use quotation marks for short quotations that are less than four lines long. Integrate short quotations into your own paragraphs.

- Set off prose quotations of four or more lines from the rest of your paragraph by indenting at least five spaces. Do not use quotation marks.

- Set off poetry quotations of more than four lines by using the same line length and punctuation of the original poem. For an example, see how "The Tyger" is set off from the text on page 72.

- Use ellipses (. . .) to indicate words that you have left out of the material you are quoting.

- Explain the quotation's significance and how it supports your thesis. Do not assume that your purpose in including the quotation is self-evident.

- Make quotations part of your own sentences. Your writing will flow smoothly if you incorporate quotations into your own sentence structure, as in the following example:

> The tentatively hopeful tone indicated by the images "freedom on the earth" and "singing on the barren air" is shattered by the phrase, "I tell you, no." The tone turns unrelentingly bitter as the speaker tells her lover that they are "captives still," trapped in a loveless relationship, watching "each other with the winter's look" and speaking with "his bitter breath."

Making Sure Your Essay Is Coherent

If your essay is coherent, your reader should be able to follow your train of thought. The chart below lists a number of signal words and phrases that will help

SIGNAL WORDS FOR COMPARISON AND CONTRAST ESSAYS	
TRANSITIONS FOR COMPARISON	TRANSITIONS FOR CONTRAST
also	in contrast with (or to)
equally	on the other hand
just	unlike
just as	different from
like	although
likewise	even though
similarly	whereas
similar	while
	however

you make your comparison and contrast essay more coherent. When you write and edit your essay, review this list to make sure you have used some of these words or phrases.

Making Sure Your Essay Is Unified

When an essay is unified, all the paragraphs relate to the essay's thesis. The essay contains no irrelevant information. To make sure your essay is unified, check every paragraph and sentence to see that they relate to the thesis. In an essay that compares the tone of two poems, everything in it should be about tone. If you discuss theme, rhythm, or personification, they should all be mentioned in connection with the tone in the two poems.

in Tutorial 4 in Chapter 2 to determine your audience and purpose and to formulate a thesis statement. Draw a Venn diagram to help you capture your topic's similarities and differences. Map out your essay either by using an outline or another method for grouping ideas. Then, prepare a first draft of the essay.

Use the checklist below to ensure that your essay is as clear as it can be. Then share it with a classmate. Make any worthwhile changes to the essay that he or she suggests. For more on revising, editing, and proofreading your essay, see Writing Power Tools, pages 303 to 304.

Planning and Writing a Comparison and Contrast Essay

Choose a topic for a comparison and contrast essay on "Winter" and "A November Landscape." Or, if you prefer, write a comparison and contrast essay on two poems of your choice. Use the strategies you learned

Checklist: Planning and Writing a Comparison and Contrast Essay

○ Did I identify an audience and purpose for my essay?

○ Did I narrow down my topic into a clear thesis statement with a limited scope?

○ Did I use organizers such as a Venn diagram or an outline to help identify similarities and differences?

○ Did I use quotations from the poems to support my points? Did I integrate the quotations into the body of my essay?

○ Did I ask a partner to edit my final draft for clarity, coherence, and unity?

○ Did I proofread my essay for grammar, syntax, and spelling errors?

Chapter 7: Drama

Learning Expectations

You will learn
• the elements of drama
• to read a script
• to identify symbols in literature
• to write dialogue

What Is Drama?

Drama is a special type of literature. Like fiction, drama uses plot and character to develop a theme. Like poetry, it uses imagery, figurative language, and sound to make us feel emotions more intensely. However, drama is unique in one key respect: it is performed by actors for an audience.

Although we may read a drama, a live performance drama demands involvement and active listening. Actors convey meaning through their words, gestures, movements, and facial expressions. The director conveys his or her vision through the actors, costumes, sets, and lighting. But you, as a member of the audience, actively interpret actions and meaning.

Comedy, Tragedy, and Melodrama

The terms comedy, tragedy, and melodrama are used to identify types of dramas. You might think that all tragedies are unbelievably sad, all melodramas unrealistic, and all comedies hilariously funny, but, in fact, some tragedies do not make you sad, some melodramas are not much more exaggerated than

real life, and some comedies are not funny at all. Comedy, tragedy, and melodrama differ mainly in their portrayal of human nature.

Not all dramas can be easily categorized. Some contain elements of tragedy and melodrama; some can be considered tragicomedies, and some have elements of tragedy, comedy, and melodrama.

Comedy

Comedy points out human weaknesses and limitations by inviting us to laugh at characters who are vain, hypocritical, foolish, or simply unaware of their own failings. Comic plots are typically implausible, with unlikely coincidences and mistaken identities at the centre of the action. True comedy always ends happily, often with reconciliation or a marriage. Comedies can be romantic or satirical. In a romantic comedy, the main characters are usually ordinary and likable, but the situations in which they find themselves are often comic. Most television situation comedies are examples of this type of comedy. In a satirical comedy, the main characters are often not particularly likable, and they are completely unaware of their character flaws. *Seinfeld* is an example of this type of comedy.

Tragedy

Tragedy portrays missed potential. In the classical tragedy of ancient Greece and Shakespeare, the main character is typically a noble person who is highly respected and admired by other characters in the play. Tragic heroes in classical tragedy are usually well-intentioned people, but because of a character flaw or an error in judgement, they suffer a fall from grace, which typically results in banishment or death. In modern tragedies—such as Arthur Miller's *Death of a Salesman*—the tragic hero is an ordinary person who never lives up to his or her potential because of a character flaw or an error in judgement or because of overwhelming circumstances. For a play to be considered a tragedy, the tragic hero must be responsible for his or her own downfall. Thus, a drama in which a stranger murders the protagonist—perhaps an ordinary young mother of two children—could not be called a tragedy. Neither could a drama in which a person dies young in an accident or from a disease. Both these incidents could be considered sad and untimely, but technically they are not tragedies.

Melodrama

Melodrama, like tragedy, portrays human anguish and suffering. Like tragic heroes, protagonists in melodrama are typically good people, but they are not necessarily the architects of their own misfortune. In melodrama, characters are often one-dimensional, the good characters overcome the evil characters, and the ending is usually happy. Conflict may be intensified by sensational incidents. For example, a jealous woman poisons her sister because both love the same man, but the sister is saved from death because her lover finds her in time. When we say that something is melodramatic, however, we mean that it is unrealistic, sensational, and exaggerated.

Elements of Drama

You are probably more familiar with drama than you think you are. Plays, feature films, television programs, and radio teleplays are all dramas. Even soap operas and advertisements offer us a form of drama. All dramas have the following elements.

Script

A script is the written version of a drama. A script is like a map for the director and the actors. It is divided into acts and scenes, and contains the *stage directions*, the *cast of characters*, and the *dialogue*. A script written for the screen is called a *screenplay*.

Directors rarely follow a script slavishly. While they try to be faithful to the meaning of an original drama, their interpretation may involve changing aspects of the script. For example, they may cut lines and even entire scenes; they may cut characters; and they may change the setting, location, or time of the play.

Acts and Scenes

Scripts are organized into acts that are, in turn, subdivided into scenes. Some brief scripts contain only one act and so are known as one-act plays. Longer scripts are typically divided into two or more acts. A new act or scene often signals a change in time and location, which requires a different set, costumes, and so forth.

Stage Directions

Stage directions are instructions for the staging of the drama that appear in the script. They typically describe the set and suggest how the actors should move, act, and speak. They may also provide instructions or guidelines for lighting, sound effects, and music.

Setting

The setting in a drama includes the location, the time, and the set. It also includes lighting and sound effects. The setting helps convey the mood and atmosphere of the play. In some dramas, it may figure as prominently as one of the characters. In others it may simply provide a venue for the action and dialogue.

Cast of Characters

The characters in a drama are presented in a cast of characters that appears at the beginning of the script. The cast of characters is sometimes called the *dramatis personae*. It usually introduces the characters in the order in which they appear and sometimes gives the reader a little background about them. For a live performance, the cast of characters, along with actor names, is presented in a program. In a film, television program, or radio teleplay, the cast of characters appears in the credits at the beginning and/or end of the program.

Characters

The number of characters in a drama varies tremendously. Some short, one-act plays have only two or three characters. Longer three-act plays have as many as 20 or 30 characters. Some films and television series have more than 50 cast members. Usually, even in a longer play, film, or television series, only six or seven of the characters play a central role in the action.

The main characters in a successful drama are *rounded*; that is, they are complex and many-sided. Characters in drama are usually at odds with each other, even more than they may be in a work of fiction or a poem. The differences among the characters may create comic situations or may result in tragedy.

Characters in a drama reveal themselves by what they say or do, or by what others say about them. The writer may use the stage directions and cast of characters to provide some insight into a particular character's personality, but there may not be a narrator to interpret events or tell us what the characters are thinking.

Plot

Successful dramas have well-defined plots with intense conflict and dramatic confrontations. Dramatic conflict is at the heart of all drama. Characters are usually in conflict with themselves or other characters. Characters create and increase conflict by arguing, feuding, taunting, or teasing. They resolve conflict by revealing their own hopes and fears and by trying to reach a compromise.

The plots of many plays follow a standard pattern. They begin with an *exposition,* in which dialogue reveals the background to the characters and the conflict. Next there is *rising action,* in which conflict escalates. This leads to the *climax* or the turning point of the action in which something is revealed or discovered. The climax is followed by *falling action* and *resolution.*

Some writers use a device called *foreshadowing* to advance their plots. Foreshadowing is the presentation of events, characters, or objects that hint at events to come. Foreshadowing often adds suspense to a drama.

Dialogue

Dialogue is a conversation between two or more people. Dialogue, along with gestures and facial expressions, is the main source of a drama's meaning. Plot and character are revealed through dialogue.

Monologue

A monologue is a long speech spoken by one character usually when alone. The monologue is a device that writers of dramas use to enable their characters to express their thoughts directly to the audience. In this way the audience can tell what a character is thinking and feeling. Sometimes, especially in Shakespearean drama, a monologue is called a soliloquy.

 ## How to Read a Drama

When you read a script you must visualize how it would appear on the stage or screen. Since there is no director or actors to interpret the action and dialogue, you must read the work critically to actively interpret its meaning. In a sense, when you read a drama, you become the director.

Below are some strategies you may find helpful when you read a script:

1. **Ease into the script.** Before you read, take some time to get ready.

   - Read the title and predict what might happen in the play.

   - Flip through the script to find out how long it is. How many acts and scenes does it have?

   - Read any stage directions you find at the beginning of the play, including the description of the setting and scenery, and the cast of characters.

   - What do the stage directions tell you about the setting? Do they appear to figure prominently in the action?

   - What does the cast of characters tell you about the characters? Who are the central characters? How do they relate to one another?

2. **Read the play.** Keep notes in your Reader Response Journal as you read. Make note of anything you do not understand so that you can come back to it when you read the play again.

   - Read the first couple of pages of the play. Can you make any predictions about what might happen in the rest of the play?

   - Keep reading. Who are the main characters? What are they like? Do they remind you of anyone you know? Think about the kinds of gestures and facial expressions the characters would use if they were on the stage. What would their voices sound like?

   - Is there dramatic conflict? Which characters are in conflict? What does the conflict seem to be about? Does the conflict tell you anything about the theme of the play?

   - Are there any incidents, characters, or objects that the writer may have included to help you predict what might happen? How does this foreshadowing add to the suspense of the drama?

   - Can you identify the climax of the play? Is the conflict resolved? How is it resolved? Did you find the ending satisfying? Does the ending take you back to earlier events and actions that may not have been significant when you first read about them?

   - Would you classify the play as a tragedy, comedy, or melodrama, or do you think it has elements of more than one of these literary categories?

   - Reflect on why you liked the play or why you did not like the play. Did the characters seem real to you? Did the play say anything interesting to you about people and relationships?

The play that follows is *Still Stands the House* by Gwen Pharis Ringwood, a Canadian playwright who was born in 1910 in Washington State but who spent most of her life in Western Canada. Her years in northern Saskatchewan and Alberta made a strong impression on her, and the prairie landscape figures prominently in the more than 25 plays she wrote. Several of her plays were broadcast on CBC radio. Gwen Pharis Ringwood also wrote stories for children and taught literature in Banff and in Edmonton. For many years she lived in Williams Lake, BC, where the Gwen Pharis Ringwood Theatre was named in her honour. *Still Stands the House* was written and first performed in 1938.

1 This could mean the house is still, or the house is still standing— an interesting play on words. The house must be central to the play.

Still Stands the House ₁

Gwen Pharis Ringwood

Cast:
Ruth Warren
Arthur Manning
Hester Warren
Bruce Warren

Scene: A living room.

The icy wind of a northern blizzard sweeps across the prairie, lashes about the old Warren farmhouse, and howls insistently at the door and windows. But the Warren house was built to withstand the menace of the Canadian winter and scornfully suffers the storm to shriek about the chimney corner, to knock at the door and rattle the windows in a wild attempt to force an entrance.

The living room of this house has about it a faded austerity, a decayed elegance that is as remote and cheerless as a hearth in which no fire is ever laid. 2 *The room has made a stern and solemn pact with the past. Once it held the warm surge of life; but as the years have gone by, it has settled in a rigid pattern of neat, uncompromising severity.*

2 I would not want to be in this cold, cheerless room during a blizzard!

As if in defiance of the room, the frost has covered the window in the rear wall with a wild and exotic design. Beside the window is an imposing leather armchair, turned toward the handsome coal stove in the Right corner. A footstool is near the chair. A door at the Center of the rear wall leads to the snow-sheeted world outside. Along the Left wall, between a closed door to the bedroom (now unused) and an open door to a kitchen, is a mahogany sideboard. Above it is a portrait of old Martin Warren, who built this house and lived in it until his death. The portrait is of a stern and handsome man in his early fifties, and in the expression of the eyes the artist has caught something of his unconquerable will.

An open staircase, winding to the bedrooms upstairs, extends into the room at Right. There is a rocking chair by the stove with a small stand-table beside it. A mahogany dining table and two matching chairs are placed at a convenient distance from the sideboard and the kitchen door. The figured wallpaper is cracked and faded. The dark rug, the heavy curtains, and the tablecloth show signs of much wear, but there is nothing of cheapness about them.

Two coal-oil lanterns have been left beside the kitchen door.

Blooming bravely on the table, in contrast to its surroundings, is a pot of lavender hyacinths.

Ruth Warren is standing near the outside door, talking to Arthur Manning, who is about to leave. Ruth is small, fair-haired, and pretty, twenty-five or twenty-six years of age. There is more strength in her than her rather delicate appearance would indicate.

She wears a soft blue house-dress, with a light wool cardigan over it. Manning is a middle-aged man of prosperous appearance. He wears a heavy overcoat over a dark business suit. His hat, gloves, and scarf are on the armchair. 3

Ruth: Do you think you'd better try to go back tonight, Mr. Manning? The roads may be drifted.

Manning: It's a bad blizzard, all right, but I don't think I'll have any trouble. There's a heater in the car, and I've just had the engine checked over.

Ruth: You'll be welcome if you care to spend the night.

Manning: Thank you, but I'm afraid I've got to get back to town. I'd hate to try it in an old car, but this one of mine can pull through anything.

Ruth: I've never seen a storm come up so quickly.

Manning: These prairie blizzards are no joke. One of my sheepherders got lost in one last year, just half a mile from the house. He froze to death out there trying to find his way. 4

Ruth: How frightful!

Manning: One of the ranch hands found him the next morning. Poor old fellow— he'd herded for me for twenty years. I never knew how he came to be out in a storm like that.

Ruth: They say when a person gets lost he begins to go round in a circle, although it seems straight ahead.

Manning: Yes, I've always heard that. The winters are the one thing I've got against this country.

Ruth: (*Wistfully*) I used to like them in town. We went skating on the river and tobogganing. But out here it's different.

Manning: If Bruce 5 sells the farm and takes this irrigated place near town, you won't notice the winter so much, Mrs. Warren.

Ruth: No. I hope he does take your offer, Mr. Manning. I want him to.

Manning: He'll never get a better. Five thousand dollars and an irrigated quarter* is a good price for a dryland farm these days.

Ruth: If only we didn't have to decide so soon.

Manning: I talked it all over with Bruce in town a couple of weeks ago, and I think he's pretty well made up his mind. All he needs to do is sign the papers.

Ruth: I thought he'd have until spring to decide.

Manning: I've got orders to close the deal before I go South next week. You tell Bruce I'll come by tomorrow or the next day, and we can get it all settled.

---

*Quarter section, 160 acres or one-fourth of a square mile, a common farm area in the West.

3 These are very precise stage directions. I wonder if the setting is an important element in the play.

4 Poor man! These prairie blizzards are no joke.

5 I wonder who Bruce is— Ruth's husband or brother?

Ruth: I'll tell him. I hope he does take it, Mr. Manning.

Manning: I know you do and you're right. I think all he needs is a little persuading. He's had a hard time here these dry years.

Ruth: I don't know what Hester *6* will say.

6 Who is Hester?

Manning: I understand she's very much attached to the place. Is it true that she never leaves the farm?

Ruth: Not often.

Manning: She'd be better off where she could get out more.

Ruth: I don't know.

Manning: I suppose all those years out here, keeping house for Bruce and her father, *7* were pretty hard on her.

7 Bruce must be Ruth's husband, and Hester must be Bruce's sister.

Ruth: The house has come to mean so much to her. But maybe she won't mind. *(Smiling hopefully)* We'll see.

The door to the bedroom, Left, is opened quietly, and Hester Warren enters the room. She closes and locks the door behind her and stands looking at the two in the room with cold surmise. Hester is forty years old. She is tall, dark, and unsmiling. The stern rigidity of her body, the bitter austerity of her mouth, and the almost arrogant dignity of her carriage seem to make her a part of the room she enters. There is bitter resentment in her dark eyes as she confronts Ruth and Manning. 8 She holds a leather-bound Bible close to her breast.

8 What a bitter-sounding woman!

Ruth: *(Startled)* Why, Hester! I thought you never unlocked that door.

Hester: *(Quietly)* No. I keep Father's room as it was.

Ruth: Then why were you—

Hester: I was reading in Father's room. I heard a stranger.

Ruth: You know Mr. Manning, Hester.

Manning: *(With forced friendliness)* I don't suppose you remember me, Miss Warren.

Hester: *(Without moving)* How do you do?

Manning: *(Embarrassed at her coldness and anxious to get away)* Well, I'll be getting on home. I'll leave these papers for Bruce to sign, Mrs. Warren. Tell him I'll come by tomorrow. He'll find it's all there, just as we talked about it. *(He lays the document on the table.)*

Ruth: Thank you, Mr. Manning.

Manning: *(Turning to go)* Take care of yourselves. Good-night. *(To Hester)* Good-night, Miss Warren.

Hester barely nods.

Ruth: You're sure you ought to try it in the storm?

Manning: Sure. There's no danger if I go right away. *(He goes out.)*

Ruth: *(Calling after him as she shuts the door)* Good-night.

Hester watches Manning out and, as Ruth returns, she looks at her suspiciously. There is a silence which Hester finally breaks.

Hester: What did he want here?

Ruth: *(Uncomfortable under Hester's scrutiny)* He just left some papers for Bruce to look over, Hester. He was in a hurry so he didn't wait to see Bruce.

Hester: I see. What has Arthur Manning got to do with Bruce?

Ruth: It's something to do with the farm, Hester. I'll put these away. *(She starts to take up the document on the table, but Hester is before her.)*

Hester: *(After a long look at the document)* A deed of sale. *(Turning angrily upon Ruth)* So this is what you've been hiding from me.

Ruth: *(Quickly)* Oh, no! Nothing's settled, Hester. Mr. Manning made an offer and Bruce wants to think it over. That's all.

Hester: *(Her eyes betraying her intense agitation)* Bruce isn't going to sell this place!

Ruth: It's just an offer. Nothing has been decided.

Hester: Your hand's in this! You've been after him to leave here.

Ruth: *(Trying to conciliate her)* Let's not quarrel. You can talk to Bruce about it, Hester.

Hester: You hate this house, *9* I know that.

Ruth: No. *(Facing Hester firmly)* But I think Bruce ought to sell.

Hester: You married him. You made your choice.

Ruth: *(Quietly)* I've not regretted that. It's just that we're so cut off and lonely here; and this is the best offer we could get. But let me put these away. *(Indicating the deed of sale)* We'll talk about it later, the three of us.

Hester: *(Allowing Ruth to take the papers)* You may as well burn them. He isn't going to sell.

Ruth: Please, Hester—we'll discuss it when Bruce comes. *(She places the document on the sideboard, then crosses to the stove.)* I'll build up the fire.

Hester: *(Takes the Bible to the sideboard and places it under her father's portrait. She stands looking up at the portrait.)* This house will not be sold. I won't allow it.

Ruth: *(Puts some coal on the fire. Shivering 10)* It's so cold it almost frightens me. The thermometer has dropped ten degrees within the hour.

Hester: I hope Bruce knows enough to get the stock in. They'll freeze where they stand if they're left out tonight. *(She moves to the window and takes her knitting from the ledge.)*

Ruth: He'll have them in. *(Crossing to the table)* Look, Hester, how the hyacinths have bloomed. I could smell them when I came in the room just now.

9 *This seems like an over-reaction.*

10 *I can almost feel how cold it is.*

Hester: Hyacinths always seem like death to me. *11*

11 *What a strange thing for Hester to say.*

Ruth: *(Her voice is young and vibrant)* Oh, no. They're birth, they're spring! They say in Greece you find them growing wild in April. *(She takes an old Wedgwood bowl from the sideboard, preparing to set the pot of hyacinths in it.)*

Hester: *(In a dry, unfriendly tone)* I've asked you not to use that Wedgwood bowl. It was my grandmother's. I don't want it broken.

Ruth: I'm sorry. *(Replacing the bowl, she gets a plain one from inside the sideboard.)* I thought the hyacinths would look so pretty in it, but I'll use the plain one.

Hester: You've gone to as much trouble for that plant as if it were a child. *(Hester sits in the rocking chair by the stove.)*

Ruth: *(Placing the hyacinths in the bowl)* They're so sweet. I like to touch them.

Hester: They'll freeze tonight, *12* I'm thinking.

12 *Why would they freeze? Surely it will not get that cold inside.*

Ruth: Not in here. We'll have to keep the fire up anyway. *(Leaving the bowl of hyacinths on the table, Ruth returns to the sideboard, taking some bright chintz from the drawer. She holds it up for Hester to see.)* I've almost finished the curtains, Hester.

Hester: *(Tonelessly)* You have?

Ruth: Don't you think they'll make this room more cheerful?

Hester: The ones we have seem good enough to me. *13*

13 *Hester hates change.*

Ruth: But they're so old.

Hester: *(Coldly)* Old things have beauty when you've eyes to see it. That velvet has a richness that you can't buy now.

Ruth: *(Moving to the window)* I want to make the room gay and happy for spring. You'll see how much difference these will make.

Hester: I've no doubt. *(Hester rises and goes to the table to avoid looking at the curtains.)*

Ruth: *(Measuring the chintz with the curtains at the window)* I wonder if I have them wide enough.

The wind rises. As if the sound has quelled her pleasure in the bright curtains, Ruth turns slowly away from the window. A touch of hysteria creeps into her voice.

Ruth: The wind swirls and shrieks *14* and raises such queer echoes in this old house! It seems to laugh at us in here, thinking we're safe, hugging the stove! As if it knew it could blow out the light and the fire and—*(Getting hold of herself)* I've never seen a blizzard when it was as cold as this. Have you, Hester?

14 *The wind shrieks like a person. That must be personification.*

Hester: *(Knitting)* Bruce was born on a night like this.

Throughout this scene Hester seldom looks at Ruth but gives all her attention to her knitting. She seems reluctant to talk and yet impelled to do so.

Ruth: I didn't know.

Hester: Father had to ride for the doctor while I stayed here with Mother.

Ruth: Alone?

Hester: Yes. I was rubbing Father's hands with snow *15* when we heard the baby crying. Then we helped the doctor bathe him.

Ruth: You were such a little girl to do so much.

Hester: After Mother died I did it all.

Ruth: I know, but it was too hard for a child. *16* I don't see how you managed.

Hester: Father always helped me with the washing.

Ruth: Not many men would stay in from the field to do that.

Hester: No. (*Her knitting drops to her lap, and for a moment she is lost in the past.*) "We'll have to lean on one another now, Daughter."—Those were his words.— And that's the way it was. I was beside him until—I never left him.

Ruth: (*At Hester's side*) You've never talked of him like this before.

Hester: (*Unconscious of Ruth*) He always liked the snow. (*Her eyes are on the portrait of her father.*) He called it a moving shroud, *17* a winding-sheet that the wind lifts and raises and lets fall again.

Ruth: It is like that.

Hester: He'd come in and say, "The snow lies deep on the summer fallow, *18* Hester. That means a good crop next year."

Ruth: I know. It's glorious in the fall with the wheat like gold on the hills. No wonder he loved it.

Hester: (*Called out of her dream, she abruptly resumes her knitting.*) There hasn't been much wheat out there these last years.

Ruth: That isn't Bruce's fault, Hester.

Hester: You have to love a place to make things grow. The land knows when you don't care about it and Bruce doesn't care about it any more. Not like Father did.

Ruth: (*Her hands raised to touch the portrait above the sideboard*) I wish I'd known your father.

Hester: (*Rising and facing Ruth with a sudden and terrible anger*) Don't touch that picture. It's mine.

Ruth: (*Startled, she faces Hester.*) Why, Hester—

Hester: Can't I have anything of my own? Must you put your fingers on everything I have?

Ruth: (*Moving to Hester*) Hester, you know I didn't mean—What is the matter with you?

Hester: I won't have you touch it. *19*

Ruth: (*Gently*) Do you hate my being here so much?

15 Why would Hester rub snow on her father's hands? Maybe for frostbite?

16 This is giving the audience background.

17 I think a shroud would be an image of death. Maybe this is foreshadowing something terrible.

18 What does fallow mean? The context suggests it is a field.

19 Hester really hates Ruth.

Hester: *(Turning away)* You've more right here than I have now, I suppose.

Ruth: *(Crossing over to the stove)* You make me feel that I've no right at all.

Hester: *(A martyr now)* I'm sorry if you don't approve of my ways. I can go, if that's what you want.

Ruth: *(Pleading)* Please—I've never had a sister, and when Bruce told me he had one, I thought we'd be such friends— *20*

Hester: *(Sitting in the chair by the stove)* We're not a family to put words to everything we feel. *(She resumes knitting.)*

Ruth: *(Trying to bridge the gulf between them)* I get too excited over things: I know it. Bruce tells me I sound affected when I say too much about the way I feel, the way I like people—or the sky in the evening. I—

Hester: *(Without looking up)* Did you get the separator *21* put up? Or shall I do it?

Ruth: *(Discouraged, Ruth turns away, and going to the table, sits down with her sewing.)* It's ready for the milk when Bruce brings it. I put it together this morning.

Hester: The lanterns are empty.

Ruth: I'll fill them in a minute.

Hester: When I managed this house, I always filled the lanterns *22* right after supper. Then they were ready.

Ruth: *(Impatiently)* I said I'd fill them, Hester, and I will. They're both there in the corner. *(She indicates the lantern at the end of the sideboard.)*

Hester: Bruce didn't take one, then?

Ruth: No.

Hester: You'd better put a lamp in the window.

Ruth: *(Lights a small lamp on the sideboard and takes it to the window.)* I wish he'd come. It's strange how women feel safer when their men are near, close enough to touch, isn't it? No matter how strong you think you are. *(As she speaks, Ruth drapes some of the chintz over the armchair.)*

Hester: I can't say that I need my strength from Bruce, or could get it if I needed it.

Ruth: That's because he's still a little boy to you. *(A pause. Then Ruth speaks hesitantly.)* Hester—

Hester: Yes?

Ruth: Will you mind the baby in the house? *23*

Hester: *(After a silence, constrainedly)* No, I won't mind. I'll keep out of the way.

Ruth: *(Warmly, commanding a response)* I don't want you to. You'll love him, Hester.

Hester: *(Harshly)* I loved Bruce, but I got no thanks for it. He feels I stand in his way now.

Ruth: *(Suddenly aware that Hester has needed and wanted love)* You mustn't say that. It isn't true.

20 Ruth is trying to reach out to Hester, but Hester is rejecting her.

21 What is a separator?

22 I wonder what they use the lanterns for?

23 Oh, Ruth is pregnant.

Hester: When he was little, after Mother died, he'd come tugging at my hand—He'd get hold of my little finger and say, "Come, Hettie—come and look." Everything was "Hettie" then.

Ruth: *(Eagerly, moving to Hester)* It will be like that again. This baby will be almost like your own.

Hester: *(As if Ruth's words were an implied reproach)* I could have married and married well if I'd had a mind to.

Ruth: I know that. I've wondered why you didn't, Hester.

Hester: The young men used to ride over here on Sunday, but I stopped that. *(A pause)* I never saw a man I'd let touch me. Maybe you don't mind that kind of thing. I do.

Ruth: *(Involuntarily; it is a cry.)* No! **24** *(Attempting to put her arm around Hester)* What hurt you?

Hester: *(Rising)* Don't try your soft ways on me. *(She moves behind the armchair, her hand falls caressingly on the back of the chair.)* I couldn't leave Bruce and Father alone. My duty was here in this house. So I stayed. *(Hester notices the chintz material draped over the chair and, taking it up, turns to Ruth angrily.)* What do you intend to do with this?

Ruth: I thought—there's enough left to make covers for the chair to match the curtains—

Hester: *(Throwing the chintz down)* This is Father's chair. I won't have it changed.

Ruth: I'm sorry, Hester. *(With spirit)* Must we keep everything the same forever?

Hester: There's nothing in this house that isn't good, that wasn't bought with care and pride by one of us who loved it. This stuff is cheap and gaudy.

Ruth: It isn't dull and falling apart with age.

Hester: Before my father died, when he was ill, he sat here in this chair where he could see them threshing from the window. It was the first time since he came here that he'd not been in the fields at harvest. Now you come—you who never knew him, who never saw him—and you won't rest until—

Ruth: Hester!

Hester: You've got no right to touch it! *(Her hands grip the back of the old chair as she stands rigid, her eyes blazing.)*

Bruce Warren enters from outside, carrying a pail of milk. He is tall and dark, about thirty years old, sensitive and bitter. His vain struggle to make the farm pay since his father's death has left him with an oppressive sense of failure. He is proud and quick to resent an imagined reproach. He has dark hair, his shoulders are a little stooped, and he moves restlessly and abruptly. Despite his moodiness, he is extremely likeable. He is

24 *Maybe Hester suffered abuse as a child.*

dressed warmly in dark trousers, a sweater under his heavy leather coat; he wears gloves, cap, and high boots. He brushes the snow from his coat as he enters.

Bruce: *(Carrying the milk into the kitchen)* Is the separator up, Ruth?

Ruth: Yes, it's all ready, Bruce. Wait, I'll help you. *(She follows him into the kitchen.)*

Hester stands at the chair a moment after they have gone; her eyes fall on the table. Slowly she goes toward it, as if drawn by something she hated. She looks down at the lavender blooms 25 for a moment. Then with a quick, angry gesture, she crushes one of the stalks. She turns away and is winding up her wool when Bruce and Ruth return.

Ruth: You must be frozen.

Bruce: *(Taking off his coat and gloves)* I'm cold, all right. God, it's a blizzard: thirty-eight below, 26 and a high wind. *(He throws his coat over a chair at the table.)*

Ruth: *(With pride)* Did you see the hyacinths? They've bloomed since yesterday.

Bruce: *(Smiling)* Yes, they're pretty. *(Touching them, he notices the broken stalk.)* Looks like one of them's broken.

Ruth: Where? *(She sees it.)* Oh, it is! And that one hadn't bloomed yet! I wonder —It wasn't broken when I—*(Ruth turns accusingly to Hester.)* Hester!

Hester: *(Returns Ruth's look calmly. Coldly)* Yes?

Ruth: Hester, did you—

Bruce: *(Going over to the fire)* Oh, Ruth, don't make such a fuss about it. It can't be helped.

Hester: I'll take care of the milk. *(She takes the small lamp from the window.)*

Ruth: I'll do it.

Hester: *(Moving towards the kitchen)* You turn the separator so slow the cream's as thin as water. 27

Ruth: *(Stung to reply)* That's not true. You never give me a chance to—

Bruce: *(Irritably)* For God's sake, don't quarrel about it. *(He sits in the chair by the stove.)*

Hester: I don't intend to quarrel. *(She goes into the kitchen.)*

Ruth follows Hester to the door. The sound of the separator comes from the kitchen. Ruth turns wearily, takes up the pot of hyacinths, 28 and places them on the stand near the stove. Then sits on the footstool.

Ruth: It's always that way.

Bruce: *(Gazing moodily at the stove)* Why don't you two try to get along? 29

A silence.

25 *The hyacinths again.*

26 *That is cold!*

27 *Oh, I see. The separator's a machine for separating milk and cream.*

28 *The hyacinths must be a symbol.*

29 *Bruce obviously does not understand his wife and sister.*

Ruth: Did you put the stock in? (*The question is merely something to fill the empty space of silence between them.*)

Bruce: Yes. That black mare may foal tonight. I'll have to look at her later on.

Ruth: It's bitter weather for a little colt to be born.

Bruce: Yes.

Another silence. Finally Ruth, to throw off the tension between them, gets up and moves her footstool over to his chair.

Ruth: I'm glad you're here. I've been lonesome for you.

Bruce: (*Putting his hand on hers*) I'm glad to be here.

Ruth: I thought of you out at the barn, trying to work in this cold.

Bruce: I was all right. I'd hate to walk far tonight, though. You can't see your hand before your face.

Ruth: (*After a look at the kitchen*) Hester's been so strange again these last few days, Bruce.

Bruce: I know it's hard, Ruth.

Ruth: It's like it was when I first came here. At everything I touch, she cries out like I'd hurt her somehow.

Bruce: Hester has to do things her own way. She's always been like that.

Ruth: If only she could like me a little. I think she almost does sometimes, but then—

Bruce: You think too much about her.

Ruth: Maybe it's because we've been shut in so close. I'm almost afraid of her lately.

Bruce: She's not had an easy life, Ruth.

Ruth: I know that. She talked about your father almost constantly today.

Bruce: His death hit us both hard. Dad ran the farm, decided everything.

Ruth: It's been six years, Bruce.

Bruce: There are things you don't count out by years.

Ruth: He wouldn't want you to go on remembering forever.

Bruce: (*Looking at the floor*) No.

Ruth: You should get free of this house. It's not good for you to stay here. It's not good for Hester. (*Getting up, she crosses to the sideboard and returns with the deed of sale, which she hands to Bruce.*) Mr. Manning left this for you. He's coming back tomorrow for it, when you've signed it.

Bruce: (*Takes the paper. Annoyed by her assurance*) He doesn't need to get so excited. I haven't decided to sign yet. He said he wouldn't need to know till spring. (*He goes over to the lamp at the table and studies the document.*)

Ruth: His company gave him orders to close the deal this week or let it go. *30*

30 I hope Bruce signs the deed. Ruth needs to get away from Hester.

Bruce: This week?

Ruth: That's what he said.

Bruce: Well, I'll think about it.

Ruth: You'll have to decide tonight, Bruce. No one else will offer you as much. Five thousand dollars and an irrigated farm a mile from town seems a good price.

Bruce: I'm not complaining about the deal. It's fair.

Ruth: *(Urgently)* You're going to take it, aren't you, Bruce?

Bruce: I don't know. God, I don't know. *(He throws the document on the table.)* I don't want to sell, Ruth. I think I'll try it another year.

Ruth: Bruce, you've struggled here too long now. You haven't had a crop, a good crop, in five years.

Bruce: I need to be told that!

Ruth: It's not your fault. But you've told me you ought to give it up, that it's too dry here.

Bruce: We may get a crop this year. We're due for one.

Ruth: If you take this offer, we'll be nearer town. We'll have water on the place. We can have a garden, and trees growing.

Bruce: That's about what those irrigated farms are—gardens.

Ruth: And, Bruce, it wouldn't be so lonely there, so cruelly lonely.

Bruce: I told you how it was before you came.

Ruth: *(Resenting his tone)* You didn't tell me you worshipped a house. That you made a god of a house and a section of land. You didn't tell me that!

Bruce: *(Angrily)* You didn't tell me that you'd moon at a window for your old friends, either. *(He stands up and throws the deed of sale on the table.)* 31

Ruth: How could I help it here?

Bruce: And you didn't tell me you'd be afraid of having a child. What kind of a woman are you that you don't want your child?

Ruth: That's not true.

Bruce: No? You cried when you knew, didn't you?

Ruth: Bruce!

Bruce: *(Going blindly on)* What makes you feel the way you do, then? Other women have children without so much fuss. Other women are glad. 32

Ruth: *(Intensely angry)* Don't speak to me like that. Keep your land. Eat and sleep and dream land, I don't care!

Bruce: *(Turning to the portrait of his father)* My father came out here and took a homestead. He broke the prairie with one plough and a team of horses. He built a house to live in out of the sod. You didn't know that, did you? He and Mother lived here in a sod shanty and struggled to make things grow. Then they built a

31 *The conflict is escalating between Ruth and Bruce.*

32 *Bruce does not understand Ruth.*

one-room shack; and when the good years came, they built this house. The finest in the country! I thought my son would have it.

Ruth: *(Moving to him)* What is there left to give a son? A house that stirs with ghosts! A piece of worn-out land where the rain never comes.

Bruce: That's not all. I don't suppose you can understand.

Ruth: *(Turning away from him, deeply hurt)* No. I don't suppose I can. You give me little chance to know how you feel about things.

Bruce: *(His anger gone)* Ruth, I didn't mean that. But you've always lived in town. *(He goes to the window and stands looking out for a moment, then turns.)* Those rocks along the fence out there, I picked up every one of them with my own hands and carried them with my own hands across the field and piled them there. I've ploughed that southern slope along the coulee* every year since I was twelve. *(His voice is torn with a kind of shame for his emotions.)* I feel about the land like Hester does about the house, I guess. I don't want to leave it. I don't want to give it up.

Ruth: *(Gently)* But it's poor land, Bruce.

Bruce sits down, gazing gloomily at the fire. Hester comes in from the kitchen with a small lamp and places it on the sideboard. Then she sits at the table, taking up her knitting. As Bruce speaks, she watches him intently.

Bruce: Yes, it's strange that in a soil that won't grow trees a man can put roots down, but he can.

Ruth: *(At his side)* You'd feel the same about another place, after a little while.

Bruce: I don't know. When I saw the wind last spring blowing the dirt away, the dirt I'd ploughed and harrowed and sowed to grain, I felt as though a part of myself was blowing away in the dust. Even now, with the land three feet under snow, I can look out and feel it waiting for the seed I've saved for it.

Ruth: But if we go, we'll be nearer other people, not cut off from everything that lives.

Bruce: You need people, don't you?

Hester: Yes. She needs them. I've seen her at the window looking toward the town. Day after day she stands there.

Bruce and Ruth, absorbed in the conflict between them, had forgotten Hester's presence. At Hester's words, Ruth turns on them both, flaming with anger.

Ruth: You two, you're so *perfect!*

---

*A steep and narrow valley cut by a stream.

Hester: *(Knitting)* We could always stand alone, the three of us. We didn't need to turn to every stranger who held his hand out.

Ruth: No! You'd sit in this husk of a house, living like shadows, until these four walls closed in on you, buried you.

Hester: I never stood at a window, looking down the road that leads to town.

Ruth: *(The pent-up hysteria of the day and the longing of months breaks through, tumbling out in her words.)* It's not for myself I look down that road, Hester. It's for the child I'm going to have. You're right, Bruce, I am afraid. It's not what you think, though, not for myself. You two and your father lived so long in this dark house that you forgot there's a world beating outside, forgot that people laugh and play sometimes. And you've shut me out! *(There is a catch in her voice.)* I never would have trampled on your thoughts if you'd given them to me. But as it is, I might as well not be a person. You'd like a shadow better that wouldn't touch your house. A child would die here. A child can't live with shadows.

Bruce: *(Much disturbed, Bruce rises and goes to her.)* Ruth! I didn't know you hated it so much.

Ruth: I thought it would change. I thought I could change it. You know now.

Bruce: *(Quietly)* Yes.

Ruth: *(Pleading)* If we go, I'll *want* this child, Bruce. Don't you see? But I'm not happy here. What kind of life will our child have? He'll be old before he's **33** out of school. *(She looks at the hyacinth on the stand.)* He'll be like this hyacinth **34** that's broken before it bloomed.

Bruce: *(Goes to the table and stands looking down at the deed of sale. His voice is tired and flat, but resolved.)* All right. I'll tell Manning I'll let him have the place.

Hester: *(Turning quickly to Bruce)* What do you mean?

Bruce: I'm going to sell the farm to Manning. He was here today.

Hester: *(Standing up, her eyes blazing)* You can't sell this house.

Bruce: *(Looking at the deed of sale)* Oh, Ruth's right. We can't make a living on the place. *(He sits down, leafing through the document.)* It's too dry. And too far from school.

Hester: It wasn't too far for you to go, or me.

Bruce: *(Irritably)* Do you think I want to sell?

Hester: *She* does. But she can't do it. *(Her voice is low.)* This house belongs to me.

Bruce: Hester, don't start that again! I wish to God the land had been divided differently, but it wasn't.

Hester: Father meant for us to stay here and keep things as they were when he was with us.

Bruce: The soil wasn't blowing away when he was farming it.

33 Who says they will have a son, not a daughter? That would be a sexist comment by today's standards, but then the play was written more than 60 years ago.

34 The hyacinths are mentioned again.

Hester: He meant for me to have the house.

Ruth: You'll go with us where we go, Hester.

Hester: *(To Ruth)* You came here. You plotted with him to take this house from me. But it's mine! **35**

Bruce: *(His voice cracks through the room.)* Stop that, Hester! I love this place as much as you do, but I'm selling it. I'm selling it, I tell you. *(As he speaks, he gets up abruptly and, taking up his coat, puts it on.)*

Hester sinks slowly into the chair, staring. Ruth tries to put her hand on Bruce's arm.

Ruth: Bruce! Not that way! Not for me. If it's that way, I don't care enough.

Bruce: *(Shaking himself free)* Oh, leave me alone!

Ruth: Bruce!

Bruce: *(Going to the door)* I'll be glad when it's over, I suppose.

Ruth: Where are you going?

Bruce: *(Taking his cap and gloves)* To look at that mare.

Ruth: Bruce!

But he has gone.

Hester: *(Getting up, she goes to her father's chair and stands behind it, facing Ruth; she moves and speaks as if she were in a dream.)* This is my house. I won't have strangers in it.

Ruth: *(At the table, without looking at Hester)* Oh, Hester! I didn't want it to be this way. I tried—

Hester: *(As if she were speaking to a stranger)* Why did you come here?

Ruth: I've hurt you. But I'm right about this. I know I'm right.

Hester: There isn't any room for you.

Ruth: Can't you see? It's for all of us.

Hester comes towards Ruth with a strange, blazing anger in her face. **36**

Hester: I know your kind. You tempted him with your bright hair.

Ruth: Hester!

Hester: Your body anointed with jasmine for his pleasure.

Ruth: Hester, don't say such things!

Hester: Oh, I know what you are! You and women like you. You put a dream around him with your arms, a sinful dream.

Ruth: *(Drawing back)* Hester!

Hester: You lift your white face to every stranger like you offered him a cup to drink from. *(Turning to Ruth, as if she had forgotten her presence, Hester looks fondly at the room.)* I'll never leave this house.

35 Hester is getting more hysterical.

36 I think Hester is going mad.

Bruce: *(Opens the door and comes in quickly and stormily. He goes into the kitchen as he speaks.)* That mare's got out. She jumped the corral. I'll have to go after her.

Ruth: *(Concerned)* Bruce, where will she be?

Bruce: *(Returning with an old blanket)* She'll be in the snowshed by the coulee. She always goes there when she's about to foal.

Hester sits in the chair by the stove, her knitting in her hand. She pays no attention to the others.

Ruth: But you can't go after her in this storm.

Bruce: I'll take this old blanket to cover the colt, if it's born yet. Where's the lantern? *(He sees the two lanterns by the kitchen door and, taking one of them to the table, lights it.)*

Ruth: It's three miles, Bruce. You mustn't go on foot. It's dangerous. **37**

Bruce: I'll have to. She'd never live through the night, or the colt either. *(He turns to go.)* You'd better go to bed. Good-night, Hester.

Ruth: Let me come with you.

Bruce: No. *(Then, as he looks at her, all resentment leaves him. He puts down the lantern, goes to her, and takes her in his arms.)* Ruth, forget what I said. You know I didn't mean—

Ruth: *(Softly)* I said things I didn't mean, too—

Bruce: I love you, Ruth. You know it, don't you?

Ruth: Bruce!

He kisses her, and for a moment their love is a flame in the room.

Bruce: Don't worry. I won't be long.

Ruth: I'll wait.

Bruce goes out. Ruth follows him to the door, and, as it closes, she stands against it for a moment. There is a silence. Hester is slowly unravelling her knitting but is unaware of it. **38** *The black wool falls in spirals about her chair.*

Hester: *(Suddenly)* It's an old house. I was born here. *(Then in a strange, calm voice that seems to come from a long distance)* You shouldn't let Bruce be so much alone. You lose him that way. He comes back to *us* then. He'll see you don't belong here unless you keep your hand on him all the time.

Ruth looks curiously at Hester but does not give her all her attention.

Hester: *(Suddenly becomes harsh)* This is my house. You can't change it. *(Ruth starts to say something but remains silent.)* Father gave it to me. There isn't any room for you. *(In a high, childlike tone, like the sound of a violin string breaking)* No room. *(She shakes her head gravely.)*

37 *I have a horrible feeling something might happen to Bruce.*

38 *Hester really is going mad.*

Ruth: *(Aware that something is wrong)* **39** Hester—

Hester: *(As if she were telling an often-recited story to a stranger)* I stayed home when Mother died and kept house for my little brother and my father. *(Her voice grows stronger.)* I was very beautiful, they said. My hair fell to my knees, and it was black as a furrow turned in spring. *(Proudly)* I can have a husband any time I want, but my duty is here with Father. You see how it is. I can't leave him.

Ruth: *(Goes quickly to Hester. With anxiety and gentleness)* Hester, what are you talking about?

Hester: That's Father chair. I'll put his Bible out. *(She starts from her chair.)*

Ruth: *(Preventing her)* Hester, your father's not here—not for six years. You speak of him as if you thought—Hester—

Hester: *(Ignoring Ruth but remaining seated)* When I was a girl I always filled the lanterns after supper. Then I was ready for his coming.

Ruth: *(In terror)* Hester, I didn't fill them! I didn't fill the lanterns! *(She runs to the kitchen door and takes up the remaining lantern.)*

Hester: *(Calmly)* Father called me the wise virgin* **40** then.

Ruth: Hester, Bruce took one! He thought I'd filled them. It will burn out and he'll be lost in the blizzard.

Hester: I always filled them.

Ruth: *(Setting the lantern on the table)* I've got to go out after Bruce. If he gets down to the coulee and the lantern goes out, he'll never find the way back. I'll have to hurry! Where's the coal oil?

Ruth goes to the kitchen and returns with a can of coal oil and a pair of galoshes. Hester watches her closely. As Ruth comes in with the oil, Hester slowly rises and goes to her.

Hester: I'll fill the lantern for you, Ruth. **41**

Ruth: *(Trying to remove the top of the can)* I can't get the top off. My hands are shaking so.

Hester: *(Taking the oil can from Ruth)* I'll fill it for you.

Ruth: Please, Hester. While I get my things on! *(Giving Hester the oil can, Ruth runs to the footstool and hurriedly puts on her galoshes.)* I'm afraid the lantern will last just long enough to get him out there. He'll be across the field before I even get outside. *(She runs up the stairs.)*

Hester: *(Standing motionless, the oil can in her hand)* You're going now. That's right. I told you you should go.

---

*St. Matthew, XXV: 1–4.

---

39 Ruth knows something is wrong with Hester, but I do not think she realizes she is mad, but the audience does—that must be irony.

40 I wonder why her father called Hester the wise virgin?

41 Why is Hester suddenly being helpful? I do not trust her.

Ruth disappears up the stairs. Hester moves a step toward the lantern, taking off the top of the coal-oil can. She hesitates and looks for a long moment after Ruth. With the strange lucidity of madness, slowly, deliberately, she places the top back again on the can and, moving behind the table, sets it on the floor without filling the lantern. Ruth hurries down the stairs excited and alarmed. She has on heavy clothes and is putting on her gloves.

Ruth: Is it ready? 42 *(Hester nods.)* Will you light it for me, Hester? Please. *(Hester lights the lantern.)* I'll put the light at the window. *(She crosses with the small lamp and places it at the window.)* Hurry, Hester! *(With a sob)* Oh, if only I can find him!

Hester crosses to Ruth and gives her the lantern. Ruth takes the lantern and goes out. A gust of wind carries the snow into the room and blows shut the door after her. Hester goes to the window.

Hester: *(Her voice is like an echo.)* The snow lies deep on the summer fallow 43— The snow is a moving shroud—a winding-sheet that the wind lifts and raises and lets fall again. *(Turning from the window)* They've gone. They won't be back now. *(With an intense excitement, Hester blows out the lamp at the window and pulls down the shades. Her eyes fall on the bowl of hyacinths in the corner. Slowly she goes to it, takes it up and, holding it away from her, carries it to the door. Opening the door, she sets the flowers outside. 44 She closes the door and locks it. Her eyes blazing with excitement, she stands with her arms across the door as if shutting the world out. Then softly she moves to the door of her father's bedroom, unlocks it, and goes in, returning at once with a pair of men's bedroom slippers. Leaving the bedroom door open, she crosses to the sideboard, takes up the Bible, and going to her father's chair, places the slippers beside it. She speaks very softly.)* I put your slippers out. *(She draws the footstool up to the chair.)* Everything will be the same now, Father. *(She opens the Bible.)* I'll read to you, Father. I'll read the one you like. *(She reads with quiet contentment.)* "And the winds blew, and beat upon the house; and it fell not: for it was founded upon a rock."*

The wind moans through the old house as the curtain falls.

42 There is lots of suspense here—it feels like the climax of the play.

43 I remember these words from earlier in the play— they show Hester's preoccupation with death.

44 Now I understand what Hester meant when she predicted the hyacinths would freeze. That must have been foreshadowing.

---

*St. Matthew, VII: 25.

Tutorial 13: Identifying Symbols in Literature

Learning Expectations

You will learn
- to identify symbols in literature
- to write a paragraph about one symbol in *Still Stands the House*

Understanding the Task

A symbol is an object, action, person, animal, or plant that represents something else—e.g., a star, a flag, a prison. Because symbols depend on the connotations the reader attributes to them, symbols suggest meanings rather than state them directly. Symbols can be found all around us. For example, a wedding ring is a piece of jewellery people wear on their ring finger as a symbol of a bond between married people.

Writers of poetry, fiction, and drama often use symbols to express ideas and emotions. For instance, a writer might use a shattered mirror as a symbol of a character's pain and suffering, a crossroads as a symbol of a choice a character must make, and a bud opening in spring as a symbol of hope and rebirth.

To recognize and understand symbols, you must read critically and perceptively. If you simply accept everything the writer says, you may not notice any symbols. But if you stop to think about why certain things appear in the work, you may recognize that some things are there for their symbolic significance.

While you should read perceptively in order to recognize symbols, you need to be careful not to get carried away. Once you start consciously looking for symbols, it is easy to see them everywhere. How can you tell if something really does have symbolic weight? Here are some suggestions:

- A symbol should have a prominent position within a work. It should be emphasized and referred to several times.

- A symbol is usually a visual image.

- Symbols are related to the theme of the work.

- Symbols may have more than one meaning, and they may mean different things to different characters.

Symbols enrich a literary work by giving us added insight into the theme and characters. However, before you can see the full significance of a symbol, you must first have a basic understanding of the theme and characters.

Getting Ready

In your journal, sketch a rough chart like the one on page 109. Then read *Still Stands the House* again. Find two symbols in the play. Ask yourself whether the symbols are valid by answering the questions in the chart. One example is done for you.

Writing About Symbols

Select one of the symbols that you have found. Write a paragraph about how the symbol relates to the theme of *Still Stands the House*. Keep the following points in mind as you plan and write your paragraph:

- Identify the title and author in your first sentence.

- Ensure your paragraph has a topic sentence.

- Select at least three supporting details from the play to support your topic sentence.
- Use quotations from the play to support your opinion.
- Avoid including irrelevant plot details.

- Use the present tense to write about the play.

When you have finished the paragraph, use the checklist below to make sure that your paragraph connects the symbol to the theme of the play.

ITEM (LITERAL MEANING)	SYMBOL (SYMBOLIC MEANING)	SUPPORTING QUOTATIONS FROM THE PLAY	HOW IS THE SYMBOL RELATED TO THE THEME OF THE PLAY?	HOW IS THE SYMBOL RELATED TO THE CHARACTERS IN THE PLAY?	DOES THE SYMBOL HAVE MORE THAN ONE MEANING?
Winter blizzard on the prairie	Death	"the icy wind of a northern blizzard sweeps across the prairie" "These prairie blizzards are no joke. One of my sheepherders got lost in one last year, just half a mile from the house. He froze to death out there trying to find his way."	The theme of the play is the struggle between life and death. The winter blizzard that freezes everything it touches is a symbol of death.	Hester represents sterility, tedium, and death; Ruth represents hope, change, and life. The winter blizzard symbolizes the triumph of death over life.	The blizzard could also be a symbol of the conflict among the characters. As well, it could symbolize the triumph of nature over humans. With its fierce, cold wind, it could also be a symbol of madness.

Checklist: Identifying Symbols in Literature

○ Does my topic sentence identify the symbol and explain how it relates to the theme of the play?

○ Did I find details from the play to support my topic sentence?

○ Have I used actual quotations from the play?

○ Is my paragraph unified? Does it contain any irrelevant details?

○ Is my paragraph coherent? Have I used connecting words to link my sentences?

○ Have I summed up my points in my concluding paragraph?

○ Have I edited and proofread my paragraph?

Tutorial 14: Writing a Brief Scene for a Drama

Learning Expectations

You will learn
- to write dialogue
- to write a scene for a drama

Understanding the Task

In groups of two, you will write a brief scene for a script. Imagine that *Still Stands the House* does not end with Hester taking the lantern from the window and placing the hyacinths outside to freeze. There is still another scene to come. The final scene will reveal what happens to Ruth and Bruce. Does someone find their bodies the next day? Do they die in each other's arms? Do they live? Does one live and one die? You decide how to end the play. Then write a convincing script that reveals character and plot.

Getting Ready

Setting

You need to decide on a setting for your scene. Will it take place in the house? Will it take place outside in the field? Perhaps it takes place in town. When will the final scene occur? Will it occur on the same night, the next day, a few days later, or a few years hence? Will the storm still be raging, or will it have passed? Will it still be winter? How will the setting you choose contribute to the atmosphere of the scene? Will anything in the setting take on symbolic significance?

Describe the setting in stage directions for the scene.

Cast of Characters

Decide who will be in your scene. You do not need to repeat information that was in the original cast of characters. However, if you have added any characters, you need to provide information about them.

Dialogue

As we discussed in Elements of Drama (pages 87–88), drama is almost totally dependent on dialogue. There may not be a narrator to tell us what the characters are thinking or to help us interpret events. Other devices, such as setting, gestures, facial expressions, and tone of voice, may help us to understand a play, but it is largely dialogue that reveals character and plot and carries the play forward. When you write the dialogue for your scene, consider the following questions:

- **Does the dialogue reflect the characters' personalities?** Through dialogue we learn the characters' thoughts, feelings, likes, dislikes, opinions, and inner struggles. If your dialogue is effective, the characters will stay true to form. Their personalities will remain consistent and will not suddenly change without good reason.

- **Does the dialogue reveal relationships among the characters?** If you introduce a new character—a police officer, for example—you must show the relationship of the new character to the existing characters. Do they know each other? How do they get along? Are they in conflict?

- **Does the dialogue provide background information?** Through dialogue we learn crucial information about the characters and plot. Use dialogue to explain how much time has elapsed and what has happened to the characters since we last saw them.

- **Does the dialogue reveal the mood we are trying to establish?** How the characters behave and what they say to each other affects the mood of the play. Think about what mood you are trying to convey, and make sure the dialogue reflects the mood.

- **Does the dialogue carry the plot of the play forward?** In most plays, dialogue advances the plot. Make sure your dialogue advances the plot. Your dialogue will deal with the resolution of the plot because your scene comes after the climax of the play.

- **Are any stage directions included to help clarify meaning?** You may want to include some stage directions about tone of voice, gestures, and facial expressions.

- **Are any monologues included?** If your scene or part of your scene has only one character, you may choose to include a monologue.

 ## Writing a Script

Write your script with your partner. Make sure you consider all of the above points as you write. After you have finished, read the dialogue aloud to make sure that it sounds as natural as possible. When you have finished, read over the following checklist to ensure you have remembered everything.

Checklist: Writing a Brief Scene for a Drama

○ Have we established the scene with stage directions that describe the setting and the cast of characters? Do our stage directions also establish the mood? Have we used stage directions elsewhere in our scene to help clarify our meaning?

○ Does the dialogue reveal the personalities of the characters? Are the words the characters speak consistent with their personalities?

○ Does the dialogue carry the plot forward? Do we deal with the resolution of the plot, rather than introduce new conflicts and characters?

○ Does the dialogue give any background information the audience needs to know?

○ Have we read the dialogue aloud?

○ Have we edited and proofread the script?

Further Explorations: Narrating and Describing

The *Further Explorations: Narrating and Describing* section extends the range of texts that you can create, interpret, and respond to. This section will offer you additional pathways for responding creatively and critically, while applying your understanding of language, form, and genre.

Stopping by Woods on a Snowy Evening

Robert Frost

Whose woods these are I think I know.
His house is in the village though;
He will not see me stopping here
To watch his woods fill up with snow.

My little horse must think it queer
To stop without a farmhouse near
Between the woods and frozen lake
The darkest evening of the year.

He gives his harness bells a shake
To ask if there is some mistake.
The only other sound's the sweep
Of easy wind and downy flake.

The woods are lovely, dark and deep,
But I have promises to keep,
And miles to go before I sleep,
And miles to go before I sleep.

Meeting at Night

Robert Browning

The gray sea and the long black land;
And the yellow half-moon large and low;
And the startled little waves that leap
In fiery ringlets from their sleep,
As I gain the cove with pushing prow,
And quench its speed i' the slushy sand.

Then a mile of warm sea-scented beach;
Three fields to cross till a farm appears;
A tap at the pane, the quick sharp scratch
And blue spurt of a lighted match,
And a voice less loud, through its joys and fears,
Than the two hearts beating each to each!

The Taxi

Amy Lowell

When I go away from you
The world beats dead
Like a slackened drum.
I call out for you against the jutted stars
And shout into the ridges of the wind.
Streets coming fast,
One after the other,
Wedge you away from me,
And lamps of the city prick my eyes
So that I can no longer see your face.
Why should I leave you,
To wound myself upon the sharp edges of the night?

We Are Going

Oodgeroo of the Tribe Noonuccal (Kath Walker)

For Grannie Coolwell

They came in to the little town
A semi-naked band subdued and silent,
All that remained of their tribe.
They came here to the place of their old bora ground[1]
Where now the many white men hurry about like ants.
Notice of estate agent reads: 'Rubbish May Be Tipped Here'.
Now it half covers the traces of the old bora ring.
They sit and are confused, they cannot say their thoughts:
'We are as strangers here now, but the white tribe are the strangers.
We belong here, we are of the old ways.
We are the corroboree[2] and the bora ground,
We are the old sacred ceremonies, the laws of the elders.
We are the wonder tales of Dream Time,[3] the tribal legends told.
We are the past, the hunts and the laughing games, the wandering camp fires.
We are the lightning-bolt over Gaphembah Hill[4]
Quick and terrible,
And the Thunderer[5] after him, that loud fellow.
We are the quiet daybreak paling the dark lagoon.
We are the shadow-ghosts creeping back as the camp fires burn low.
We are nature and the past, all the old ways
Gone now and scattered.
The scrubs are gone, the hunting and the laughter.
The eagle is gone, the emu and the kangaroo are gone from this place.
The bora ring is gone.
The corroboree is gone.
And we are going.'

---

1. The term *bora* is applied both to the most solemn of Aboriginal rites, in which a young boy is admitted to the rights of manhood, and to the site of the ceremony.

2. Aboriginal dance ceremony

3. The time of mythic events

4. On Stradbroke Island, behind Myora Springs and near Moongalba, where the author lives

5. Thunder; Aboriginal beliefs tend to be localized, rather than universal among the various tribes, and mythic figures, such as Thunderer, are often attached to specific sites or regions.

Africa

Maya Angelou

Thus she had lain
sugar cane sweet
deserts her hair
golden her feet
mountains her breasts
two Niles[1] her tears
Thus she has lain
Black through the years.

Over the white seas
rime white and cold
brigands ungentled
icicle bold
took her young daughters
sold her strong sons
churched her with Jesus
bled her with guns.
Thus she has lain.

Now she is rising
remember her pain
remember the losses
her screams loud and vain
remember her riches
her history slain
now she is striding
although she had lain.

---

1. The Nile, an ancient African river

Marriage Is a Private Affair

Chinua Achebe

"Have you written to your dad yet?" asked Nene one afternoon as she sat with Nnaemeka in her room at 16 Kasanga Street, Lagos.[1]

"No. I've been thinking about it. I think it's better to tell him when I get home on leave!"

"But why? Your leave is such a long way off yet—six whole weeks. He should be let into our happiness now."

Nnaemeka was silent for a while, and then began very slowly as if he groped for his words: "I wish I were sure it would be happiness to him."

"Of course it must," replied Nene, a little surprised. "Why shouldn't it?"

"You have lived in Lagos all your life, and you know very little about people in remote parts of the country."

"That's what you always say. But I don't believe anybody will be so unlike other people that they will be unhappy when their sons are engaged to marry."

"Yes. They are most unhappy if the engagement is not arranged by them. In our case it's worse—you are not even an Ibo."[2]

This was said so seriously and so bluntly that Nene could not find speech immediately. In the cosmopolitan atmosphere of the city it had always seemed to her something of a joke that a person's tribe could determine whom he married.

At last she said, "You don't really mean that he will object to your marrying me simply on that account? I had always thought you Ibos were kindly disposed to other people."

"So we are. But when it comes to marriage, well, it's not quite so simple. And this," he added, "is not peculiar to the Ibos. If your father were alive and lived in the heart of Ibibio-land he would be exactly like my father."

"I don't know. But anyway, as your father is so fond of you, I'm sure he will forgive you soon enough. Come on then, be a good boy and send him a nice lovely letter. . . ."

"It would not be wise to break the news to him by writing. A letter will bring it upon him with a shock. I'm quite sure about that."

"All right, honey, suit yourself. You know your father."

As Nnaemeka walked home that evening he turned over in his mind the different ways of overcoming his father's opposition, especially now that he had gone and found a girl for him. He had thought of showing his letter to Nene but decided on second thought not to, at least for the moment. He read it again when he got home and couldn't help smiling to himself. He remembered Ugoye quite well, an Amazon[3] of a girl who used to beat up all the boys, himself included, on the way to the stream, a complete dunce at school.

> I have found a girl who will suite you admirably—Ugoye Nweke, the eldest daughter of our neighbour, Jacob Nweke. She has a proper Christian upbringing. When she stopped schooling some years ago her father (a man of sound judgment) sent her to live in the house of a pastor where she

has received all the training a wife could need. Her Sunday School teacher has told me that she reads her Bible very fluently. I hope we shall begin negotiations when you come home in December.

On the second evening of his return from Lagos Nnaemeka sat with his father under a cassia tree. This was the old man's retreat where he went to read his Bible when the parching December sun had set and a fresh, reviving wind blew on the leaves.

"Father," began Nnaemeka suddenly, "I have come to ask forgiveness."

"Forgiveness? For what, my son?" he asked in amazement.

"It's about this marriage question."

"Which marriage question?"

"I can't—we must—I mean it is impossible for me to marry Nweke's daughter."

"Impossible? Why?" asked his father.

"I don't love her."

"Nobody said you did. Why should you?" he asked.

"Marriage today is different. . . ."

"Look here, my son," interrupted his father, "nothing is different. What one looks for in a wife are a good character and a Christian background."

Nnaemeka saw there was no hope along the present line of argument.

"Moreover," he said, "I am engaged to marry another girl who has all of Ugoye's good qualities, and who. . . ."

His father did not believe his ears. "What did you say?" he asked slowly and disconcertingly.

"She is a good Christian," his son went on, "and a teacher in a Girls' School in Lagos."

"Teacher, did you say? If you consider that a qualification for a good wife I should like to point out to you, Emeka, that no Christian woman should teach. St. Paul in his letter to the Corinthians says that women should keep silence."[4] He rose slowly from his seat and paced forwards and backwards. This was his pet subject, and he condemned vehemently those church leaders who encouraged women to teach in their schools. After he had spent his emotion on a long homily he at last came back to his son's engagement, in a seemingly milder tone.

"Whose daughter is she, anyway?"

"She is Nene Atang."

"What!" All the mildness was gone again. "Did you say Neneataga, what does that mean?"

"Nene Atang from Calabar.[5] She is the only girl I can marry." This was a very rash reply and Nnaemeka expected the storm to burst. But it did not. His father merely walked away into his room. This was most unexpected and perplexed Nnaemeka. His father's silence was infinitely more menacing than a flood of threatening speech. That night the old man did not eat.

When he sent for Nnaemeka a day later he applied all possible ways of dissuasion. But the young man's heart was hardened, and his father eventually gave him up as lost.

"I owe it to you, my son, as a duty to show you what is right and what is wrong. Whoever put this idea into your head might as well have cut your throat. It is Satan's work." He waved his son away.

"You will change your mind, Father, when you know Nene."

"I shall never see her," was the reply. From that night the father scarcely spoke to his son. He did not, however, cease hoping that he would realize how serious was the danger he was heading for. Day and night he put him in his prayers.

Nnaemeka, for his own part, was very deeply affected by his father's grief. But he kept hoping that it would pass away. If it had occurred to him that never in the history of his people had a man married a woman who spoke a different tongue, he might have been less optimistic. "It has never been heard," was the verdict of an old man speaking a few weeks later. In that short sentence he spoke for all of his people. This man had come with others to commiserate with Okeke when news went round about his son's behaviour. By that time the son had gone back to Lagos.

"It has never been heard," said the old man again with a sad shake of his head.

"What did Our Lord[6] say?" asked another gentleman. "Sons shall rise against their Fathers; it is there in the Holy Book."

"It is the beginning of the end," said another.

The discussion thus tending to become theological, Madubogwu, a highly practical man, brought it down once more to the ordinary level.

"Have you thought of consulting a native doctor about your son?" he asked Nnaemeka's father.

"He isn't sick," was the reply.

"What is he then? The boy's mind is diseased and only a good herbalist can bring him back to his right senses. The medicine he requires is *Amalile*, the same that women apply with success to recapture their husbands' straying affection."

"Madubogwu is right," said another gentleman. "This thing calls for medicine."

"I shall not call in a native doctor." Nnaemeka's father was known to be obstinately ahead of his more superstitious neighbours in these matters. "I will not be another Mrs. Ochuba. If my son wants to kill himself let him do it with his own hands. It is not for me to help him."

"But it was her fault," said Madubogwu. "She ought to have gone to an honest herbalist. She was a clever woman, nevertheless."

"She was a wicked murderess," said Jonathan who rarely argued with his neighbours because, he often said, they were incapable of reasoning. "The medicine was prepared for her husband, it was his name they called in its preparation and I am sure it would have been perfectly beneficial to him. It was wicked to put it into the herbalist's food, and say you were only trying it out."

Six months later, Nnaemeka was showing his young wife a short letter from his father:

It amazes me that you could be so unfeeling as to send me your wedding picture. I would have sent it back. But on further thought I decided just to cut off your wife and send it back to you because I have nothing to do with her. How I wish that I had nothing to do with you either.

When Nene read through this letter and looked at the mutilated picture her eyes filled with tears, and she began to sob.

"Don't cry, my darling," said her husband. "He is essentially good-natured and will one day look more kindly on our marriage." But years passed and that one day did not come.

For eight years, Okeke would have nothing to do with his son, Nnaemeka. Only three times (when Nnaemeka asked to come home and spend his leave) did he write to him.

"I can't have you in my house," he replied on one occasion. "It can be of no interest to me where or how you spend your leave—or your life, for that matter."

The prejudice against Nnaemeka's marriage was not confined to his little village. In Lagos, especially among his people who worked there, it showed itself in a different way. Their women, when they met at their village meeting were not hostile to Nene. Rather, they paid her such excessive deference as to make her feel she was not one of them. But as time went on, Nene gradually broke through some of this prejudice and even began to make friends among them. Slowly and grudgingly they began to admit that she kept her home much better than most of them.

The story eventually got to the little village in the heart of the Ibo country that Nnaemeka and his young wife were a most happy couple. But his father was one of the few people who knew nothing about this. He always displayed so much temper whenever his son's name was mentioned that everyone avoided it in his presence. By a tremendous effort of will he had succeeded in pushing his son to the back of his mind. The strain had nearly killed him but he had persevered, and won.

Then one day he received a letter from Nene, and in spite of himself he began to glance through it perfunctorily until all of a sudden the expression on his face changed and he began to read more carefully.

> . . . Our two sons, from the day they learnt that they have a grandfather, have insisted on being taken to him. I find it impossible to tell them that you will not see them. I implore you to allow Nnaemeka to bring them home for a short time during his leave next month. I shall remain here in Lagos . . .

The old man at once felt the resolution he had built up over so many years falling in. He was telling himself that he must not give in. He tried to steel his heart against all emotional appeals. It was a re-enactment of that other struggle. He leaned against a window and looked out. The sky was overcast with heavy black clouds and a high wind began to blow filling the air with dust and dry leaves. It was one of those rare occasions when even Nature takes a hand in a human fight. Very soon it began to rain, the first rain in the year. It came down in large sharp drops and was accompanied by the lightning and thunder which mark a change of season. Okeke was trying hard not to think of his two grandsons. But he knew he was now fighting a losing battle. He tried to hum a favourite hymn but the pattering of large rain drops on the roof broke up the tune. His mind immediately returned to the children. How could he shut his door against them? By a curious mental process he imagined them standing, sad and forsaken, under the harsh angry weather—shut out from his house.

That night he hardly slept, from remorse—and a vague fear that he might die without making it up to them.

---

1. Lagos: capital of Nigeria

2. Ibo: a people in southern Nigeria

3. Amazon: a strong, aggressive woman. The Amazons were a race of warrior women in Greek mythology.

4. St. Paul . . . should keep silence: St. Paul was an early Christian apostle and author of several books in the Christian Bible. In his first letter to the early church in Corinth, he criticized the Corinthians' practice of allowing women to preach.

5. Calabar: city in southeastern Nigeria

6. Our Lord: Christ

Further Explorations in Narration and Description

1. Imagine that you are Okeke, the father in the short story "Marriage Is a Private Affair." Decide how you are going to respond to the letter from your daughter-in-law, Nene. You may choose to write Nene a letter, or you may choose to send her a poem expressing your feelings.

2. Write a poem, short story, personal essay, or literary essay on one of the following themes:

   • the alienation of a person from a group

   • the imposition of one culture on another

   • conflict that occurs between children and their parents when the parents try to retain the old ways and values and the children want to change

   If you choose to write a literary essay, refer to at least two literary works in your response.

3. In groups of three or four, share and discuss your personal responses to the poems "Africa" (page 115) and "We Are Going" (page 114). Then create a visual or musical collage that represents your response to one of the poems.

4. In groups of three or four, read aloud Justin Trudeau's eulogy to his father (pages 43 to 45). Then read the poem that Justin Trudeau quotes in his speech, "Stopping by Woods on a Snowy Evening" (page 112). Share and discuss your individual responses to the pieces. Then, as a group, write and share with the class a brief explanation of the connection between the eulogy and Robert Frost's poem.

5. With a partner, create a character of a grandmother or grandfather, either from your own imagination or based on the qualities of your own grandparents. Then write a short dramatic piece in which a grandchild (someone your own age) learns something about his or her history or culture from the grandparent.

6. Read the poems "Meeting at Night" (page 113) and "The Taxi" (page 113). Write a descriptive essay or a poem about the anticipation of meeting a loved one or the sadness at having to part. Whichever form you choose, try to use strong, fresh images in your writing.

SECTION 2: EXPLAINING AND REPORTING

An explanation is a piece of writing that answers a question. It may be something about which the reader is curious—for example, "Why does lightning occur?" or "What causes a heart attack?" Or it may be a question of practical relevance to the reader such as, "How do I set up my new stereo system?" or "How do I get to City Hall?" Explanations always provide the reader with information about what something means or how something is done, organized, formed, or used. Clear, precise explanations are crucially important in daily life and in the workplace.

The reading selections in this section of the text are all explanations. Although they vary in purpose and in form, all the selections give clear, precise, practical information about a thing, a process, or an idea.

Some of the selections in this section are reports. A report is a document that provides the reader with an objective, factual account or explanation in a particular format. Reports have headings, numbered lists, and they often use graphs, charts, and tables to present information.

The tutorials in this section are intended to help you understand the various devices and structures writers use when writing explanations. They are also designed to help you write your own explanations, whether these be study notes, summaries, essays, or reports.

Chapter 8: The Informational Essay

Learning Expectations

You will learn
- to find and identify paragraph strategies in informational essays
- to use the Internet to do research
- to evaluate the information you find on the Internet

What Is an Informational Essay?

If you are like most people, you probably buy glossy magazines, or at least you flip through them when you are waiting to see your dentist or to board a plane. Glossy magazines are full of informational essays. You will find articles that tell you how to bake a decadent chocolate cake, who is dating whom in Hollywood, where to find the best bike trails, what to wear for the current season, when to travel to New Zealand, what causes marital breakdown, and so on. The list is endless.

An informational essay is a brief, non-fiction composition whose primary purpose is to explain an item, process, or idea. The informational essay is one of the most common forms of writing. Many newspaper and magazine articles are actually informational essays. They explain an item, process, or idea by answering the questions how, who, what, where, when, or why. Some articles answer all six questions. Others answer just one. No matter how many questions they answer, the primary purpose of all informational articles and essays is to explain something to the reader.

Elements of an Informational Essay

Most informational essays share some of the following elements:

1. **A clearly stated or implied thesis that expresses the main idea of the essay.** A thesis statement in an informational essay usually appears in the first two or three paragraphs, but, occasionally, it appears in the middle or at the end of an essay.

2. **Well-chosen examples that support the main points.** Examples are essential in informational essays because they enable the reader to visualize the object, process, or idea that the writer is explaining.

3. **Paragraphs that use a variety of organizational strategies.** Writers of informational essays organize their paragraphs in a variety of ways. For example, in an informational essay about World War II fighter planes, the writer may *narrate* a story about a particular bombing raid in her opening paragraph; she may *define* a fighter plane in her second paragraph; she may *classify* types of fighter planes in her third and fourth paragraphs; and she may *compare and contrast* fighter planes in her fifth and sixth paragraphs. In her concluding paragraph she may return to the story she opened with, and *narrate* the final sentences of her essay. Some essays rely more on one organizational strategy than others. For example, a writer may choose to write an entire essay that compares and contrasts fighter planes.

4. **Illustrative material that helps to explain the essay or article.** Many writers and magazine editors use

sidebars, charts, tables, photographs, cartoons, and drawings to help explain or illustrate the writer's thesis. Many magazine editors also use these elements to add visual appeal to their magazine.

How to Read an Informational Essay

Below are some strategies for reading informational essays. If you are reading for recreation, you may not use them as consciously as when you read for information and research. However, they are useful strategies no matter what kind of reading you are doing.

- Look at the essay's title and author. Do you know anything about the topic? Have you read anything else by this author? Predict possibilities: what could this essay be about?

- Read the text of the essay once without reading any illustrative material in the sidebars or boxes. Did you recognize the point that the writer is making? What will you look for when you read the essay again?

- Look at the structure of the essay. Has the author used headings to divide the paragraphs? Read any headings and highlighted extracts from the essay. How do structures and related clues (headings, topic sentences, italics or boldface) help us determine the important details of the essay? How long is the essay?

- Is there any illustrative material used in the essay? Are there sidebars or boxes? Do their titles tell you anything about the article? Are there tables, charts, or other illustrations? Read their captions (the words above, below, or beside them). How do the illustrations relate to the essay and the essay's main idea?

- Read the essay again more carefully. What does the author actually say? What does the author lead you to believe? Can you pick out a thesis statement, or is the thesis implied?

The essay that follows is called "Blowing the Whistle on Concussions" by Polly Shulman, a science writer in New York City and a Sunday book critic for *Newsday*. The essay was published in Fall 2000 in a special issue of *Scientific American* called *Building the Elite Athlete: The Science and Technology of Sport*.

Blowing the Whistle on Concussions [1]

Polly Shulman

1 *Title: an interesting play on words.*

Immediately after being elbowed in the jaw by Boston Bruin Hal Gill during a March 4 hockey game, Eric Lindros's world went yellow. The star center of the Philadelphia Flyers fell to the ice. He was helped into the locker room by the team's trainer, then vomited. He complained of a bad headache and strangely colored vision. Team doctors gave him heat packs and ibuprofen and then put him back in the lineup for another four games. "I wanted to keep playing," despite the telltale signs of a concussion, Lindros told reporters. "That's the mentality of a player— 'Everything's going to be fine, it's going to go away,' and you just keep on playing." He added, "I knew that things were not good, and I tried to convey that through my symptoms. But I was not going to pull myself out of the game. I wanted the team to pull me out. I was hoping as the week went on that they would do that."

It was nine days before team doctors sent Lindros to a headache specialist, who referred him to James P. Kelly, an expert in sports-related concussions who is based at Northwestern University Medical School. Kelly diagnosed Lindros with a moderate concussion. Playing in subsequent games would put the athlete at serious risk: a second concussive hit sustained before the first one had healed could cause permanent brain damage or even death. **2**

2 *It would have been extremely dangerous for Lindros to continue to play hockey with a concussion.*

Lindros did not recover well. He sat out for 10 weeks, returning only for the crucial last two games of the Eastern Conference finals in May. He had played just eight minutes in Game 7 when he was elbowed again, this time by New Jersey Devil Scott Stevens. Lindros went down hard. It was his fourth concussion of the season and his sixth in two years. In the following days doctors said that Lindros should hang up his skates, and the sports media conjectured widely about the 27-year-old's premature retirement. And yet in July rumors arose that he might be traded, with several teams said to be interested. Lindros is a perfect example of the dangers that sports-related concussions pose. According to the Centers for Disease Control and Prevention, 20 percent of the brain injuries that occur yearly in the U.S. can be attributed to athletics. That's more than 300,000 concussions. *3* High school, college and amateur athletes receive most of these injuries, because there are so many more of these players than there are pros. "This is a major public health issue that's been given short shrift," says Michael W. Collins of the Henry Ford Hospital in Detroit. "It's underrecognized, underdiagnosed and misdiagnosed. It's happening with alarming frequency at the high school, college and professional levels." *4*

A single blow to the head can cause a whole range of symptoms, from problems with balance and coordination to impaired decision making, failing memory and personality changes. Unless the injury is severe, patients generally recover with time. But most athletes return to games or practices far too soon. A second blow before a concussion is fully healed has a far greater chance of imposing more serious, longer-lasting harm. There is also the risk of death from "second impact syndrome," a rare condition in which the brain swells fatally. Furthermore, "there's growing evidence that not only are you more

3 This statistic is alarming.

4 Here is the thesis of the article.

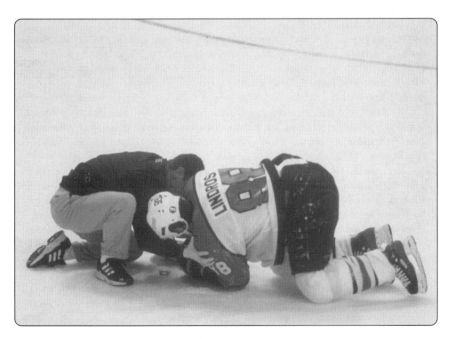

Cold as Ice: Relations between Eric Lindros and Philadelphia Flyers management chilled this spring after he accused the team doctors of mistreating his many concussions.

5 I could get a concussion, or one of my friends could.

6 Everyone involved with sports should learn to recognize the symptoms of a concussion.

likely to have another concussion if you've had one, but the problems accumulate," Kelly says.

Although the professional-athlete cases get the media attention, the thousands of kids playing youth hockey, football and soccer, the thousands of high school and college athletes, and the thousands of weekend jocks are in even greater danger, *5* because it is far less probable that they, their coaches or their parents will recognize the symptoms of concussion. *6* Scientists are trying to develop guidelines to help amateurs as well as pros recognize the signs of severities of concussions, but it is an inexact science. And there are currently no treatments that make concussions heal faster. . . .

HARD TO DIAGNOSE

Part of the trouble in diagnosing concussion is that the symptoms can be very subtle. People might dismiss a headache or altered vision as signs of stress or fatigue.

A HEADS UP ON HEADERS

Concern about concussions in youth soccer has surged as rapidly as the sport's popularity has. Some scientists are now questioning the wisdom of "heading" the ball, at least for players under 12 years old. Others disagree, citing one study that found that by far the most concussions in soccer come from collisions with other players, especially when more than one are trying to head the ball.

"All of us suspect that the momentum of a ball on a young child's head, especially if it hits them when they're not ready, is a possible concussion scenario," says James P. Kelly, an expert in sports-related concussions who is based at Northwestern University Medical School. "But we have very little evidence that heading the ball per se is dangerous."

Also under debate is the long-lasting effect of years of headers. A 1999 study of amateur adult soccer players, swimmers and runners in the Netherlands (the average age was 25) found that on tests of memory and planning soccer players performed the least well. Some of the researchers concluded that the soccer players were suffering from chronic traumatic brain injury, or "punch-drunk syndrome," and oppose heading the ball on the basis of this study. Other scientists, however, think that factors such as head collisions and regular drinking could account for the lower scores.

Most physicians say that more testing is needed before concluding that headers should be banned, at a minimum for young players. But some concerned parents are clamoring for protective headgear, and entrepreneurial operations have surfaced to offer it. The armor varies from glorified cloth headbands to neoprene helmets. Whether they work, or are needed, is up in the air.

"People joke, 'I got my bell rung,' but getting your bell rung means there's been some neurological change in the brain," Collins explains. People commonly think that concussion results from a knockout blow, but most concussions don't involve loss of consciousness. **7** The primary symptoms that often go unrecognized include balance trouble, headaches, dizziness, subtle personality change and cognitive problems. Sometimes injured athletes will have difficulty calling up old memories or forming new ones.

Complicating the subjective recognition of symptoms is the athlete's desire to underemphasize injury. Young athletes are taught to "play through the pain." Few players want to sit out a stretch of important games, much less an entire season. One of the hardest challenges, Kelly says, "is getting the athletes to honestly report their symptoms and pull in the reins on themselves a bit. **8** As much as it's admirable that the athletes are serious about getting back at it, they have to understand that these problems are very serious."

Collins agrees. Brain injuries demand more caution than orthopedic injuries do, he says; because there are no pain receptors in the brain, an individual doesn't experience direct pain with a concussion. This adds to the confusion when trying to judge symptoms. Doctors maintain that to be safe, athletes who are symptomatic following a blow to the head should be kept off the playing field and return only after the symptoms have disappeared. For more severe concussions, players should be free of symptoms for up to two weeks before resuming play [see box on page 130]. . . .

WHAT EXACTLY IS A CONCUSSION?

There is great misconception among the public about what a concussion actually is. It is not a bruise to the brain. It is a harsh chemical imbalance within the gray matter. A brain inside a skull is like a person riding inside a car with no seat belt, **9** explains David A. Hovda, a neuroscientist at the University of California at Los Angeles School of Medicine. If the skull halts or spins suddenly as a result of a collision, abrupt stop or whiplash motion, the unrestrained brain mass will slam up against the inside of the skull. The brain tissue is not physically damaged, except in the worst cases. But a devastating cascade of chemical reactions is unleashed.

The slam causes all the brain cells, or neurons, to fire at once, for several milliseconds. This extreme mass-firing sends the brain into a panic. Neurons across the brain release neurotransmitters—the chemicals that carry signals between them. "It's like a very brief seizure," Hovda says. A sinister wave of electrical activity

7 Wow—I always thought that a concussion would knock you out.

8 All people who play sports have to realize that a concussion is dangerous and should not be ignored. That includes me!

9 The seat belt example makes it easy to visualize the brain hitting the skull.

10 *This is getting a bit complicated. Maybe I should read the last couple of paragraphs again.*

11 *I like the potato chip example. It helps me to imagine how the cells swell and crush against the skull.*

12 *If the cells are exhausted and cannot produce the chemicals needed, the brain cannot function properly.*

spreads across the brain as the flood of neurotransmitters, especially glutamate, tells neurons everywhere to fire even more. The cells scramble in vain to regain a normal, neutral state so they can be ready to fire again. 10

This scrambling consumes a lot of energy. But the neurons can't regenerate the energy they lose. The frantic firing causes the neurons to absorb excess electrically charged calcium and sodium and to spit out potassium. The calcium clogs the mitochondria—the cell structures that make energy—preventing them from doing their job. So just when the neurons most need energy, they can't produce it.

Meanwhile the wash of calcium and potassium causes the brain's blood vessels to constrict, right when the neurons need more glucose from blood to fuel their attempts to recover. "We call this an energy crisis," Hovda says. A prolonged energy crisis can kill cells, resulting in permanent brain damage.

The extra sodium entering the brain cells can create more trouble, too. It makes them take in water—the way eating salty potato chips makes you thirsty. The water swells the cells, pushing them up against the skull. 11 If the swelling is extreme, the expanding brain will start to crush itself against the skull; neurons, or even the entire brain, can die.

The cascade of chemical events peaks rapidly, but it takes a long time for the cascade to tail off and for the brain to settle neurons back to normal. Although no one knows quite how long is needed for the self-correction in humans, Hovda and his colleagues have done some suggestive studies in rats. Potassium, they found, rushes out of the cells for minutes, calcium rushes in for days, and sodium rushes in for hours to days. The constriction of blood vessels can also last for days. There is a damning after-effect as well: once the brain manages to increase metabolism to meet the cells' high energy demands, it goes into a state of metabolic depression. The brain "sort of gets exhausted," as Hovda describes it. 12 The exhaustion lasts longer than the other chemical effects do.

The more severe the concussion, the longer the cascade continues. If a second concussion interrupts the brain's quest for equilibrium, Hovda says, a new cascade starts on top of the first one. The resulting damage is not just additive but multiplicative.

The chemical cascade helps explain the symptoms of concussion. "The cells in the brain have to fire in order for you to learn or remember something," Hovda says. "If they can't fire because they can't pump the chemicals where they have to go, or are exhausted, then you can't learn." Learning and retrieving information also require your cells to produce certain proteins. Protein synthesis takes energy—exactly what the concussed brain is short of. "It's not that the information isn't there," Hovda says. "It's that you can't access it."

Blows that twist the head—such as the elbow to Lindros's jaw or a right cross in boxing—cause worse harm than head-on hits. While setting off the chemical cascade, the wrenching action can also stretch or even sever neuronal pathways, adding permanent, local damage to the trauma.

Physicians try to treat certain symptoms of concussion by administering painkillers for headaches or antidepressants for some personality problems. But so far there's no effective treatment for the concussion itself except time. "I find it very depressing," Hovda says. "In the last 10 to 20 years there have been more than 25 clinical trials of treatments for head injury, and none of them have been successful. The problem is that the treatments target a particular part of the cascade. But no one knows how long these cascades last, so a drug given at one point may be beneficial but may be detrimental later.". . .

Doctors agree that the benefits of playing most sports far outweigh the risks. "Most of us are interested in making sports safer and elevating the level of competition so that it is not just one step away from a brawl," Kelly says. Equipment can help. Helmets should fit properly and be hard, so that blows bounce off rather than twist the head. Mouth guards can absorb force and reduce it from the joint of the jaw. Training can help, too; athletes should work on their neck muscles, because a strong neck can carry the force of a blow away from the head into the torso.

Leagues should also impose rules that emphasize head safety, and referees should enforce them. *13* But most of all, doctors, coaches, trainers, parents and athletes themselves need to understand the symptoms of concussion so that they can guard against the dangers posed by repeat blows to the head. After all, we're not like cartoon characters who can survive any number of anvils dropped on the head. For thousands of sports enthusiasts as well as pros, paying close attention to those seemingly minor symptoms will help protect the athlete's most important piece of gear: the brain.

13 I like these suggestions. Leagues should impose and enforce rules to keep players safe.

14 *This chart is useful because it describes the various stages of sports-related concussions. I hope coaches will take this seriously.*

HOW SERIOUS IS A BLOW? *14*

The American Academy of Neurology has issued the following guidelines for recognizing and managing sports-related concussions:

GRADE 1	
Symptoms:	No loss of consciousness; transient confusion, mental-status abnormalities last less than 15 minutes.
Management:	Remove the athlete from the activity; examine immediately and at five-minute intervals. Allow to return to sports that day only if symptoms resolve within 15 minutes. Any athlete who incurs a second Grade 1 concussion the same day should be removed from sports until symptom-free for one week.
GRADE 2	
Symptoms:	No loss of consciousness; transient confusion; mental-status abnormalities last longer than 15 minutes.
Management:	Remove the athlete from the activity; examine frequently to assess the evolution of symptoms. Get more extensive diagnostic evaluation if symptoms persist or worsen for longer than one week. Remove from sports activity until symptom-free for one week. Any athlete who incurs a Grade 2 concussion subsequent to a Grade 1 concussion on the same day should be removed from sports until symptom-free for two weeks.
GRADE 3	
Symptoms:	Loss of consciousness, either brief (seconds) or prolonged (minutes or longer).
Management:	Remove the athlete from sports until symptom-free for one week if the loss of consciousness is brief, for two weeks if the loss of consciousness is prolonged. If still unconscious or if abnormal neurological signs are present at the time of initial evaluation, the athlete should be transported by ambulance to the nearest emergency department. If a subsequent brain scan shows brain swelling, contusion or other intracranial pathology, the athlete should be removed from sports for the season and be discouraged from returning to contact sports.

Tutorial 15: Identifying Paragraph Strategies in Informational Essays

Learning Expectation

You will learn how to recognize paragraph strategies in informational essays.

PARAGRAPH OR ESSAY	HOW THE ORGANIZATIONAL STRATEGY WORKS
Definition	defines something
Example	uses examples
Description	uses descriptive details
Narration	uses anecdotes as examples
Comparison and contrast	explains similarities and differences
Classification	classifies items or ideas
Cause and effect	explains causes and effects or reasons and results
Problem and solution	explains problems and offers possible solutions

Understanding the Task

An informational essay is really an *explanation*. Explanations provide you with a complete understanding of a topic or a clear picture of why or how something happens. As you learned in the introduction to this chapter, writers use organizational strategies to make their explanations clear. The chart on this page lists some of these organizational strategies and shows you how they work. Sometimes whole essays are built around one organizational strategy. More often, writers use a variety of organizational strategies in one essay. Sometimes, they use more than one strategy in a single paragraph. In this tutorial, we will explore some of these strategies, and we will look at how some of them are used in "Blowing the Whistle on Concussions."

Getting Ready

Definition

A definition answers the question, "What is it?" Occasionally the purpose of an entire informational essay is to define a complex or abstract term for its readers. More often, informational essays begin with the definition of a term before going on to explore other aspects of the topic. For example, an essay on lightning might begin with a definition such as:

Lightning is a flash of light across the sky, resulting from a discharge of electricity in the atmosphere.

This definition gives you some idea of what lightning is, but further details are necessary if you want to know about the types of lightning, the causes of lightning, and the frequency of lightning.

Skim through the essay "Blowing the Whistle on Concussions." Find the author's definition of concussion. The definition is longer than the definition of lightning in the above example. Why do you think the author devotes more than one sentence to answering the question, "What exactly is a concussion?"

Examples

Examples help clarify explanations for readers. Without examples, most explanations would be vague, imprecise, impossible to visualize, and difficult to remember. Consider the following:

People interact with a variety of institutions.

Without examples, the meaning of the above sentence is obscure. The reader does not even know what the writer means by "institutions." Now consider the same sentence with the addition of examples. Is the meaning of the word "institutions" now clearer?

People interact with a variety of institutions, such as the workplace, banks, phone companies, utilities, and municipal governments.

Description

As you learned in the first section of this book, written descriptions paint word pictures for readers. Informational essays use adjectives and nouns to describe size, shape, weight, texture, colour, quality, or quantity, all of which add to the reader's understanding of the topic. To return to the example of lightning, adjectives such as *forked*, *sheet*, or *ribbon* help to give you a precise picture of the lightning.

Descriptions not only depend on adjectives and nouns, they also require specific details. The following explanation of bears' hibernation describes in great detail what bears eat, when they eat, and how much weight they gain.

To prepare their bodies for hibernation, bears will eat enormous quantities of berries, insects, nuts, and fish throughout the late summer and early autumn. In order to sustain their bodies for four to five months of winter hibernation, bears must accumulate large amounts of body fat, and some gain as much as 14 kilograms of weight per week. During this period of intense eating, bears may

sleep very little, as they spend the majority of their time foraging for food.

Narration

Some examples take the form of anecdotes. As we discussed in the chapter on biography (pages 30 to 45), an anecdote is a brief personal narrative, like a very short story. Magazine articles frequently use anecdotes to engage their readers' interest. Anecdotes help readers feel involved in the essay because they make the subject of the essay seem more personal for the reader. Consider the following:

As a little girl in Puerto Rico, Louisa Rodriguez dreamed of becoming "a pediatrician—a doctor for the little kids in my hometown." Last year, this smart, funny, 30-year-old pediatrician became a doctor for all Canadians when she chose to open the first health care clinic for street people in the downtown core.

Notice how this introduction uses an anecdote from Louisa's childhood to introduce her. How does this technique grab your attention as a reader?

Comparison and Contrast

Paragraphs and essays that are developed using comparison point out similarities between two like ideas or things. Paragraphs that are developed using contrast point out differences. Some compositions point out both. Writers often use the comparison–contrast pattern to describe advantages and disadvantages.

Writers also use comparison and contrast in individual sentences to help clarify explanations. Readers can more readily understand complex technical or medical terms if they are compared and contrasted with familiar processes or situations. How does comparison and contrast in this paragraph help you understand the definition of a concussion?

There is great misconception among the public about what a concussion actually is. It is not a bruise to the brain. It is a harsh chemical imbalance within the gray matter. A brain inside a skull is like a person riding inside a car with no seat belt, explains David A. Hovda, a neuroscientist at the University of California at Los Angeles School of Medicine. If the skull halts or spins suddenly as a result of a collision, abrupt stop or whiplash motion, the unrestrained brain mass will slam up against the inside of the skull. The brain tissue is not physically damaged, except in the worst cases. But a devastating cascade of chemical reactions is unleashed.

Classification

Essays and paragraphs that use the classification pattern organize their information according to type or class. Topics are organized into groups or categories based on shared characteristics and differences. A paragraph on types of lightning might classify them as sheet, fork, or ribbon. A paragraph on cholesterol might classify it into two types: good and bad. An essay on minerals may group them into three categories: metallics, nonmetallics, and fossil fuels.

Cause and Effect

The cause-and-effect organizational strategy answers one or more of the following questions:

- Why does this happen?

- What are the causes of this?

- What are the reasons for this?

- What are the results of this?

- What are the effects or consequences of this?

Entire essays are often organized using a cause-and-effect strategy. For example, you might write a history essay about the causes and effects of a World War II battle, or a social studies essay on the reasons for marital breakdown. The cause-and-effect strategy

is also commonly used in individual paragraphs within a longer essay. You often find it when the words "if . . . then" or "when . . . then" are used, as in the following examples.

When opposed electrical charges build up in a cloud, then lightning occurs.

If the rain continues, then the level of water in the river will rise and overflow its banks, flooding the downtown area.

Problem and Solution

The problem and solution strategy is similar in structure to cause and effect, and the two strategies are often used in combination. Paragraphs and essays that use the problem and solution strategy typically start by identifying a problem. The body of the paragraph or essay either explores the problem further, identifies potential solutions, or both. The overarching strategy of "Blowing the Whistle on Concussions" is problem and solution, used in combination with cause and effect. The author begins her essay by

PARAGRAPH STRATEGY	SENTENCE FROM PARAGRAPH THAT USES THE STRATEGY
Definition	
Example	
Description	
Narration (anecdote)	
Comparison and contrast	A brain inside a skull is like a person riding inside a car with no seat belt.
Classification	
Cause and effect	
Problem and solution	

identifying concussions as a problem. She discusses the causes and effects of concussion in the body of her essay, and she concludes with suggestions—or solutions—for preventing concussions.

Identifying Paragraph Strategies in Informational Essays

Copy the chart on page 133 into your journal or onto a piece of paper. Using the chart as a guide, see how many paragraph strategies you can identify in "Blowing the Whistle on Concussions." You may find that some strategies are used in more than one paragraph, and you may also find that some strategies are not used at all. Write a key sentence that identifies the strategy on the chart. Hint: Do not just look for the strategies in the main essay. The comparison and contrast strategy is done for you. Study the boxes as well. Use the checklist below to help you identify the strategies.

Checklist: Identifying Paragraph Strategies in Informational Essays

○ Are there any definitions in the paragraph?

○ Are there examples? Do any of them take the form of anecdotes (or narration)?

○ Are there descriptive passages?

○ Are two things compared (and contrasted) in the paragraph?

○ Do any of the paragraphs classify items or ideas?

○ Do any of the paragraphs discuss causes and effects or reasons?

Tutorial 16: Finding and Evaluating Information on the Internet

Learning Expectations

You will learn
- to use the Internet to do research
- to evaluate the information you find on the Internet

Understanding the Task

You may be already acquainted with the Internet in your daily life. For many people, it provides information and entertainment as well as access to e-mail. You can read the latest news on the Internet; you can find the best places to visit on spring break; you can check out your favourite TV shows, movie stars, or musicians, and you can keep in touch with your friends. Besides these functions, the Internet can be a powerful tool for doing research.

The Internet is a huge, interconnected network that grows exponentially every day. The World Wide Web (known as the Web) is part of the Internet. It is a multimedia global database that combines text, pictures, sound, and animation to explore practically every subject known to humankind. Information that used to be available only in library books, sometimes only in remote libraries in big cities or in other countries, is now readily accessible to everyone via the Web.

In 2000, there were estimated to be over seven million Web sites, an increase of 50 percent since 1999. Clearly, those numbers mean that a great deal of material is available on the Web to everyone. Of course, those same sites are not all the work of experts: anyone who can build a Web page is free to publish on the Web. Unlike book publication, a process that demands careful editing and review of materials by experts in a particular field, much Web publication is done by amateurs, unrestricted by demands of reliability or credibility. Although many sites are reputable and authoritative, some are the work of individuals who do not have to comply with any rules or expectations about their content.

Getting Ready

The breadth of information on the World Wide Web means that getting relevant, reliable research material from it is a skill. It also means that you must learn how to evaluate the materials you find in order to have confidence in their validity. Since a simple search may well yield over 1000 results, narrowing down your search and finding the best materials available are key to successful use of the Web for research. In this tutorial you will practise finding and evaluating information on the Web.

Web Terminology

When searching the Internet for information, it is helpful to be familiar with Web terminology. The chart on page 136 reviews key terms and provides basic definitions.

WEB TERMINOLOGY	DESCRIPTION
Web site	A source of information containing Web pages or screens.
Web pages	Screens within Web sites containing information.
Home page	The first page of a Web site. Like a title page of a book, it orients you to the site.
Menu	The table of contents of a Web site. The menu often appears at the left of the home page.
Hypertext	A code in which Web pages are written that allows the combination of graphics, video, sounds, and links to other Web sites.
HTML	An abbreviation of *Hypertext Mark-up Language*.
URL	A *uniform resource locator*, or the formal address of a page. An example is <www.bartleby.com>
Links	Parts of a Web page that allow you to move around the page, to other pages in the site, and to other sites. Links may be in the form of pictures, text, or hot spots. Text links are underlined; hot spots are identified by a small hand that appears when you place your cursor on the spot.
Browser	To access any Web page, you need a browser such as Netscape Navigator or Internet Explorer. Browsers allow you to search for Web sites and bookmark (save) Web sites you want to refer to again.
Search engines	Software that allows you to search the Web. Examples are AltaVista, Yahoo, and Google.
Download	To retrieve a copy of information from a remote source to your computer, i.e., from a computer or Web site.
Robot	A computer program written to retrieve, sort, and store information when related to an *indexer*. The robot actually does the "indexing" or the filtering.
Indexer	A program that can grab a file and take words into a database or alternate file to create an index. An indexer is used for Web searches. An indexer is basically a programmable filter run by a robot.

Learning to Search the Web

Research on the Web is often the best source for current news and for popular materials. It may be less useful for information on history or less-popular subject matter. It is best to be familiar with accessing typical library sources before you turn to the Internet. That way, you will have a better understanding of the value of what you find.

1. Go to the search engine of your choice by opening your browser and clicking on Search. Note that some search engines (such as AltaVista and Hotbot) use a robot and an indexer to seek information and provide keyword searches. Others,

such as Yahoo and Webcrawler, are directories with professional editors who index sites. These will allow you to search by subject as well. Experience and experimenting will show you which engines give you the best results. Here are some URLs for search engines:

- <www.yahoo.com>

- <www.altavista.com>

- <www.google.com>

- <www.excite.com>

- <www.webcrawler.com>

- <www.infoseek.com>
- <www.hotbot.com>

2. Narrow the search by using options such as "all the words" or "the exact phrase." Although search engines vary in what they find and in the exact instructions for finding information, all of them have help files that may be accessed to narrow down a search to a manageable size. Suppose you are trying to find information on the devastation of the world's rain forests. Here are some combinations of words that may help you narrow down your search:

- If you type in *rainforest AND deforestation*, you get materials with both terms in that order.

- If you type *rainforest OR deforestation*, you get a broader search of either term separately.

- If you type *rainforest AND deforestation NOT Brazil*, you get a search that eliminates documents with the word Brazil in them.

- If you type *rainforest deforestation*, the search will be confined to those words grouped together.

- If you type *rainforest NEAR deforestation*, you will get (on some engines, such as AltaVista) documents where the two words are within ten words of each other.

Keeping Track of Valuable Information
- Keep track of reference sites that may be useful to you. Many free guides and resource materials can be found in the reference sources below (and in associated links).

  - Roget's Thesaurus
    <www.thesaurus.com>

  - Encyclopedia Britannica
    <www.britannica.com>

  - The Voice of the Shuttle: Web page for Humanities Research
    <vos.ucsb.edu>

  - Bartleby Library
    <www.bartleby.com>

- Save materials you find. It is often a good idea to download material from a Web site onto a diskette. This step is important because Web sites may change from day to day, and the material you find today may not be accessible tomorrow. Keep a log to tell you when you referenced the Web sites you used.

- To avoid plagiarism, it is a good idea to take "notes" by cutting and pasting text from a Web site in another font so that it is easy to tell where your words stop and someone else's words begin.

- Record important Web sites among your bookmarks or in your favourites folder for easy reference.

Documenting Web Sources
The same rules apply as to written sources. If an author's name is given, list your Web site by that author's name, last name first. Then follow that with the title of the Web site. Next, list the date the site was last updated, followed by the date of your access to the site. Finally, include the URL, enclosed in angle brackets (<>), so that the reader can easily find your source. For example, if you were doing research on artists who created paintings based on the plays of Shakespeare, you might document a Web source in the following manner:

Rusche, Harry. Shakespeare Illustrated. 13 Sept. 2000. 20 May 2001 <http://www.cc.emory.edu/ENGLISH/classes/Shakespeare_Illustrated/Shakespeare.html>.

Assessing Web Sites for Credibility
You should search the Internet with a healthy sense of doubt and some clear objectivity, because you may encounter some of the following situations:

- Information may be limited with brief text based on only a few sources.

- Information may be biased—the site may be a fan site, a commercial site trying to sell a product, or a site created by someone with a particular, individual point of view.

- Information may be difficult to verify, or the reputation and reliability of the author may be unknown.

Here are some guidelines for evaluating Web sites:

1. **Consider the source.** It is often a good idea to note the extension on the address. A site that ends in *.gov* comes from the government; one that ends in *.com* may well be a commercial site, which, while informative, may also be trying to sell you something; *.edu* denotes that the source is an educational institution; *.ca* is short for Canada (different initials are used to indicate the country from which the information originates).

2. **Consider authorship.**

   - Who wrote the materials on the Web site, if an author is named?

   - Is that person a recognized authority on the subject?

3. **Consider the date.**

   - Has the site been updated recently? (This information is often at the bottom of the main Web page.) Is information current and therefore relevant to your research topic?

4. **Consider the evidence.**

   - What kind of support is included for the information? Are there facts, interviews, statistics, and things that may be checked out?

   - Is the evidence convincing to you?

5. **Consider bias and motivation.**

   - Can you detect bias in the author's point of view?

   - Is the intent of the site polemical, political, or otherwise biased?

6. **Consider commercial influences.**

   - Do banners and advertisements clutter up the Web site?

   - Does the site intend to sell you something instead of just provide information?

7. **Consider readability and ease of navigation.**

   - For a Web page to be convincing, it should be visually appealing and easy to read. Web pages contain images as well as text; to be credible, information must be presented in a way that is appropriate to the subject matter.

Check out these Web sites on how to assess on-line materials:

- Wolfgram Memorial Library <www2.widener.edu/Wolfgram-Memorial-Library/webevaluation/webeval.htm>

- UCLA College Library: Thinking Critically about World Wide Web Resources <www.library.ucla.edu/libraries/college/help/critical/index.htm>

Finding and Evaluating Information on the Internet

Work in pairs for the following assignment. Go to the search engine of your choice and seek out information on one of the following topics.

- DNA in medical research
- Grizzly bears in the Canadian Rockies
- Pollution in the Great Lakes
- Wayne Gretzky
- Natalie McMaster
- Ann-Marie MacDonald
- Jim Carrey

Choose two of the sites you find most authoritative and consider why you believe them to be trustworthy. Also choose one that you feel is not convincing and explain why, using the criteria on the previous page, with detailed references to the page you chose. Include a Works Cited page with documented Web sources. For information on citing Internet and other electronic sources, see Tutorial 22 on page 169. Attach a page to your Works Cited for partner reflections and include the following information:

1. We were on the right track with our research about _____ , but what we did not know was _____ .

2. We had some trouble but we solved it by _____ .

3. A question we are curious about and want to find the answer to is _____ .

4. One piece of advice that we would give someone else working on a similar project is _____ .

Checklist: Finding and Evaluating Information on the Internet

○ Did we try different methods of narrowing down the search?

○ Did we consider the source of the Web site?

○ Can we trust the author of this site?

○ Is the information current?

○ Is there evidence (or research) to support the information on the site?

○ Does the site seem to be biased?

○ Can we detect any commercial influences?

○ Is the site readable and visually friendly?

Chapter 9: Procedures

What Is a Procedure?

Procedures provide precise directions and diagrams for accomplishing tasks. Baking a cake, programming a VCR, and putting together a piece of assemble-it-yourself furniture are all tasks that can be accomplished. Effective procedures are goal-oriented; the reader can clearly visualize the result and can follow the steps in the procedure to achieve that result. If you follow a procedure properly, you should be able to duplicate the task exactly.

The purpose of a procedure is always to explain a process to the reader in the most clear and direct manner possible. Although a procedure sometimes does contain paragraphs, it is typically more skeletal in form, containing a list of materials and numbered steps. The tone of a procedure is always matter-of-fact, although some writers of procedures do try to make the procedure sound interesting and fun, as well as straightforward.

Elements of a Procedure

Procedures usually have at least some of the following elements:

- **A writer who is an authority on the subject.** The writer is either an expert on the subject or has researched the subject thoroughly.

- **A clear statement of the questions or problem.** This is typically found in the title or in the first line. For example, the title of a recipe might be, "How to Make French Toast." For a science investigation the problem might be stated as, "What is the effect of carbon dioxide on a flame?"

- **A description of required materials.** Following the problem statement there may be a description of the materials required to complete the procedure. In some instances the materials are defined or illustrated.

- **A sequence containing complete instructions.** These step-by-step instructions explain how to accomplish the procedure. They are presented in a logical, coherent sequence and are often numbered. For the reader to follow the directions, no vital step can be omitted.

- **Chronologic order.** The steps in the sequence are usually presented in chronologic order so that the reader can re-create the order of steps or understand the exact order of events.

- **Criteria by which to evaluate the procedure's success.** These enable the reader to determine if the procedures have been followed correctly. They typically appear at the end of the procedure.

- **Diagrams to illustrate how to complete the procedure.** Effective diagrams are usually clearly labelled.

- **Plain language.** Effective procedures are written in plain, clear language. If the readers are subject experts, more technical language is used.

How to Read a Procedure

Because the purpose of a procedure is to explain a process to its readers as clearly as possible, there are no hidden meanings. When you read a procedure your goal should be to understand it well enough to duplicate the task. Below are some tips for reading a procedure.

- Look carefully at the title. Does the title tell you anything about the procedure? What do you already know about this process?

- Does the procedure call for any materials? If it does, ensure that you gather the materials together before you begin the procedure.

- Look at the steps in the procedure. How many are there? Are the steps presented in chronologic order? Do they give you a sense of how much time the procedure will take?

- Examine any diagrams for labels and definitions of parts. How can they help you understand the procedure?

- Notice that the instructions are usually numbered so that you can follow the steps in the proper sequence. Seldom can you skip a step.

- Observe the verb at the beginning of each instruction, and the commanding tone that tells you what to do.

- When you have completed the procedure, check the conclusion to see if you have completed it successfully.

The procedure that follows is about running a successful product display at a company called Magic Books. Imagine that you have just been hired by Magic Books and that one of your first tasks is to set up and run a product display. Read the procedure. Did you ponder the same points as the person who wrote the margin notes? After reading the procedure, turn to the tutorials that follow.

Magic Books [1]

Our realities become your illusions.

Marlene Jennings

1   I wonder if Magic Books is
a bookstore or a publisher.

A. Introduction

The product display is a key marketing strategy for Magic Books. The main purpose of the product display is to promote our new titles to booksellers and the general public. *2* Displays are held at the following venues:

2   This could be a memo
addressed to people who
work at Magic Books.

- international and Canadian book fairs

- launches for new books

- conferences where authors of our books are speaking

We expect all product displays and employees working at them to project confidence, creativity, and professionalism. To achieve this goal, everyone involved in the displays must follow the standard operating procedures that follow. Consult the diagram that is appended to the procedures for precise placement of product.

B. Procedures for Setting Up the Display

1. Check with the conference coordinator to ensure that our supplier, Better Displays has delivered and set up bookshelves, a display table, and chairs at our booth. If there is a problem with delivery or the equipment, phone Jim on his cell phone at 244-7176 immediately.

2. Unpack the boxes that have been sent by the publisher to the display area. Unpack the box marked with a large purple X first. It is the supplies box, containing items you will need to set up the display. Use the checklist inside to ensure that you have all supplies and resources for the display (reproduced as "Display Checklist.")

3   These instructions are
straightforward. They
would be easy to follow.

3. Place ten copies of each of *Easy Magic Tricks*, *Magic for Kids*, and *More Amazing Magic* on the bookshelves behind the display table. Display all titles with their covers facing out, and their spines to your left, assuming you are facing the bookshelves behind the display table. *3* Follow these directions when placing the titles on the shelves.

- Place *Easy Magic Tricks* in the bookshelf to your left.
- Place *Magic for Kids* in the central bookshelf.
- Place *More Amazing Magic* in the bookshelf to your right.
- See diagram of a Magic Books Product Display.

4. Place the posters advertising the three new titles on the wall of the booth, above the bookshelves. Situate the posters above the titles they advertise. *4* For example, place the poster for *Easy Magic Tricks* above the bookshelf displaying *Easy Magic Tricks*. Attach the posters to the wall with the poster glue that is in the supplies box.

5. Place the brochures for the three new titles on the display table in front of the bookshelf. Make sure that you put each brochure in front of the book that it is advertising. See the diagram of a Magic Books Product Display on page 145.

6. Place the small poster advertising the draw for the magic costume toward the back of the display table, in the centre. Prop it up with a display stand. Place the jar (which will hold the ballots for the draw) in front of the poster. Both the jar and display stand are in the supplies box.

7. Keep our catalogues in an accessible spot behind or under the display table.

8. Ask the conference coordinator to ensure that empty boxes are removed.

C. Display Checklist

Place a check mark beside each item as you unpack the boxes and set up your display: *5*

	Setup	Takedown
1. Display Area		
• Bookshelves	___	___
• Display table and two chairs	___	___
2. Supplies	___	___
• Tape and tape gun	___	___
• Scissors	___	___
• Poster glue	___	___
• Jar and ballots for draw	___	___
• Cash box with float	___	___
• Packing slips	___	___
• "Back in 5 Minutes" sign	___	___

4 It is a good thing these points are numbered. It would be easy to lose track.

5 This checklist is a great idea. It would help you keep track of items.

	Setup	Takedown
3. Resources		
• 2 boxes (50 per) of *Easy Magic Tricks*	___	___
• 2 boxes (50 per) of *Magic for Kids*	___	___
• 2 boxes (50 per) of *More Amazing Magic*	___	___
• 1 box (1000 per) of Magic Books brochures	___	___
• 1 box for posters and catalogues	___	___

D. Procedures for Working at the Booth

1. Wear your name tag.

2. Keep the booth tidy.

3. Do not eat or chew gum at the booth. *6*

4. Ask a neighbouring publisher to watch the booth when you require a "bio" break. Leave the cardboard note that says "Back in 5 Minutes" in a prominent position on the display table. You will find it in the supplies box.

5. Never sit down when there is a customer at the booth.

6. Ask customers if they need help, even if they do not ask for it.

7. Tell receptive customers about our new titles and how well they are being received.

8. Give every customer a brochure.

9. Give away a catalogue only if a customer asks for it. We have a limited supply.

10. Ask each customer to fill out a draw ballot for the magic costume, and deposit it in the draw jar. Make sure you secure customers' names and addresses on the ballots.

11. At 4:00 P.M. on the final day of the display, draw the winning name from the glass jar. Phone Cynthia Jones in the marketing department (ext. #345) to give her the name and address of the winner. Use your cell phone so you do not have to leave the booth.

E. Procedures for Taking Down the Display

1. Ask the conference coordinator to bring your empty boxes to the booth.

2. Make sure that a representative from Better Displays comes to take down the bookshelves and tables.

6 *This seems like common sense!*

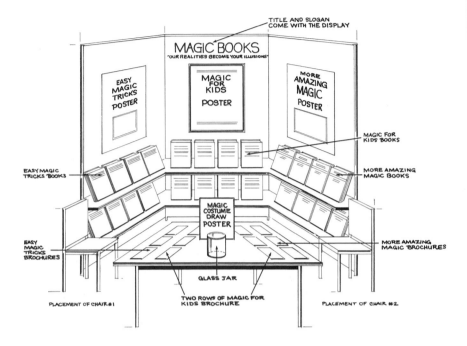

3. Pack the remaining books, posters, and brochures in the same boxes in which they were sent.

4. Leave the supplies box open until the end because you will need the tape gun, and the packing slips. Use the checklist to ensure that you do not leave anything behind. *7*

5. Tape the packing slips onto the outside of the boxes.

7 This is a handy instruction.

F. Evaluating the Success of the Display

The display may be deemed to have been successful if we made contact with a large number of participants at the venue, and if participants stayed at the booth long enough to see some of our product. To gauge the success of the display, use the following indicators:

1. The number of draw ballots.

2. The number of specific requests for follow-up contact.

3. The number of brochures and flyers distributed.

4. The number of book sales.

Tutorial 17: Comparing Two Procedures

Learning Expectation

You will learn the key features of procedures.

Understanding the Task

If you have ever tried to follow a new recipe or assemble something using a manual, you know that even simple procedures can be difficult to follow. The key is to read the procedure carefully. If you do not concentrate when you are reading the list of ingredients in a recipe, for example, you are likely to find you are missing an important ingredient halfway through the process.

Getting Ready

Procedures vary from simple three-step instructions with no diagrams to complex technical manuals. Learning how to approach a procedure will help you no matter what your purpose.

Studying the Title

People have a tendency to skip over titles of procedures, but they are worth studying, because they actually tell you quite a bit about the procedures themselves. Look at the following titles. What do they tell you about the procedures?

- Basic Wiring for the Home
- Easy Dinners You Can Make in Ten Minutes
- Planning a Sit-Down Dinner for Eight
- Garden Projects for Woodworkers
- Instructions for Your Barclay's Dryer
- User's Manual for Color Jet Printer: TL200

You probably found yourself saying about each of these titles, "That sounds like something I could do" or "I do not have the expertise for that" or "I'm not interested in doing that." Most titles tell you the subject of the procedure and something about its level. Words such as *basic*, *simple*, and *easy* indicate that the procedure is for beginners. A word such as *advanced* tells you that you may not have the expertise to follow the procedure.

Studying the Definitions

All useful procedures should provide definitions of words that readers may not understand. Names of materials should be defined, as should any specialized terminology. Before beginning a procedure, scan the document to find any words that you do not understand. If definitions are not provided, look up the words in the dictionary.

Studying the List of Materials

If the procedure includes a list of materials, equipment, or ingredients, look at this carefully. Make sure you understand the definition of each item, then gather the items together. If you are preparing a recipe, for example, retrieve all the ingredients you need and measure them out in the required amounts before you begin the procedure.

 ### Reading the Steps of the Procedure

The steps of the procedure—sometimes called the sequence—are the body of the document. Read through these steps to get an idea of the complete task. Are the instructions clear? If there is anything you do not understand, read the instructions again. If something still is not clear, ask someone else to read the procedure. Do not start the procedure unless everything is clear. Otherwise you may get stuck halfway through. Do you have a sense of the time the task will take? Make sure you have set aside enough time to follow the procedure. If you are pressed for time, you may grow frustrated and give up easily. Do you think you might need someone to help you?

Check the steps in the procedure to see if there are any items you may need that are missing from the list of materials. Some procedures are not edited carefully, and items are sometimes omitted.

Examining Any Diagrams

Examine any diagrams in the procedure carefully. Look at the title, caption, and labels. Do the diagrams contain definitions of parts that may help clarify something that is not clear? If there is something in a diagram that you do not understand, read the text near the diagram to see if you can find an explanation. Use the title and keywords from the diagram to locate the same words in the list of materials and the steps.

See Tutorial 19 for more information on examining diagrams.

Studying the Conclusion

Most procedures have a section called *Conclusions* or *Results*. Others have an unlabelled section or diagram that serves a similar purpose. These sections tell you how you can expect the procedure to turn out. A recipe might tell you that a successful cheese soufflé is supposed to rise fifteen centimetres from the top of the soufflé pan. A user's manual for assembling a chest of drawers may show you a diagram of the assembled chest. A science experiment may tell you the results of a particular experiment.

 Comparing Two Procedures

The following procedure for boxing text on page 148 is from a chapter called "Borders, Boxes, and Shading" from *Word 2000 for Windows for Dummies*. Study the form and content of the document, and compare it with "Magic Books: Procedures for Running a Product Display." Use the checklist on page 148 to compare the effectiveness of each procedure. Discuss similarities and differences in the two procedures with other classmates.

 Boxing in Small Bits of Text or Paragraphs

Word allows you to stick a box around any bit of text or paragraph in your document. For example, you can box in a title, or draw a box around an "aside" paragraph or sidebar, or put a box around a single word. Follow these steps for boxing text:

1. Choose the text you want to box.

It is best to select the text you want to put into a box: either a word, a few words, several paragraphs, or an entire page.

If nothing is selected as a block, Word boxes in the paragraph the toothpick cursor is blinking in.

2. **Choose the Format → Borders and Shading command.**

The Borders and Shading dialog box opens. Make sure the Borders tab is chosen. (If not, click that tab with the mouse.)

3. **Select the type of border you want from the Setting column.**

Four preset, easy-to-use, pop-n-fresh border styles are available; do not bother with the Custom style until you fully figure this out. Just click the style of paragraph border you want. My favorite is Shadow.

Optionally you can choose a line style from the Style list.

The Color drop-down list sets the border color. (The "Automatic" color is black.)

The Width drop-down list sets the line width.

Observe the Preview window to see how the border affects your text.

4. **Choose Text or Paragraph from the Apply To list.**

Word is usually smart with this. If you select only one word or any bit of text less than a paragraph, Word assumes you want to box in only that text. Even so, you can choose Paragraph or Text from the list.

5. **Click OK.**

Your text now has a box around it.

Checklist: Comparing Two Procedures

○ How carefully do the titles state the task? Could either of them be more precise?

○ How are the materials or resources addressed in each procedure?

○ How easy would it be to follow the steps in the two procedures?

○ Did both writers use plain language? Could jargon be a barrier to understanding in either of the procedures?

○ If there were diagrams, were they helpful?

○ What specific features helped you the most?

Tutorial 18: Writing a Procedure

Learning Expectation

You will write a procedure that a partner can follow.

Understanding the Task

Writing a procedure may at first seem like a simple task, particularly if you are an expert on the subject of the procedure. However, even writing about a familiar procedure that you follow every day can be more complex than you think. In this tutorial, we will outline steps for you to follow and strategies for you to consider when you plan and write a procedure. You will then write a procedure for a partner to follow.

④ Getting Ready

To write an effective procedure you need to consider your audience and purpose. You then need to state the problem, develop a list of materials, and determine a logical sequence of steps. Finally, you need to provide a means for your readers to determine if they have followed the procedure properly.

Considering Your Audience and Purpose

Ask yourself why your readers are reading your procedure. Most likely, they want to learn how to carry out a particular task or make a specific item themselves. Ask yourself the following questions:

- How familiar are my readers with the subject?
- How familiar are my readers with the procedure?
- What is my readers' level of experience?
- What is their level of vocabulary?

Your audience's reason for reading your procedure will influence your purpose. This may seem obvious, but it is surprising how many user manuals are difficult to follow because the writer has not thought about why and how the reader will use the document.

If you are writing your procedure for specialists, you will be expected to use specialized vocabulary. For example, a procedure on installing a newly designed part in a vehicle written for mechanical engineers would likely use highly technical language. However, if you are writing for novices, you should use simple vocabulary and plain language.

Stating the Problem

If you are writing a procedure that provides solutions to a problem or answers to a question, state the problem clearly either in the title of the procedure or in the first paragraph, or both.

Selecting a Title

Select a title for your procedure that will communicate the exact nature of the procedure for the level of reader for which it is intended.

Deciding on Materials

Decide if your procedure needs a list of materials. Some procedures do not strictly require a list of materials, but it is useful to make up a draft list even if it does not make it into your final document. The list will help clarify what materials are required for your procedure.

Defining Any Unfamiliar Terms

Define any unfamiliar term that your reader may need to know to complete the procedure, including the names of special equipment or materials. There are several ways to define an unfamiliar term: you can describe it; you can explain how it is unique; you can compare it with other similar items; and you can give your reader examples.

Deciding on the Sequence

After you decide on a rough sequence of steps, try following the steps yourself. Record each step as you complete it. Then look at your list of steps. Would someone else be able to follow them? Think about the task itself. Did you complete it yourself in a logical way? Is there a better way of doing any of the steps? Have you missed any steps? Have you taken shortcuts that a novice may not be able to copy? Have you included any unnecessary steps or irrelevant details?

You may find that some of your steps are substeps of larger categories. In these cases, you may choose to organize your steps into sections rather than in one unbroken list of steps and substeps. No matter which way you organize them, your steps should be organized in logical and chronologic order, and they should be numbered. If you choose to use substeps, number your main steps 1, 2, 3, and so on, and your substeps, 1.1, 1.2, 1.3, and so on.

Avoiding Missing Steps

Writers of procedures sometimes leave out a step or forget to explain something that the reader needs to know. To ensure that no steps are missing, ask someone who is not familiar with the process to read your sequence in draft form.

Thinking About Safety

Always keep your readers' safety uppermost in mind. Many procedures require the use of tools or dangerous equipment. You cannot take anything for granted when it comes to safety. For example, if you are writing procedures for washing a coffee grinder, you must tell your reader to unplug the appliance. If you fail to mention this, your readers could lose a finger or, worse, electrocute themselves. Missed steps and imprecise definitions can result in injury or death.

Considering Diagrams

Would diagrams help make the procedure clear for your readers? Think about parts of the procedure that the reader may find particularly difficult. How might a diagram with labels help clarify the procedure? How will you integrate your diagrams with the text? See Chapter 10 for more about diagrams.

Deciding on Conclusions or Results

How will your readers know if they have mastered the procedure? Will you include a heading called *Conclusions* or *Results* that tells your readers how they know they did the procedure correctly? Perhaps you will use a diagram to show the results for which they should be aiming.

Writing a Draft of a Procedure

When you write your procedure, keep the audience in mind at all times. Think about their purpose, their safety, and how to make the process more straightforward. Try to pay attention to the following:

- Provide the right amount of detail. *Do not* include detailed descriptions of items and steps that are obvious. *Do* include detailed descriptions for items and steps that are likely new to your reader.

- Give precise measurements. If your procedure requires measurements, make sure your measurements are exact.

- Include diagrams of complex procedures. If something is particularly difficult to explain in words, include a diagram and make sure it is integrated with your text.

- Use plain, simple language. If you have to use any technical terms, define them. Try to avoid long, complex sentences.

- Use directive verbs for each step. Examples are *stir, measure, select, place,* and *patch.*

Editing and Revising Your Procedure

When you have finished the first draft of your document, try using it to run though the procedure again. Then ask a friend who is unfamiliar with the process to do the same. Can you both do the procedure using your draft? Did either of you find any missing steps or information? Are the steps presented in logical, chronologic order? Are safety terms addressed? Are unfamiliar terms defined? Are precise measurements given? Do diagrams clarify the procedure? Is plain language used throughout the document? Are directive verbs used?

Finally, proofread your document for any grammatical, punctuation, or spelling errors. If it is letter perfect, your procedure is complete.

Writing a Procedure

You will plan and write a procedure. Choice topics include backing a car out of a driveway, checking tire pressure, or applying mascara. Imagine that your reader is someone who has no experience executing the procedure you are about to describe. Write the procedures using the checklist below. Be forewarned that it may take longer than you think!

Partner Role-Play: When you have finished a draft of the procedure, find a partner. One of you will role-play the part of the person who has never backed a car out of a driveway. This means trying hard to forget everything you know about driving a car. Using your partner's procedures, try to back a car out of a drive-way. Then reverse roles. Then revise your procedures using the checklist below as a guide. What did this activity teach you about writing a procedure?

Checklist: Writing a Procedure

- ◯ Did I keep my reader in mind at all times?

- ◯ Did I define terms that my reader might not understand?

- ◯ Did I include a list of materials?

- ◯ Did I divide the body of my procedure—the sequence—into numbered, logical, chronologic steps?

- ◯ Did I try following my own procedure?

- ◯ Did I consider diagrams for anything difficult to explain?

- ◯ Did I write my procedure in plain English?

- ◯ Did I edit and proofread my procedure?

Chapter 10: Graphics

What Are Graphics?

Graphics are pictures—such as drawings, photographs, diagrams, charts, and graphs—that explain and clarify accompanying text. For example, a municipality's annual report may use a pie graph to show the various uses of tax dollars. From examining this pie graph, you may see that the largest proportion of taxes was spent on education. Later, you may remember this information because you saw it in visual form.

In addition to providing clarity, graphics can also save space by conveying a wealth of information in visual form. For example, the annual report of a company may use a line graph to show the fluctuation of product sales over the year. If this was explained in writing only, you would probably have to read several pages of text to understand the sales trend, but the line graph shows you the sales trend in one glance.

Elements of Graphics

Effective graphics have at least some of the following elements:

- **Visual appeal.** Graphic elements use basic shapes and lines and a variety of colours to catch your eye and make information easy to understand.

- **Labels.** Short, specific terms identify items or parts of the graphic.

- **Titles.** Titles identify the subject and purpose of the graphic.

- **Proximity to text.** Graphics are usually placed very close to the related text.

- **Compactness.** Graphic elements take relatively little space compared with the amount of information they convey.

Types and Uses of Graphics

Tables
Tables organize details into columns and rows, often condensing into a small space information that might take several paragraphs to explain or describe.

Charts and Flowcharts
Because charts illustrate relationships among elements, they allow you to compare those elements. A flowchart may show you a sequence of steps or events, or it may show the lines of responsibility and communication in an organization. Flowcharts may use arrows, boxed items, or circles. You will find an illustration of the communication process in Oral Communication Power Tools on page 322.

Diagrams
Diagrams are generally simple line drawings that represent an object. You may find a diagram of the

parts of a tree or flower in a gardening book, or of ways to cut a cake in a cookbook.

Timelines

Timelines show the order in which events happened, usually by placing the events along a line.

Pie Graphs or Charts

Pie graphs or charts are named for their circular shape and for the division of circles that look like pieces of a pie. Just as a whole pie is divided among a number of people, so the pie graph shows the divisions, relationship, and size of the parts of any whole amount.

Bar Graphs

Bar graphs are most commonly used to compare different amounts, quantities, or levels. The bars may be vertical or horizontal, and they are generally side by side so that you can compare one element with another. See page 154 for an example.

Line Graphs

Line graphs are used to show change over time. (See page 183 in Chapter 12 for an example of a line graph.)

 ## How to Read Graphics

Visuals or graphics are designed to make information and instructions easy to understand and remember.

To read graphics effectively, you have to read them differently from the way you read words. When reading words, you begin at the left side of a line and proceed to the right side of the page. You also read from the top of the page to the bottom. When reading graphics, you may have to read from the bottom to the top and from the right to the left. You may even have to read diagonally from bottom left to top right, or vice versa. Try to be flexible when you read a graphic. The following tips should help you read, interpret, and understand graphics:

- Orient yourself to the diagram, chart, table, or graph. Is the title at the top or the bottom? The title placement may be a good indicator of the starting point for reading the graphic.

- Check to see whether a source has been provided for the information represented. How does the source help you judge the reliability of the information?

- Think about the features of the particular form so that you know how to read the information. What are the column or row headings? What labels can you find?

- Follow the flow of the graphic. Do arrows take you from one place to another? How high is each bar compared with its neighbour? Are there big pieces of the pie that your eye is drawn toward?

- Connect the graphic to the text you have read. How do the diagrams and flowcharts help you follow the instructions? How do the tables and graphs support or extend the explanation?

Study the graphic images that appear in this chapter. One is a bar graph that accompanies the explanation, "Why Rock Stars Go Deaf." The other is a set of diagrams accompanying procedures for repairing lamps. When you look at the bar graph on noise, consider the amount of information that has been included in a small space. When you look at the procedures and diagrams of the lamp, try to imagine yourself following instructions to repair parts of it.

Why Rock Stars Go Deaf

John Watkins

What do artists Pete Townsend (of The Who), Eric Clapton, and Ted Nugent have in common? They have all experienced hearing loss from prolonged exposure to the noise of their own music. *1* It is widely accepted that exposure to excessive levels of sound energy can cause damage to hearing; however, a subject of considerable debate is whether music as a sound source can be compared with industrial noise in terms of risk to hearing for those who perform it.

Music tends to be intermittent in nature, with frequent breaks for the performers between songs and sections. Also, sound within songs or pieces can vary dramatically in level. These characteristics may allow the ear some scope for rest and recovery between exposures. Nonetheless, studies undertaken into the hearing loss of musicians indicate that sound levels received by stage performers fluctuate from 90 to 130 decibels. Hearing safety standards suggest that prolonged exposure to 85 decibels or more can cause permanent hearing loss. *2* The average person can get a sense of how these levels compare by referring to the graph "Approximate Noise Levels of Everyday Sounds" below.

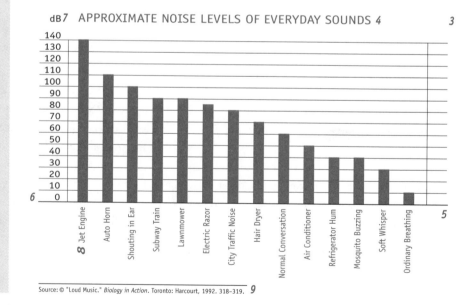

dB *7* APPROXIMATE NOISE LEVELS OF EVERYDAY SOUNDS *4*   *3*

6

8 Jet Engine, Auto Horn, Shouting in Ear, Subway Train, Lawnmower, Electric Razor, City Traffic Noise, Hair Dryer, Normal Conversation, Air Conditioner, Refrigerator Hum, Mosquito Buzzing, Soft Whisper, Ordinary Breathing   *5*

Source: © "Loud Music." *Biology in Action*. Toronto: Harcourt, 1992. 318–319. *9*

Margin notes:

1 Standing in front of speakers must be deafening!

2 It sounds as if you have to listen to a lot of loud music for damage to be done.

3 This is a bar graph.

4 The title identifies the content of the chart.

5 The x-axis lists the everyday noises.

6 The y-axis tells me how much noise is produced by each sound.

7 dB must stand for decibels.

8 The decibel level of rock music is almost as high as a jet engine!

9 The source seems to be a science text. Should be reliable.

Repairing Lamps

Most plug-in incandescent lamps are electrically alike. They all have a socket, switch, cord, and plug. And these are the four elements that may wear out. Replacing the defective part is usually all that is necessary to restore the lamp. Low-voltage lamps have a transformer that also may need to be replaced. On some low-voltage models, you may be able to unscrew the defective transformer and install a new one.

The typical parts of an incandescent lamp are shown in the illustration at right. *2* Some lamps, though, whether they are incandescent or low-voltage, are assembled with rivets instead of nuts and bolts and cannot be taken apart and repaired.

Anatomy of a Lamp 1

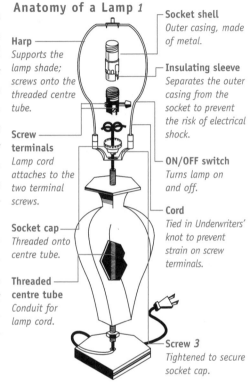

Harp
Supports the lamp shade; screws onto the threaded centre tube.

Screw terminals
Lamp cord attaches to the two terminal screws.

Socket cap
Threaded onto centre tube.

Threaded centre tube
Conduit for lamp cord.

Socket shell
Outer casing, made of metal.

Insulating sleeve
Separates the outer casing from the socket to prevent the risk of electrical shock.

ON/OFF switch
Turns lamp on and off.

Cord
Tied in Underwriters' knot to prevent strain on screw terminals.

Screw 3
Tightened to secure socket cap.

1   *The title tells me that this diagram shows the parts of a lamp.*

2   *The text directs me to the diagram.*

3   *The labels on this diagram are very clear.*

Quick Fix

Cleaning and Adjusting the Socket Tab

If a lamp doesn't work, check that it is plugged in, and that the bulb is not loose or burned out. If you still have not solved the problem, unplug the lamp, unscrew the bulb, and inspect the socket tab. If the tab is too flat, it will not make contact with the base of the bulb. To raise the socket tab, use a standard screwdriver to gently pry it up, as shown. Also use the tip of the screwdriver to scrape dirt from the tab. If the lamp still does not work, replace the socket. *5*

Socket 4

Socket tab

4   *This gives me a close-up of the socket from a different angle than the Anatomy of a Lamp diagram.*

5   *This whole procedure is written in plain language.*

Tutorial 19: Analyzing Diagrams

Learning Expectations

You will learn
- the strategies and skills required to interpret and analyze diagrams
- to analyze the effectiveness of diagrams

Understanding the Task

Diagrams are most often used to help you picture actual, physical objects. When you are attempting to understand an explanation, or trying to complete the steps of a procedure, a diagram can be a valuable, even essential, aid to your understanding. Learning to read the key features of diagrams will assist you with many tasks throughout your life.

Getting Ready

Studying the Title
The titles of diagrams are usually pretty straightforward. What you read is what you see in the diagram. Consider the following titles and think about what you would expect to see in the diagram:

- How the Ear Works
- The Oil Pan
- Cutting a Round Cake Into Sixteen Pieces
- Building a Cold Frame for Plants

Even without the diagram above or below the title, you can probably form a picture in your mind of what you will see. The title also allows you to double-check that you are examining the correct diagram for the process you plan to undertake. "How-to" books in particular are often full of diagrams, so when you are following instructions from these books, check the title to make sure you are using the correct diagram.

In the diagram "Anatomy of a Lamp," what inference can you make from the choice of the word *anatomy*?

Determining the Type of Diagram
A diagram can be as simple as a very sketchy map that you draw for friends to show them how to get to your home. In creating this map, you likely assume that certain locations and street names are familiar to your friends. As soon as you establish enough points of common understanding, the rest is easy. In a similar way, diagrams attempt to be friendly for the reader.

- A *cutaway* diagram asks you to imagine that the surface layer has been removed from an object, or that a clean slice has been taken right out of it. This type of diagram allows you to see the inner workings of the object.

- An *exploded* diagram asks you to picture an object as if gravity has been removed and all the pieces are loose and floating a little bit away from each other. The pieces stay in relatively the same place they would when the object is together, but they are separate from each other. If you think of puzzle pieces that have been laid out in exactly the right places to match up, but they have not been hooked together, you have the idea of an exploded diagram. An exploded diagram allows you to develop a clear understanding of how to put something together.

- A *combination* diagram may show an exploded object, but with some elements cut away so that you can see the inner workings as well.

- A *close-up* or *detail* diagram narrows the field to one portion of the larger diagram so that you can see more features of this smaller part of the whole object. The detail is helpful if you have to perform a process specific to that part of the object.

What kind of diagram is "Anatomy of a Lamp"? Why is this type of diagram appropriate? What type of diagram illustrates "Cleaning and Adjusting the Socket Tab"?

Looking at the Labels

Some diagrams can be interpreted without labels. In these cases, the picture says everything.

However, most diagrams provide labels to clearly indicate individual features, parts, or components of the whole object. The labels may be connected to the individual components by lines or arrows to ensure that you can make no mistake in identifying them.

How are the labels in "Anatomy of a Lamp" made even more meaningful?

Testing the Diagram

The true test of any diagram is whether it helps you make sense of the accompanying text. Most often, you have to read through the text, examine the diagram to acquaint yourself with the various parts and terms, and then read through the text again. When you read the text a second time, always ask yourself, "How did the diagram help me to understand this explanation or procedure?"

Analyzing Diagrams

Study the text and graphics for "Repairing Lamps." Decide if these are effective diagrams. Write a short paragraph describing the strengths and weaknesses of the diagrams. In your assessment, think about the function of the large diagram and the smaller diagram and how they do or do not help you understand the procedure. Remember that sometimes the simplest diagrams are the most effective. Would the procedure be easy to follow if either of the diagrams were eliminated? Use the checklist below as a guide to help you write the paragraph.

Checklist: Analyzing Diagrams

- ❍ How effective are the titles of the diagrams?

- ❍ What is the purpose of the two diagrams?

- ❍ How do the labels help me understand the procedure? Would I have understood the procedure better with more or fewer labels, or with more or less detailed labels?

- ❍ How do the different diagrams help me understand the procedure?

- ❍ Are the diagrams well integrated with the text? If they are not well integrated, is my understanding of the procedure hindered?

Tutorial 20: Creating a Graphic for a Document

Learning Expectation

You will create a graphic for a procedure or explanation.

Getting Ready

Learning how to create graphics and insert them into your procedures, explanations, and reports will immediately give your work a professional look. Once only accomplished graphic artists could create graphics to accompany text. With today's high-powered computers, anyone can create a graphic. You do not even have to be able to draw. In this tutorial you will learn how to create a graphic that accompanies a procedure or explanation. As you will see, the creation of a graphic is similar to the writing process itself, starting with thinking about your audience and finishing with proofreading your work.

④ Considering Your Audience and Purpose

As you learned in Chapter 9 on procedures, when you write an explanation or a procedure, you must be keenly aware of your audience. Are you writing for someone with subject-specific knowledge or for a person who knows very little about the subject? Is your purpose to inform an expert or to instruct someone who has no experience of this subject at all? Ask yourself the following questions:

- What type of visual would work best in this situation?

- How should I construct and label my visual?

- What do I want the reader to do with this visual?

If you are writing for an expert audience, your labels can be minimal and the information can be conveyed in a chart, graph, or table that allows the readers to draw some of their own comparisons and conclusions. If you are writing for an uninformed audience, your graphics must be very clear, perhaps in the form of a diagram, and the text must correspond to the graphic.

Choosing the Graphic

The type of graphic will depend on the topic of your explanation or procedure. Consider what you have written. Which part of your writing requires visual support? Do you want your graphic to support the entire idea of the explanation or procedure? Choose a table to summarize large amounts of information in a relatively small space. Decide on a bar graph or a pie chart if you want the reader to make comparisons and draw conclusions. Use a diagram to illustrate the tricky part of a procedure or the materials required to carry out the steps of the procedure.

Using Technology

Computer word processing software allows you to create tables and text boxes, or draw circles and lines. Practise using some of these features on a Clean Page or New Document before you insert your graphic into your text. Here are some of the things you can do:

- Choose Table from the tool bar and indicate the number of rows and columns you require. A quick way to add more rows is to use the tab key in the very last cell of the table.

- Click on the circle or line in the drawing tool bar to draw a pie chart and the lines dividing it. Right click on top of your circle to add text around the circle or inside of it. This is one way to label your graphic.

- Choose Format from the tool bar to find borders and shading to create boxes or to differentiate one bar from the next in a bar graph.

- Remember that you can use the semicircular, left-facing arrow to Undo any effect you created by mistake or wish to remove. (Simply click on Edit in your toolbar, and then on the arrow.)

- You can create a table in Microsoft Word and convert it to a graph. Simply choose Insert on the toolbar, go to Object, and click on Microsoft Graph. Follow the directions to create a colourful graph.

Integrating the Graphic with the Text

Once you create a graphic, you need to choose the location in the text where it will work best to support your reader's understanding. Ensure that you provide a reference to your graphic, either directly with a clear statement, or indirectly by placing the graphic very close to the appropriate text.

Creating a Graphic for a Document

Plan a brief procedure or explanation, such as directions from the school to your home. Choose a graphic—either a table, chart, graph, or diagram—to illustrate your document. Plan the content of your graphic, and either draw it with a computer or by hand. Label your graphic and give it a title. Then ensure that it is integrated with your text. When you have a satisfactory draft of your graphic and procedure (or explanation), exchange documents with a classmate. Once your classmate is satisfied that your graphic and procedure are clear, proofread the document for accuracy. If you are using numbers, be sure to double-check them.

Testing and Revising Your Graphic

Ask a friend or writing partner to read your procedure or explanation and to examine your graphic. Was your friend able to make the connection? Was the graphic helpful, a true aid to clear understanding? Depending on the response you receive, you may have to revise your graphic or your text to make a better connection between the two.

Checklist: Creating a Graphic for a Document

- ❍ Did I clearly identify my audience?

- ❍ Is the graphic suitable to the purpose of my procedure or explanation?

- ❍ Does the graphic support the reader's understanding of the text?

- ❍ Is the graphic integrated with the text, providing clear links?

- ❍ Does the graphic allow the reader to draw key information from the visual?

- ❍ Did I test the effectiveness of my graphic on a friendly but sincere audience?

- ❍ Did I revise my graphic as necessary?

- ❍ Did I proofread my graphic?

Chapter 11: Notes

Learning Expectations

You will learn
- to take effective notes
- to read for main ideas
- to read a textbook
- to take notes from research sources
- to cite research sources in an essay

Why Take Notes?

Taking notes can help you improve your reading, writing, research, and listening skills. To take useful notes you must do more than simply scribble a few words on a page. You must concentrate intensely to grasp key ideas and information. Good note taking does not come naturally to everyone, but it is a skill that you can easily learn.

Note Taking for Different Purposes

The purpose of taking notes is to isolate key ideas, to clarify your thoughts, and to remember main points. However, the type of notes you take varies, depending on whether you are listening, reading, writing, or doing research.

Listening

Note taking in class can help you learn the material and reduce the need for last-minute cramming before a test or exam. Research on human memory shows that individuals forget 60 percent of random information that they hear within 24 hours. To help remember what you learn in class, take notes in class, read them after school, and read them again before the next class. Review them once a week before the exam. When you study for the exam, you will be surprised at how much you already know.

When taking notes, listen hard to what the teacher is saying. If you feel your mind wandering, bring it back. Do not try to write everything down. Write down the main points in your own words.

Reading

Taking notes when you read can engage your interest in the subject matter. It can also help you understand and remember what you read. Your notes will vary, depending on your purpose for reading and the type of reading you are doing. If you are reading a story for enjoyment, you may choose not to take any notes, or you may write your personal response in your journal. If you are learning a chapter of a textbook for class, you will probably want to make detailed notes about the main ideas contained in the chapter. If you are reading an article for a research paper, be sure to take careful notes that include bibliographic information about the source. See Reading Power Tools, pages 260 to 262 for more information on strategies for different types of reading.

Writing

As we have seen throughout this book, taking notes can help you prepare to write. Brainstorming on paper and freewriting can help you find something to write about. Writing notes in a rough outline can help you organize your thoughts. Few people begin writing without first taking notes and continuing to jot down points as they revise.

Research

Taking notes when you do research is essential. Notes help you remember where you found information so that you can properly document your sources. Good note taking during the research process can save enormous amounts of time when you write your paper. You will not need to run around looking for the books and magazines that you used to write your paper. Everything will be in front of you.

When you do research, write information from another source in your own words. This will help you understand the main idea. It will also help you avoid accidentally plagiarizing someone else's work.

How to Take Notes When You Read

As we noted above, how you read depends on your purpose for reading and the type of material you are reading. The following tips will help you when you are reading mainly for information, and when you are reading textbooks, newspaper or magazine articles, reports, Web sites, and other reference sources.

- Review any knowledge you already have on the subject.

- Skim the work and read chapter titles, headings, and subheadings.

- Read any chapter objectives, overviews, and summaries.

- Look at any visuals, captions, labels, and explanatory notes.

- If the reading selection is long, divide it into parts or sections.

- Make a note of key terms. Read any definitions provided.

- Read the section and take notes about main ideas.

- Write notes in your own words to ensure you understand the concepts.

- Be concise. Using point form will save space.

- Be neat and organized so that you can read your own notes.

The selection that follows is taken from a high school geography textbook. Read the selection, then turn to Tutorial 21, where you will learn more about taking notes from textbooks.

A Renewable Resource? ₁

Ralph Krueger, Ray Corder, John Koegler

Forests, like fish, have been important to our country from the days of its earliest inhabitants. To the first explorers and settlers from Europe, . . . the forests were both awesome and beneficial. Today forests provide more kinds of products and benefits to Canadians than do fish. Indeed, forest products make up a larger part of our export trade than do the combined exports of farm, fish, and mineral products. Forest industries create many more jobs than does fishing in hundreds of communities across Canada.

In some ways, forest and fish resources are remarkably alike. Both are renewable resources, and if managed wisely, they can produce abundant harvests year after year. Both forest and fish industries have a history of over-harvesting and of harvesting in harmful ways that hinder or prevent the resource from renewing itself. Fish and trees alike are threatened by competition for the land or water they need. Just as power dams and offshore oil wells compete for use of the fish environment, so mines, parks, and farms compete for forest land. Unless our forest and fish resources are better managed, Canada could face shortages in the future. 2

Distribution of Forest Land

Trees are the most common type of natural vegetation in the Canadian landscape. A natural vegetation map . . . shows the distribution of forests across Canada from our southern border to the northern tree line. Most of Canada's ecozones . . . are forested.

Forest land can be divided into two types: productive forest land and unproductive forest land. Productive forest land is land that can produce, on 10 percent or more of its area, trees with a trunk diameter of at least ten centimetres. Trees of this size are useful for commercial purposes. The parts of Canada that provide the greatest volumes of *commercial forest* have the largest land areas of productive forest, as well as much precipitation and warmer annual temperatures.

Timber grows fastest on the Pacific coast and in the mixed forest region of southern Ontario, but the largest area of productive forest in Canada is in Québec.

Forest Species

Forest species can be classified as belonging to one of two main groups: *deciduous* trees and *coniferous* trees. In Canada's major forested regions, there are more species of coniferous trees than of deciduous trees, and the coniferous trees provide a greater volume of wood (Table 8.2). The greatest volume of *conifers* is in British Columbia, while Ontario and Québec produce most of Canada's deciduous timber.

Many coniferous and deciduous trees have shapes that are easily identified. As you read about different species of trees in this chapter, you might refer to a guide to trees that shows their typical shapes.

Threats to Our Forests

In all regions, forests face a variety of hazards that threaten their productivity. Anything that reduces the growth rate of trees damages forest resources. Some of these dangers are natural and have always been present. Others are caused or increased by human activity. These dangers fall into two classes: natural hazards and human disturbances. Not all species of trees are able to adapt to environmental changes, and some do not survive under altered conditions.

Natural Hazards

Natural hazards such as storms, extremes of weather, insects, disease, and fire have serious effects on forest resources. The following text outlines how natural hazards may harm the forest environment.

Extremes of weather affect forests in many ways. A period of time when precipitation is much below average is harmful to trees. It can slow their growth and weaken them, making them more liable to disease. On the other hand, above-average precipitation for a period of years harms trees that cannot tolerate much moisture. Violent windstorms sometimes uproot large areas of trees. Unusually warm periods in early spring kill conifers in certain areas, 3 such as the eastern edge of the Rocky Mountains. Here the sudden warmth and sunlight increase transpiration,

3 *There are many natural hazards that can cause harm to the forest environment.*

and the still-frozen ground cannot supply the moisture to replace the moisture the trees lose by this process. As a result the needles dry out, and the trees die. Severe thunderstorms often ignite forest fires.

Insects and disease can be a menace to our forests. Insects often *defoliate* trees, and then the weakened trees are attacked by disease. Insects and disease infest every forested area, but they do not usually damage the trees severely. Forests where there are only one or two species of trees and where all the trees are about the same age are most likely to suffer from insect and disease epidemics. The most severe insect damage occurs in the forests of Ontario, Québec, and New Brunswick. In these provinces, in the mid-1980s, insects were defoliating between 20 000 and 30 000ha of forest each year.

By far the most serious pest in eastern Canadian forests is the spruce budworm. This insect kills coniferous trees by eating their needles; . . . it prefers the tender needles near the ends of the branches. The damaged needles turn yellow and fall to the ground. The damage caused by the spruce budworm accounts for over one-third of the timber losses from insect and disease attacks in all of Canada. Despite this insect's name, its favourite food is the balsam fir. Spruce budworm epidemics are cyclical: that is, . . . years of heavy infestation are followed by years with almost no budworm damage. The damage from annual budworm attacks is limited by an increase in natural predators such as birds. Over the years, however, the area of forest land infested by the spruce budworm has increased.

Glossary 4

4   *These definitions are useful to help me understand the terminology the writer uses.*

commercial forest: woodland area with trees that are large enough and accessible enough to make harvesting them a profitable operation
conifer: tree or shrub that bears its seeds in cones
coniferous: cone-bearing [tree]
deciduous: broad-leaved [trees] that shed their leaves each year
defoliate: remove leaves from a plant

TABLE 8.1: AREA OF FOREST AND OTHER LAND USES IN CANADA (000 KM2) *5*

Productive forest land	2 433
Unproductive forest land	2 096
Total forest land	4 529
Agricultural land	730
Other non-forest land	3 952
Total land area	9 211

Source: Data from Forestry Canada, 1986

Note: "Other non-forest land" is treeless land unsuitable for farming: it includes tundra, ice-covered areas, grassland, and rocky areas above the tree line.

5 This table provides me with specific information about how many different types of trees there are in Canada.

TABLE 8.2: CANADIAN FOREST VOLUME BY SPECIES (000 000 M3)

CONIFERS		
Spruce	7 146	
Jack and lodgepole pine	4 087	
Balsam fir	2 827	
Hemlock	1 278	
Cedar	885	
Douglas fir	696	
Other coniferous	915	
Total coniferous		17 834
DECIDUOUS		
Poplar (aspen)	2 979	
Birch	1 124	
Maple	652	
Other deciduous	565	
Total deciduous		5 320
Total Forest Volume		23 154

Source: Data from Forestry Canada, 1986

Note: Forest volume includes only trees with a trunk diameter of 10 cm or greater, less the stump and top.

Tutorial 21: Taking Notes From a Textbook

Learning Expectations

You will learn
- to identify common elements in textbook writing
- to take detailed notes on textbook material

Understanding the Task

Textbooks are designed to help you learn. Therefore, they contain elements that you do not typically see in other books. These elements help you identify and clarify key concepts.

Getting Ready

Before you read a textbook chapter, skim through it to identify elements, such as key terms, tables, and figures. Below is a description of some of the more common textbook elements.

Common Textbook Elements
Headings
Textbooks typically have main headings and subheadings. The main headings represent the broad topics in a chapter. The subheadings represent more specific topics. You can tell whether a heading is a main heading or a subheading by the size of type that is used. Look at the Table of Contents in this textbook, and decide whether the size of type indicates a main heading or a subheading.

Keywords
In many textbooks, keywords are highlighted in **bold**, *italics*, or colour. Keywords are usually defined in a glossary at the back of the book or in the margin of the text. Whenever you see a keyword, read the definition and make a note of both the word and the definition.

Objectives, Overviews, and Summaries
Chapter objectives list the learning expectations for the chapter. Chapter overviews and summaries list the main ideas in a textbook chapter. They might be located at the beginning or the end of the chapter. Read the objectives, overview, and summary before you read the chapter.

Boxes
Some textbooks contain material that is set off from the main text in boxes. Boxes contain specific examples and stories about the topic under discussion. Boxes illustrate main ideas; they seldom introduce main ideas that are not in the text.

Tables
Tables use columns and rows to convey large amounts of information. They help simplify concepts and enable you to see connections among items at a glance. Tables have titles, captions, and labels that explain the information they contain. Tables are often identified with two numbers separated by a decimal point. The first number refers to the chapter number where the table is found and the second number refers to the number of the table. For example, Table 2.3 would be the third table in Chapter 2.

Figures

Figures consist of graphs, charts, diagrams, maps, drawings, and photographs. Like tables, figures can convey large amounts of information and complex concepts. Titles, captions, labels, and information in the text help you interpret figures. Figures are identified in the same way as tables. For example, Figure 5.7 would be the seventh figure in Chapter 5.

Activities

Textbooks often contain questions for you to answer and activities for you to do. Activities help you learn by doing, not just by reading.

Scan the excerpt on forestry to see how many of the above elements it contains. Answer the questions indicated in the chart Taking Notes From a Textbook. Compare your answers with a partner.

Taking Detailed Notes

After you have skimmed the text for its elements and made preliminary notes about any key terms, you are ready to take detailed notes. Work your way through the chapter, section by section. Write down the main headings and subheadings. Then, for each paragraph, write down the main idea and supporting details. Aside from the headings, put the information in your own words. This will help you remember it. Use point form and be concise. Some students leave a left margin to write questions next to main headings or subheadings. To study for a test, they cover up the headings and supporting details to test themselves with key questions. Think about which strategies work best for you.

Method One

One useful method for taking detailed notes is to divide your page into three columns. On the left, write down major headings and subheadings. In the middle, record the main idea of each paragraph. On the right, record supporting details. This method

TAKING NOTES FROM A TEXTBOOK	
ELEMENT	FORESTS AND FORESTRY
What are the main headings?	
Are there any subheadings?	
What are the keywords and their definitions?	
Are there learning objectives or a chapter summary?	
What are the topics of any boxes?	
How many tables are there? What are the table topics?	
How many figures are there? What are the figure topics?	
Are there any questions and activities?	
Are there additional elements that may help me understand the main ideas?	

forces you to distinguish main ideas from supporting details. It also provides you with useful study notes. If you want to review only the main ideas, read the two left-hand columns only. If you want more detail, read the right-hand column as well. See the example on page 168, based on the selection on forestry.

A variation of Method One is the two-column format. Simply divide your page in half. On the left, write down all the headings and main ideas, and on the right, the supporting details.

Method Two

A second useful method for note taking is to make a graphic representation of the main and supporting ideas. Some people use mind-maps and webs (see Writing Power Tools, pages 277 to 279); others use flowcharts, and still others use storyboards. Some use a combination of one of these methods. In the example on page 168, the note taker has used the combina-

HEADINGS	MAIN IDEA	SUPPORTING DETAILS
THREATS TO OUR FORESTS		
Natural hazards	weather extremes harm forests	low rain fall—weaken
		high rain fall—harm
		windstorms—uproot
		severe thunderstorms—fire
		unseasonable warmth, early spring—kill BC conifers

tion of a storyboard and a hierarchical storyboard to create an original diagram that will help her remember the material. This method is particularly useful for people who remember pictures better than they remember words.

 Taking Notes From a Textbook

Go back to the beginning of the selection on forestry. Make sure you have taken preliminary notes about chapter elements and key terms. Then make notes about the selection, using one of the methods discussed in this chapter.

Compare chapter notes with a partner. How did you identify key words, main ideas, or, supporting details? Which note-taking format works best for you?

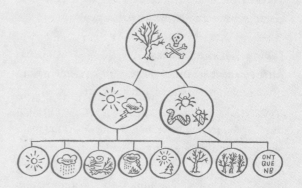

Checklist: Taking Notes From a Textbook

○ Did I skim the chapter looking for textbook elements?

○ Did I make note of any key terms and their definitions?

○ Did I make note of the main headings and subheadings?

○ Was I able to find the main idea and key supporting details in each paragraph?

○ Did I select a note-taking method that would work best for me?

Tutorial 22: Taking Notes for Research

Learning Expectations

You will learn
- to take notes from research sources
- to prepare a Works Cited list

Understanding the Task

When you write an essay using other people's ideas and research, you must document those sources in a Works Cited list. If you do not document your sources, you are plagiarizing, which is a serious offence. There are three reasons why documentation is required:

- to give credit to the people who first had the ideas or gathered the information you are citing

- to tell your readers exactly where your information is from, so they can evaluate the validity of your source

- to enable your readers to do some further research on the topic

In order for your readers to be able to find your sources themselves, you must write detailed and accurate citations. This means marking the exact place in your essay where you have used source material and including a Works Cited list at the end of your essay. To create detailed and accurate citations, you must first take careful notes.

Getting Ready

Some people find preparing accurate and detailed references a tedious task. You may ask yourself, "Does it really matter if I put a period there instead of a comma?" or "Does it matter if I put the author's last name or first name first?" The answer is that it does matter. If every writer used a different style for references, readers would waste time trying to figure out what was meant. They may have difficulty finding a source because the citation was too confusing. Universal standards mean that nobody is confused, and all people receive credit for their work.

Taking Notes as You Work

To save time preparing your Works Cited list, take notes as you work. Every time you come across a source that you think might be useful for your essay, make a note of the full bibliographic citation. Then you will have all the information you need when you prepare your references. If you forget to take notes as you go along, you will have to scramble to track down your sources just before your essay is due. Chances are you will not be able to find the information or recall where you found it.

Web sites create a particular problem for researchers who do not take accurate notes. Many Web sites are updated daily, so if you have not recorded the information, you may find that it has disappeared the next time you access the site. As well, you must be meticulous when recording a URL. They can often be up to 30 characters long, and it is easy to make a mistake, especially if you hurry. To double-check that you have recorded the correct URL, try to access the site using the URL you have just written down.

Making Sure Your Notes Are Complete

It is not enough to scribble down an author's name beside a note. In order to prepare a proper Works Cited list, you need to make note of the following:

- the author and/or editor

- the title and edition

- the publisher and the place and date of publication

- the volume and issue number of the magazine or journal

- the page numbers from which the information was taken

- for a Web site, the URL and the date you accessed the source

Using Index Cards to Take Research Notes

A useful method for recording research notes is to use a separate index card for each citation. If you change the order of ideas in your essay, you can shuffle the cards to reflect the new order. Write clearly and legibly on your cards. Otherwise, when you come to write your Works Cited list in your essay, you might not be able to read your own handwriting. Large index cards are best because they give you more space to record both the information you want to use for your essay and the source where you found it.

Below is an example of a note card.

Margaret Ward

The Family Dynamic: A Canadian Perspective. 2nd ed.

Nelson, Toronto, 1998

Page 56

"In our society, marriage is the norm—most people marry at some point in their lives."

Technological Tip

When using the computer to take research notes, be sure to follow these steps:

1. Create a separate master folder (or directory) for your essay.

2. Create folders within the master folder for your notes and Works Cited list.

3. Keep all the notes for each source in a separate file.

4. Use different fonts to distinguish notes on different source materials.

5. Use a table to keep a log of your notes.

Using the Computer to Take Notes

You may prefer to use your computer to take research notes. The computer makes it easy for you to move information around, but this also makes it more likely that you will lose track of where the note came from. See the Technological Tip on page 170 for more information on how to use the computer to take research notes.

Marking Places in Your Essay

You need to mark the sentences in your essay in which you have used other people's ideas and research. The clearest way to cite a source is to refer to it both in the sentence itself and in parentheses at the end of the sentence. If you do not include information about the work in the sentence, then more information should be placed in the parentheses. The point to remember is to include enough information to guide your readers to the Works Cited list at the end of your essay. In the following example, all that is needed in parentheses is the page number since the name of the author is given in the sentence. In the second example, the name and page number are included in parentheses because the author's name is not included in the sentence.

Example 1

Author Margaret Ward points out that our values and traditions influence the mate we select (56).

Example 2

Our values and traditions influence the mates we select (Ward 56).

Creating a Works Cited List

As just mentioned, a Works Cited list should appear at the end of your essay. A Works Cited list contains full bibliographic entries for all the works that you have cited in your essay. It appears on a new page following the end of your essay. The entries appear in alphabetical order. The entry for the above source would be the following:

Ward, Margaret. <u>The Family Dynamic: A Canadian Perspective</u>. 2nd ed. Toronto: Nelson, 1998.

Entries in your Works Cited list should begin flush with the left margin. If an entry runs more than one line, indent the subsequent line or lines by half an inch. This is called a *hanging indent* (see Technological Tip, below).

For an example of a Works Cited list as well as in-text citations, see the essay "The Death Penalty: Justice for None" in Chapter 14.

Books in your Works Cited list should include the following information:

- author(s)
- title and subtitle
- publisher

Technological Tip

Most word processing packages will enable you to create a hanging indent. Follow these steps:

- Highlight the text you want to indent.

- Click on Format on your toolbar.

- Click on Paragraph.

- Go to Special and click on Hanging.

- publisher's city
- publication date

Magazine, newspaper, and journal articles should include the following information:

- author(s)
- article title
- title of the magazine, newspaper, or journal
- volume and issue numbers
- publication date
- page numbers

See the box on page 173 for details on how to document different types of books, magazines, and newspapers. The box on page 174 shows you the proper form for documenting nonprint sources.

Internet sources should contain the following information:

- author (if known)
- title of the item or article (where there is no title, use a description such as Home Page)
- version number, if not part of the title, or the volume or issue of a journal
- date of electronic publication or latest update (if known)
- date you accessed the source

- URL in angle brackets like this: <URL>

(See Technological Tips below and on page 174, for more information regarding URLs.)

Because the Internet contains such a wide array of information, there are as many potential variations of Internet sources as there are print sources. The following Web sites will provide you with everything you need to know about citing Internet sources:

- <www.mla.org> Once you are in the site, click on the section on MLA Style. Then click on Frequently Asked Questions About MLA Style, and finally on HOW DO I DOCUMENT SOURCES FROM THE WORLD WIDE WEB IN MY WORKS-CITED LIST? This will give you more detailed information if you need it.

- <http://node.on.ca/support/citing.html> This site contains information on doing electronic citations in a number of different styles, including MLA and the University of Chicago styles. To keep yourself from becoming confused, it is best to stick to one bibliographic style.

The box on page 175 gives examples of how to document information you find on the Internet. All Works Cited entries for Web sources should contain the following information: author's name (last name first), document title, date of internet publication, date you accessed the information, and the <URL>.

Technological Tip

Most newspapers keep their articles posted on the Web for only a few days, so that URLs for these articles quickly become obsolete. If you are looking for a newspaper article that has an outdated URL, try typing in the first part of the address, which is typically the newspaper's general URL. You can probably find the article you are looking for by searching the newspaper's electronic archives. Some newspapers charge for this service.

Citing Print Sources

Book by one author

Ressor, Baynard. <u>The Canadian Constitution in Historical Perspective</u>. Scarborough: Prentice-Hall, 1992.

Book by two or three authors

Dasgupta, Geri and Nell Waldman. <u>Reading and Writing Basics: Sentence Strategies for Canadian Students</u>. Toronto: Nelson, 2000.

Book by more than three authors

Mancuso, Maureen, et al. <u>A Question of Ethics: Canadians Speak Out</u>. Toronto: Oxford, 1998.

Book by an editor

Smandych, Russell C., ed. <u>Youth Justice: History, Legislation and Reform</u>. Toronto: Harcourt, 2001.

Article (or story) from an edited collection

Reitsma-Street, Marge. "Justice for Canadian Girls: A 1990s Update." <u>Youth Justice: History, Legislation and Reform</u>. Ed. Russell C. Smandych. Toronto: Harcourt, 2001, 169–195.

Book not in a first edition

Levine, John, Carol Baroudi, and Margaret Levine Young. <u>The Internet for Dummies</u>. 7th ed. Foster City, CA: IDG Books Worldwide, 2000.

Newspaper article (For unsigned articles, begin the citation with the title of the article.)

Nolen, Stephanie. "Barak Wins Reprieve as Bullets Fly." <u>The Globe and Mail</u> 31 Oct. 2000, Nat'l. ed.: A15.

Magazine article

McClelland, Susan. "All in the Family." <u>Maclean's</u> 30 Oct. 2000: 50.

Article in an encyclopedia (For unsigned articles, begin the entry with the title of the article.)

Campbell, Ian A. "Cypress Hills." <u>The Canadian Encyclopedia</u>. 2nd ed. Edmonton: Hurtig, 1988.

Practice with Research Sources

Go to the library and find three sources, either for a project you are working on or a subject that interests you. One of the three sources should be from a newspaper, magazine, or journal; another should be from the Web. Record the information you need to prepare a Works Cited list without removing any items from the library. Then write up your three sources using proper bibliographic form.

Find a partner and exchange your lists of sources. Each partner should edit the other person's Works Cited list for accuracy and then track down the works on the list. The checklist on page 175 may help you with this activity.

Citing Nonprint Sources

Interview

Chang, Mark. Personal Interview. 15 May 2001.

Film

Everyone Says I Love You. Dir. Woody Allen. Miramax, 1997.

Videocassette (When citing a videocassette, include the year the film was released and the year it appeared on video. For recent films the dates may often be the same.)

The Perfect Storm. Dir. Wolfgang Petersen. 2000. Videocassette. Home Box Office and Warner Bros., 2000.

Television program

"Episode Five: A Question of Loyalties." Canada: A People's History. CBC, Toronto. 12 Nov. 2000.

Recording

Krall, Diana. Stepping Out. Justin Time Records, 1993.

Song

Krall, Diana. "Body and Soul." Stepping Out. Justin Time Records, 1993.

CD-ROM

Digital Image Archive for Physiological Psychology. CD-ROM. Needham Heights, MA: Allyn & Bacon, 1998.

Technological Tip

When you enter a URL for a Web site in your document, some word processing programs automatically underline the URL. To remove the underlining, simply highlight the URL and click on the U symbol on your toolbar.

Citing Internet Sources

Personal site

Cousins, Leah. Home Page. 1 March 2001. 1 May 2001 <www.chass.utofino.ca:6060/~Leah/index.html>. (This is not a real URL; it is only an example.)

Professional site

The History Channel Online. 2001. History Channel. 19 Feb. 2001 <http://historychannel.com/>.

Document within a professional site

"Canada: A People's History." 2001. CBC Online. 30 Jan 2001 <http://cbc.ca/history/>.

Article on the Web

Wente, Margaret. "Medical Care That's Not Even Fit for a Horse." The Globe And Mail Web Centre. 14 Oct 2000. 16 Oct 2000 <http://archives.theglobeandmail.com/%3D10&>.

Encyclopedia article

"Tornadoes." Britannica.com. 1999–2000. Encyclopedia Britannica. 12 Dec 2000. <http://www.brittan-ica.com/bcom/eb/article/0/0,5716,1.9120+1+106250,00.html?query=tornado>.

E-mail

Buckingham, Rachel. Re: "Text of Speech on Advertising." E-mail to Rick Saunders. 15 April 2001.

Checklist: Taking Notes for Research

❍ Has my partner used proper bibliographic style for his or her Works Cited list?

❍ Have I checked the library's microfiche and indexes to see if the items are in the library?

❍ Have I checked any URLs provided in the sources? If the URL is incorrect, have I tried using a search engine to find the document?

Chapter 12: Reports

What Is a Report?

A report is an account that provides information to its readers. Reports can be delivered orally or on the computer screen, but most often they are written documents. No matter what line of work you choose, chances are you will be required to write a report. Reports range from informal half-page sales activity reports, to 200-page financial reports, to proposals for overhauling entire systems.

There are two basic types of report: the informational report presents the facts of a situation, but does not analyze or interpret those facts; the analytical report analyzes a situation and recommends a course of action. The primary purpose of both types of report is to provide information that others can use to make decisions. These could be decisions about anything work-related, from changing a procedure to hiring more staff.

Elements of a Report

The audience for most reports that you write in the workplace will be your manager and co-workers. Managers rely on reports from their employees to provide information and advice they can trust. They do not want to waste time wading through poorly organized documents. Reports should be clearly organized so that readers can immediately grasp the essential points. Good reports contain the following elements:

- **Headings and subheadings.** Reports are divided into sections. The heading at the beginning of the section identifies the subject of that section. In longer reports, sections are divided into smaller sections, each of which is introduced by a subheading. Headings in longer reports are numbered. The headings make it easier for readers to navigate the report. Readers know immediately what a specific section is about. Those who are short of time can use the headings to scan the document and focus on essential information.

- **Graphics.** Many reports contain tables, charts, graphs, and other illustrations. Graphics have several benefits. They add visual appeal to a document that might otherwise be boring and difficult to read. They can also save considerable space. A typical table, for example, can replace several paragraphs of text. Graphics make it easy to high-light essential information.

- **Summary.** Most analytical reports begin with a sum-mary. The summary is typically one paragraph long and provides an overview of the most important points. The summary is not an introduction; it is a short version of the report. Its primary purpose is to provide the busy manager or worker with a brief synopsis of the report's key points. Because informa-tional reports are usually short and straightforward, they often do not include summaries.

- **Introduction.** The introduction follows the sum-mary. It typically includes information on the purpose of the report, the background or reasons for the report, and the method the writer has used to research the report. The method may include questionnaires, interviews, or Internet or library research.

- **Discussion.** This is the body of the report. In short informational reports it includes the facts presented in point or paragraph form. In analytical reports it includes a discussion of research findings. In longer reports, it is usually subdivided into smaller head-ings. It can be organized by topic or category, chronologically, or by order of importance.

- **Conclusions and/or recommendations.** Most brief informational reports contain neither conclusions nor recommendations, but analytical reports typi-cally have one or both. Conclusions are interpreta-tions based on findings. Recommendations are suggested courses of action.

 ## How to Read a Report

Ease Into the Report

Before you read the report, take time to familiarize yourself with the format and content, following these suggestions:

- Read the title page. Do you know anything about the subject or the authors of the report?

- Check the length of the document. How many pages is it? Estimate the time it will take you to read it and grasp the main points.

- Scan the report for headings and subheadings. What do the headings and subheadings tell you about the content of the report?

- Look at any graphics in the report. Read the cap-tions that accompany the graphics.

- Read the summary twice, or until you have an understanding of the report's key points.

Read the Report

Read the report slowly, one section at a time. Reread any sections that are not immediately clear.

- Read the introduction first. Can you identify the purpose of the report? What research methods has the writer used?

- Read the body of the report. Does the writer pre-sent any findings?

- If there is anything you do not understand about the graphics, read pages 152 to 153 on how to interpret graphics.

- Before you read any conclusions or recommenda-tions, try to predict what they will be.

The following report is an analytical report writ-ten for the vice-president of sales and marketing at a company called Mitchum's Foods. Mitchum's pro-vides cafeteria services to high schools and colleges. Using the above guidelines, read the report, and make a few notes. How do the notes in the margin compare with your own? When you have read the report twice, work through the tutorials that follow.

An Assessment of the Revenue Decline at Bowen Community College's Cafeteria

Prepared for:

Tina Cunningham

Vice-President, Sales and Marketing

Mitchum's Foods

Prepared by:

Mario Beruti

Emily Humbert

Marketing Coordinators

May 15, 2001

A. Summary

In 2000, cafeteria revenues at Bowen Community College were $37 700 (33%) less than they were in 1999. This serious situation for Mitchum's Foods prompted the need for an investigation, the results of which are written in this report. In the course of our investigation, we found that a new restaurant across from the school has taken much of our business. Our research, which included a survey and focus groups, shows that students and staff are dissatisfied with the lunch services offered by their cafeteria. To reverse the revenue decline, we make five recommendations:

1. Delete the hot luncheon special from the menu, and offer hamburgers instead.

2. Delete the prepared sandwiches from the menu, and offer a sandwich bar instead.

3. Delete tossed salads from the menu, and offer a salad bar instead.

4. Hire three part-time employees to prepare and serve sandwiches, hamburgers, and fries during the lunch periods.

5. Continue the assessment with an investigation into costs and their potential impact on profits. *1*

1   *The focus of this report is to look at why revenues dropped by 33% in one year and to provide some solutions for the problem.*

B. Introduction

Between January 1, 2000, and December 31, 2000, revenues at the cafeteria at Bowen Community College dropped by $37 700 (33%) when compared with revenues for the same period in 1999. This report analyzes the reasons for the revenue decline, and provides recommendations for restoring revenues to their former levels.

We used the following methods to analyze the revenue decline:

- 2300 questionnaires were sent to all students and staff at Bowen Community College. Two hundred people completed the questionnaire, giving us a rate of return of 8.7%.

- Three focus groups *2* were held, each with six students and one teacher. The purpose of the focus groups was to gather suggestions from students and staff for improvements to the cafeteria service.

- An investigation was completed of all competitors located within one square mile of the college.

C. Assessment of Current Situation

1. Mandate of Bowen Cafeteria

Mitchum's Foods signed a five-year contract in 1998 with Bowen Community College. Our mandate is to provide cafeteria services to students and staff from 7:30 a.m. until 3:00 p.m. We serve breakfast from 7:30 a.m. to 9:00 a.m. and lunch from 11:30 a.m. to 1:30 p.m. Coffee, tea, and other beverages are served throughout the day.

2. Overall Revenue Picture

In 1999, total revenues were $113 500. In 2000, they were $75 800, which represents a decline of $37 700 (33%). In 2000, breakfast revenues were unchanged from 1999 at $15 200. Lunch revenues were $51 500, which represents a decline of $35 300 (41%). *3* Beverage revenues were $9100, which represents a decline of $2600 (22%). Sales receipts show that beverage revenues declined only during the lunch period. See Table 1 in Appendix A for a comparison of 1999 and 2000 revenues.

3. Categories of Lunch Foods

Mitchum's serves four categories of lunch foods at Bowen Cafeteria. They are as follows:

- a hot special served daily consisting of meat, or a pasta dish with a meat sauce, potatoes or rice, and a vegetable

2 A focus group sounds like a good idea because you get to hear from people personally.

3 The revenue seemed to decline most during the lunch times.

- French fries with gravy
- prepared sandwiches (salmon, tuna, roast beef, ham and cheese, cheese and tomato)
- a tossed salad (with French, Thousand Island or Ranch dressing)

4. Revenue Decline by Food Category

Our analysis included a detailed study of the sales and revenue pattern of the specific lunch foods itemized above. Significant findings were as follows:

- Revenues from hot specials have fallen by $13 500 (41%).
- Revenues from prepared sandwiches have fallen by $10 000 (45%).
- Revenues from French fries and gravy have fallen by $8700 (36%).
- Revenues from tossed salad sales have fallen by $3100 (42%). *4*

See Table 2 in Appendix A for a comparison of lunch revenues in 1999 and 2000.

4   These percentages all seem very close in number.

D. Reasons for Revenue Decline

1. Opening of a New Restaurant

Our investigation of restaurants within one square mile of the college indicates that a new restaurant called Ricky's opened on February 5, 2000. It is located on Fifth Street, directly opposite Bowen Community College. Ricky's serves a wide selection of fresh food. The writers of this report had lunch at Ricky's three times, and found the following:

- The menu includes charcoal burgers, fries, a salad bar, and a sandwich bar.
- Prices at Ricky's are low (a charcoal hamburger and fries is $7.00).
- Service is quick. The average time from order to delivery of food is four minutes.
- Service includes take-out.

2. Quality of New Restaurant

Of the 200 students and instructors who returned their questionnaire, 60% had tried Ricky's and reported that they liked the wide selection and the quality of the food. Ninety-five percent *5* of the students and staff who had tried Ricky's said that:

5   Wow—95% of the people polled seemed to prefer the new restaurant to the school cafeteria.

- the quality of the food at Ricky's is superior to the food at the college cafeteria

- the food is fresher at Ricky's than at the cafeteria

- the selection at Ricky's is better

- service is as fast at Ricky's as it is at the college cafeteria

E. Recommendations for Increasing Revenues

The following recommendations are based on comments received in the focus groups, answers given on the questionnaires, and research into the competition:

1. Delete the Hot Special from the Menu 6
Seventy-four percent of survey respondents said that they would order a hamburger rather than the hot special if hamburgers were on the menu. Focus group participants reported that the hot special is "tasteless" and "unappealing."

2. Buy a Charcoal Grill to Cook Hamburgers
Clearly the charcoal hamburgers and fries at Ricky's are selling well. Fifty-five percent of our survey respondents had ordered a Ricky's hamburger more than once, and cited the hamburgers as a reason for buying lunch at Ricky's rather than the school cafeteria.

3. Delete Prepared Sandwiches from the Menu
Seventy-seven percent of survey respondents said they would not buy prepared sandwiches if fresh sandwiches were available. 7 Focus group participants said that the prepared sandwiches were "soggy" and "tasteless."

4. Start a Sandwich Bar
Thirty-five percent of our survey respondents had bought a fresh sandwich from Ricky's at least three times. They cited the variety of breads and the freshness of Ricky's ingredients as reasons for buying his sandwiches. We recommend starting a sandwich bar staffed by two individuals between 11:30 a.m. and 1:30 p.m. The sandwich bar would provide an assortment of breads and rolls, luncheon meats, cheeses, tuna salad, and salmon salad.

6   *The captions here make it easy to see the specific recommendations.*

7   *Many of those surveyed did not like this item on the menu, so this sounds like a good recommendation.*

5. Delete Tossed Salads from the Menu

Ninety-five percent of survey respondents said they would not order a tossed salad if a salad bar were available. Focus group participants said the tossed salads were "bland" and "tasteless."

6. Start a Salad Bar

Thirty-four percent of our survey respondents had bought salads from Ricky's salad bar at least four times. They cited the variety of salad materials and the freshness of the ingredients as reasons for buying a salad at Ricky's. Currently, the school cafeteria does not have a salad bar. We recommend starting a salad bar, with a variety of salads, toppings, and dressings.

7. Hire Three Part-Time Employees

Current staffing consists of two full-time staff members who work from 7:30 a.m. until 3:30 p.m. The sandwich bar and the charcoal grill will create a need for more staff because employees will need to prepare the sandwiches and burgers on demand. We recommend hiring three additional employees for two hours per day, two to make sandwiches and another to cook hamburgers on the grill. The existing staff members will operate the two cash registers during the lunch periods.

7. Conduct Further Research Into Costs

It was beyond the scope of this report to research costs. We recommend that more research be undertaken to determine the costs of implementing these changes and their impact on profitability.

APPENDIX A

8 *This table makes it easy to see where most of the decline in revenue has occurred.*

TABLE 1: A COMPARISON OF 1999 AND 2000 REVENUES BY FOOD CATEGORY 8		
FOOD CATEGORY	1999 REVENUES	2000 REVENUES
Breakfast	$15 200	$15 200
Lunch	$86 800	$51 500
Beverages	$11 700	$9 100
Total	$113 500	$75 800

TABLE 2: A COMPARISON OF 1999 AND 2000 REVENUES BY LUNCH FOOD CATEGORY

LUNCH FOOD CATEGORY	1999 REVENUES	2000 REVENUES
Hot special	$33 000	$19 500
Prepared sandwiches	$22 300	$12 300
French fries and gravy	$24 100	$15 400
Tossed salad	$7 400	$4 300
Total	$86 800	$51 500

FIGURE 1: A COMPARISON OF 1999 AND 2000 REVENUES, MONTH BY MONTH *9*

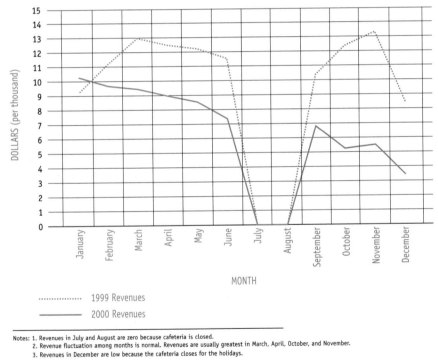

1999 Revenues

2000 Revenues

Notes: 1. Revenues in July and August are zero because cafeteria is closed.
2. Revenue fluctuation among months is normal. Revenues are usually greatest in March, April, October, and November.
3. Revenues in December are low because the cafeteria closes for the holidays.

9 This line graph really shows a downward trend in revenues. No wonder the company is concerned.

Tutorial 23: Looking for Visual Cues

Learning Expectations

You will learn
- the visual elements of a report
- to use visuals to help you read a report

Understanding the Task

You may not have read many reports, but you have undoubtedly read countless textbooks, books, and magazines. You have probably also looked at numerous Web sites, job postings, sample résumés, and letters. Have you ever thought about what makes some documents more visually appealing than others? The key to visual impact is a good page design.

Getting Ready

The purpose of informational documents such as reports and the examples mentioned above is to convey information. This type of writing usually contains visual cues or signposts that help you find what you need easily. Examples of visual cues are headings, terms in **bold** or *italics*, numbered and bulleted lists, and the white space on the page. Visual cues work by creating an expectation in the reader's mind. For example, if you are reading a text or a report that has subheadings in a certain size and style of font, you know that every time you see that particular font, it indicates a subheading.

Consistency of Visual Cues

In order for visual cues to be useful they must be used consistently. It is easy for the reader to become confused if they are applied haphazardly. If a font in Times New Roman 14 is used for one main heading and **Arial Black** 12 is used for the next main heading, the reader will not realize that both are meant to be main headings.

Effective Use of Headings

Most effective reports use both main headings and subheadings. To provide useful visual cues for the reader, headings should not only be consistent, they should be short, descriptive and specific, and parallel.

- **Headings should be short.** If headings are too long they can be difficult to follow, and readers can easily become confused. Compare the following two headings. Which one is easier to read?

  Details Staff Need to Know in Case the Photocopy Machine Breaks Down

  Tips for Fixing the Photocopier

- **Headings should be descriptive and specific.** Headings should enable a reader to grasp the intent of a report without having to read it. Compare the following two headings. Which one is more descriptive and specific?

  Software Applications Available for Word Processing

  Using Word for Windows 2000

- **Headings should be parallel.** When a subheading is parallel, its grammatical construction is consistent with other subheadings. In the following example, the first three headings are not parallel, and the second three are parallel. Can you see the difference?

Opening a File
How to Format a Document
Print a Document

Opening a File
Formatting a Document
Printing a Document

Numbered and Bulleted Lists

Lists indicate that the writer has a number of points to make and make it easier for the reader to distinguish one point from another. Lists can be prepared with numbers or bullets. Numbers are preferred if the writer refers to an item in the list in the body of the report.

- **Lists should not be too long.** The most effective lists are neither too long nor too short. Lists with more than 10 points are often best grouped into smaller lists. Sometimes lists with fewer than three points could just as effectively be put into paragraph form.

- **Lists should be parallel.** Like headings, items in lists are easier to read if they are grammatically parallel. In the example below, one list is not parallel; the other list is parallel. Which do you find easier to read?

1. Even if customers don't ask for help, you should still ask them if you can help them find something.
2. Our new titles are being received well. You should let customers know this.
3. All customers should receive our brochures.

1. Ask customers if they need help, even if they don't ask for it.
2. Tell customers about our three new titles, and how well they are being received.
3. Give every customer our three brochures.

Evaluating Visual Cues in a Report

Read the excerpt in the box on page 186. Did you find the excerpt difficult to read? Make a note every time a visual clue is used inconsistently, using the checklist on page 187 as a guide. With a partner, review the excerpt again, and find the following:

- an example of a heading that is too long

- an example of a heading that is not descriptive and specific

- an example of a heading that is not parallel

Without looking back at the original report on page 178, rewrite the three headings so that they are more effective. Now look back at the report. How do your headings compare with the original?

Comparing the Use of Visual Cues in a Report and Other Documents

With a partner, select three types of documents from the following list:

- a report

- a magazine article

- a résumé

- a chapter in a reference book

- a chapter in a textbook

- an encyclopedia article

Excerpt from Bowen Community College Cafeteria Report

(Sample Report Excerpt)

Recommendations for Increasing Revenues

Delete the Hot Special from the Menu and Buy a Charcoal Grill to Cook Hamburgers

Seventy-four percent of survey respondents said that they would order a hamburger rather than the hot special if hamburgers were on the menu. Focus group participants reported that the hot special is "tasteless" and "unappealing."

Clearly the charcoal hamburgers and fries at Ricky's are selling well. Fifty-five percent of survey respondents cited the hamburgers as a reason for buying lunch at Ricky's.

Sandwiches Should Be Deleted from the Menu.

Seventy-seven percent of survey respondents said they would not buy prepared sandwiches if fresh sandwiches were available. Focus group participants said that the prepared sandwiches were "soggy" and "tasteless."

Sandwich Bar

Thirty-five percent of our survey respondents had bought a fresh sandwich from Ricky's at least three times. They cited the variety of breads and the **freshness** of Ricky's ingredients as reasons for buying his sandwiches.

- The sandwich bar should be staffed by two individuals between 11:30 a.m. and 1:30.p.m.

- An assortment of breads should be provided.

A Salad Bar Would Help Increase Revenues

Thirty-four percent of our survey respondents had bought salads from Ricky's salad bar at least four times. They cited the *variety* of salad materials and the freshness of the ingredients as reasons for buying salad at Ricky's. Focus group participants said the cafeteria's tossed salads were "bland" and "tasteless."

Employees and Costs

Current staffing consists of two full-time staff members who work from 7:30 a.m. until 3:30 p.m. The sandwich bar and the charcoal grill will create a need for more staff. Employees will need to prepare the sandwiches and burgers on demand. We recommend hiring three additional employees for two hours per day.

It was beyond the scope of this report to research costs. We recommend that more research be undertaken to determine the costs of implementing these changes and their impact on profitability.

Analyze and evaluate the use of visual cues in each document by answering the following questions. Use the checklist below as you work.

- How does the document use bullets, bolding, italics, underlining, typeface, and colour? What do they signal to the reader? Are they applied consistently throughout the document? How do they help you read and understand the document? Are they effective? How could they be improved?

- Are there headings in the document? How are they used? How do they help you read and understand the document? Are they effective? How could they be improved?

- Are there lists in the document? How are they used? How do they help you read and understand the document? Are they effective? Are there a sufficient number of lists? Could there be more?

- Are there other visuals in the document? How are they used? Are they effective? How could they be improved?

Compare the use of visual cues in the three documents. Which uses visual cues most effectively and why?

Checklist: Looking for Visual Cues

- ○ Are the typefaces consistent? What do they signal to the reader? Are they effective?

- ○ Has the author applied bullets, boldface, italics, underlining, and other visuals consistently? What do they signal to the reader?

- ○ Is spacing applied consistently in the report? What does the spacing indicate?

- ○ By reading only the headings, can we determine the content of the document?

- ○ Are the headings short, specific, and descriptive?

- ○ Are the headings used consistently?

- ○ Are any lists parallel?

Tutorial 24: Planning and Writing a Report

Learning Expectation

You will learn to plan and write a report.

Understanding the Task

Good writing skills are essential to career success. Almost all careers require some writing, and no matter what field you choose, others will evaluate your performance based, at least in part, on your writing ability. In this tutorial, you will work as part of a group to research what kind of writing skills employers are seeking. Then you will write a report that assesses your own writing skills and provides an action plan for improving those skills to meet the objectives of the workplace.

Getting Ready

Before you start to work on your report, ask yourself the following questions:

- **What is the purpose of my report?** Is your purpose to provide the facts in a situation or to do some research and analysis and make conclusions and/or recommendations?

- **What type of report will I write?** If your purpose is to provide facts with no analysis, you will write an *informational report*. If you are expected to provide facts, analysis, conclusions, or recommendations, you will write an *analytical report*.

- **Who is the audience for my report?** A report is like any other piece of writing. Before you begin,

you need to identify your audience. To help in this task, ask yourself the following questions:

- How will my audience use my report?

- What does my audience already know about the subject?

- What key facts does my audience need to know?

- What level of language would work best with this audience?

- What tone would work best with this audience?

- **What research do I need to do?** You may need to do some research in order to write your report. This may involve library research or Internet research (see Chapter 8, Tutorial 16), or it may involve conducting original research through questionnaires or interviews. No matter what kind of research is required, you will need to start the process by formulating research questions.

Devising a Work Plan

After you have answered the above questions, the next step in writing a report is to devise a work plan. The plan should identify the tasks you need to do and the dates by which you need to complete them. A work plan for an analytic report might look something like this:

TASK	DUE DATE
Internet and library research	January 22
Interview research	January 24
Outline	January 24
First draft of text	January 29
Editing and proofreading	January 30
Final draft	February 1

Devising an Outline

Once research has been gathered from various sources, you are ready to devise an outline. When planning your outline, think about the headings, the order in which you will present information and ideas, and the graphics.

- **Headings.** Give your main headings titles, and label them with letters (A, B, C, etc.). Give your subsections titles and number them. Your heading titles, letters, and numbers will make the report easier for your readers to follow. A number of standard main headings can be used, depending on the purpose of your report.

- **Order of ideas.** When devising the outline, think about the order in which to present ideas and information. Each main section of the report could be organized differently, depending on what makes the best sense for that particular section. Look at the box to the right for the different ways you can organize sections of a report.

- **Graphics.** Decide what graphics, if any, you plan to include in your report. Brief informational reports do not require graphics. However, graphics are used in analytical reports to add visual appeal and to simplify complex information. Graphics should be presented in an appendix. An appendix is a page or pages that appear at the end of the report so the flow of the narrative is not disrupted. See Chapter 10 for more on graphics.

Writing the First Draft of the Report

Reports should be written in a professional, objective style, using plain language. Keep the following tips in mind as you write:

- **Use the active voice.** Verbs may be active or passive, depending on whether the subject of the verb is acting (active voice) or being acted upon (passive voice) (see Technological Tip, page 190). Reports

METHOD OF ORGANIZATION	EXAMPLE
CHRONOLOGIC ORDER: The organization is according to time.	The body of a procedural (informational) report could organize events according to the sequence in which they typically happen.
SPATIAL ORDER: The organization is according to location or geography.	Portions of a sales report could give a geographic breakdown organized by province and territory.
CLASSIFICATION: The topic is divided into class or type.	An analytic report about animals on the endangered species list could classify research findings according to the different species.
CAUSE AND EFFECT: The causes are discussed first, followed by the effects. Or one cause and effect are discussed, followed by a second cause and effect, etc.	An analytic report about contaminated soil could organize research findings by discussing first the causes of soil contamination, followed by the effects.
PROBLEM AND SOLUTION: The problems are discussed first, followed by the solutions. Or one problem is discussed followed by one solution, followed by a second problem and solution, etc.	An analytic report on computer problems could organize its body by first identifying the problems, then discussing the solution.
ORDER OF IMPORTANCE: Start with the most important point, and work down to the least important point.	A list of recommendations may start with the most important recommendation and end with a less important one.

often make for dull reading because the writer has used the passive voice. The active voice is more powerful and precise than the passive voice.

Occasionally, the passive voice may be the better choice. Choose the passive voice:

– when the person or agent that performed the action is not known, for example:

Farzin's bicycle was stolen from his garage last night.

– when you want to de-emphasize the subject that performed the action, for example:

Farzin's bicycle was stolen by one of his roomates.

For more information on active and passive voice, see page 302 of Writing Power Tools.

- **Use specific details and examples.** Specific, concrete details will make your report clearer. Try to be as precise and exact as you can.

- **Make your report visually appealing.** Use visual features such as white space, headings, and numbered and bulleted lists to make your report visually appealing and easy to read (see Technological Tip on page 191). The key to using these features in any document is to make sure that they are applied consistently and that their structure is parallel. See Tutorial 23 for more on visuals.

Editing the First Draft

When you have completed a first draft, read the report through once aloud, then once silently. Try to imagine you are reading someone else's report. Ask yourself the following questions:

- Have I used headings that are appropriate to my purpose?

- Have I put the details in a particular order? Have I used connecting words that guide the reader through the report?

- Have I included specific details that will enable the reader to grasp what I am saying?

- Have I used a professional, objective tone?

- Have I used too much of the passive voice?

- Are my headings, lists, and other features applied consistently?

- Are my headings and lists parallel in structure?

- Do my graphics help explain the content of the report?

Once you are satisfied with your report, ask a partner to read it and give you feedback.

Writing the Final Draft

As you write the final draft, keep the above list of details in mind. When you are finished, edit and proofread your work for grammar, syntax, and

Technological Tip

Most word processing programs highlight sentences written in the passive voice, giving you an opportunity to rewrite the sentence in the active voice. Be sure to use this feature if you are working with a computer.

spelling. Workplace reports reflect the person who wrote the report. To project a professional image, they must be error free. Ask a partner to proofread your report to make sure that there are no errors.

Planning and Writing a Report

Group Research Plan

In groups of four, develop a research plan for investigating the writing skills required in the workplace. Read pages 324 to 327 on working in groups and Tutorials 16 and 22 on research before you begin. Also, consider questions listed under the heading "Getting Ready" on page 188. Then divide up the tasks: two group members could do library and Internet research while the other two conduct an interview. When the group has gathered the information, each person should use it to prepare an individual report that details the following:

- the writing skills required in the workplace
- an analysis of your own writing skills, including strengths and weaknesses
- an action plan (or recommendations) for attaining the level of skill required in the workplace

Plan and write the report using the strategies discussed in this tutorial and in the checklist below. When you are satisfied with the content of your report, select an appropriate format, and publish it, referring to pages 315 to 316 of Writing Power Tools for guidelines.

Technological Tip

Icons on the toolbar of your word processing program will allow you to automatically number or bullet items in your report.

Checklist: Planning and Writing a Report

○ Have I kept my audience and purpose firmly in mind?

○ Has my group done the necessary research?

○ Have I created a work plan and an outline?

○ Have I labelled and numbered my headings?

○ Have I selected an appropriate order?

○ Have I used effective graphics?

○ Has a partner provided feedback on my report?

○ Have I edited and proofread my report?

Further Explorations: Explaining and Reporting

The *Further Explorations: Explaining and Reporting* section extends the range of texts you can create, interpret, and respond to. This section will offer you additional pathways to responding creatively and critically, while applying your understanding of language, form, and genre.

The Cellular Phone Virus in Japan

Miki Uniya

Cellular phones have not been available at reasonable prices in Japan until lately. This fact notwithstanding, the Japanese have, en masse, succumbed to the lure of the new technology. As a result, our lifestyle appears to have become more convenient, for we can call people anytime, anywhere. However, the convenience has also had another price: people have been getting overwhelmed by the spreading *cellular phone virus*, in the office, on the road, in high-school, and even at home.

For example, the virus is often found in the office. When I was working in the sales promotion section of a hotel, I always had to take a cellular phone or a pager wherever I went. The ring was merciless and called me even if I was relaxing during lunch time. Usually, such a ring at break time meant there was a serious problem in which I was involved, or it was urgent. Therefore, the ring became an ominous presentiment to me. Similarly, my colleagues, as well, used to turn pale whenever their phones rang. My boss's plight was pitiful too. In Japanese companies, no important decisions are made at once. Each decision is examined through many steps, and the boss at each level has to endorse it. Therefore, when an important and urgent problem arose, we called our boss. The phone would ring for him, even though he would be bathing in a hot spring on his holiday! Cellular phones victimized my boss too.

This restless syndrome is not only confined to the office. Many Japanese people spend a couple of hours commuting and hope such commuting hours would be a transient resting time before or after the business war. With the cellular phone as a virulent weapon, however, a truce in the war is now impossible; the phone rings in a train, a bus, a car, or even an elevator. Of course, as there are many people who carry the viral phones with them, they all start frantically checking their pockets and bags all at once when the phone rings. In this way, the virus of one ring spreads among the many people afflicted with phones and creates an upsurge of the nervous and restless syndrome among them. To make matters worse, not only the ring, but also the abnormally loud voices that follow in its wake spur the irritation on further: Urgent changes of schedule, explanations of location, secret rendezvous, a horse laugh at a nonsense joke—these kinds of conversations catch the ears of people around the phone no matter how hard they cover and protect their ears. The voices on the phones are abnormally loud because, transmitted from vehicles, normal voices don't carry clearly and loudly enough to the receivers. Needless to say, people can no longer peacefully enjoy beautiful scenery, and novels to and from work.

This phone virus is spreading even among high-school students. Cellular phones and pagers are becoming essential fashion items for them, since they don't want to be out of date. During class, they send messages such as "How are you?" and "I'm sleepy" to each other through pagers. As the vibration system of the bell makes no noise, their secret fun is not noticed by teachers. Yet there is anxiety among the students about being detected by the teachers, and the teachers are puzzled and annoyed by the restlessness they perceive in the class. The nervous and restless syndrome also extends to dates. A girl is sometimes paged or called by other boyfriends when she is on a date. The undesirable call often leads to quarrels, so the couple are nervous and restless while dating. Wise students, of course, have two pagers and use them separately hoping to avoid the syndromes: for instance, Takeshi would be bell A and Ken and Toru would be B in Akiko's system. When she meets Takeshi, "bell A," she would turn off bell B. Immediate conflict on the date is avoided. But anxiety about Ken and Toru would trouble her all through the date and even later.

The only place that can now be regarded as a sanctuary from such a virus should be the home. However, even if we don't need to use cellular phones at home, which is not always the case, answering machines and fax machines take their place and don't let us relax. My mother is one of the victims of the phone virus. She has a large number of friends and acquaintances because of her sociable nature. Yet she had managed to deal with appointments with them successfully and without tension until she was given an answering machine as a Christmas present by me. The answering machine works very well and records all important and trivial messages from everyone who calls her. Then, after she comes homes, she starts taking notes from the machines and returns every call. Such phone calls are sometimes about tiresome meetings and local cleaning campaigns she doesn't want to know about. Naturally, she has become busier and looks tired out from dealing with all these phone calls. Her aching back, the result of sitting and calling the many people who have called her, seems to begrudge the gift I gave her for Christmas. I never meant to give her the free gift of the phone virus, though. The outbreak of the virus at home is not only confined to the activities of real phones. As people come to use cellular phones in daily life, the people on TV 9 (in soap operas, documentaries, and commercials) have also come to use them very often. The sound of phone calls on TV echoes over the house incessantly and, each time it happens, family members dash to the phone under the misapprehension that it is a real call, only to be frustrated and upset. There is no place to escape from the cellular epidemic.

Japanese people are complete in the grip of the phone virus, no matter where they are. Whether in the office, on the road, in school or at home, they carry the virus with them.

Unlike the cold virus or HIV, the phone virus doesn't show apparent physical damage. Yet the negative psychological conditions it triggers are real. The more nervous and anxious people are made by the phone, the more psychological harm they are exposed to; this harm is at least as deadly as any physical damage, if not more.

Further Explorations in Explaining and Reporting

1. Form groups of three. Each member of the group should bring to class procedures, instructions, user manuals, and reports from a variety of sources. Discuss whether the use of language is appropriate to the intended reader. Select one item, and rewrite it to adapt to another type of reader. Be sure to include an explanation of your audience, as this will affect your choice of language. When you have finished the piece, everyone should edit it. One person should be responsible for inputting the changes, another for proofreading, and the third for formatting and publishing the document.

2. Write either a summary or a review of a film of your choice. See pages 345 to 346 of Media Power Tools on writing film reviews before you decide what form to use.

3. Choose either of the following subjects as a topic for a report or informational essay:

   • the benefits of television to children

   • violence on television, and its impact on children

   • the consequences of cellular phone use

   • Canadian codes and regulations concerning sex and violence on television

   When you have finished writing the document, format it and publish it, using the guidelines on pages 315 to 316 of Writing Power Tools.

4. Form groups of three. Think of something that you think needs to be improved or a problem that needs to be solved in your school or community. See the following examples:

   • Creating more green space for the community

   • Implementing a procedure for welcoming new students

   Decide what you want to say about your topic, and determine your audience and purpose. Then write a report or essay to address the issue. Format and publish your report.

5. Research the origins of the English language, using the questions who? what? when? where? why? and how? Write either an informational essay or a short report on the major influences on the development of the English language. Ask a classmate to edit your work, and incorporate appropriate feedback into your revisions. Format and publish your work.

6. Form groups of four. Imagine that you work for a young, independent filmmaker who has asked you to arrange financing of $200 000 for a new film that she wants to make. Before you begin, she wants to see a proposal in report form on how you will go about finding the financing. Research the financial end of film production, and produce a brief report. All group members should edit the report.

SECTION 3: PERSUADING

Persuasion is quite different from the expressive narratives and descriptive passages you read in Section 1 and the explanations and reports you read in Section 2. As its name suggests, persuasive writing makes no pretence at being objective. Persuasive writing is a vehicle for the writer's opinion, and it often actively seeks to change the reader's mind.

Successful persuasive writing is based on a logical argument and emotional appeals to the reader. Although persuasive writing does not purport to be objective, it must be based on an argument that is supported by factual evidence.

Advertising is a special type of persuasion. Rarely based on logical argument, it depends almost solely on emotional appeals to the audience.

The tutorials in this section will help you detect bias and weak or illogical arguments in editorials, persuasive essays, advertising, and debates. They will also show you how to write strong editorials and persuasive letters of application.

Chapter 13: Editorials

What Is an Editorial?

An editorial is a brief, written commentary on a specific topic. Editorials express opinions, beliefs, or judgements. They are usually written by newspaper or magazine editors or by guest writers. Most newspapers have a section devoted to editorials called The Editorial Page. This section of the newspaper contains several editorial and opinion pieces as well as letters to the editor. The letters are often readers' responses to recent editorials.

Most magazines contain an editorial written by the editor that comments on one of the stories in the magazine. Some magazine editors use a story as a springboard to discuss a specific issue.

Good editorial writers must do more than express their opinions; they must write persuasively. Persuasion is the art of convincing another person to accept an opinion.

Elements of an Editorial

Most editorials have these five elements:

1. **A proposition.** This statement tells you the writer's opinion on the topic. It usually appears in the introduction, but in some editorials it appears in the middle or end. Occasionally, a proposition is implied rather than stated explicitly.

2. **A context.** The context for an editorial is the circumstance that prompts the writer to express the opinion. It tells you why the writer considers the topic worthwhile and why we should care. Some editorial writers create a context as a vehicle to express their opinion. Others start with the context (or circumstance) that prompts them to form the opinion. The context for an editorial on the need for more subsidized daycare spaces may be a proposed government bill. The context for an editorial on why a candidate should not become prime minister may be a speech the candidate made on the campaign trail.

3. **Evidence to support the proposition.** Editorial writers use evidence to bring their readers around to their point of view. This evidence may be based on fact or expert opinion. It may be objective evidence, or it may be biased. Editorial writers are not concerned with presenting an unbiased, objective view of events. They freely express their biases and present evidence to support these biases. Good editorials make a clear distinction between facts and opinions.

4. **Logical and emotional language.** Most editorial writers use vivid language that appeals to our minds (logical language) and to our hearts (emotional language). Whether they use mainly logical or emotional language depends on the issue they are discussing. An editorial about the cruelty of deer hunting might use descriptions of orphaned fawns to appeal to the readers' emotions. The

author would not mention that in some years there are so many deer in a given area that they cannot find enough food. An editorial about the need for more computers in school might appeal to the readers' logic or common sense with descriptions of high school dropout rates. Most effective editorials use a combination of logical and emotional language.

5. **Brevity.** Editorials are brief; most are only a few paragraphs long. Therefore, editorial writers must make every word count.

 ## How to Read an Editorial

Remember that the writer of an editorial wants you to share his or her opinion. To achieve this objective, the writer might present clear, well-reasoned arguments that are supported with evidence. However, the writer might have deliberately excluded some facts that would have supported the opposing point of view. He or she might also have used language that appeals to your emotions.

You need to read editorials with an open yet critical mind. Being critical does not mean being nit-picky. It means using sound reasoning to think for yourself and form your own opinions. Here are some tips to keep in mind as you develop your critical reading skills:

- Scan the article to find out the title and subject of the editorial and information about the author.

- Question everything the writer says. Just because this writer's words are in print does not mean that you should agree with his or her ideas.

- Be aware of your own biases. If you disagree with the author's opinion, do you have sound evidence to support an opposing point of view?

- Pay attention to the author's biases. Why might the author be expressing this opinion? Is the author qualified to write about this subject?

- Distinguish between the author's opinions and the facts presented in the editorial.

- Notice whether the writer appeals to your logic, to your emotions, or to both.

- Notice words that trigger an emotional response. How do these words make you feel?

The editorial that follows is written by Margaret Wente, a columnist with *The Globe and Mail*. Read the editorial that follows. Which sentence best captures her proposition? Which sentence best captures the context? Assess the evidence the writer presents to support her opinion. Write notes about the piece in your journal. Indicate why you agree or disagree with the writer. After reading the editorial, try the tutorials that follow.

Medical Care That's Not Even Fit for a Horse [1]

Margaret Wente

1 *The title of this piece lets me know that the writer has a definite opinion about medical care.*

Tino Martinez is a horse doctor in Victoria. He has a portable ultrasound unit that he uses on his patients. It shows him pictures of their innards so he can check their pregnancies and figure out what's causing their lameness. So when the local hospital offered him an old ultrasound unit for free, he was enthusiastic.

Then he tried to use it, and all he got was a fuzzy blur.

"I thought I was doing something wrong," he told me. "So I got one of the hospital technicians to help me out." But he wasn't doing anything wrong. The unit was simply an antique. "It was useless. My portable machine was of much better quality."

The hospital tried to donate it to the Third World, but the Third World turned it down, too.

Fortunately for human patients, the hospital now has a nice new machine. But plenty of hospital backrooms are medical museums of obsolete technology, where highly trained radiologists do their best to diagnose your brain tumour, your breast cancer or your blocked artery with equipment that scarcely works. **2** Once upon a time, it was state of the art. So was a Tandy computer from Radio Shack.

2 *This writer believes that many hospitals use equipment that barely works because it is so old.*

One leading Ottawa hospital made do with an angiography machine that was 25 years old. These machines show pictures of your blood vessels, so that doctors can decide whether you need a heart bypass. The machine was so decrepit that it would jam midway through a test, and the (fortunately) anesthetized patient would have to be moved while the technicians got it going again.

"In most hospitals, it's almost impossible to replace equipment until it dies," says Ian Hammond, the radiologist who told me this story. "It's crisis management. Most hospitals are running deficits, and one piece of expensive X-ray equipment might cost you a million dollars. *3* So do you buy that? Or do you buy incubators, instead?"

So much for our nation's capital.

In Saskatoon, one hospital's angiography machine has broken down 45 times in the past six months, and the ultrasound unit needs to be shut off because it's no good. The radiologists have identified $14-million in new equipment they need right now. The Saskatoon health authority's total budget for new equipment is $1-million. *4*

Rapid technological advances have put expensive tools such as CT scanners and MRIs at the heart of good patient care.

"When I started in medicine, if nobody knew what was wrong with you, we cut you open and looked inside," says Dr. Hammond. Today, they use technology, not knives, to look inside. "This equipment has revolutionized medicine."

Unlike emergency-room crises, the equipment crisis doesn't yield sexy headlines or dead teenagers or pictures of sick people stacked in hallways. Most of us have no idea that the machine that scans our liver might be rejected by a horse vet. We like to think that, even if we have to wait, our technology is state of the art.

And so it is—for Greece, maybe.

Never mind the United States. Most of Europe is better fixed than we are. *5* Very little of our aging technology was replaced during the health-care funding famine of the '90s. Many major hospitals haven't had a capital-replacement budget *6* for a decade.

We're paying the price now. More than half of Canada's X-ray, ultrasound, and other imaging equipment has outlived its useful life. Hospitals depend on their own fundraising to buy their MRIs, and breakthrough technology like that is in acutely short supply. Demand is so heavy that even some private MRI clinics have waiting lists.

"In Europe," says one expert, "there would be a total revolt of the medical community."

Luckily, Allan Rock has promised to fix all this. The new health-care funding deal includes a billion dollars for new X-ray machines and CT scanners, and so we can all vote for the Liberals because they've saved health care just in the nick of time. *7*

Unluckily, we probably need $2-billion or $3-billion to catch up to, say, Austria.

Also, Mr. Rock can't easily fix the dramatic shortage of radiologists, which, to be fair, he didn't create. That began in the early '90s, when provincial governments deliberately decided to reduce the number of doctors in Canada by cutting medical-school enrolment. The idea was that fewer doctors meant lower billings.

3 The reason given here for the poor equipment is a lack of money.

4 These figures would mean that the hospital in Saskatoon will not get the equipment it needs.

5 Why does most of Europe have better medical equipment?

6 How is a capital replacement budget *different* from a regular budget?

7 In the nick of time— this sounds sarcastic!

It worked like a charm, except now there's a terrible doctor shortage, and the supply of radiologists is plunging just as demand for them is exploding. Some towns are so desperate that, as *Globe and Mail* reporter Lisa Priest discovered, they're letting doctors practise as radiology specialists even though they've repeatedly flunked the specialty exams. *8*

8 *This sounds like a dangerous practice!*

So much for health-policy experts.

I've learned that a lot of people get upset when you criticize the health-care system. It's as if you'd said something disloyal or attacked the flag. A lot of us would still like to believe that, for all its flaws, our health care, like Canada, is the best. I remember when we used to brag that it was a competitive advantage. But the truth is that it's turned into a competitive liability. A horse can get a better scan than a person can.

Anyone care to chip in for an MRI?

Tutorial 25: Distinguishing Facts From Expert Opinions

Learning Expectations

You will learn

- to distinguish between a fact and an opinion
- to recognize expert opinions
- to recognize bias in an editorial

Understanding the Task

People often do not read editorials critically, believing that the writer knows more about the subject than they do. They tend to think, "If it's in print, it must be true." In fact, much of what is in print is a shading of the truth. If you learn to read editorials critically, you will be able to detect bias and insufficient evidence. One way to improve your critical reading skills is to learn to distinguish facts from opinions.

Getting Ready

Think of an editorial as a prosecutor's case. The prosecutor (writer) presents a proposition, and builds a case around this proposition. Members of the jury (you, the reader) decide if the evidence is sufficient to support the proposition.

Propositions

An effective editorial contains a proposition backed up by facts and the expert opinion of others. The proposition is like a thesis statement: it tells the reader the writer's position on the subject of the essay. It can be located anywhere in the editorial, but usually it is near the beginning or the end. Occasionally, the proposition is implied rather than stated outright. Read over "Medical Care That's Not Even Fit for a Horse." Can you locate the writer's proposition?

A proposition is the writer's *judgement* about something. A judgement is different from a *preference*. A preference is an expression of belief based on one's tastes and biases, as in, "I like Gina's pizza better than Joe's pizza." A judgement is an expression of belief backed up by objective evidence.

Most editorial writers do not just present the facts; they also interpret those facts. Like prosecution lawyers, they only present the facts that support their case. They encourage their readers to agree with their judgement.

 ### Recognizing Facts and Opinions

Editorial writers use facts as evidence for their points of view. A statement of fact can be shown to be true or false. Unlike opinions, facts can be checked to see if they are correct. Read the following list of sentences and decide whether they are statements of facts or opinions.

1. It was a perfect evening: calm, cool, and clear.
2. Rome is the capital of France.
3. Metropolitan Toronto has the largest population of any Canadian city.
4. The wonderful thing about e-mail is that you save on long-distance telephone bills.

Sentence 1 is an opinion. Sentence 2 is a statement of fact that happens to be false—Paris is the capital of France. Sentence 3 is a statement of fact that is true. What about sentence 4? This is a little less obvious because most people who use e-mail probably do save on their long-distance bills. However, the word *wonderful* signifies that this is an opinion, and that there is a cost associated with having a computer and Internet access.

Opinions are sometimes easy to recognize because they use qualifier words that express values, feelings, and judgements. Some examples of qualifier words are *perfect*, *wonderful*, *best*, and *most*. Other words to look for when trying to spot opinions are words that express doubt such as *probably*, *may*, *might*, *would*, and *could*. Some opinions, however, do not use these words and are harder to spot.

Recognizing Expert Opinions

Expert opinions are the opinions of people who are considered to be authorities in their field. How do you know if someone is an expert? Experts should have the following characteristics:

- They should have authority because of their position, education, or experience.

- They should be knowledgeable about the topic.

Recognizing Bias

No matter how many facts they cite to support a proposition, editorials are seldom free from bias. A bias is a tendency to look at things in one way, ignoring other points of view. When you read an editorial, ask yourself about other points of view on the issue.

Imagine what an opposing editorial would say. Look over "Medical Care That's Not Even Fit for a Horse" again. What might the health minister's proposition be if he were to write an opposing piece?

One way to recognize bias is to look for loaded words—words that trigger an emotional response. Notice how the words in the following two sentences create different impressions:

The lawyer cunningly avoided the reporter's questions.

The lawyer walked past the reporters on her way to a meeting.

The first sentence is biased because it makes judgements about the lawyer's behaviour. The second sentence is unbiased because it avoids making a judgement.

Look for three examples of loaded words in "Medical Care That's Not Even Fit for a Horse." Compare your examples with a classmate's. Did you choose the same ones? How do these word choices demonstrate the author's attitude toward the topic?

Distinguishing Facts From Expert Opinions

Find three facts and three expert opinions in "Medical Care That's Not Even Fit for a Horse." Use the following checklist to help you distinguish facts from opinions and to determine if the opinions are from experts.

Checklist: Distinguishing Facts from Expert Opinions

○ Can the facts be shown to be true or false; that is, can they be verified?

○ Do the opinions use qualifier words?

○ Does this expert have authority based on position, knowledge, education, or experience?

○ Would this person's authority be generally recognized in the community?

Tutorial 26: Writing an Editorial

Learning Expectation

You will learn to plan and write an editorial.

Understanding the Task

To write a good editorial, you should feel strongly about something. A passionate interest in your subject will help convince readers that your editorial is worth reading. Take a few minutes to brainstorm things about which you feel strongly and passionately. Choose one of these topics for an editorial and use the brainstorming strategies discussed on pages 277 to 279 of Writing Power Tools to develop your ideas.

Getting Ready

Forming a Preliminary Proposition

A proposition is like a thesis statement. It is a single sentence that tells your readers your judgement about something. Once you have found a topic about which you feel passionate, write a sentence containing your judgement. This proposition is preliminary. It may change once you consider other elements of your editorial, such as your audience, purpose, and supporting details. The following are examples of preliminary propositions:

Winning medals should be the only goal of Canadian athletes at the Olympics.

To improve Canadian children's fitness, we must make four hours per week of physical education compulsory in elementary school.

The use of animals for cosmetic testing should be banned because it promotes cruelty to animals.

Ⓐ Determining Your Audience and Purpose

Although the purpose of an editorial is to persuade your readers that you are right, you may want to do more than bring them over to your side. You may want your readers to act on the opinion you have expressed. Perhaps you want them to change their behaviour or to write to their member of Parliament.

Your audience will determine everything about your editorial: your purpose, your final proposition, the evidence you use, the level of language, and your tone. Here are some of the questions to ask yourself about your audience:

- Does the audience understand the issue?

- Does the audience share my opinion?

- What is my purpose in addressing this audience?

- Do I want this audience to share my opinion?

- Do I want this audience to change their behaviour?

- What key facts does this particular audience need to know?

- What level of language would work best with this audience?

- What tone would work best with this audience?

The following chart illustrates how an editorial on banning the use of animals in cosmetic testing could be developed quite differently depending on the audience and purpose.

In your journal, draw a rough sketch of a chart similar to the one below. Once you decide on your audience and purpose, complete the chart, including a revised proposition, details about your audience and purpose, and ideas for the tone and supporting details.

Assembling Reasons to Support Your Proposition

Once your proposition is clearly stated, you need to assemble reasons or facts to support it. As you learned in Tutorial 25, facts are statements that can be proved to be true. When finding facts that support your opinion, use reliable sources such as books, encyclopedias, CD-ROMS, or magazines that have a

good reputation. The Internet may seem like a reliable source, but, in fact, some information presented on the Internet is false. You can also use expert opinions to back up your opinion. See Tutorial 25 in this chapter for ideas on how to recognize expert opinions.

Presenting Your Evidence

Once you have established the evidence that supports your opinion, you need to arrange your evidence in order. The usual arrangement for an editorial is climactic order, which means building from least important to most important. In climactic order, you save your most compelling evidence for your last paragraph. This ensures that your editorial ends with your most important point. Use an outline to plan the order in which you will present your evidence.

TOPIC: THE USE OF ANIMALS FOR COSMETIC TESTING				
AUDIENCE	PURPOSE	PROPOSITION	TONE	SUPPORTING EVIDENCE
• Readers of a magazine about animal rights and conservation • Animal lovers who oppose the use of animals for cosmetic testing	I want my readers to write to their member of Parliament asking that the use of animals in cosmetic testing be banned.	The use of animals in cosmetic testing should be banned because it promotes unnecessary cruelty to animals.	Appeal to readers' emotions with language and examples of sick animals. Tone: outraged	Include facts on numbers of animals maimed or killed in cosmetic testing.
• Readers of cosmetics industry trade journal • Members of the cosmetics industry who likely support the status quo	I want my readers to stop using animals for cosmetic testing.	The use of animals should be banned: it is unnecessarily cruel, and, contrary to popular belief, it does not make cosmetics any safer for humans.	Appeal to common sense and logic because the cosmetics industry may be tired of emotional appeals. Tone: matter-of-fact	Include facts about alternatives to animal research. Use examples of firms that do not use animal testing. Show that eliminating animal research will not hurt profits.

Writing Your Editorial

Finally, you are ready to begin writing. As you write, remember that vivid language that appeals to logic and emotions will help hook your readers. When you are finished, make sure that you have used some of the strategies in the checklist below.

Checklist: Writing an Editorial

○ Did I choose a topic about which I feel passionate?

○ Did I write a preliminary proposition based on my audience and purpose?

○ Did I research my topic?

○ Did I find facts and expert opinions?

○ Did I prepare an outline for my editorial?

○ Did I use vivid language that appeals to my readers' logic and emotion?

○ Did I present my arguments in a compelling order?

○ Did I edit and proofread my final draft?

Chapter 14: The Persuasive Essay

What Is a Persuasive Essay?

A persuasive essay is a short, non-fiction composition. Its purpose is to convince the reader to think or act in a certain way. A good persuasive essay must have a strong, clearly stated thesis—sometimes called a proposition—and a logical line of reasoning that the reader can follow.

Newspaper and magazine editorials, opinion pieces, and columns are all examples of persuasive essays.

Elements of a Persuasive Essay

A persuasive essay only succeeds if it convinces its readers to share its writer's views. A good persuasive essay has at least some of the following elements:

• **A clearly stated thesis or proposition that expresses the writer's opinion.** Words such as *should*, *ought*, and *must* help make thesis statements strong.

• **An emotional appeal.** Most writers of persuasive essays use emotion to get the readers to feel strongly about their argument. Often persuasive essays begin with an emotional appeal.

• **Well-chosen examples that support the main points.** Without examples, a persuasive essay can be flat and unconvincing.

• **Firm evidence to support the main points.** The evidence should consist of facts, expert opinions, and examples.

• **A line of argument that answers critics in advance.** Writers who anticipate, confront, and refute opposing arguments show their readers that they are knowledgeable about the other side of the issue. By answering objections in advance, these writers strengthen their own position.

• **An argument that depends on logic.** Although persuasive essays often do appeal to their reader's emotions, the argument should be based on logic.

• **Arguments presented in a logical or climactic order.** Persuasive essays can be organized in a number of different ways, but many writers present their arguments in a logical progression, often in the order of importance, saving their most important point for last.

• **Conclusions that predict.** Some writers use their conclusion to predict what will happen if their argument is not believed or acted upon. Others point out what will happen if their arguments are taken seriously.

How to Read a Persuasive Essay

Here are some strategies for getting the most from reading a persuasive essay:

- Look at the essay's title and author. Do you know anything about the subject or the author? Do you already have your own opinion about the subject?

- Read the essay through once. Did you recognize the point that the writer is trying to make?

- Read the essay again more carefully. Can you pick out the author's thesis statement? In what part of the essay did you find it? Why do you think the author chose to place it there?

- Do you find the writer's arguments to be convincing? Evaluate the examples and evidence that the writer presents. Does the evidence consist of facts and expert opinions?

- How are the arguments presented? Has the writer presented the arguments in climactic order or some other order? Why do you think the author chose this method of organizing material?

- Are the arguments logical? Does the writer make any leaps in logic that you find hard to follow?

- Does the writer rely heavily on emotional appeals? If emotional appeals are used, are they justified or are they exaggerated?

- Has the writer answered the critics in advance? Are counterarguments presented and refuted? How convincing is the author in dealing with counter-arguments?

Keep these questions in mind as you read the persuasive essay that follows. "The Death Penalty: Justice for None" was written in 2000 by Canadian writer Heather Meredith.

The Death Penalty: Justice for None ₁

Heather Meredith

1 The title tells me that the writer does not think that the death penalty provides justice.

Lorenzo Norwood is mentally challenged. Severely learning disabled, he failed grade one, and his life went downhill from there. At the age of thirty, unemployed and frustrated, Norwood tried to buy a bottle of wine from a convenience store clerk. When Norwood was twenty cents short, the two argued. The clerk flew into a rage, hit Norwood with a baseball bat and chased him down the street. Norwood later met up with Herbert Joyner, a convicted criminal, who convinced him to take revenge on the clerk. That evening, the pair returned to the store and started a fire. The clerk died in the fire.

Joyner, who had some money stashed away, was able to hire his own lawyer. He was sentenced to fifteen years in prison, and released after seven years. Norwood, who had to settle for a court appointed lawyer because he couldn't afford one of his own, was sentenced to death by lethal injection ("Mental Retardation and the Death Penalty"). **2**

2 This sounds as though Norwood was given the death penalty not for his crime but because he was too poor to afford a good lawyer.

If he had lived in Canada, Western Europe, or most South American countries, Lorenzo Norwood would have received a prison term. But he has the misfortune to live in the United States of America where the death penalty is legal in 38 states ("State by State"). While countries the world over are abolishing the death penalty, the United States is executing more people every year. In 1989, the United States executed 16 people; in 1999, it executed 98, a sixfold increase ("Number of Executions"). Some states have expanded the number of crimes that are punishable by death, and are executing people who committed crimes as juveniles (Dieter, "Perspectives"). In this environment, people like Lorenzo Norwood don't stand much of a chance.

3 The opening sentence of this paragraph tells the reader the author's main point—that the death penalty is inhumane and unjust.

The death penalty in the United States should be abolished because it is inhumane and unjust. **3** Supporters of the death penalty think that executions are humane because they are quick and painless. They aren't. In Texas in 1998, Joseph Cannon was being given a lethal injection when the needle popped out of his vein.

The executioners jabbed a weeping Cannon with the needle for fifteen minutes before they finally found a suitable vein ("Botched Executions"). Two similarly disturbing incidents occurred in 2000. In Florida, it took 33 minutes for executioners to find a vein large enough to administer a lethal drug to Bennie Demps ("Botched Executions"). In Missouri, Bert Leroy Hunter coughed, gasped, and convulsed in an adverse reaction to the lethal drugs. A lawyer who witnessed his execution said he suffered a "violent and agonizing death." The Death Penalty Information Center cites thirty-two executions since 1982 in which the prisoner died in excruciating pain ("Botched Executions"). It doesn't seem to matter what form the execution takes—lethal injection, asphyxiation, or electric chair. None can be counted on to administer a pain-free death. *4*

Some people support the death penalty because they believe that it costs less than keeping a convicted criminal in jail for life (Constanzo 9). In fact, the death penalty costs more. In Texas, a death penalty case costs an average of $2.3 million, about three times the cost of imprisoning a high-risk offender for forty years (Constanzo 10). Governments frequently spend a great deal of money prosecuting high-profile murder cases. The cost of a capital trial is about six times higher than other murder trials, and the appeals process is also expensive (Constanzo 11).

Supporters of capital punishment believe that the death penalty is a deterrent. The evidence doesn't support this. When U.S. homicide rates are compared with countries that don't have the death penalty, their rates are much higher. For example, the homicide rate in the United States is more than four times higher than it is in Canada, where capital punishment is illegal ("Homicide Statistics"). When the Bureau of Justice Statistics studied 1999 murder rates in four regions of the United States, it found that the south carried out 80% of the total executions, yet had the highest murder rate ("Deterrence"). In contrast, the northeast accounts for 1% of the executions and had the lowest murder rate. Recent studies of California and Oklahoma, two states that resumed executions after a twenty-five-year moratorium, found that murder rates actually increased after executions were resumed ("Deterrence"). *5*

Some people think it is only fair to kill those who have killed others. However, sentencing in the United States is far from even-handed. Blacks and other minorities receive the death penalty far more often than whites; Americans who murder white people are almost twice as likely to be executed than Americans who murder black people; and 98% of prosecutors responsible for death penalty decisions are white ("Race and the Death Penalty"). Arguing against the death penalty, Justice Harry Blackman pointed out that "the death penalty remains fraught with arbitrariness, discrimination, caprice, and mistake" and that "race continues to play a

4 *How horrible! These examples show that execution can be torture.*

5 *These statistics seem to support the belief that the death penalty is not a deterrent.*

major role in determining who shall live and who shall die" (Constanzo 2). In Georgia, those convicted of murdering white people are more than four times as likely to receive the death penalty than those convicted of murdering black people ("Race and the Death Penalty"). The situation is similar in other southern states. However, these kinds of inequities are not restricted to the south. A recent study of Philadelphia sentencing practices revealed that black defendants have a 38% higher death sentence rate than white defendants ("Race and the Death Penalty"). The researchers cited racial discrimination as the underlying cause of the disparity. 6

6 *These statistics support the judge's statement that race seems to play a role in many death penalty cases.*

Inequality also exists in the courts. Well-off defendants can afford to pay for a high-priced defence team, but poor defendants must settle for a defence lawyer appointed by the state. Michael Kroll, former director of the Death Penalty Information Center, maintains that in the southern states, lawyers assigned to capital cases often work for less than minimum wage. Sister Prejean, author of the book, *Dead Man Walking*, notes that public defenders are so overburdened with clients that they sometimes don't have time for pre-trial interviews, let alone for research and investigation (49). Little wonder that public defenders are not able to defend their clients against the well-resourced prosecution teams that handle most capital cases. Both Sister Prejean and Michael Kroll speak of incidents where defence attorneys showed up for court completely ill prepared or even drunk, and cases where lawyers who have never tried a criminal case are assigned to represent convicted murderers.

Those who suffer most from the inequities of the courts are the young and the mentally deficient. In 1999, Sean Sellers was on death row for crimes he committed when he was sixteen. Pleas from such eminent leaders as Bishop Desmond Tutu fell on deaf ears. Sellers was killed in the electric chair despite evidence of mental illness (Dieter, "The Death Penalty"). Only five other countries have executed juveniles since 1990—Iran, Nigeria, Pakistan, Saudia Arabia, and Yemen—but the United States executed more in that time than any other country (Dieter, "The Death Penalty"). Numerous international human rights organizations have denounced the execution of juveniles, the mentally deficient, and the mentally ill.

Surely the most egregious injustice of all is the execution of innocent people. Had Canadians Donald Marshall, David Milgaard, and Guy-Paul Morin lived in the United States, they would have been executed long before their innocence was discovered. Since 1973, over 80 people have been released from death row in U.S. jails because of new evidence of their innocence ("Innocence and the Death Penalty"). 7 Some of these stories are heart-wrenching, like the story of Rolando Cruz who was convicted of murdering a ten-year-old girl, and spent ten years on death row before being released. Another man had confessed to the crime but

7 *Sentencing an innocent person to death is definitely not just.*

prosecutors had it in for Cruz. Five members of the prosecuting team have since been charged with obstruction of justice.

In 1972, Supreme Court Justice Thurgood Marshall argued that popular support for the death penalty was based on ignorance. If Americans knew the facts about capital punishment, he claimed, "the great mass of citizens would conclude that the death penalty was immoral and therefore unconstitutional" (Ellsworth 33). In the almost thirty years since Marshall made this pronouncement, support for the death penalty has increased to an all-time high. *8*

Public interest in crime and safety seems also to have increased, judging by the crimes showcased on nightly newscasts and on popular television programs like *Law and Order*. In spite of this extensive media coverage, few programs reveal the inequities in the U.S. justice system and the cruel nature of death by execution. Surely, if more Americans knew the plight of Lorenzo Norwood and the hundreds of others like him on death row, they would fight to abolish the death penalty.

8 Why has support for the death penalty recently increased?

Works Cited

Costanzo, Mark and Lawrence T. White. "An Overview of the Death Penalty and Capital Trials: History, Current Status, Legal Procedures, and Cost." Journal of Social Issues 50.2 (1994): 1–18.

Dieter, Richard C. "International Perspectives on the Death Penalty: A Costly Isolation for the U.S." Oct. 1999. Death Penalty Information Center. 25 Oct. 2000 <http://www.deathpenaltyinfo.org/internationalreport.html>.

———. "The Death Penalty in Black and White: Who Lives, Who Dies, Who Decides." June 1998. Death Penalty Information Center. 25 Oct. 2000 <http://www.deathpenaltyinfo.org/racerpt.html>.

Ellsworth, Phoebe C. and Samuel R. Gross. "Hardening of the Attitudes: Americans' Views on the Death Penalty." Journal of Social Issues 50.2 (1994): 19–52.

"Facts About Deterrence and the Death Penalty." 21 Oct. 2000. Death Penalty Information Center. 22 Oct. 2000 <http://www.deathpenaltyinfo.org/deter.html>.

"Homicide Offences, Number and Rate." 26 Oct. 2000. Statistics Canada. 26 Oct. 2000 <http://www.statcan.ca/english/Pgdb/State/Justice/legal12a.htm>.

"Innocence and the Death Penalty." 22 Oct. 2000 Death Penalty Information Center. 23 Oct. 2000 <http://www.deathpenaltyinfo.org/innoc.html>.

Kroll, Michael. "Chattahoochee Judicial District: Buckle of the Death Belt: The Death Penalty in Microcosm." 1991. Death Penalty Information Center. 24 Oct. 2000 <http://www.deathpenaltyinfo.org/dpic.r11.html>.

"Mental Retardation and the Death Penalty." 22 Oct. 2000. <u>Death Penalty Information Center</u>. 23 Oct. 2000 <http://www.deathpenaltyinfo.org/dpicmr.html>.

"Number of Executions Since 1976." 22 Oct. 2000. <u>Death Penalty Information Center</u>. 23 Oct. 2000 <http://www.deathpenaltyinfo.org/dpicexec.html>.

"Post-Furman Botched Executions." 21 Oct. 2000. <u>Death Penalty Information Center</u>. 22 Oct. 2000 <http://www.deathpenaltyinfo.org/botched.html>.

Prejean, Sister Helen. <u>Dead Man Walking</u>. New York: Vintage Books, 1994.

"Race and the Death Penalty." 22 Oct. 2000 <u>Death Penalty Information Center</u>. 23 Oct. 2000 <http://www.deathpenaltyinfo.org/race.html>.

"State by State Death Penalty Information." 22 Oct. 2000. <u>Death Penalty Information Center</u>. 23 Oct. 2000 <http://www.deathpenaltyinfo.org/first-page.html>.

Tutorial 27: Evaluating Supporting Details in a Persuasive Essay

Learning Expectations

You will learn
- to assess the validity of a persuasive essay
- how to check research sources

Understanding the Task

A good persuasive essay appeals to different sides of our brain—to the left side, which we use for logic, mathematics, and reasoning, and to the right side, which we use to feel emotions. An essay full of facts and statistics may make a logical argument, but without emotional power it is unlikely to convince you of anything. An essay full of eloquent words, heartfelt passion, and personal anecdotes may move you, but it will be unconvincing if it lacks facts. In this tutorial, you will evaluate the supporting details in a persuasive essay for their validity.

Getting Ready

Writers of persuasive essays use three techniques to convince their readers that their argument is valid: they appeal to their readers' emotions; they anticipate and refute their objections; and they appeal to their reason or common sense.

Identifying Emotional Appeals

Appealing to the reader's emotions can help strengthen a logical argument. Emotional appeals typ-

ically consist of vivid descriptions or moving anecdotes about real people. They add human interest to an argument. A writer arguing that our health care system is in trouble may use an anecdote about a patient who dies while waiting for an operation. The more details the writer gives you about the patient, the more you will probably empathize with the person. A single example like this adds nothing logical to the argument, but it personalizes the situation. It says, "We're talking about more than an abstract system. We're talking about real people like you and me."

- Do the emotional appeals in "The Death Penalty: Justice for None" help convince you that the writer's argument is valid?

- How would the essay have been different without these emotional appeals?

Identifying Refutations

Refutation is the anticipation of objections or opposing arguments. Writers of persuasive essays anticipate their readers' reactions so that they can respond to objections. Writers use refutation to show their readers that they have considered all sides of the question. This adds to their authority. You might respond to an essay without refutations by saying to yourself, "Hey, what about this?" and "I happen to know that's false."

- What refutations does the writer of "The Death Penalty: Justice for None" use?

- Can you think of another refutation that the writer has not used?

Identifying Logical Appeals

All persuasive essays use logical appeals, some more successfully than others. Logical appeals are based on reason. The writer must establish a clear relationship between his or her stated position (the thesis statement) and proof or evidence that supports this position.

- Did you find a stated thesis in "The Death Penalty: Justice for None," or is the thesis implied?

- If the thesis is stated, in what paragraph did you locate it?

Key to the successful defence of a thesis statement are reliable supporting details. Persuasive essays use four types of supporting details: examples, facts, expert opinions, and personal experiences. These types of supporting details are not necessarily mutually exclusive. For instance, an example can also be a fact.

- **Examples.** *Examples* are concrete details that illustrate the writer's point. They give the readers reasons for accepting the writer's argument. Some examples are facts because they can be verified. Others are not facts because they cannot be verified.

- **Facts.** *Facts* are information that can be verified. They can be figures, statistics, or examples. The following is a fact: The *Titanic* struck an iceberg on April 14, 1912. *Statistics* are numerical facts. They can add authoritative weight to any argument. Be particularly suspicious of them, however. Although statistics themselves are facts, they are easily manipulated. For example, politicians from opposing parties may use the same set of statistics to reach completely different conclusions.

- **Expert opinions.** These are the views of reputable, knowledgeable individuals who are qualified to be consulted on the subject of the essay.

- **Personal experiences.** Writers' own experiences can give their essays credibility, especially if they have a background in the subject of the essay. For example, the personal experience of a journalist could give an essay on ethics and the media considerable weight. Personal experiences are always examples. If they can be verified, they are also facts.

Evaluating Sources

Although it is relatively easy to distinguish between an example and a statistic, how do you know if an author's facts and statistics are real? For all you know, Lorenzo Norwood, mentioned in "The Death Penalty: Justice for None," may not exist.

Writers of convincing persuasive essays name their sources. Be suspicious of any fact or statistic that lacks a source. In most editorials and newspaper and magazine articles, the sources are contained in the article itself. In most academic essays, the sources are identified both in the essay as references and in the Works Cited list at the end of the essay. This list makes it easy for the reader to verify information.

When checking a writer's bibliography for reliability, ask yourself the following questions:

- **Are the sources up-to-date?** The writer should have provided the dates in the Works Cited list.

- **Has the writer relied too heavily on only one or two sources?** Does the Works Cited list contain a range of books and articles? Has the writer relied too heavily on the Internet as a source?

- **Are the sources impartial?** Does the publisher of any of the sources have a vested interest in the topic? For example, one might question a statistic on handgun murders that came from the National Rifle Association. Similarly, one might question a statistic on the same subject that came from an anti-gun lobby group.

Evaluating Supporting Details

Roughly sketch the chart below in your journal. Then identify three different types of supporting detail from the essay "The Death Penalty: Justice for None." Decide if each detail is an example, a fact, a statistic, an expert opinion, or a personal experience. (Remember that some supporting details may fall into more than one category.) Then check in the Works Cited list to see if the sources for the information you have identified are up-to-date, impartial, and reliable. Use the checklist below as a guide.

SUPPORTING DETAIL	EXAMPLE	FACT	STATISTIC	EXPERT OPINION	PERSONAL EXPERIENCE	SOURCE

Checklist: Evaluating Supporting Details in a Persuasive Essay

○ Have I identified the supporting details as examples, facts, statistics, expert opinions, or personal experiences?

○ Are the sources up-to-date?

○ Has the writer relied too heavily on one source?

○ Are the sources reliable and impartial?

Tutorial 28: Using Logic in a Debate

Learning Expectation

You will learn to use and identify logic in a debate.

Understanding the Task

If you can master good persuasive skills, they will help you in all aspects of your life. Being persuasive does not mean bullying people into doing things, or being less than straightforward to get others to see things your way. It means using common sense to plan and structure your arguments. It also means recognizing weaknesses in your own and other people's arguments. Your task in this editorial is to engage in a debate with some of your classmates.

Getting Ready

Planning an Argument

Few people plan what they are going to say ahead of time unless they are giving a speech or a presentation. However, planning ahead will help you hone your persuasive skills. Once you have mastered the art of persuasion, you can reduce the time you spend planning what to say. The steps to follow when you plan are similar to those you follow when you write an editorial or a persuasive essay. Here are some questions to answer as you plan to win an argument or a debate:

1. **What is my purpose?** What do you want to achieve? Do you want the person to agree with you? Do you want the person to act in a certain way, to change his or her beliefs?

2. **What is the other person's position?** What are the person's views on this issue? How is the person likely to respond? What logical arguments can you develop in anticipation of the response?

3. **How will the other person react emotionally?** From what you know about the person, how will he or she respond? Will the person get angry or upset? Will the person grow silent? How will this, in turn, affect you? How can you prepare for the response?

4. **To what emotional appeals will the person respond?** Some people are more likely than others to respond to emotional appeals. If the person is likely to respond positively to an emotional appeal, what can you say that will support your argument?

5. **What should I avoid saying?** What makes this person angry? Make a list of things you should avoid mentioning. Writing these down will help you remember them.

6. **What evidence should I use?** Do you need to do some research to find some evidence, or do you already have examples, facts, statistics, and expert opinions that support your argument?

7. **What order should I use?** Consider the order in which you will raise your points. Will you handle objections first? Will you save your strongest argument for the end? Be prepared to change course if the other person raises a different point.

Recognizing Fallacies

To win an argument or debate, half the battle is in the preparation; the other half is in recognizing weaknesses in your own and your opponent's arguments. How do you know if someone is being logical? You look for fallacies, which are gaps in logic or illogical statements. Here are eight different kinds of fallacies:

1. **Generalizations.** Generalizations occur when the writer takes a specific example and applies it falsely to all similar situations. Generalizations often lead to stereotypes. Examples:

   Canadians are quiet and peaceful people.

   People who believe in gun control are bleeding-heart liberals.

2. **Leaps in logic.** Leaps in logic occur when the writer jumps to conclusions with insufficient supporting evidence. Examples:

   If Canada restored the death penalty, crime would decrease.

   Pradeep and Rosa like working at Superstore. Therefore, it must be a great place to work.

3. **Coincidence.** Writers sometimes suggest that one event causes another, when, in fact, any connection is purely coincidental. Politicians occasionally take credit for things that are, in fact, coincidence. Examples:

   The decrease in crime in Allington County is because of the death penalty.

   The policies of our government have resulted in a robust economy.

4. **Non sequiturs.** *Non sequitur* is Latin for "does not follow." A non sequitur is an argument that does not arise logically out of the argument being presented, as in the following example on capital punishment. There is not enough of a logical relationship between capital punishment and euthanasia to make the first example work. The second example is a non sequitur because it is impossible to prove. Examples:

   Capital punishment is illegal in Canada. Therefore, euthanasia should be illegal as well.

   Juliette failed her course because of cutbacks to the educational system.

5. **Either/or reasoning.** This is a statement that falsely presents two choices as the only alternatives. Parents often use either/or reasoning to discipline their children. Examples:

   The United States must either abolish the death penalty or be ostracized by the international community.

   Either you go to bed by 10:30 or your grades will drop.

6. **Ad hominem arguments.** These are personal attacks that denigrate a person's character rather than criticize his or her views. Examples:

   Anyone who believes in the death penalty is stupid.

   The candidate's attitude proves he is a racist.

7. **Circular or repetitive arguments.** These are arguments that go nowhere. They state the obvious;

they do not add any information, and they finish in the same place as they started. Examples:

Executions should be abolished because they kill people.

We should stay home if we don't want to go out.

8. **The bandwagon effect.** This argument says, "Since everyone is doing it, it must be acceptable." Advertisers frequently use the bandwagon effect to get people to buy their product. Their advertisements often carry subtexts like this one: "If you want to be part of the 'in crowd,' you'd better buy our product." Children frequently use this line of argument when they are trying to get their own way. Examples:

Since everyone else has a tattoo, I want one too.

I'm not too young to have my own place. All my friends live away from home.

 ## Using Logic in a Debate

Divide into groups of four. Then divide again into two sets of partners. The four of you should choose a scenario for a debate from the three below. Each partnership should have a debater and an observer. One debater plans and presents the argument, while the other debater presents the opposing argument. The observers should listen to the debate carefully, and use the checklist on page 219 to make a note every time a debater uses a fallacy.

Scenario One: You have learned to drive using a friend's car, and you have just passed your driver's test. Your parents are opposed to you driving because they think you are too young. They have always been strict and somewhat overprotective. You want to use their car now, but they are refusing to lend it to you until you are 18. One debater will play the role of the 16-year-old. The other debater will play the role of one of the parents.

Scenario Two: You sell athletic clothing for a small clothing manufacturer. One of your large clients—a popular sportswear store—has recently dropped your line because the owner says it is too expensive. The client is known to be a "tough sell." The word in the industry is that the client does not give new items enough exposure or time to become established. You have been successful with other accounts, but you stand to lose a big bonus if you cannot win back the lost business. You need to convince the owner of the sportswear store to give your line another chance. One debater will play the role of the salesperson. The other debater will play the role of the store owner.

Scenario Three: Choose a controversial issue that you would like to debate, such as gun control, tattoos and body piercing, vegetarianism, the use of animals in experiments, or violence on television. Or choose an issue to do with your school. For example, one set of partners could argue that the school needs a new building; the other could counter with arguments opposing the building. Use your imagination.

After you have finished the debate, meet as a group to discuss it. The observers should present their feedback, and the four of you should decide whether you agree with their observations. The debaters should address the following:

- How did your preparation help to make your arguments stronger?

- What emotional appeals did you consciously use?

- How did the opposing debater respond to these emotional appeals?

- If you used facts in presenting your argument, how did your opponent respond to them?

- Were you aware of using any fallacies? Were you able to identify your partner's fallacies and address them during the argument?

Finally, as a group discuss what you learned about persuasion from debating experience, and devise an action plan for approaching another debate in the future.

Checklist: Using Logic in a Debate

- ◯ Does the debater use any generalizations, leaps in logic, or non sequiturs?

- ◯ Does the debater confuse a coincidence with a cause?

- ◯ Does the debater make any personal attacks?

- ◯ Does the debater use circular arguments?

- ◯ Does the debater use either/or reasoning?

- ◯ Does the debater make use of the bandwagon effect?

Chapter 15: Advertising

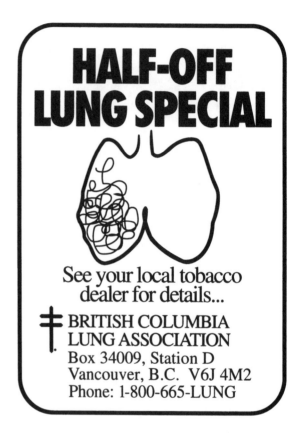

What Is an Advertisement?

There is no doubt about it—advertisements are everywhere. In fact, they are so much a part of our lives that sometimes we forget that their purpose is usually to persuade us to spend money. We see advertisements in magazines, on television, on billboards, on the Internet, on buses, in shopping malls—almost everywhere. Many of us are exposed to hundreds of advertisements a day. Since advertisers must compete for our attention, they are constantly looking for ways to make their advertisements louder, brighter, funnier, or more shocking. Media experts are beginning to wonder what effect this barrage of images is having on people.

Most advertisements are intended to draw your attention to goods or services that the advertiser wants you to buy. On the other hand, some advertisements (often called public service announcements) are designed to increase your awareness of certain health, safety, environmental, or other social concerns. These include antismoking advertisements, drinking and driving advertisements, and campaigns from charities such as United Way.

Elements of Advertisements

Advertisements use words and images to persuade us to buy or do something that often involves changing our consumer habits or behaviour. Advertisements share at least some of the following characteristics:

- Advertisements are always biased. For example, the creators of car advertisements are biased in favour of their own vehicles.

- Advertisements typically appeal to emotions and desires rather than reason. Advertisers use emotive language and images to convince us that we should buy their product, contribute to their cause, or change our behaviour.

- Some advertisements have a slogan, which is a short, memorable message. Examples of slogans are Nike's "Just Do It" and Microsoft's "Where do you want to go today?"

Characteristics of Advertisements

Most advertisements fall into the following three categories:

- **Brand name.** These types of advertisements promote a specific brand-name product such as Nike shoes, Fuji film, Kellogg's Cornflakes, and so on. Advertisers want to develop brand loyalty in the consumer.

- **General types of products or services.** These advertisements are designed to increase consumption of products or services as a whole rather than a particular brand. All those advertisements you see on TV about milk, cheese, and eggs are examples of this kind of advertising.

- **Advocacy advertising.** These advertisements promote a particular viewpoint or, during elections, a particular political candidate. For example, Mothers Against Drunk Driving (MADD) produces advocacy TV advertisements, and recycling campaigns promote the benefits of reducing consumption and of recycling. Political advocacy advertisements attempt to make voters feel that one political party or candidate is better than the others.

How to Read an Advertisement

This list of questions will help you view advertisements more critically:

- What is the purpose of the advertisement? What does it want the reader to do or feel?

- Who is the intended audience for this advertisement?

- Is this an example of brand advertising, product advertising, or advocacy advertising?

- How are the advertisers getting my attention?

- What is the bias in the advertisement?

- What emotions does this advertisement evoke in me? Which words or images produce this emotion?

- What desires does this advertisement evoke in me? Which words or images produce this desire?

- What facts are presented?

On the following page you will find a car advertisement for the Audi A8. Examine the advertisement, then complete the following tutorials.

Nappa leather.

Burled walnut.

Hairpin curves.

Fluid acceleration.

Goosebumps.

Mix thoroughly.

Stir.

Add olive.

1 *I think libation may mean an offering of wine, perhaps to the Gods.*

2 *The advertisement is trying to sell me on safety as well as luxury.*

3 *I have no idea what Tiptronic means, but maybe Audi has made up the word to rhyme with supersonic.*

Part luxury car. Part performance sedan. The elegantly appointed Audi A8 is, truly, the ultimate libation *1* for the spirits. A sophisticated mixture of engineering brilliance, luxury prowess and safety. A visionary leap from Audi and Alcoa, the unique all-aluminum Audi Space Frame in the A8 takes the luxury car to a place where lighter is stronger and safer. *2* And with a potent V8 delivering unbridled

acceleration through a five-speed Tiptronic® *3* transmission, this sedan handles like a performance car. More than another luxury-class car, it's the future of luxury. The A8 also offers the distinction of our class-exclusive FrontTrak™ front-wheel drive or legendary quattro® all-wheel drive. The A8. One part luxury. One part performance. One part soul-stirring perfection.

†National Highway Traffic Safety Administration 35 mph frontal crash test into a fixed barrier. The 1998 Audi A8 was awarded 5 star ratings for both driver and front passenger protection. Call 1-800-FOR-AUDI or visit us at www.audiusa.com for more information.

"Audi," "quattro," "A8" and the four rings emblem are registered trademarks of AUDI AG. "Tiptronic" is a registered trademark of Dr. Ing h.c.F. Porsche AG. © 1999 Audi of America, Inc.

Tutorial 29: Analyzing an Advertisement

Learning Expectations

You will learn
- to identify emotive language and images in advertising
- how advertisers create an advertisement by appealing to an audience's emotions

 **Understanding the Task**

Words and images have not only literal meanings, they also create feelings and imply a sense of values. Advertisers are aware that their choice of words and images can influence the way we respond to things and even the way we feel about ourselves. Indeed, in today's highly competitive advertising world, it is more important for advertisers to sell feelings and attitudes than it is to sell the products themselves. In this tutorial, you will learn how advertisers create advertisements that appeal to our emotions, thereby persuading us to do or buy something. Then, with a partner, you will analyze the emotional impact of advertisements from two media forms.

Getting Ready

Advertisers use words and images that evoke emotional responses such as sensual pleasure, sexual longing, fear, guilt, and shock. They appeal to our need for love, security, acceptance, social status, and wealth, and our desire for youth, beauty, and excitement. An advertisement for jeans implies that when you wear that brand of jeans, you will be as youthful and alluring as the young men and women in the photograph. An advertisement for low-fat ice cream promises that you will be slim and beautiful if you eat the ice cream. An advertisement for tires implies that the driver's children will be safe with those tires on the family vehicle. This is persuasion at a purely emotional level.

The Power of Words and Images

Look closely at the words used in the car advertisement. Besides the Audi A8 sedan, what is the advertisement selling?

Nappa leather.
Burled walnut.
Hairpin curves.
Fluid acceleration.
Goosebumps.
Mix thoroughly.
Stir.
Add olive.

"Nappa leather" and "burled walnut" convey images that suggest elegance and comfort. The Audi does not just have a leather and wood interior; it has a special type of leather and a special type of wood. The words appeal to our need for social status. "Fluid acceleration" suggests effortless power and comfort, appealing to our desire for speed and comfortable elegance.

Notice how the advertisers have used the word "curves" instead of the word *bends* or *turns*. Why do you think they made this choice?

"Goosebumps" might seem an odd word to use. Why do you think the advertisers included this word?

The caption ends with an implied metaphor—a comparison of two things. To what is the Audi being compared? Why does the writer use a metaphor rather than stating the point directly?

Below is a rewritten version of the advertisement.

> The Audi A8 sedan has leather seats and a wood-trimmed dashboard. It handles hairpin turns, speeds up smoothly, and can be invigorating to drive. It is like a martini.

Without the words "nappa," "burled walnut," "curves," and "fluid acceleration," the car loses its aura of elegance, comfort, and sophistication. The modifier "wood-trimmed" evokes a simple, plastic dashboard, edged with a strip of wood, a crude interior with none of the polish and craftsmanship implied in the words "burled walnut."

Without the implied martini metaphor, the advertisement loses its cleverness. With the martini metaphor, the makers of Audi try to forge a bond with their readers by subtly suggesting, "We are sophisticated, elegant people who like our luxury cars and our martinis, too. But we are not going to state this outright. If you're one of us, you'll understand what we're saying."

Images, Personality, and Tone

Advertisers choose images that establish a carefully selected *personality* and set up in the mind of the viewer a connection between the product and a need, emotion, desire, or lifestyle. This personality sets the tone for the advertisement. Just as a paragraph or literary work can convey almost any tone, so can an advertisement; it might be elegant, sexy, sophisticated, reassuring, ironic, or angry.

- What is the tone of the Audi advertisement?

- Now look at the advertisement on page 220. What is the tone of this advertisement? What emotional reaction does this advertisement evoke? Does it persuade you not to smoke? If so, why is the advertisement effective?

Persuasive Methods Used to Evoke Emotional Responses

As we have just seen, advertisers manipulate words and images to evoke an emotional response. They use standard methods to do this. You will probably recognize some of the methods described below. After you read this list, find a partner and discuss which of these methods the Audi A8 advertisement uses. For each method, decide on the emotional response the creators of the advertisement were trying to evoke in consumers.

- **Special words.** Advertising has its own special language. Creators of advertisements use familiar and unfamiliar words to make you think they mean something special or important. These words spark an emotional response in consumers. People are convinced that an SUV with "hydroglide four-wheel drive" must be a superior product.

- **Euphemisms.** Euphemisms are mild or vague expressions that substitute for words that are considered too direct, harsh, or honest. Advertisers use euphemisms all the time when dealing with delicate subjects such as death, weight, bodily functions, and potentially hazardous products. Thus, advertisements for pesticides use the euphemism "crop protection industry."

- **Flattery.** Advertisers sometimes flatter their audience by suggesting they are intelligent, stylish, on the cutting edge, or just better than the average person. They use flattery to make their audience feel good about themselves and to associate those good feelings with the product. You have probably seen advertisements that state or imply that *intelligent people* or *smart shoppers* use their product.

- **Celebrity endorsement.** Some advertisers hire celebrities, such as movie stars and athletes, to sell their products. The reason is simple: the audience likes the celebrity, so if the celebrity uses the product, then so will the audience. Even though the audience knows the celebrity is getting paid for the endorsement, this technique is known to work. That is why you see so many sports stars, singers, and actors selling products on TV.

- **Normal-people endorsement.** This is almost the opposite of celebrity endorsement. In this approach, advertisers use real people (or actors hired to play real people) to make you think that everyday people just like you use the product.

- **Professional endorsement.** Some advertisers secure endorsements from professionals or professional organizations, such as the Canadian Dental Association or the Canadian Toy Testing Council. A stamp of approval from organizations such as these can help persuade consumers that a product is the best or safest on the market.

- **Statistics and numbers.** Advertisers like to use numbers because people believe facts. If a household cleaner kills 98 percent of household germs, it must be effective. If four out of five doctors recommend a pain reliever for a headache, it must work. The thing to remember is that statistics and numbers can be made to say just about anything. The only way to validate statistics and numbers is to investigate the research methods of advertisers used in their data collection.

- **Bandwagon.** This approach suggests that everyone should follow the latest trend. The latest wrinkle on this approach is *branding*, which implies that you are a nobody unless you are wearing the right brand. Advertisers for products like

these often design advertisements with no words except for the brand name itself. They make clothing with the brand name in a prominent position so that when you wear their clothes, you are telling the world that you have jumped on the bandwagon. What you are actually doing is selling the product for the manufacturer.

- **Right or wrong.** In this approach to selling products, the advertiser suggests that there are only two groups: those who use the product and who are therefore smart, wise, and above the crowd, and those who do not and who are therefore stupid, foolish, and stuck in the hordes of ordinary people. Many commercials on TV show the smart person who made the right choice of credit card, car, airline, or computer breezing through the worst situations possible, while the poor fool who made the wrong choice ends up losing everything.

- **The enemy.** You may not realize it, but many advertisements are based on the premise that out there is an enemy that will get you unless you get it first. Plaque, ring around the collar, lawn weeds, household germs, you name it—the enemy is out there and needs to be defeated.

Analyzing and Comparing Two Advertisements

In groups of four, select two advertisements of your choice from the following list. One must be a print advertisement and the other a multimedia advertisement.

- television commercial
- video or film advertisement
- radio advertisement
- Internet advertisement
- magazine advertisement

- newspaper advertisement

- billboard

- poster

Read pages 324 to 327 of Oral Communication Power Tools on working in groups and pages 328 to 330 on making presentations. Then prepare a brief group presentation to the class.

Start your presentation by describing the two advertisements that your group selected. Then state what emotional response each advertisement is designed to evoke. Analyze how language and images are used in the different media to create this emotional response and to persuade viewers to buy or do something. Look specifically at the words, images, and layout of the print advertisement, and the words, images, and sequence of shots in the multimedia advertisement.

Divide your presentation into parts, so that each group member speaks about one aspect of the two advertisements. Before you give the presentation in front of the class, be sure to have at least one rehearsal, in which all the group members practise saying their parts aloud. Use the checklist below to assist you as you write and practise your presentation.

Checklist: Analyzing an Advertisement

○ What emotional response or responses are the advertisements designed to evoke?

○ To what needs or desires are the advertisements designed to appeal?

○ How have the advertisers used words and images to evoke emotional responses?

○ How do words and images contribute to the "personality" or tone of each advertisement?

○ How does the design of the advertisements (page layout, shots, or sequence of shots) contribute to the purpose, "personality," and tone?

○ Which, if any, of the persuasive methods described on pages 225 to 226 have the advertisers used to evoke particular emotional responses? How have they used these methods?

○ Which advertisement is the most persuasive, and why?

○ Did we edit and proofread our work?

○ Did we practise giving the presentation aloud?

Tutorial 30: Planning and Presenting an Advertising Campaign to a Client

Learning Expectations

You will learn
- the elements that advertisers use to create emotional appeal
- to describe, explain, and analyze the choices you make in the creation of a commercial
- different production issues that arise in print and multimedia advertising

Understanding the Task

In this tutorial, you will learn about some of the decisions that advertisers make when they design their campaigns. Then, as part of an advertising team, you will plan and create an advertising campaign. At the end of the process, you will describe, explain, and justify your choices to a client.

Getting Ready

Advertisers make deliberate choices about what their advertisements will contain. Absolutely nothing in an advertisement is there by accident. If you can learn to look at an advertisement through the eyes of an advertiser, you will become a better critic.

Identifying a Target Market

Before embarking on an advertising campaign, advertisers must know the customers for whom their products are intended. They use surveys, focus groups, and in-depth interviews to identify the people most likely to buy their product or contribute to their cause. Once these people have been identified, they are known as the *target market*. The target market is usually specific: advertisers typically know the age range, sex, income level, marital status, occupation, and even favourite leisure activities of targeted consumers. What market do you think the makers of the Audi advertisement were targeting? What clues in the advertisement give this away?

Through research, advertisers can predict how groups of people are likely to respond to a particular advertisement or advertising campaign. For example, through focus-group research a maker of children's pain relievers may discover that mothers 25 to 40 years of age have a strong emotional reaction to photographs of a sick child. This knowledge may lead to an advertising campaign that uses a sick child in bed as its central image.

Creating a Plan

Advertisers use every element of an advertising campaign to evoke a particular emotion or set of emotions. Typically, at the beginning of the creative process, they make a plan that they present to the client for approval. If the client approves the plan, it is used as a basis for the advertisement. The plan usually includes the details about the target market and other elements of the campaign.

The Advertising Plan

Target market: This portion of the plan identifies the target market and its characteristics, including, as mentioned above, age range, sex, income range,

marital status, and occupation. Depending on the advertisement, it may also include even more details about the target market. For some campaigns, marketers gather very precise and personal details about their target market, such as the following:

- place of residence—region, city, area of the city, and even, in some cases, exact names and addresses

- number of children and their dates of birth

- charitable donations made in the past year or two

- magazines and newspapers typically read

- stores where groceries or other items are typically purchased

- credit cards used

- type of vehicle last purchased, and date of purchase

Purpose: The explicit purpose of the advertisement is stated.

Campaign: This section describes the various ways the advertisers plan to reach the target market. In large campaigns to launch a new product, this might include television advertisements, magazine advertisements, billboards, in-store posters, and brochures mailed to the target market.

Timing: The exact time of the year the campaign will be released is indicated. If the campaign is for a new garden hose, it might be launched in April or May. If it is for a new children's toy, it will probably be launched in the fall, when people are beginning to shop for the holidays.

Desired emotional response: The plan should explain the emotional need or desire to which the campaign is designed to appeal and the emotional response it aims to evoke. As discussed in the last tutorial, the need might be for enjoyment, safety, social status, or wealth. The emotional response might be happiness, security, sensual pleasure, passion, fear, guilt, shock, or something else.

Theme: Most advertising campaigns include a predominant theme that is based on the desired emotional response. A planned theme for a car advertisement might be "To keep your family safe from harm, buy brand X." What do you think the makers of the Audi A8 advertisement intended as a theme?

Characters: This portion of the plan describes what characters will be in the advertisement and how they will be used. It describes the characters in detail, and explains why they have been selected, why they will appeal to the target market, and how they will evoke the desired emotional response.

Setting: The setting is described, with an explanation of how it will contribute to the emotional appeal of the advertisement.

Story: Every advertisement tells a story. This section of the plan explains the story and how it connects to the desired emotional response.

Point of view: This portion explains from whose point of view the advertisement will be made or the story will be told. Some advertisements are obviously made from the point of the view of the consumer who is looking at the advertisement. Others, particularly multimedia advertisements, are made from the point of view of one of the characters in the advertisement.

Composition: This portion describes how text, images, music, sound, and colour will work together to create the desired emotional impact. The plan for a print advertisement would explain the details of a pose and the positioning of text and images on a page. The plan for a multimedia advertisement would explain the composition of each shot. Both would explain how details of composition contribute to the emotional appeal of the advertisement.

Copy/script: This portion of the plan describes how words will be used in the advertisement to evoke an emotional response. There might be printed words on the page and screen, dialogue, or a voice-over—an unseen narrator explaining or reinforcing the images on the screen.

Designing a Storyboard

When advertisers plan an advertisement, they use a technique called storyboarding. A storyboard is a drawing or series of drawings that map out the advertisement. For a print advertisement, this is likely to be a simple sketch. For a multimedia advertisement, it is likely to be a sequence of shots that will be used in a film, television program, video, or commercial. The sketches indicate the camera shots and what will be visible in each shot. Beneath the sketches are written directions for the music, lyrics, sound effects, and any copy that will appear on the screen. For more information on multimedia production techniques, see pages 337 to 340 in Media Power Tools.

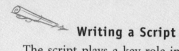

Writing a Script

The script plays a key role in any commercial that uses sound. Unlike a film or television script, a script for a television commercial often consists of only a voice-over—a narrator explaining the feeling you get when you drive a particular car, or the effect a certain cologne has on women, or the reason why you should feel secure in the hands of a particular mutual fund manager. Some commercials have dialogue between two or more people. Typically, dialogue is restricted to a few words, and is followed by a voice-over.

Planning and Presenting an Advertising Campaign to a Client

Form groups of four. Before you begin the activity, read pages 321 to 327 in Oral Communication Power Tools on working cooperatively in a group. Imagine that you are members of a creative team for an advertising firm. You have been assigned the following tasks:

* Prepare a plan for an advertising campaign for one of the following:

  – a United Way campaign

  – an anti-drinking-and-driving campaign

  – a new commercial product of your choice

The campaign should contain two advertisements using different media from the following list:

  – a newspaper advertisement

  – a magazine advertisement

  – a poster

  – a billboard

– any other print advertisement

– a television commercial

– a video commercial

• Prepare a storyboard with copy for a print advertisement and a storyboard and script for a multimedia advertisement.

• Present your plans and your storyboards to the client.

When you are ready to present, assign each person a key segment of the presentation. One person could explain the target market; another could describe the campaign itself and timing issues; a third person could present the storyboards; and the fourth person could sum up the key success factors in the campaign.

Leave enough time to practise making your presentation to the client as polished as possible. Throughout the activity, imagine that you really are young professionals working for an advertising agency. Make sure you practise making your presentation to the client ahead of time. Use the checklist below to assist you as you work on this activity.

As you work on the project, each member of the team should keep a log detailing challenges and issues that arose during production. After the presentation, meet as a group and compare notes. What did the group find were the biggest challenges? What were the main differences between preparing the print advertisement and the multimedia advertisement? What would you do differently if you could start this activity over again? What did this activity teach you about the world of work?

Checklist: Planning and Presenting an Advertising Campaign to a Client

❍ Have we identified a specific target audience?

❍ Have we identified a specific need or desire and an emotional response?

❍ Do the elements of the storyboard flow together and reflect our purpose?

❍ Does the copy on the print advertisement connect with the visual elements?

❍ Do the sound effects, music, and/or lyrics of the commercial connect with the visual elements?

❍ Do both the print copy and the script for the commercial use specific and appropriate language that reflects our purpose?

❍ Have we revised, edited, and proofread our document and rehearsed our presentation?

❍ Have we discussed the different challenges involved with print and multimedia production?

Chapter 16: Letters of Application

Learning Expectations

You will learn
- to recognize an effective letter of application
- to write a persuasive letter of application

What Is a Letter of Application?

A letter of application, also called a cover letter, is a letter you send to a potential employer when applying for a job. The letter may be written either to respond to an advertised job or to inquire about any potential openings. Although it often accompanies a résumé, a letter of application does not simply restate all the information in the résumé; rather, it details the reasons why the writer is qualified for the job.

Elements of a Letter of Application

A good letter of application is like a personal sales pitch. In it you have an opportunity to introduce yourself to a potential employer and to prove that you are the best person for the job. The most persuasive letters of application have the following characteristics:

- **They look attractive and are easy to read.** Because it forms the reader's first impression of the applicant, the letter must look and sound professional. It should be printed on high-quality paper and follow standard business letter format (see Tutorial 32). A persuasive letter of application has no spelling, grammar, or punctuation mistakes. Even one careless error weakens the credibility of the writer.

- **They are personalized to a particular job and employer.** A letter of application is not a form letter. It must consider the expectations of the reader and the needs of a particular job. It commands attention by addressing the reader by name, and it identifies the particular job sought. It then highlights only the work history, skills, and personality traits that are most relevant to the job. Skills that are not applicable to the job are not mentioned in the letter.

- **They are concise and persuasive.** A letter of application is usually limited to about three or four paragraphs on one page. In such a relatively short space, however, the letter introduces the writer and argues convincingly that he or she should be interviewed for the job.

How to Read a Letter of Application

At this point in your life, you are probably writing more applications than you are reading them. But by reading your own or your friends' letters as if you were an employer, you may find ways to improve your writing.

As you read a letter of application, imagine what an employer would be looking for. Consider the following questions:

- Does the letter writer sound literate? Are there any mistakes in grammar, spelling, or punctuation?

- Does the writer use proper letter form?

- Does the writer address the employer by name and position?

- If responding to an advertisement, has the writer carefully read it and responded specifically to what it requested? If there was no advertisement, has the writer demonstrated that he or she has researched the company and knows what employment skills (or requirements) are needed?

- Does the letter reveal the writer's applicable skills and experience in a polite yet persuasive manner? Does the person seem right for the job?

- Might the letter set the writer apart from other applicants?

The sample on the following page is a letter of application for an advertised position.

Solicited Letter of Application

1   *This letter looks professional. As an employer, I would be impressed.*

2   *I like the way this student relates her work experience to the likely requirements of the new job.*

3   *It is interesting that she does not discuss where she goes to school or any school achievements. I guess they may not be as relevant as the gardening experience.*

4   *I guess Chandra Sakar can find out where the student goes to school by looking at her résumé.*

154 Albert Avenue South *1*
Somewhere, ON
S7H 5K9
(519) 123-4567
e-mail: mlau@somewhere.net

May 01, 2001

Ms. Chandra Sakar
Manager of Human Resources
Northern Landscapers
Somewhere, ON N7P 3H4

Dear Ms. Sakar,

I am writing to apply for one of the student gardener positions that were advertised in the April 22 issue of *The Herald*.

You specified that you are looking for students who have had gardening or landscaping experience. Last summer I was a gardener for the parks department of the City of Somewhere where, with other students, I prepared flower beds, mowed lawns, and planted trees. The experience taught me how to work efficiently and cooperatively on a team, as well as a great deal about plants and park maintenance. *2*

I am a positive, dependable individual whose work is completed thoroughly, accurately, and on time. Because I enjoy physical labour, gardening, and working with others, I feel sure that I would be a productive and enthusiastic gardener for Northern Landscapers. *3*

Enclosed you will find a résumé that provides details about my skills and experience. *4* At your convenience, I would like to meet to discuss how I can contribute to Northern Landscapers.

Sincerely,

Mei Lau

Mei Lau

Enclosure

Tutorial 31: Revising a Letter of Application

Learning Expectations

You will learn
- words to use in letters of application
- the difference between formal and informal language

Understanding the Task

Your letter of application has to distinguish you from other applicants by using assertive words and language. Descriptive adjectives and strong action words help to clarify what you are capable of doing for the employer. In this tutorial, you will work with a partner to revise and improve a letter of application.

 ## Getting Ready

Action Words

When describing your relevant work history in a letter of application, use action words to show what your experience has taught you. For example, if applying for a job in retail, instead of simply stating, "I worked in a video store," briefly describe the skills you have acquired from the experience. "Working in a video store taught me how to interact with the public, manage inventory, and handle money." Notice how all the verbs in the second sentence give a better impression of what you are capable of doing.

When describing yourself to a potential employer, remember to use adjectives frequently. For instance, instead of stating simply, "I am a student," you might present a more accurate picture of yourself by stating, "I am a dedicated student" or "I am an honour roll student." The tables below and on page 236 show examples of effective action words that highlight the skills and personal traits that employers often seek.

A good application letter highlights those skills and attributes that are relevant to the particular job for which you are applying. If you are applying for a sales position, do not emphasize your scheduling skills, your eye for detail, and your accuracy. Instead, emphasize your listening and selling skills and your outgoing nature. Be careful, however, not to misrepresent yourself.

ACTION WORDS DESCRIBING SKILLS		
COMMUNICATION SKILLS	ORGANIZATIONAL SKILLS	LEADERSHIP SKILLS
interacting	scheduling	supervising
writing	coordinating	managing
coaching	programming	problem solving
demonstrating	planning	motivating
listening		decision making
selling		

ADJECTIVES DESCRIBING PERSONAL TRAITS			
A STRONG WORK ETHIC	A POSITIVE ATTITUDE	PERSONAL VALUES	WORKING STYLE
hard-working	enthusiastic	responsible	organized
industrious	positive	reliable	thorough
dedicated	motivated	dependable	accurate
conscientious	energetic	honest	innovative
efficient	outgoing	trustworthy	creative

If you are actually a quiet, reserved person, do not tell your prospective employer that you are outgoing.

Employers want to know as much about you as you can convey in a short letter. Try to pick action words and adjectives from more than one of the categories in the boxes above and on page 235. Rather than saying that you are efficient, hard-working, industrious, and dedicated, state that you are hard-working, reliable, positive, and organized, or whatever combination of words best describes you.

Read the letter of application on page 234. Find all the action words and adjectives that the writer uses to describe her skills and attributes. How many words are there? With a partner, discuss why you would or would not interview Mei Lau based on her letter of application.

The Right Style

The words you choose and how you present them determine the style of your letter, and the style, in turn, reflects your relationship with the reader. In an e-mail message to a friend in a chat room, you write differently than you would in a research paper for a science class. The language written in a chat room is colloquial and personal; thoughts and ideas are conveyed in a chatty, casual manner. The language in a research paper is formal and impersonal; facts and information are conveyed in a serious, careful manner.

The style of a letter of application, and other business letters, should be informal, somewhere between the colloquial and formal styles. An informal style conveys a respectful, capable, and professional tone yet is not too distant and impersonal. The following list compares the different degrees of style:

- **Colloquial style.** This casual style is used in personal letters, e-mails, or journals. The vocabulary is casual and brief, with short, simple sentences and paragraphs. Sentences may even be fragmented. It sounds much like speaking and may include slang, colloquialisms, or contractions. The first and second persons, I and you, are used.

- **Informal style.** This style is to varying degrees used in most books, newspaper and magazine articles, and business letters. The vocabulary is still somewhat personal and friendly, but the grammar is more precise and careful. The sentences are complete and correct. The first and second persons may be used when necessary, but slang, colloquialisms, and contractions should be used sparingly. This textbook is an example of informal style.

- **Formal style.** The formal style is used mainly in academic, scientific, or technical writings. The vocabulary is often specialized to the topic or is quite technical. There is no mention of the first or second persons, so it is always impersonal. The sentences and paragraphs are always complete, correct, and often long and complex.

Read the following excerpts from three application letters written in varying degrees of formality. Notice how the words and style of the language affect the relationship between the writer and reader.

- **Colloquial:**

  I just love dogs and showing them at dog shows, so I'm sure that working at DogLand would be awesome. I can't wait to hear if you decide to hire me on.

- **Informal:**

  Because of my experience grooming and handling dogs at local dog shows, I am confident that I would be a capable and enthusiastic employee at DogLand. I would like very much to speak with you personally about the advertised position.

- **Formal:**

  The applicant is familiar with canine grooming, presentation, and obedience training. Such experience qualifies this applicant to be an employee at DogLand.

For more information on style and tone, see Writing Power Tools, pages 284 to 287.

 ## Revising a Letter of Application

On the next page, you will find a letter of application written by a grade 12 student. With a partner, evaluate the letter. Decide if you would hire Claire. Then on your own rewrite the letter using the checklist below. Use your imagination to provide details. Compare your letter with your partner's. Did you use any of the same action words and attributes? Did you use a similar style?

Checklist: Revising a Letter of Application

- ○ Did I make a note of all the ways the letter could be improved?

- ○ In my revision, did I use action words to describe skills?

- ○ Did I use adjectives to describe a range of personal attributes?

- ○ Did I establish a professional tone?

- ○ Did I edit and proofread my letter?

Letter of Application

Mr. Michael Nuncio
General Manager
Freshest Foods
123 Manchester Rd.
Anywhere, BC.

Dear Mr. Nuncio,

I saw the ad for a cashier in the paper and I would like to apply for it.

I am in grade 12 at Brandon Collegiate. I am a good student. My best subjects are math and French. I am active in the school and I love sports. This year I am on the volleyball and basketball team. Every year I am involved in the school play. In grade ten I did the lighting. Last year I was the set desiner. And this year I was the stage manager.

On Tuesday evenings and Saturdays I volunter at a senior citizen's home. I'm really into helping other people out.

A friend of mine works at your store. She really likes her job. So I think I would like to work there to.

Sincerely,

Claire Atkinson

Tutorial 32: Writing a Letter of Application

Learning Expectations

You will learn to write a letter of application.

Understanding the Task

When you write a letter of application, you are summarizing your résumé for the potential employer. You highlight how your skills and experience can be applied to the job you are seeking. This tutorial will demonstrate ways in which you can prepare and write a convincing letter of application.

Getting Ready

(4) Considering Your Audience

The first step when writing a letter of application is to consider who the reader is and what the reader's expectations are. Plan the letter accordingly. If the letter is in response to a job that is advertised, first look at the job description and note exactly what the employer is looking for. List the experiences you have that qualify you for the position. Then infer from the advertisement any other skills or attributes the employer may be seeking. Think what other qualifications you may have that, although not specifically requested in the advertisement, may nevertheless be helpful in the job.

The following advertisement for a summer job appeared in a newspaper:

Wanted: Senior high school student willing to train as a summer camp counsellor at Camp Lake View. Duties include supervising children in camp activities and assisting with the preparation of the daily itinerary.

Read the notes on page 240 that a student made about the advertisement before writing a letter of application for the job. Notice how the student reads beyond the vague job description and considers what skills and traits would impress the employers.

Of course, you must also be honest about your personal traits. If the thought of taking control of a situation and telling others what to do makes you terrified, do not say that you are a leader. At the same time, acknowledge your accomplishments. If you deliver papers every morning on a large paper route with relatively few problems, you can honestly say that you are dependable and hard-working.

If you write a letter hoping either to find an unadvertised job or to create a new one for yourself, you may not know what will be required of you. In this case, research the business to get a good idea of what is needed. Most public libraries have directories and information on Canadian businesses. What is it about the company that interests you in working there? Make notes of how you think you could be of service to the business. If an article about Camp Lake View had been printed, rather than an advertisement, you might still write a letter applying for a job there. Your letter might look something like the one on page 241.

Notes for a Letter of Application

- **What the employers are looking for:**
  - They may not want someone too young, as they have specified that they want a "senior" high school student.
  - "Supervising children" means they need someone who is responsible, sensible, safety conscious, and confident being with children. They are probably looking for someone with leadership abilities.
  - "Assisting with the preparation of the daily itinerary" may mean they want someone to help plan and type an itinerary, or it may mean that they want someone to carry out the itinerary. Either way this means they need someone who can work cooperatively with others. Maybe computer skills would also help here.
  - They might need someone who is familiar with a variety of camping activities.
  - They probably need someone who is enthusiastic about camping.

- **Experience and personality:**
  - I take part in many different camping activities by being a member of the school's Outdoor Education Club.
  - My swimming and first-aid certificates would probably be very useful at a camp.
  - I help coach my younger brother's soccer team, so I have some experience working with kids.
  - I really enjoy camping and being with kids.
  - I am enthusiastic and cooperative.
  - I have good computer skills.

---

(4) Using Standard Business Letter Format

Once you have finished your notes and have a list of what you want to say, you can start assembling your letter. Your letter must be well organized so that you can say all you need to in a short space. The best way to do this is to follow the basic format for a business letter, as follows (see also the Technological Tip, page 241). The sample application letter on page 241 is labelled to roughly correspond with the following items.

1. **Return address and date.** Put your full mailing address at the top of the page. Include your telephone number and e-mail address, if you have one. Make it easy for the employer to contact you.

Unsolicited Letter of Application

331 Whitewood Road *1*
Anywhere, ON
S7H 5K9
(403) 123-4567
e-mail: biggs@anywhere.net

May 15, 2001 *2*

Ms. Joanne Hite *3*
Director of Student Counsellors
Lake View Camp
Box 202, Lake View, AB T2N 4F6

Dear Ms. Hite,

I am writing to express my strong interest in being a camp counsellor at Lake View Camp this summer. *4*

The article that appeared in *The Examiner* on February 12 indicated that your camp offers a wide range of activities to children from ages eight through twelve, including swimming, hiking, and canoeing. *5* As an active member of our school outdoor education program for the past three years, I have acquired skills in all these areas. This year, I successfully completed my Level 12 swimming course and a first-aid course, both of which qualify me to supervise swimming activities. I also help coach a youth soccer team, an experience that has allowed me to develop confidence and patience when dealing with children. *6*

I am a mature, responsible grade 12 student who works well with others and has strong leadership skills. Because I thoroughly enjoy being outdoors and working with children, I know I could be a competent and enthusiastic counsellor. *7*

Please find enclosed my résumé, which outlines my skills and experience in detail. I look forward to discussing with you in person how I can contribute to your program at Lake View Camp. Next week I will call you to discuss the possibility of an interview. *8*

Sincerely,

Stephen Biggs

Enclosure

1	Return address
2	Date
3	Name and title of contact person and company address
4	Identify the position sought
5	Indicate that you have knowledge of the company
6	Indicate that your skills are relevant to the job requirements
7	Highlight your personal qualities in connection with the job
8	Ask for an interview

Technological Tip

Many computer software programs offer standard letter templates or "wizards" that walk you through the creation of a standard business letter format.

2. **Company address and greeting.** Put the full name and address of the person or company to whom the letter is going to be sent. This appears flush with the left-hand margin. Use the name and title of a contact person mentioned. If necessary, phone the company to get the name of a contact person. Use the person's name in the greeting. If a name is not available, address the letter with "Dear Sir or Madam."

3. **Body.**

   a. **Identify the job you are seeking and where you found out about it.** If the job was not advertised, show your knowledge of the business by suggesting what the reader may need. For example: "I read in the *Free Press* that your sporting goods department is expanding, and I am writing to ask that you consider me should you need sales representatives."

   b. **Describe your work experience and skills that are relevant to the job requirements.** If necessary, you can state how your skills are relevant to the employer. For example, "By successfully completing a babysitting course and a first-aid course, I have the safety and leadership skills that are essential when working with children."

   c. **Include a brief paragraph highlighting how your personal qualities make you suitable for the job.** You may not have a lot of experience yet, so this paragraph gives you the opportunity to express your enthusiasm and willingness to learn.

4. **Closing.** In the concluding paragraph, ask for an interview or, if the letter is unsolicited, offer to call the contact person at a specific time. For example, you could say "I will call you next week to discuss the possibility of arranging an interview." Refer the reader to the enclosed résumé, if appropriate.

In the final salutation, remember to sign your signature in ink above your typed name.

Proofreading and Delivering the Letter of Application

Once you have finished a draft of your letter, you must carefully proofread it as many times as necessary until it says exactly what you want it to say and is free of any spelling, grammar, and punctuation errors. One careless mistake can undermine all your efforts and make you seem sloppy and incompetent. Ask a friend or family member to edit and proofread the letter for you.

Double-check that your return address, phone number, and e-mail address are complete and correct. A perfect letter of application is useless if the reader cannot contact you. For this reason, unless otherwise requested, application letters should always be mailed or handed in personally rather than sent by e-mail. Because technologies and capabilities vary from one business to the next, your e-mail could lose its format or the employer may not even be able to open it. Of course, you can always send an e-mail version as well as a mail- or hand-delivered hard copy. Unless otherwise indicated in an advertisement for a job, it is a good idea to include your résumé as an enclosure with your letter. Include the word *enclosure* after your name at the bottom of your letter.

Writing a Letter of Application

Practise writing a letter of application for yourself (or for an imaginary applicant) for one of the following jobs. Or write an unsolicited letter for a job you know you would like. Use the checklist on page 243 to help guide you in the process.

Wanted: A mature, reliable person to work in a golf shop. Duties include booking tee times, greeting golfers, renting out equipment, and receiving payment.

Wanted: A busy office requires a competent clerk to help the secretaries file invoices and type letters, reports, and memos. Some computer skills are required.

Wanted: The Jean Shop is looking for outgoing sales associates to join their sales team. Experience not required, but must be willing to learn.

Checklist: Writing a Letter of Application

- ◯ Did I read the advertisement carefully to get a sense of what skills and qualities the employer requires?

- ◯ Did I write notes on what the employer needs and how my education, experience, skills, or personality traits match the position?

- ◯ For an unsolicited letter, did I research the company and the job?

- ◯ Did I address the letter using the reader's name and position?

- ◯ Did I identify the job I am seeking in the letter, and explain how I found out about it? If the letter is for an unadvertised job, have I shown that I have some knowledge of the reader's business?

- ◯ Does my letter show how my skills and qualities could benefit the company?

- ◯ Is my letter written in a polite yet friendly tone?

- ◯ Have I used strong action words to describe my skills and qualities?

- ◯ Have I concluded my letter by asking for an interview?

- ◯ Have I asked a friend or relative to edit and proofread my letter?

- ◯ Have I proofread my letter carefully to make sure it is letter-perfect and that no information is missing?

Further Explorations: Persuading

The *Further Explorations: Persuading* section extends the range of texts you can create, interpret, and respond to. This section will offer you additional pathways for responding creatively and critically, while applying your understanding of language, form, and genre.

For Canada and First Nations

Phil Fontaine

Much noise is made about the new century, but for most Canadians the turn of a calendar page is of little more than symbolic significance, and we go on with our lives. And far too often, for far too many Canadians, daily life focuses on the grim realities of mere survival. This is true for most First Nations Canadians.

Even so, the advent of a new century in human history powerfully engages the mind and spirit with creative and hopeful visions. It also provides a unique opportunity to examine ourselves and our values and to ask: what are we doing, and where are we going, as individuals, as communities and as a nation?

I address these questions from the perspective of my culture and my people, the Anishinabe—the Ojibway—and on behalf of all First Nations. My perspective is founded in my roots—as a member of a nation that has a treaty with the Crown, a community and a culture with a distinctive language, traditions, values, and history—but is enriched by many years of practical experience in service of my people and Canada as Chief of my own community, as senior federal public servant, and provincial leader of First Nations in Manitoba.

In many respects, Canada is the envy of the world. We are seen to have the freedom to create and fulfill opportunities, in a growing economy that appears prosperous and stable. We are a land of opportunity for immigrants from every part of the world. Despite controversy over the means, Canada is moving aggressively to cope with and position itself to profit from economic globalization, the reduction of international trade barriers and the rapid growth of new technologies. Canadian governments have acted radically and boldly on the fiscal front, sharply reducing the growth of deficits and debt.

Confederation is undergoing restructuring, with the federal and provincial governments eagerly collaborating in fundamental shifts in jurisdictional roles. While these measures have been painful for Canadians in terms of social and economic security, ostensibly they will better enable us to meet the future social and economic needs of the nation.

These recent developments prove that the Confederation is flexible; exigencies of the future can be accommodated; nothing is impossible if the will exists.

And yet, Canada's house remains seriously out of order where First Nations and other Aboriginals are concerned. This, too, cries out for bold and radical measures, and I fear Canada does not have much time left to act.

The depressing and shameful litany of the social and economic effects of dispossession, marginalization and exclusion of First Nations from the opportunities and prosperity of Canada are well-documented and do not require recitation here. Suffice it to say that Canada continues to ignore the incalculable loss of productivity and potential contribution to the national well-being of some one million Aboriginal Canadians. History suggests that continuation of the paradigm of the past will not lead us to resolve this most pressing of Canada's social and economic problems. We need creative new approaches. We must build new bridges and forge new relationships within the national community.

This country has the capacity, and the national interest, to facilitate the necessary development of First Nations' hope, dignity, and productivity. What is required is the political and national will.

How do we get there? As a first step, I propose a national commitment to a concerted and sustained effort, by key sectors of Canadian society, to establish a new social, economic, and political compact between Canada and its indigenous peoples. This would involve the participation, in partnership with First Nations and other Aboriginal peoples, and in roles appropriate to their legal, economic and moral obligations, of the federal and provincial governments, corporate Canada, major social institutions, and the peoples of Canada.

The rationale, blueprint, and framework for this historical undertaking are in place, in the findings of the Royal Commission on Aboriginal Peoples, the Manitoba Aboriginal Justice Inquiry and other studies. More study and delay is not necessary. We know the issues, the problems and the necessary solutions. We also know the national human, economic and fiscal costs of complacency and inaction.

I call for the convening of a unique national summit for the development of a national plan of action, to be in place and with implementation under way as we reach the dawn of the 21st century. It is essential, for the future of Canada and of First Nations, that this plan of action include such matters as definitive resolution of treaty and aboriginal rights; restoration of First Nations governing jurisdictions; and an integrated approach to investment in human capital, development of the economic sustainability of indigenous communities, measures to instill and ensure social health and stability for indigenous peoples and the provision of a viable environmental basis for the First Peoples, including matters of land, water and other natural resources.

We must all dare to be innovative in striving to achieve the necessary reconciliation, healing and productive investment in our collective future. Let us turn away from those who seek to revise the history of Canada and to ignore its fundamental problems, from those who lack vision and a sense of justice and fairness, and from those who dishonourably and speciously argue against catering to "special interests."

The stark reality is that, as concerns the present conditions and future prospects of First Nations, the interests at stake are those of all Canadians, Aboriginal and non-Aboriginal alike. Do we and our governments have the vision and will to meet this challenge? The next century beckons us.

Spiked!
News from Developing Nations
Vanessa Baird

Good hard news combines novelty and drama within a limited timescale. Ideal events are natural or political catastrophes such as aircrashes, earthquakes, cyclones, famines and coups.

When the Third World does break into the rich world's consciousness it is usually with one of these events. As a result Western perceptions of Africa, Asia and Latin America as zones of chaos and misery are often exaggerated. Peter Adamson, co-founder of *New Internationalist*, regularly gives 16- and 17-year-olds and their teachers a questionnaire asking them what percentage of the world's children are "visibly malnourished." The usual answer is 50-70 percent. The true answer is one to two percent.

One reason positive stories don't get told is because they tend to unfold slowly, undramatically. Increasing female literacy in a state in Bangladesh can't compete with a flood, although the links between a mother's education and her children's chances of survival are direct and proven and the number of lives saved by educating women is likely to far exceed lives lost in a flood.

Positive stories also tend to show people quietly getting on with development. But the mainstream Western media is hooked on narratives about its own people going out and saving the world. It's a form of collective narcissism that actually obstructs visions: you cannot see through mirrors. It's also inherently racist.

Dominant Technology
A handful of huge media empires, such as Time Warner and Rupert Murdoch's News Corp., is rapidly gaining control of every conceivable communications means and outlet—from old-established independent newspapers to Hollywood studios to cable, satellite and telephone companies.

Journalist and academic Ben Bagdikian has vividly outlined the ideal scenario for today's media mogul, whereby a magazine article generates a TV series, a movie screenplay, a sound track, a hit single, cable re-runs and worldwide distribution of videocassettes. All the companies and players involved are, of course, owned by the mogul.

At a time when some developing countries, like Brazil, India, Korea and Uruguay are becoming prolific media and news producers, there might be a real chance of realizing the 1970s dream of reversing the North-South flow of information. But, in the wake of the recent GATT free-trade agreements, the technology-rich Western media empires have *carte blanche* to flood and dominate world markets as never before.

Windows Not Mirrors

The media are too important for us to permit this concentration of power. A practical step would be to extend and apply anti-monopoly legislation or trust laws to restrict ownership. One news medium per owner would free up the market and the media to be more imaginative and more receptive to news from different perspectives—from the South, from women, from indigenous groups.

It may also allow more diverse forms of journalism to flourish. When you come down to it, any communicator worth his or her salt should be able to make us feel for another person's situation, whoever and wherever they are. The best medium of communication remains not the fibre-optic cable, but the common thread of humanity. The moving, insightful and at times subjective work of some women war correspondents—such as Maggie O'Kane's eyewitness accounts from Bosnia for *The Guardian*—demonstrates the positive value of human-response journalism and of a fresh approach.

If, however, the media moguls have their way we are likely to end up with news from distant places and about other peoples only as an offshoot of commercial advertising.

It already happens. For the past 20 years the gradual genocide of the Buddhist Jumma people by Muslim Bangladeshi Government forces had been ignored in the mainstream media. Then, suddenly, the plight of the Jummas hit the news. Why? Hollywood star Richard Gere, himself a Buddhist, made a special plea for them while opening the winter sales at Harrods, London's most prestigious store.

It's good that he cares. But are we only going to hear such stories as part of another story about a famous shop and a Western celebrity who is, broadly speaking, "a local man"?

Perhaps it's time for the dominant countries of the world and their media to junk the need to have reflections of themselves, their prowess and their preoccupations in all they see. That way we might end up with a media that is closer to what is has often grandly claimed to be—a window on the world.

Further Explorations in Persuasion

1. With a partner, write an advertisement for the sale of the farm in "Still Stands the House" (page 90). Before you begin, decide on your target market, and consider whether the advertisement will appear in the newspaper, on the real estate channel on television, or in a magazine.

2. Write a comparative essay on the recommendations made by Carol Geddes in "Growing Up Native" (page 16) and by former First Nations Chief Phil Fontaine in "For Canada and First Nations" (page 244). When you have written a first draft, ask a classmate to edit your work, and incorporate appropriate feedback to make revisions.

3. Canada is a multicultural society that respects differences in culture, behaviour, and values. Yet, as some of the selections in this book attest, prejudice and discrimination exist in Canada. Write an informational essay, a persuasive essay, or an editorial on prejudice and discrimination, referring to the comments or stories of at least two writers in this book. As you plan your essay or editorial, consider at least one of the following questions:

   • How does a dominant culture impose its culture on a marginalized group?

   • How does a dominant culture perpetuate stereotypes?

4. You have bought a product that is defective, and you want your money back. Decide whether you are going to write a letter or complain in person. Map out the arguments you intend to use, engage in a dialogue with a partner who plays the part of the store manager, and then write a letter using appropriate language and format.

5. Form groups of four. Two students are editors working for a book publisher; the other two are members of the publisher's editorial board. Choose one of the selections from Section 1 of this book. Imagine that the two editors have read the manuscript and that they believe it has potential. They must convince members of the editorial board to publish the work. Based on the information provided by the editors, the members of the editorial board then decide whether or not to accept the work for publication. Choose one of the following forms for this activity:

   • an oral presentation and response

   • a report and a written response to the report

   • a persuasive letter and a reply

6. You work in the marketing department of a large publisher that has just accepted a new book for publication. The editor, who is convinced it will be a bestseller, is relying on the marketing team to publicize the book. In groups of three, prepare a publicity campaign to publicize the book in advance of publication. Remember that before you can write the campaign, you need to identify the target market. All group members should edit the report. One person should be responsible for inputting the changes, another for proofreading, and the third for formatting and publishing the document.

SECTION 4: POWER TOOLS

Power Tools comprises four chapters for you to use as a reference when you are working on the tutorials in the first three sections of the text:

- Reading Power Tools
- Writing Power Tools
- Oral Communication Power Tools
- Media Power Tools

The Reading Power Tools section offers you strategies for becoming a better reader. You will find valuable information on reading different genres for different purposes, as well as tips for how to improve your vocabulary.

The Writing Power Tools section helps you become a better writer by offering a range of strategies, from finding a topic to peer editing to proofreading. Grammar and punctuation checklists and a troubleshooting guide on the top five writing problems should also help you as you edit and proofread your work.

The Oral Communication Power Tools section offers you strategies for improving your speaking and listening skills in order to communicate and work effectively in groups. These tools should help you hone your speaking skills, and enhance your contribution to group activities.

The Media Power Tools section will help you analyze media processes. It will improve your understanding of films, television programs, and other media.

Each section contains Your Turn activities that offer suggestions for practising specific strategies. To get the most out of Power Tools, practise using some of the strategies, and then use those that work best for you.

Reading Power Tools

Reading involves more than recognizing words and their meanings as they appear on a page. Whether you are reading for enjoyment, appreciation, or information, you are engaging in an active process that involves thinking, reasoning, questioning, comparing, interpreting, and evaluating. In this chapter, we explore strategies that will deepen and strengthen your reading experience.

 ## Setting a Purpose for Reading

When you approach a reading task, you should think about your purpose for reading. Your purpose will influence how closely you look at the words and sentences and how carefully you consider the ideas in those words and sentences.

- Are you reading simply to enjoy a good story or poem?

- Are you reading to understand characters or ideas?

- Are you reading to appreciate language and point of view?

- Are you reading to gather information and make notes for a research paper or to find ideas and facts to help you reach a major decision?

- Are you reading to discover how to do something?

Generally speaking, you tend to read either for enjoyment, appreciation, or information.

Reading for Enjoyment

You read short stories, novels, poetry, or drama for enjoyment. You can immerse yourself in a time, place, and mood; understand and feel what the narrator and characters feel; and become involved in the events. To become involved, you willingly suspend your disbelief; that is, you choose to allow yourself to believe the situations that the author, poet, or playwright has created. You put yourself in the author's hands and read along for the adventure and experience. As you read for enjoyment, especially when you have finished reading, ask yourself the following questions:

- Is this place like or unlike places where I have been?

- Is this time—whether past, present, or future—like or unlike times I have experienced?

- Are the characters similar to or different from characters I have met and known? Did they react to situations and behave in a way I would have acted or behaved?

- Have I experienced situations like the ones described or am I interested in these situations because they are ones that I will encounter at some point in my life?

- Which words help me to appreciate the sensory aspects of the experience?

Reading for Appreciation

You read editorials, biographies, accounts of significant events, stories, drama, and poetry for appreciation. You can involve yourself in the point of view, the ideas, and the language. You can admire the creation of the author—the imagination, the ability to convey genuine experiences, the wealth of supporting detail, the strength of argument, and the choice of words. As you read for appreciation, ask yourself the following questions:

- What do I already know about this topic? Do I know details that the author clearly does not or has chosen not to include?

- What is the author's bias?

- Do I agree with the author's point of view on this subject?

- Is there sufficient evidence to support the author's point of view?

- Has the author considered the most important ideas?

- Which words are key to revealing the point of view?

- Which words may have been carefully chosen because they are "loaded" with significant meaning?

- What questions do I still have about this subject?

When you read for appreciation, you tend to think about what you have read and whether or not you agree with the point of view for some time after you have finished reading.

Reading for Information

You read newspaper and magazine articles, advertisements, textbooks, Web sites, encyclopedias, and other reference works for information. Generally, you have a question in your mind, a task you need to accomplish, or a topic you need to research. You may read to find out the best stereo equipment to purchase or to discover which used cars offer the best value and the greatest reliability. You may read to research information on an unfamiliar topic for a class assignment, such as the uses of lasers in industry and medicine.

As you read for information, keep the following questions in mind:

- What do I already know about this topic?
- Will this article, book, or advertisement offer me new information?
- Was it written recently enough to offer current information?
- How much of this text do I need to read to get the key information?
- Where should I begin to read and conclude my reading?
- Are there pictures, graphs, or diagrams that will give me extra information or help to explain the information in the article?
- Do I still need to read more on this topic to get a clear picture in my mind?

When you read for information, you want to draw out the key details that you require. You may be satisfied with the pieces you have read, or you may decide that you need to do more reading immediately or at some time in the future.

Your Turn

- Make a list of the 10 most recent things you have read. Were they novels, magazine articles, advertisements, textbooks for school subjects, newspaper articles, e-mails from friends, reminder notes from a parent, research for an assignment?

- Write your purpose for reading beside each item. Did you read for appreciation, enjoyment, or information?

 Varying the Pace or Speed of Reading

Your purpose for reading helps you determine how carefully you pay attention to the words and sentences you read. Your purpose for reading plus the nature of the information can determine the pace or speed at which you read.

- You may read a novel quickly, simply to enjoy the story and discover the final resolution of the conflict. On the other hand, you may wish to enjoy the language and description in the novel; thus, you will read it more slowly.

- You may read the biography of a famous scientist carefully and slowly as you encounter many new terms, and perhaps take notes for an assignment.

- You may skim through the first few paragraphs of a news report or a magazine article just to get a sense of the information in it, and to determine whether it holds interest for you.

- You may scan a page of the telephone book to find a name and street address or telephone number.

- You may scroll through a site on the Internet, clicking the various links and quickly checking to see whether a screen holds information you need.

When words, phrases, and subject matter are familiar, you can read text more quickly. If terms are new, or very specific to a subject, you may find that your reading slows down as you wrestle with pronunciation or check the meaning of unfamiliar language.

Generally speaking, being able to read at a fairly quick pace aids in your comprehension of what you read. The faster you get the big picture of the ideas in an entire chapter or editorial, the more ready you are to grapple with their meaning, to make decisions about how useful the information is to you, or decide whether you agree with the point of view. The more time you must spend actually decoding a word—sounding it out, breaking it down into smaller understandable bits, or looking up its meaning in a dictionary—the less you can understand the bigger picture of the entire piece.

Three techniques can help you to read more efficiently and quickly: skimming, scanning, and rereading.

Skimming

Skimming is a type of quick reading that gives you a general sense of a chapter, article, story, or other type of text. Skimming helps you decide whether or not you wish to read a piece in depth, either because it interests you or because it contains information you need. Different people have different techniques for skimming.

- Some people choose to read just the first sentence or just the last sentence of each paragraph.

- Other people read a couple of sentences in each paragraph.

- Some people read the first couple of paragraphs, two or three middle paragraphs, and the final one or two paragraphs of a piece.

- Some people skim the entire piece, but read only a few keywords in each sentence, skipping common, frequently occurring words such as *the, and, because,* and concentrating on nouns and verbs to get the main ideas.

You will have to discover which method works best for you. Most important, you will have to practise skimming, forcing your eyes to move quickly across the lines of words on the page or the computer screen. Some readers have a habit of subvocalizing, or silently saying each word in their heads or even with their mouths as if they were reading aloud. To skim proficiently, you must train yourself not to say each word in your head or pronounce each word with your lips and tongue. Let your eyes do the work.

Power Tools Tip

Skimming is also a useful strategy for pre-reading. You can skim a chapter in a textbook, looking only at the title and subheadings and then stopping to think about what you already know on the topic or to make predictions about the information you will discover.

Technological Tip

A number of Internet sites allow you to download sample exercises to increase your reading speed. Using the keywords *speed reading*, use your search engine to locate and record several of these sites.

Your Turn

- Choose several pages of unfamiliar reading from one of your subject-area textbooks.

- Flip through the pages, reading only the subheadings and noticing the pictures or diagrams. Make some mental predictions about the subject of the pages based on the subheadings.

- Now skim by reading the first and last sentence of each paragraph as quickly as you can. Were your predictions correct? Did you discover information that you did not expect?

- Read one entire paragraph to confirm the impression you got from reading the first and last sentence.

Scanning

Scanning is another type of quick reading that helps you locate very specific pieces of information on a page. Just as with skimming, there are different methods for scanning.

Focus Method

You may choose to use the focus method of scanning. Think of your eyes as a pair of binoculars looking for one red bird in a tree. You move your binoculars quickly from side to side, up and down, or diagonally until you have located only that red bird. You try to disregard anything else that your eyes may encounter. Now think about finding a year such as 1867, or a name such as John A. Macdonald, on the page of text or on the computer screen. Let your eyes zoom across the lines on the page, or up and down, or diagonally across it. Try to ignore everything on that page that is not a year or a name. Let your eyes pounce on the date or name when you find it.

Finger-Pointer Method

You may also wish to use the finger-pointer method of scanning. Let your finger run quickly under the lines of words, horizontally, vertically, or diagonally on the page. Again, ignore anything that is not the date, name, place, or number for which you are looking. Remind your brain that a date has numbers, or that the name of a person or place begins with a capital letter, and keep that finger moving quickly so that your eyes move with it.

Scanning is a particularly helpful type of reading when you are searching for a telephone number or trying to find a word in the index of a book.

Rereading and Monitoring Your Reading Comprehension

At first thought, rereading may seem like a strategy that will actually slow you down. In fact, when you reread sentences, paragraphs, or pages, you are helping yourself to understand the material better. There are several purposes for rereading:

- You may wish to reread a lengthy sentence that did not quite make sense to you because of its elaborate structure. Reading it again helps you get a better sense of all the pieces—the clauses and phrases—of the sentence.

- You may reread a sentence or two to check the meaning of an unfamiliar word based on the context—the other words and phrases around it. For example, consider the sentence, "She practised her dives over and over again in a seemingly *redundant* cycle, to teach her body to perform the motions without thinking about them." You can get some sense of the word *redundant*, which means "repetitive to the point of being unnecessary," by rereading the sentence, which talks about practising over and over again.

- You may reread a paragraph or two to refresh your memory after you have spent some time away from a text.

- You may also reread a piece of text after you have looked up a number of unfamiliar or specialized terms in a glossary or dictionary so that you will now understand what it means as a whole.

Rereading is a good way to monitor and improve your comprehension of what you read. When you reread and fix up your difficulties in understanding, you can then continue with your reading.

Another way to monitor your comprehension, especially with unfamiliar or specialized information for which you do not have a lot of prior knowledge, is a simple method called *click or clunk*. After reading one or several paragraphs, stop and ask yourself, "Does this click—do I get it? Or does this clunk because I haven't got a clue?" If it clicks, then continue reading. If the piece clunks, then you should use some of the rereading techniques suggested above.

Making Predictions About Content

Before you read, and while you are reading, you can make predictions about the content of the piece you are reading. If you pick up a science textbook, you can predict some of the ideas, words, and even pictures you may encounter. If you choose to read a novel or short story, you understand that there will be characters

Your Turn

- The next time you are in a bookstore or library, choose a magazine on a topic with which you are only slightly familiar.

- Flip the magazine open to one of the articles and read a half-column of the text.

- Stop and ask yourself, "Did it click or clunk?"

- If it clicked, continue reading and monitoring your understanding every few paragraphs.

- If the information clunked, ask yourself: "Would rereading several sentences be helpful? Is there terminology that is unfamiliar to me? What can I do to assist my comprehension?"

in conflict within a certain setting. If you read directions for installing a light switch, you can be sure that you will encounter technical terms and diagrams. Your prior knowledge, combined with your sense of the features and organization of various types of reading material, helps you make predictions.

Prior Knowledge

Most people can understand new information more clearly and easily when they see how it fits with information they already know. In your life, you have learned many things—from classes and books as well as from personal experience. This learned and practical information you have acquired is called *prior knowledge.* To be a capable reader of new information, think of the prior knowledge to which you can attach new learning, which will help you make predictions about what you are reading.

For example, if you are preparing to read an article on the uses of lasers in industry, consider what you know about lasers:

- I have heard advertisements for laser eye surgery.
- I have seen lasers being used to make incisions for other types of surgery on TV medical programs.
- I recall that laser pointers were banned at school because they could injure someone's eyes.

Your prior knowledge about lasers can help you make predictions about how lasers may be used in industry: for cutting patterns into paper, cutting through metals, or even for carving wood. You might also predict that safety precautions would be required for the use of lasers in industry.

Asking Questions of the Text, the Author, and Yourself

Often, we have the impression that because something has been written down, especially in a newspaper, a book, or on a computer screen, that it must be true. That is not always the case. Prior knowledge allows you to evaluate or make judge-

Your Turn

Before reading part of a chapter in a textbook or a magazine article, read the subheading or title and ask yourself, "What do I already know about this topic? Based on what I know, what predictions can I make about the information I will find here?"

ments about what you have read and to ask questions of the text, the author, and yourself. Based on your own experience and learning, you can assess the relevance of the information.

- Does it speak to you about something significant in your life—your interests, your need for a certain type of information?

- Does the text have a certain bias? Do you agree or disagree with the point of view? An author may write, for instance, about prejudice toward female workers on construction sites or about the way car salesmen try to sell women cars based on power and engine size, not recognizing that women place safety and economy first. You must ask yourself, "Is this my own experience, or an experience similar to that of someone I know? Do I fit the description of the people in these illustrations, or am I different?"

- Did the author's personal life experiences and the larger societal context influence the choice of details and point of view? Is that background similar to or different from your own? Does the information about the author make any difference to the ideas in the text, or do they easily stand on their own?

- Are the ideas and information relevant in the context of your life and times?

These questions will help you assess the relevance and bias of what you have read and decide whether a statement is a fact or an opinion and whether an experience is realistic or imagined.

Your Turn

- The next time you read a newspaper editorial and find yourself disagreeing strongly with the point of view expressed, ask yourself why you disagree.

- What assumptions and biases did the author express? How do they differ from your own experiences? What factors might have influenced the author's point of view?

- What questions would you like to ask this author based on what you read and the way you reacted?

Making Predictions Based on Text Features and Organization

Your familiarity with certain features of a text also allows you to make predictions about what you will read. A *text* is anything that has features that you are able to read. Some examples of texts are newspaper articles, short stories, biographies, advertisements, textbooks, billboards, and even photographs and films. Because of your experience, you know that the text of a concert ticket is different from the text of a restaurant menu. You expect that a textbook page will have a different appearance from the pages of a novel.

Think, for example, of what you expect to see on a concert ticket:

- the name of the event or group
- the date of the event
- the location of the concert
- the price of your admission to this concert
- letters and numbers indicating the location of your seat
- the starting time

Your Turn

- What expectations do you have about what should appear on a restaurant menu?

- What features would you expect to see on the pages of a science or geography textbook? What predictions can you make after reading a chapter title or a subheading? Where would you predict you could find definitions of unfamiliar terms?

- Think about what you can *read* in a photograph—the setting, the facial expressions of people, perhaps the situation (such as a birthday party), and other details.

Predicting and Confirming During Reading

While you are reading, you can also make predictions about what is coming next, and as you continue to read, you can confirm whether or not your predictions were correct.

Fiction

As you read fiction, it is common for you to anticipate events or changes to characters and their attitudes. For example, when you read that a young man has accepted a dare to jump off a bridge into a rocky river, you can predict that (a) he will be successful, and his friends will consider him brave and athletic; or (b) he will be unsuccessful, injuring himself seriously on the rocks below, and his parents will consider him foolish for accepting the dare. As you continue to read, you will discover which alternative is correct and be able to evaluate how you feel about the outcome.

Non-Fiction

As you read non-fiction pieces, such as an editorial or an essay, you might make predictions based on the author's choice of language. If you encounter phrases such as *fresh strategy*, *new thinking*, and *refreshing personality* in an editorial about a new chief executive officer for a major car company, you can predict that the author favours the person and her ideas. Further reading, especially of the concluding paragraph, will help you confirm your prediction and evaluate whether or not you agree with the writer.

Textbooks

As you read textbook chapters, you can predict that when you encounter new terms near the beginning of the chapter, they will be explained and perhaps illustrated by its conclusion. For example, a history textbook refers to the Renaissance and the *concept of humanism* at the beginning of the chapter. You can predict that you will discover when the Renaissance occurred, what it was, and what the term *humanism* means. As you continue to read, you will develop a sense of these words, adding to your personal knowledge, or you will realize that you may need to consult another source to find the meaning.

Understanding the Organization of Different Texts

When you are reading to find information, it is important to know how the organization of different texts can assist you in locating the specific information you need. Reading non-fiction text is different from reading fiction.

Strategies for Reading Different Genres

When you read a short story, novel, poem, or drama, you usually begin at the beginning and read sequentially to the end of the piece. The first sentence or line is your entry point into the story or thought, and meaning unfolds as you read through the text. Usually there are no pictures or diagrams to support your understanding or add to your knowledge of the text, but your knowledge of the structure of these texts helps you to draw meaning from them.

Stories

In a story or novel, you expect that the setting, characters, situation, and conflict will be introduced in the first few paragraphs or chapters, that there will be various complications as the story unfolds, and that events and characters will reach a satisfactory end point.

Drama

In the text of a drama, you will likely encounter a list of characters and a description of the setting before the action of the play begins with dialogue—the words of the characters. Often the dialogue also indicates physical actions for the actors on stage. For example, in Shakespeare's *Macbeth*, Banquo says to his son, "Take my sword." Clearly, the son must step forward and take the sword from his father's hand.

Poetry

With a poem, you may discover that thoughts and ideas, or characters and situations, are revealed little by little throughout the lines of the poem, especially through the diction and imagery of the poem. For example, in the poem "High Flight," by John Magee, words such as "slipped the surly bonds," "laughter-silvered wings," "tumbling mirth," "wheeled and soared," and "eager craft" indicate the poet's enjoyment of flying.

Non-Fiction

When you read non-fiction texts, you will not always find it necessary to begin at the first sentence and read every word on every page right through to the end of the chapter or book. If you are reading an editorial, a true account of an event, or a biography, you will likely wish to follow the argument or the chronology of events through from beginning to end. If you are reading a news report or a magazine article, you may decide that you have acquired enough key information after reading only a few paragraphs. Some types of reading material are designed specifically to allow you to read and use only small bits of information at a time. Think, for example, of a telephone or recipe book, an encyclopedia, or a first-aid manual. Think of other examples of texts that are designed to encourage brief, purposeful reading experiences.

Strategies for Reading Textbooks

When you read school textbooks for subjects such as science, geography, history, or mathematics, you may use a combination of reading strategies, sometimes reading only small bits of text, and other times reading large chunks from beginning to end. Again, you must consider your purpose for reading.

- Are you reading to answer questions provided by the teacher or at the end of the chapter? For example, you might need to write solutions to problems in a mathematics textbook. For this purpose, you will read a small but relevant chunk of text.

- Are you reading to find and define terms or new vocabulary? For example, you might read a science textbook to discover the meaning of various biologic terms such as *epithelial, dermis,* or *epidermis*. For this purpose, you may have to read most of a chapter, but you might also have to navigate the textbook pages to find the necessary information more quickly.

- Are you reading to understand a situation or a series of events? For example, you might read about the formation of the earth's crust in a geography textbook or about the causes of World War I in a history text. For these purposes, you would likely have to read a fairly large chunk, perhaps from the beginning of the chapter to the end.

Making Inferences and Drawing Conclusions

As you read, some information is very obvious to you and is spelled out in *explicit* details of colour, shape, size, dates, street addresses, personality characteristics, facts and figures, and descriptions of events. But sometimes you must also *read between the lines* or fill in the details to get the true picture of what an author wishes to convey. You are providing *implicit* details, things that are implied or suggested.

If an author writes, "It was a perfect morning in June," your own experience of a perfect morning in June completes the picture even if the author adds no other details. You may envision a sunny day with blue sky and a few fluffy clouds, a warm breeze, the singing of birds, and the fragrance of flowers and freshly cut grass. Or the author may write, "It was a typical day in late November," and you recall a grey, overcast day in November with a bit of fog in the air, and the beginnings of a cool breeze, based on your prior knowledge of November days.

When you fill in these implied details in your mind, you are making *inferences*. Inferences are conclusions that you reach based on your prior knowledge and on clues that you find in the text. For example, the author may write of a competition between Philip and Emil, the winner receiving a pair of tickets for gold seats at a hockey game. When the author does not describe the actual competition, but concludes the story with the line, "Emil had never seen a better game," you can draw the conclusion that Emil was the winner.

Looking for Clues and Noticing Diction

To make an inference or draw a conclusion, you must often synthesize or put together significant details or clues from several parts of a text, especially in non-fiction. You make inferences, as well, from the diction—the particular words and phrases that an author chooses to use. Examine the following passage, looking carefully at the author's diction or word choice. What general impression do you get about this situation from the words that are used? Which words in particular create this impression? What clues allow you to make inferences about the subject of Ahmad's decision?

It was a typical November day, and Ahmad's mood was as grim as the weather as he walked toward the hospital. He faced a crucial decision with no easy avenues leading to the right choice. The leaden sky weighed upon him just as the concrete under his feet felt hard and unforgiving. The cold needles of rain that began to fall provided no relief from the hard truth of this moment, and yet it had to be faced. His brother deserved the second chance at life that Ahmad could provide.

Notice how so many of the words the author has chosen imply the difficulty and weight of Ahmad's decision and the grimness of his mood. While the paragraph concentrates on Ahmad's decision, the details about the hospital in the first sentence and his brother's second chance in the last sentence help us make inferences or draw some conclusions about his decision.

Your Turn

- With a partner, decide what inferences might be drawn from the following situations.

  - A young man carrying a bouquet of roses arrives at the home of a young woman.

  - A young man carrying a bouquet of lilies arrives at the home of a young woman.

- With a partner, explore the difference between the denotation and possible connotations of the italicized words in the following expressions:

  - She was a *pitbull* in any debate.

  - She was a *ballerina* in any debate.

Denotation and Connotation of Words

Another aspect of diction allows us to make inferences based on word choices. The actual meaning of words is called their *denotation*, but they also have one or more implied meanings, referred to as *connotation*. Connotation means the other ideas that we associate with a word. For example, think of the connotation of the word *plain*; it may be an advantage to be plain-spoken, but you might not want to be considered a plain person. Now think of the word *iron*; iron resolve suggests a strong character, while an iron heart indicates an unsympathetic person.

Assessing Context and Relevance

You should approach everything you read with a perceptive and critical eye, which means reading carefully and deeply. It also means being aware of things that perhaps are not evident in the text itself—things such as the date of publication, the social context, and the author's background.

Checking the Date of Publication

When you are doing research, check the date of publication of everything you read, especially anything scientific, medical, technical, or geographic. Science and technology are changing at such a rapid pace that information that was current even six months ago may now be completely out of date.

Understanding the Context

The date of publication affects the context in which a work has been written. All writers are products of their own experiences; what occurs socially, culturally, and politically in their environment will be reflected to some extent in what they write. A novel written in the early 1900s, for example, may present a different perspective on the role of women in the workplace than one written within the past five years. Understanding the time period in which a work is written will allow you to appreciate more fully the work itself. You probably noticed that the introductions to some of the reading selections in this book tell you when the selection was written. Use this information to think about the social, cultural, and political context of the work. How would your impression of "Long, Long After School" be different if it had been written in the 1990s instead of the 1930s?

Technological Tip

If you are not sure about how current an article or book may be, try searching the Internet to find any recent developments in the field.

Detecting Assumptions, Omissions, and Biases

Everything you read has a point of view. Even the most dry, matter-of-fact procedure reflects the point of view of its writer, who chose to present the information in a certain way. In the hands of another writer, the procedure may be completely different.

When a writer's point of view is unbalanced, we say it is biased. Bias is the tendency to see a subject from only one perspective, to make assumptions, and to ignore or omit other legitimate perspectives and evidence that supports these perspectives. Biased writing is typically most evident in persuasive writing, but it can occur in informational writing as well. Here are four things to look for to help you identify biased writing:

- **Is the point of view balanced?** Ask yourself if all sides of the story have been presented. Has the author raised and addressed different points of view, or have these been ignored or omitted? Are assumptions and opinions supported with facts? For more about facts and opinions see Tutorial 25.

- **Is the writing fair and equitable?** Some writing contains assumptions and stereotypes about people. For example, women may be portrayed as poor drivers and men as poor housekeepers. Advertisers are particularly prone to using stereotypes, but watch out for them in all your reading.

- **Does the writer rely more on emotional language than on facts?** Most writers of persuasive pieces use emotional language to trigger an emotional response in their readers. If the writer uses more emotional language—or loaded words—than facts, then the piece is probably biased. See Tutorial 25 for more about emotional language.

- **Who is the author?** Find out all you can about the author. If a person writing about the nutritional benefits of a new dietary supplement works for the company that manufactures the supplement, you can be sure that the piece is biased, and you need to evaluate the information with this bias in mind.

 ## Strategies for Reading Longer Works

When you read a short story or a novel, you usually become involved in the lives of the characters and may be content to let events carry you along. However, when you are reading a complex work with a detailed story line or several subplots, you may need strategies for keeping track of who is who and what is happening. Similarly, when you encounter a lengthy chapter or an editorial with a fairly involved argument, you may feel you are losing control of what you are reading. When words become a blur, sentences and paragraphs do not make sense, or you have completely lost your train of thought, use one or more of the following strategies for controlling your reading and comprehension of longer text.

Strategies for Reading Longer Novels and Poems

Two useful strategies for approaching longer fictional writing pieces are chunking the text and using graphic organizers.

Chunking the Text

Fortunately, chapters in a novel divide the text into manageable chunks to read. However, as you move through a novel—especially if you put it down and pick it up at a later time—you may need to reread the conclusion of the previous chapter or skim the first and last pages of the previous two chapters to remind yourself of the characters and situations. Some chapters have titles that allow you to make predictions about their content. At the end of the chapter, you can reflect on the author's choice of title. If the chapter has no title, when you have finished reading it, consider what title you could give it.

Longer poems may be divided into stanzas, or they may be one continuous piece. Read the poem over once to get a general sense of its content and meaning. Then go back to the beginning and mentally divide the poem into an introductory section, one or more middle sections, and a concluding section. You may wish to use pencil annotations on your own copy of the poem (do not write in your textbook) or use small stick-on notes to indicate the various sections. Now go back and reread each section, concentrating on the images, ideas, and overall meaning. You may have to look up unfamiliar words. You may wish to stop and consider the denotation and connotation of some of the words and images the poet has used. When you have concluded your closer examination of each chunk, read the entire poem one more time to synthesize your understanding of it either mentally or on paper, and consider your reaction to it.

Using Graphic Organizers to Summarize Literary Works

For longer works, sketching a plot line or drawing a diagram of relationships can help you keep track of characters and events. This strategy can also help you understand and interpret shorter works. Use your sketches and diagrams when you prepare written summaries.

Below are two useful methods to help you summarize a story or a play.

- **Sequence of events.** Try using a flowchart to record a series of events:

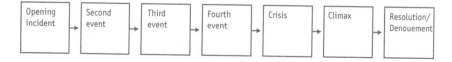

- **Plot summary diagram.** Try plotting the key events of a story or play on a line, beginning with the initial conflict or crisis, continuing with the complications that cause the conflict to escalate, and leading up to the climax and resolution or denouement. A summary diagram for *Still Stands the House* might look something like this:

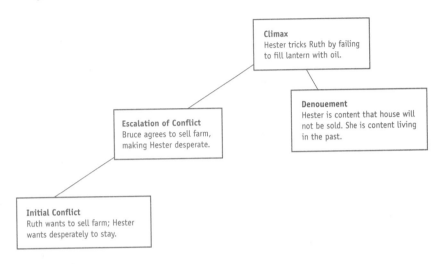

Below are two strategies for understanding characters and relationships.

- **Character chart.** Use a chart to keep track of details about characters and events in which they are involved.

CHARACTER	BRIEF DESCRIPTION	KEY EVENTS/SITUATIONS
Ruth	Small, fair, pretty, mid-20s. Compassionate, sensible, practical, outgoing, loves people. Tries to understand Hester.	Meets with Manning about selling farm. Conflict with Hester about selling the farm. Conflict with Bruce about selling the farm. Goes after Bruce into the snowstorm.

- **Diagram of relationships.** Try using a web to keep track of complex relationships among characters. Write the characters' names in boxes, and then add labelled arrows to show relationships, feelings, beliefs, and attitudes. Use two-way arrows to indicate something that is shared. A sample of a partial web appears on page 268, summarizing the relationships of the three main characters in *Still Stands the House*:

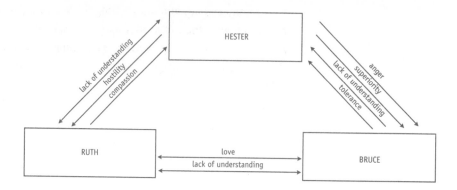

HESTER

lack of understanding
hostility
compassion

anger
superiority
lack of understanding
tolerance

RUTH

love
lack of understanding

BRUCE

Your Turn

- The next time you read a novel, make a character chart or web.

- Use one method for keeping track of events to summarize the next story that you read.

- Use stick-on notes to indicate chunks or sections in a lengthy poem. Give each section a name based on the key details or actions.

Strategies for Reading Longer Works of Non-Fiction

Four strategies can be used for reading longer non-fiction pieces: chunking the text, highlighting the text, creating titles, and using graphic organizers.

Chunking the Text

- Skim the text first to get a sense of its general subject and direction. While you are skimming, try to divide the text into the introduction, the body, and the conclusion.

- Usually the introduction and conclusion are closely tied together, and you may wish to read them together before you read the entire piece.

- Now go back to the introduction and identify the thesis or major argument and some of the key areas that will be explored. The introduction should serve as a road map, telling you the author's ultimate destination and some of the ways he or she will get there.

- Read the body paragraphs of the piece, stopping after each one to consider the significant illustrations and ideas.

- Read the conclusion and compare it with the introduction. Were the issues raised in the introduction confirmed in the conclusion? Were all the arguments tied together with a firm statement? Did the author accomplish the purpose stated in the introduction?

Highlighting the Text

- For this strategy, if you are not using your own text, use a photocopy of one or two pages of a textbook or a book borrowed from the library.

- Read the introductory paragraph and highlight what you believe to be the thesis statement. Remember, one definition of a thesis is *topic + point of view*. Also highlight some of the words that indicate key ideas or subtopics you believe the author will develop.

- Highlight the topic sentence in the second, third, and fourth paragraphs, and so on. Highlight one key illustration, proof, or example in each paragraph.

- In the conclusion, highlight what you believe to be the strongest statement of the author's position. Highlight any of these words that also appeared in the introduction.

Creating Titles

In editorials or essays, each paragraph often has a distinct enough argument or character that you can give it a title. Read the paragraph; stop and think about the main idea developed or illustrated, and then write a short title in pencil on your copy of the piece (not in your textbook) or in your notebook under the title of the whole piece. Continue in the same manner for the remaining paragraphs.

Your Turn

- Using stick-on notes and a newspaper editorial, give each paragraph a title based on the ideas and examples it contains. Put all of your stick-on notes on a sheet of paper and decide whether you agree with the order in which ideas were developed and with the key arguments.

- With a copy of the same editorial, highlight what you believe to be the thesis of the piece. Then highlight a topic sentence in each of the body paragraphs. Compare the sentences you have highlighted with the work of a partner. What was the same? What was different?

Using Graphic Organizers

Graphic organizers can help you focus on the main arguments and supporting details of a piece, or they can help you summarize the points of view held by various people on a certain event or situation. Two examples appear below.

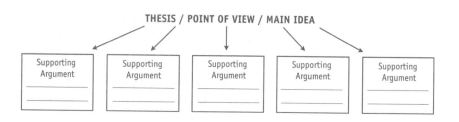

THESIS / POINT OF VIEW / MAIN IDEA

| Supporting Argument | Supporting Argument | Supporting Argument | Supporting Argument | Supporting Argument |

POINT OF VIEW WEB

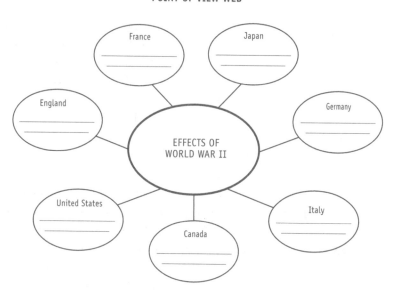

These techniques can help you control your reading process and will allow you to do some thinking about smaller sections of a longer piece. As you process these smaller sections, you should understand the whole piece better.

Building Your Vocabulary

Becoming a better, more versatile reader means developing a strong vocabulary. Without an extensive vocabulary, reading can be slow and your comprehension can be hindered. In this section, we will explore ways to increase your vocabulary.

Learning Words in Context

As you learned earlier in the book, one way to figure out the meaning of a word is to look at its context, or the other words, sentences, and paragraphs that surround the word. The extract below is from an essay called "Teletrance." Clues to the meaning of the word "teletrance" are given in the surrounding words or sentences.

Indeed, the fixed attention indicated by the unblinking stare, slack facial muscles, and immobile body posture are exactly the signs a hypnotherapist observes when deciding an individual has entered a hypnotic state. This passive, usually induced *"teletrance"* mode of consciousness competes with what might be called "participatory consciousness."

Looking for Synonyms in the Context

A synonym is a word that means the same (or nearly the same) as another word, such as *chesterfield, couch,* and *sofa.* The following example contains three words that are similar in meaning:

I was told to *stop* running. The coach said *halt.* In this way, my progress was *arrested*.

In this example, *stop, halt,* and *arrested* mean virtually the same thing.

Searching for synonyms is a method of deciphering the meaning of unfamiliar words. Suppose you were to come across the above example in your reading but did not know the meaning of the word *arrested.* Clues to the word's meaning are supplied in the synonyms *stop* and *halt.* Notice how the synonyms in the following examples clarify the meaning of the words in italics.

The *indigent* woman was so poor that she had no money for food or shelter.

Mark only *exacerbated* the situation by offending the police officer. He ended up making things worse.

They named their youngest child *Serendipity* because she brought luck and unexpected joy to their lives.

Looking for Signal Words in the Context

We have discussed signal words in several chapters in this book. Just as it is important to use signal words when you write, it is also important to notice them as you read. Signal words can indirectly help you define an unfamiliar word.

How do the signal words help you define the italicized words in the following sentences?

Sarah is usually *loquacious*, but in class today she did not say a word.

Although his mother had great charm and *charisma*, John is quiet and retiring.

My boss is usually *magnanimous*. However, this year no one received a Christmas bonus.

Using the Context to Distinguish Homonyms

The English language is so rich and complex that even the best readers and writers confuse and misunderstand words. Homonyms are words that have the same sound and sometimes the same spelling but differ in meaning. Below are some examples of homonyms:

- cite, sight, site
- hare, hair
- plain, plane
- right, write
- fine, fine

- where, wear
- whether, weather
- principal, principle
- carrot, carat

Use the context to distinguish words that sound the same but mean different things. See the Glossary of Usage on pages 316 to 319 of Writing Power Tools for other examples of homonyms and commonly confused words.

Recording New Words in a Notebook

Another way to build your vocabulary is to record new words and their meanings when you come across them. You can use a section of your Thought Book (see page 276), your Reader Response Journal, or a separate notebook. In order to remember the new words, you need to look at the words often. It is also a good idea to practise using them, either in conversation or in writing.

Using Vocabulary Cards

Another effective method is to use index cards to make vocabulary cards. Write the word you want to learn on one side of the card. On the other side, write its meaning, a synonym, and an antonym (a word that has the opposite meaning).

Perhaps select a word for each weekday. Put the cards for the week in your knapsack. When you have a spare moment, read your word for the day. At the end of the week, review all five words.

Technological Tip

You can use the computer to make a list of words and definitions to build you vocabulary. The advantage of using a computer is that you can easily erase words once you feel confident you know them; you can also manipulate words and definitions and put them into tables and lists.

 ## Improving Your Reading Skills

The following chart is a summary of most of the topics from this chapter and some reading strategies from other chapters. Use it to improve your reading and vocabulary skills.

BEFORE READING, I CAN . . .	WHILE I READ, I CAN . . .	AFTER READING, I CAN . . .
• scan for new vocabulary • use a highlighter to identify difficult terms • learn new terms from a glossary or dictionary • skim to connect with prior knowledge • make predictions • turn subheadings into questions • examine graphics—pictures, charts, or diagrams • chunk text into manageable pieces using stick-on notes	• confirm predictions • make new predictions • decide whether my reading clicks or clunks • adjust my reading pace • reread words, sentences, or paragraphs • visualize or make mental images of what I am reading • examine pictures, charts, or diagrams • make inferences • use graphic organizers • highlight key details • look for words that signal text organization or patterns • define unfamiliar vocabulary with stick-on notes	• confirm my predictions • make notes • use a graphic organizer to record key details • reread to find supporting details • scan for accurate details • give each paragraph a title based on its content • consider the author's point of view and biases • decide whether the text is factual or imaginative • evaluate how graphics support or relate to text • evaluate my own responses to what I've read • create questions I would ask the author • use the ideas and viewpoints of others to deepen my understanding

Writing Power Tools

Writing is not a linear process. Few, if any, writers begin with a blank page, follow a prescribed number of steps in precise sequence, and finish with a published work. For most of us, writing is a process of discovery in which we take one step forward, one back, and maybe one to the side to follow a new angle. The strategies described in this chapter have been separated from one another to make them easier to discuss. In reality, you will likely use several strategies at once and find some more useful than others.

 ## Finding Something to Write About

Most writers will advise you to write about the things you know best—your own thoughts, feelings, and experiences. As you move through each day of your life, you record instantaneous impressions of places, people, and events. In a sense, you carry on an interior monologue, a conversation with yourself. Consider the following examples:

- As you walk into a classroom, you may remember, "Uh-oh, I forgot to finish the assignment for this class. I'm going to have to keep a low profile, or try to scribble down a few lines while other things are happening."

- In history class you see a film in which Martin Luther King Jr. gives his "I Have a Dream" speech and are struck by its power. You think, "Wow, that guy could talk! I can see how he was able to inspire so many people to take action to stop racial discrimination."

- After school, you head to the field for soccer practice, reflecting on your skills as a player: "Today I'll show the coach that I've been practising some of those moves she taught us last time. I think I've really developed some skill."

If you pause to listen to yourself, you will find many thoughts, ideas, and feelings inside your head that you may be able to use as topics for writing. Sometimes you feel so strongly about a subject that you want to write about it. Many people, for example, write about their strong feelings in letters to the editor of a newspaper or they record them in a personal journal. At other times, you will be asked to write about a particular topic or to choose your own topic for a piece of writing for history or geography class.

- For geography class, you might write a letter to the editor of the local newspaper about ways to protect the environment in your community.

- For history class, you might research and write a persuasive essay about the most important prime minister of Canada in the twentieth century.

In each of the above writing situations, you would use evidence and details from various sources to support your own ideas and point of view.

The following sections describe strategies you can use to generate ideas for writing.

Recording Your Interior Monologue

Find a quiet space during the day to sit down and record your interior monologue using a notebook as an informal journal. For about 15 minutes, write down the thoughts, feelings, and ideas that have been in your head during the day. Write words, lists, or phrases. Use sketches or diagrams if you enjoy recording ideas in a more visual way.

As you examine your notebook entry, you may observe several things:

- The notes do not flow together smoothly; they seem quite disjointed, representing random thoughts.

- There is no consistent attempt to use complete sentences, capital letters, or proper punctuation.

- There are some significant ideas that could lead to longer pieces of writing.

Your Turn

- For five days, take 10 minutes at some quiet point to record your interior monologue. What thoughts are running through your mind? What are you saying to yourself? What questions do you ask yourself? Do you ever give yourself orders?

- After the five days, look back over your entries to see if there are common themes or patterns to your interior monologue. What questions have you answered? What commands did you follow? Should you try to change some of your thinking—for example, be more positive or upbeat? Should you turn some thoughts into a checklist of things to do so that you get some persistent themes out of your head and put them into action?

If you keep such a journal, you will find that you can mine it for good writing ideas by rereading a number of entries. Which items could someone write about in greater detail?

Keeping an Idea or Thought Book

Many successful writers and artists keep an idea or thought book. This may be similar to a journal, but the aim is not so much to register inner thoughts as to report outward happenings and influences that can then be used to inspire a piece of writing or artwork. In their thought books, writers record descriptions of people or incidents they have observed; quotations or lines from songs; conversations between friends or relatives; bits of poetry; lists of their favourite movies, restaurants, books, and people; sketches of interesting things; impressions of a winter evening or fall day; and anything else that may provide ideas for writing. Some writers have drawn heavily on their idea books or journals to reconstruct entire scenes and dialogues for novels or stories. The details they have recorded lend authenticity to their writing.

Explore your idea book for inspiration when you have moments of writer's block or to create realistic detail when you need to support a thesis or a creative concept.

Your Turn

- Keep your own idea book. Buy a blank notebook with lined pages. Anytime you get a good idea, hear an interesting phrase or sentence, eat a great meal, or see an enjoyable movie, make a note about your experience.

- Add quotations, descriptions, song lyrics, items from restaurant menus, and any other details you think would add interest to a piece of writing in the future.

- Keep lists, recording your three favourite places, five foods you will never eat again, your top five heroes, your favourite 10 movies and books, your three favourite CDs, and so on.

- Record your reactions to current events, politicians, sports activities, concerts, or movies.

Keeping a Reader Response Journal

A reader response journal is a specific type of journal in which you record your reactions to the things you read. In this journal, you can record your impressions of your reading; you can also ask questions, make comparisons, and express your reactions and opinions. Writing about the things you read can help you make connections and release ideas that you may not be aware of until you start writing. These ideas can serve as inspiration for essays and assignments. You can use a reader response journal for anything you read, from fiction to news articles and editorials to procedures and advertisements.

Technological Tip

Try keeping a journal on your computer. The advantage of a computer is that you have unlimited space in which to write; the disadvantage is that, unless you carry a portable computer with you everywhere, you may not have your journal with you when you want to jot things down.

Brainstorming

Another helpful strategy for finding ideas is brainstorming. To brainstorm, you choose a topic and then write down as many related ideas as come to mind within a given period of time. Brainstorming works even better when you try it with one or more partners. Some rules for brainstorming are

- Accept all ideas and write them down.

- Do not censor anyone else's idea by saying it is silly, stupid, or far-fetched. Some useful ideas have come from brainstorming sessions.

- Do not think logically or in a linear fashion. Branch out all over the place.

- Build on others' ideas, using each new thought as a springboard for fresh ideas.

- Do not worry about correct grammar, punctuation, or spelling. Just get the ideas down here.

Examine this sample of brainstorming around the issue of ways to make a community more environmentally friendly:

- plant more trees, bushes, and flowers
- flowers and trees along the main streets of the town
- more receptacles for garbage
- receptacles for glass, newspapers, etc. on all main corners—in parks, too
- recycling and recycling depot
- reduce garbage
- composting
- semi-annual clean-up of parks and natural areas
- school competition for who can gather the most garbage
- ban pop cans and gum chewing at stores and malls
- special receptacles for chewed gum
- convert chewed gum to something useful—bumpers for sandboxes?

Can you see that all ideas were accepted and were not necessarily recorded in a logical way? Which ideas seem far-fetched? How do some ideas build on others? How would you organize this information to create a plan for your municipality? What would you include and what would you omit?

 Webbing

Some people prefer to record their brainstorming visually so that they can see how one idea leads to another. A simple web pattern using bubble or balloon shapes provides a visual structure that may also help you organize subtopics for your writing. Here is an example of a web showing some of the ideas brainstormed above on the topic of the environment:

Freewriting

If you are unable to think of anything to write or of ways to approach a subject, try doing some freewriting. When you freewrite, you let the words flow, without stopping to reflect about what you have written. The idea is to let one idea lead to another. Here are some tips for getting the most from freewriting:

- Set yourself a time limit of no more than 10 minutes.

- Write as much as you can about as many different subjects that occur to you, or on a subject that you have already chosen.

- Ignore grammar, spelling, punctuation, and sentence structure. Stopping to think about these things can inhibit the flow of ideas.

- At the end of the time limit, read over what you have written and circle the most promising ideas. Then, using one of those ideas as the focus, start the process again.

Technological Tip

If you are freewriting on your computer, try turning the monitor off. You may find that you will write more freely if you cannot see what you are writing. After you have typed for a few minutes, print out what you have written and highlight the best ideas.

Ensuring Your Topic Is Specific

Once you have a general idea for a topic, you need to make sure it is suitable for a writing topic. Your topic should be specific. It is easier to write on a specific topic than on a broad topic. Topics that are too broad lead to generalizations. In the left margin of the box below are topics that are too broad for an essay. Copy the chart and try making them more specific. Is there a particular example that could be associated with your topic?

BROAD TOPIC	SPECIFIC TOPIC
Canadian heroes	
sleep	
planes	
the environment	

Choosing a Form for Your Writing

As you are generating and narrowing down topics, you need to think about the form your writing will take. You may be planning to write a short story, a poem, or a personal essay, or perhaps your teacher has assigned a procedure, a persuasive essay, or a research report. Most of the writing you do in senior high school will likely be informational, analytic, and persuasive, and it will require some research.

Considering Your Audience

The most important consideration in writing, next to having something to say, is knowing your audience. Knowing and understanding your audience will have a great influence on what and how you write. Often, you write to inform yourself, to make your ideas and feelings more clear to you. But human beings are social animals, and being able to share your thoughts with others and get some feedback is usually important. Many times, you will write *on demand*, producing a piece for a particular person or group of people. The following questions will help you become aware of the background of your audience:

- Does the audience feel the same way that you do?

- Has the audience had the same experience?

- Will the audience understand your ideas or appreciate the way you have said something?

- Is your audience someone special enough to share some of your most private thoughts and accept them because they come from you?

Sharing with an audience, whether one person or many people, and getting valid feedback from that audience adds significance and resonance to your creative effort. Sharing a research report or essay with someone else is one way to ensure that your ideas are clear and that your sentences flow smoothly from one paragraph to the next.

When considering how to write for your audience, think first of who that audience is and what will help them understand and relate to your writing. Think of how you correspond with a friend or family member via e-mail. You probably write very informally, using pet names, adding family expressions, and perhaps even including joking insults. Consider whether you can use this same style with every piece of writing.

Every author must address the following questions, either unconsciously in the early drafts of a piece of writing or consciously during the revising and rewriting process:

- How would you write a letter about the environment to the mayor differently than a letter to a brother or sister?

- How would word choices in a thank-you note to your grandmother differ from the choices you would use in a note to a classmate at school?

- Why would you not write a formal essay on a drama such as *Hamlet* using colloquial language to explain your point of view?

- Would you write to an insurance company about a recent car accident using the same words and details that you shared with friends?

④ Determining Your Purpose

Your intended audience will influence your purpose. Suppose you have chosen sleep as your topic. In an *expressive* piece, your purpose might be to entertain your readers with a humorous story about a sleepwalker. In an *informational* piece, your purpose might be to explain the causes of insomnia or to report on the mattresses most likely to result in a good night's sleep. In a *persuasive* piece, it might be to persuade your readers to buy a particular mattress or to convince them that sleeping pills are addictive.

The main purpose of expressive writing is often to make the reader feel an emotion—to feel sadness or joy, to laugh, or to be deeply moved. The main purpose of informational and analytic writing is to make the reader understand. The main purpose of persuasive writing is often to make a reader think and feel the way the writer thinks and feels.

Using the Assignment to Clarify Your Purpose

If your teacher has given you an assignment, use the wording to determine and clarify your purpose. If it gives you a precise topic, read the description of the task very carefully and consider what it is asking you to do. Verbs, nouns, and adjectives can make a difference to your understanding of the task. As you read the assignment description, underline the verbs and nouns that give you a sense of the job and a clear picture of the final product. Consider the following example. Some of the keywords have been underlined to make the assignment more clear.

In an essay of 1500 words, explain the causes of the "Quiet Revolution" in Quebec, examining the key social and cultural factors, as well as the political climate of the early 1960s.

First, the assignment tells you that you are to write an essay, so immediately you know that you will be expected to adhere to essay form (with a thesis statement, body paragraphs, and so on). Second, you are told that your essay is to be 1500 words. Notice that the teacher has not specified the number of pages. An essay of 1500 words would likely fill five to six double-spaced, typed pages. Third, the assignment gives you a clear sense of the type of essay you must write: in an essay that asks you to explain something, you are expected to provide information—in this case, on the causes of the Quiet Revolution—not to persuade or interpret.

Here's a second example:

Who is most responsible for the tragic events of *Macbeth*? In a well-argued essay, at least three pages in length, support your point of view with specific references to the play.

Clearly you must choose one or more characters from the play and assign each some responsibility for the tragic outcome—the deaths of Banquo, Macduff's family, and Lady Macbeth, and the tragic waste of Macbeth's talents as a leader. Then you must provide examples of specific events, decisions, and words that support your point of view. The word "most" is a key factor in your task, since it indicates that some element of comparison is necessary in your essay; to flesh out that comparative information will likely take the three or more pages indicated.

In determining the specific aspects and purpose of your task, it is helpful to understand the meaning of some typical task-related verbs. Examine the chart on the following page to clarify your sense of task verbs.

TASK VERB	EXPLANATION	SAMPLE TASK
ANALYZE	Break something down into its components in order to examine each element.	*Analyze the failure of the United States in stopping the advance of Communist rule in Vietnam.*
COMPARE	Show similarities and differences.	*Compare the physical features and economy of British Columbia and Alberta.*
CONTRAST	Show only differences.	*Contrast the concluding decades of the nineteenth and twentieth centuries.*
DEFINE	Give a clear, concise, and accurate statement of essential information about the class of a thing or person and its distinguishing characteristics.	*Define "extended metaphor." Define the essential characteristics of leadership.*
DESCRIBE	Provide specific details, especially colour, size, shape, facts, measurements, and, in some circumstances, feelings.	*Describe the effects of WWII bombing on European cities.*
DISCUSS	Write about something from different points of view, providing illustrated arguments for and against.	*Discuss genetically altered food.*
EXPLAIN	Tell how something works or came to be. Outline the steps you took to solve a problem.	*Explain the phenomenon of lightning. Explain solutions to the garbage crisis.*
ILLUSTRATE	Provide examples that create a clear picture in the reader's mind (similar to "describe").	*Illustrate the effects of good nutrition on health. Illustrate your answer with many references to the poem.*
JUSTIFY	Provide the reasons that explain an action or decision.	*Justify Trudeau's decision to invoke the War Measures Act. Justify Macbeth's decision to have Banquo murdered.*
PREDICT	Draw conclusions/make inferences from available evidence or details provided to suggest future events.	*Predict the outcome of the next election. Predict the consequences of Lenny's actions in* Of Mice and Men.
PROVE	Provide evidence— examples or illustrations— to support a stated point of view.	*Prove that Nelson Mandela is a man of principle and patience.*

- Choose a question from a textbook or an assignment and underline what you believe to be the keywords.

- Find the task verb and check its meaning and the example provided in the chart. Then write three to five short, simple sentences stating the purpose and various aspects of your task.

④ Using the Appropriate Style and Diction

Style is the distinctive manner in which a writer puts thoughts together. Style involves diction (word choices), sentence structure, and the arrangement of paragraphs. The style of some writers is so distinctive that readers recognize it immediately. A document written in a formal style might have a complex sentence structure with varied sentences, a specialized or sophisticated vocabulary, and correct grammar. A document written in a colloquial style might have a simple sentence structure; a limited vocabulary with clichés and common, everyday expressions; and, possibly, incorrect grammar. A document in an informal style would lie somewhere in between. Your audience and purpose are key determinants of style. Ask yourself these questions before you select the appropriate style for your document:

- Is my audience one person or many people?

- Does my audience have interests, tastes, and cultural background similar to my own or different from mine?

- Is my audience the same age, younger, or older than I am?

- Am I writing for a business audience, the general public, my peers, or some specialized group?

- Should I use a formal or informal style with careful sentence structure, no slang or abbreviations, clear punctuation, and correct spelling?

- Or can I be less formal, using colloquial (street language) expressions, expressive punctuation, and creative sentence structure to imitate the partial thoughts or run-on thinking of some of my characters?

- Should I write in the first person, using *I*, or should I be more formal in my approach and write in the objective third person?

The chart on pages 286 to 287 demonstrates styles of documents for different audiences and purposes.

④ Using the Appropriate Tone

As you learned in Chapter 4 on the short story, tone is the expression of the writer's attitude toward his or her writing and the audience. Think of tone as the way a writer's voice would sound if the writing were read aloud. When you write, you create tone through your choice of words and your selection and arrangement of details and images.

Notice how the tone, diction, and style changes in the charts on pages 286 and 287 depending on the audience, purpose, and form.

Observe the specific words and images the writer of the essay "The Death Penalty: Justice for None" uses to create an angry tone:

These court appointed defense lawyers are often *appallingly* inadequate.

Consider how the tone changes when the word in italics is replaced by other words:

These court appointed defense lawyers are often inadequately prepared.

Notice how word changes affect the tone of the sentences in this chart.

SENTENCE	TONE
I was astounded and outraged by the rudeness of some city drivers.	Angry/outraged
I found learning to drive in the city to be an extremely frustrating experience.	Irritated/frustrated
Learning to drive in the city requires confidence, preparation, and patience.	Matter-of-fact/ straightforward

Style and tone are closely related. A letter written in an informal style could have a number of different tones, depending on the word choice of the writer. For example, the tone might be warm and friendly; it might be romantic; it might be irritated. Some styles and tones, however, do tend to go together. For example, most documents that are written in a formal style have an impersonal tone. Just as your audience and purpose determine your style, they also determine your tone.

AUDIENCE	PURPOSE	FORM	DICTION, STYLE, AND TONE
FORMAL • University professors • Lawyers • Scientists • Physicians • Engineers • Other specialists	• To discuss research findings • To present complex information • To give a legal, scientific, medical, or technical explanation • To describe a complex process	• Journal articles • Highly specialized books • Scientific, medical, and technical papers • Legal statutes and opinions • Government documents • Business reports • University essays	• Complete, correct, and proper diction with no contractions • Specialized vocabulary • Correct spelling, grammar, and punctuation • Formal third-person voice. No use of the first or second person (*I* and *you*) • Impersonal tone
COLLOQUIAL • Workplace • School work • Business • Politics • Strangers • Older or more distant relatives	• To explain or inform • To persuade • To narrate and describe • To apply • To thank • To inquire • To make a complaint • To entertain	• Most essays • Procedures and instructions • Magazine articles • Textbooks and reference books • Workplace, business, and other letters • Workplace e-mail • Some works of literature	• Complete, correct, and proper diction; some contractions may be used • Plain language • Correct spelling, grammar, and punctuation • First-, second-, or third-person voice • Typically tone is respectful, but may have more personal warmth than formal documents

Continued on next page

AUDIENCE	PURPOSE	FORM	DICTION, STYLE, AND TONE
COLLOQUIAL • Family • Friends • Classmates • Co-workers • Children • Self	• To entertain, inform, persuade, and share news, stories, gossip, and opinions	• Some works of literature • Notes • Letters • Personal e-mail • Journals • Diaries	• Creative licence in use of fragments and run-on sentences • Colloquialisms and contractions • Expressive punctuation • First and second person used

 ## Power Tools Tip

You can convert first person to third person easily by removing the initial phrase "I think that . . ." or similar constructions. For example:

1. Original sentences written in first person:

    I think that in society today, too many people have little consideration for the needs and well-being of others. *I* observe and experience the rude behaviour of ignorant people everywhere.

2. Revised sentences written in third person:

    In society today, too many people have little consideration for the needs and well-being of others. Ignorant people demonstrate their rude behaviour everywhere.

 ## *Your Turn*

Choose and review two recent assignments you wrote for English or another subject, and consider some of the following questions:

*   Was I truly aware of my audience? Was I writing for the teacher, other classmates, or someone else?

*   What was my purpose and did I accomplish it?

*   Were my style and tone appropriate for my audience?

*   Did I observe the appropriate elements of form, such as correct paragraphing, spelling, and punctuation?

Finding Supporting Details

All writing—whether it is creative, personal, informational, persuasive, or analytic—needs to be backed up with examples and supporting details. If you are writing a creative or personal piece, you may be able to supply those examples and details from your own imagination and memory. However, if you are writing an informational, persuasive, or analytic piece, you will have to prepare a research plan in order to find and select information to use in your writing.

Making Research Plans

When making a research plan in preparation for writing an essay, an explanation, or a report, you need to consider a number of things, including your prior knowledge of the topic, the best places to find information, and the most valid and available sources of information.

The best way to begin gathering information on your topic is to think about what you know already. After reading the assignment description carefully, take some time to think about what you do know. Ask yourself:

- What has stayed in my mind from any reading and discussion I have done on this topic?

- What information do I need to review or retrieve?

- What do I think about this information? Where will it fit in the context of my task?

 ## Using Journalists' Questions

Journalists ask themselves six questions when they are writing a magazine or newspaper article: Who? What? When? Where? Why? How? Answering these six questions will help you find out as much as possible about your topic. Or you may find that the six questions can help you determine a purpose and establish a direction for your research. If you begin the research process knowing what you want to find out, your research is more likely to be successful.

Your next step is to determine what you still need to know, find, or discover. Before you begin your research, ask yourself:

- What are my greatest information gaps?

- What primary and secondary sources do I require for my research?

- Where can I find these sources?

- Do I have easy access to my sources, or will I have to make special arrangements?

You will likely wish to use a combination of print sources (books, periodicals, and reference works such as encyclopedias) and electronic sources (CD-ROMs and the Internet). The following chart defines primary and secondary sources; a variety of sources can be categorized using these terms.

TYPE OF SOURCE	WHAT IS IT?	PURPOSE
PRIMARY	These are original documents, such as contracts, certificates, or deeds. They are also works such as novels, poems, and plays. People who were participants in, or witnesses to, events are also primary sources.	These provide an authentic voice for some types of assignments. If you were writing about the effects of war, you might read the poetry of Siegfried Sassoon or Wilfred Owen, soldiers and friends in World War I. You might also interview a veteran of World War II to get a personal account of conditions during the war.
SECONDARY	These are not original authors or documents; they are often analytic accounts written by people who were not participants or original authors.	These sources may be appropriate to validate an idea or a thesis. If you were writing about the political ideas that were evident in a novel or play, you might wish to read accounts of the author's time period to see the connections.

Your Turn

For your next assignment in science, history, or geography, make a research plan, using the following questions as a guide:

- Can I find primary sources, or will secondary sources be most available and suitable?

- What information on my topic is available in the school or local library?

- Are there any CD-ROMs that might be appropriate sources?

- What search terms from the assigned question can I type into an Internet search engine? Can I quickly determine which sites might be most useful and reliable?

Deciding on a Thesis

When you have chosen a topic, decided on the appropriate form, audience, and purpose, and done your research, you are then ready to put all of your ideas together. At this point, you need to develop a clear focus for your writing. If you are writing fiction or poetry, your focus will be the theme of the work. If you are writing an essay, your central focus will be your thesis. One approach to the development of a thesis is to see it as the answer to a key question; your thesis then becomes a statement of belief. Your thesis is the thread that holds the entire piece of writing together. Spend some time developing a strong thesis. Without one, your writing will lack in focus.

Some professional essays have implied theses. That is, the writer never states his or her thesis, but the reader infers the main point from the content of the essay. It is not recommended that you use an implied thesis for school assignments. If you want your meaning to be clear, your point should be easy to grasp. The one exception is if you are writing a narrative essay, in which case a stated thesis can either ruin any element of surprise or state the obvious. For a demonstration of this, look at the narrative student essay on pages 293 to 295. You will see that in the first draft, the student placed her thesis statement at the end of the first paragraph. However, she realized that her thesis statement was obvious and unoriginal, so in her final draft she did not state her thesis.

Organizing Your Ideas and Information

Once you have gathered information for your piece, you need to organize your ideas into a coherent structure. How you organize your ideas and supporting details will depend largely on what you are writing. The chart on page 291 indicates the most common methods for organizing and ordering some types of writing, with chapter references to places in the book where these methods are explored in greater detail.

Preparing an Outline

Some writers use an outline to help them organize their ideas; others simply start to draft their essays; others use a brainstorming web to organize their ideas. If you choose this latter approach, you can group ideas in your web by using the following methods:

- colour coding similar ideas and details

- drawing arrows to connect ideas

- using a numbering system to connect ideas

ORDER OF IDEAS	TYPE OF WRITING	FOR MORE DETAILS
Spatial order	Descriptive paragraphs, essays, fiction, stage directions in drama	Descriptive Essays, Chapter 1
Time chronologic, flashbacks, and foreshadowing	Descriptive and narrative essays, procedures and instructions, fiction, drama, letters	Descriptive Essays, Chapter 1 Narrative Essays, Chapter 2 Procedures, Chapter 9
Logical order	Informational essays, process essays, procedures and instructions, persuasive essays, reports, letters	Persuasive Essays, Chapter 14
Climactic order	Persuasive essays, reports, and letters	Persuasive Essays, Chapter 14

Note: You may wish to vary the organizational method. If you are explaining a new idea or persuading someone to do something, you must consider the best way of organizing ideas to reach your reader. For example, in a persuasive essay you may choose to relate an anecdote and use chronologic order, if you were arguing that a series of events led to a particular war.

In Tutorial 8, you will find an example of a formal outline. On the next page is an example of notes and a brainstorming web that a student generated for an essay on her first job. Instead of doing a formal outline, the student used a numbering system to group her ideas for the first draft of her essay.

Planning Your Paragraphs

Writers use strategies to develop their paragraphs. One strategy is to state a cause and then explain the effects of the cause. Another is to compare two items. As you plan, think about the strategies you will use for individual paragraphs. See Tutorial 15 for details about these strategies.

If you are having difficulty organizing paragraphs into subtopics, imagine that you are arranging slides to show an audience. What would you choose first, second, third, and so on? What sentences would explain each slide? Consider a science report on the topic of whether bees communicate:

- Picture 1: Think of what the organization of bees in a hive suggests about their ability to communicate. This information will form your first paragraph.

- Picture 2: Imagine a field of clover where many bees are extracting nectar from the flowers. This is the main job of worker bees. Now you have paragraph two.

- Picture 3: Imagine a bee returning to a hive and communicating to other workers the location of the field. How does that bee tell them where to find the nectar? Paragraph three will describe bee communication.

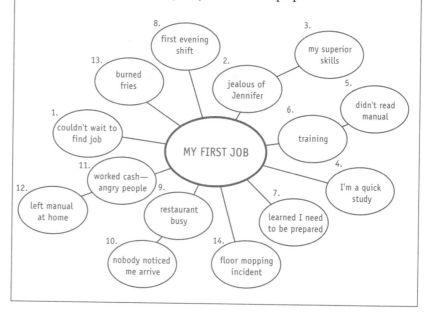

Brainstorming Web

Student essay: My First Job
Essay form: Personal narrative essay
Audience: My classmates
Purpose: To entertain and to inform
Style: Informal
Tone: Superior, but also humble
Thesis: To succeed at a new job, you have to be prepared.

8. first evening shift
3. my superior skills
13. burned fries
2. jealous of Jennifer
5. didn't read manual
1. couldn't wait to find job
6. training
MY FIRST JOB
4. I'm a quick study
11. worked cash—angry people
12. left manual at home
9. restaurant busy
7. learned I need to be prepared
10. nobody noticed me arrive
14. floor mopping incident

Writing Your Drafts

Most writers will advise you to let your ideas flow as you write your first draft. Use your plan or your outline (if you have one) as a rough guide, but otherwise write without worrying too much about sentence structure, grammar, and spelling. There are no limits to the number of drafts you can write, so, unless you have left a writing assignment to the last minute, you have time to revise your writing until you are satisfied with it. See the beginning of the first draft of the student essay "My First Job," on the next page. Have a look at the notes the student has written about changes she intends to make to this first draft.

Your Turn

For your next writing topic, imagine that you are putting together a slide show related to that topic.

- What are some key pictures you wish to give your audience? Try to see each of those pictures in vivid detail. These will be the subtopics for your piece of writing.

- Arrange the slides in a pleasing order. Should they be chronologic? Should they be logical, developing a reasonable argument or story? Should they be arranged in order of excitement from the least exciting to the most dramatic? Now you have an appropriate order for your subtopics.

- Consider how you will frame the slides. What introductory information should you supply? What commentary should accompany each of the slides? What afterthoughts will you present? These reflections will provide your introduction, some of your key details for subtopic paragraphs, and your conclusion.

First Draft of "My First Job"

Need a more vivid beginning —why do I want to work at the restaurant?

When I was sixteen, I got a job at a hamburger joint near

my house. My older sister Jennifer already worked there. I

was envious of her working there and I couldn't wait to be

old enough to work at the restaurant myself. I didn't think

that Jennifer was good at her job. She sometimes spills^ed drinks

on the customers, and she often had trouble balancing her cash reg-

ister. I was smarter in school and more coordinated than

Jennifer. And a better worker. But I underestimated my sister.

She is a very hard worker. I also overestimated my own tal-

ents. Im a good student and a fast learner, so I didn't think I

needed to pay attention in the training session or read the

training manual. I've learned that to be successful at a new

job you have to be prepared.

My first day of work was an evening shift. I arrived on

time at 6:00 to find the restaurant extremely busy. Some of

them were mad because it seemed as if they had been kept

waiting for some time. I wasn't sure what the prob'

was so busy that nobody saw w

I think this gives too much away. Write the second draft so that the reader can detect my arrogant attitude without being told.

Thesis statement sounds obvious . . . and flat.

I think it would be hard for the reader to visualize the chaos in the restaurant—need more images.

Find better word . . . busy is too vague.

Final Draft of "My First Job" by Katie Evered

My First Job

When I was 16, I got my first job working part-time at a Burgers Galore restaurant around the corner from my house. My older sister, Jennifer, already worked there. I used to watch with envy as she left the house looking spiffier than usual in her crisp, freshly laundered uniform. Now, it was my turn to enter the world of work: I could not wait.

Jennifer, as only an older sister could, had warned me about things that could go wrong, and I remember how upset she was when she spilled a large Coke all over a customer's white shirt, and when her cash register was short $200.00. But Jennifer's stories did not concern me; she is disorganized and clumsy, and she has to work hard to compensate for her lack of natural gifts. Besides, she had not had the benefit of an intensive training session as I had. True, I had not read the manual, and at times I had daydreamed when the trainer was talking, but that did not worry me because, unlike Jennifer, I am a fast learner.

I arrived at work promptly at 6:00 p.m. to find the restaurant in a state of chaos. Two lines of about 30 people snaked around the tables. I could hardly hear myself think above the screams of a hungry toddler and the loud tones of several angry customers. Six tense-looking staff members were tripping over one another to cope with the customers. No one noticed my arrival. Finally, a blond young man with a furrowed brow and a stiff back barked at me to get over to till number three.

"Oh, and bring your training manual with you," he added, "You're going to need it!"

My heart sank as I remembered that my training manual was sitting unopened on my desk at home.

At least 30 people surged toward my till. A scowling man with a round, red face complained that the delay was making him late

Your Turn

- Reread the beginning of the first draft of the student essay, "My First Job." What specific problems can you identify in the first draft? How have these problems been addressed in the final draft?

Starting New Paragraphs

Readers expect most stories, essays, and some reports and procedures to be divided into paragraphs. The beginning of a new paragraph tells the reader to expect a change. Specifically, use a new paragraph in the following instances:

- **To introduce a new topic.** Use a new paragraph when you move from one topic to another.

- **To change time or place.** Use a new paragraph when you change the setting, time, or place.

- **To emphasize a point.** If you want to emphasize a particular idea or event, you can put it in a paragraph by itself. Be careful when using this technique, because it can disrupt the flow of your essay.

- **To introduce dialogue.** If you are using dialogue, begin a new paragraph each time someone begins to speak or the speaker changes.

Use signal words such as *however*, *next*, and *finally* to link your paragraphs and give your writing coherence. See Tutorials 2 and 4 for more about coherence.

Writing Beginnings and Endings

Your beginnings and endings will vary, depending on the form of your writing. These can be the most difficult paragraphs to write, because, in many ways, they are the most important: your introduction should entice your readers to read more; your conclusion should leave them with a sense of completion and satisfaction.

Writing the Opening Paragraph

Your opening paragraph for an informational or persuasive essay or report should give the reader a roadmap to the rest of the piece. Somewhere in that paragraph, you should state your thesis. Other strategies to consider include the following:

- Ask a rhetorical question—a probing question to which you are not expecting an answer—to make a point or to set the stage for your thesis statement. The balance of your essay should then explore answers to the question.

- Begin with a key quotation or an unusual statistic or fact to provoke the reader's interest.

- Begin with an interesting anecdote that illustrates what you will discuss in the essay.

- Your opening paragraph for a story or personal essay should establish the setting, the mood, and the voice of the narrator.

Writing the Concluding Paragraph

Conclude your essay with a paragraph that returns to some of the elements in the introductory paragraph. Here are some strategies that may work for you:

- Restate your thesis using different words and from a new perspective gained from writing the essay.

- Answer the rhetorical question that you posed at the beginning of the essay or ask another rhetorical question that leads to your concluding comments.

- Challenge your readers to take action.

- Leave the reader with something more to ponder.

- If you started with an anecdote, refer to the same anecdote in your conclusion.

- If you started with a quotation, conclude with another quotation.

There are many ways to conclude a story: you could end it with the *denouement* phase of the plot, in which actions and motivations are explained; or you could end it with a sudden revelation or a twist; or, if you prefer, you could end your story in the middle of the action, explaining nothing and leaving it up to the reader to interpret the ending.

Your Turn

- Reread the final draft of "My First Job." What techniques does the student use to open her essay? What technique would you use to close her essay?

Writing Sentences

Your choices of sentence structure, details, and words will depend on your audience, and whether you want a high interest or *POW!* factor, a high degree of reader involvement, or a more dignified, objective approach to a very factual matter. In this section, we explore some things to keep in mind as you write and revise your sentences.

Using Variety in Sentence Structure

Any piece of writing that is interesting to read contains sentences of varying lengths and construction. Writing that lacks sentence variety tends to be monotonous to read.

Consider the following sentences, all of which are short and of the same simple construction:

The chaos finally subsided. There was a sudden lull. The manager asked me to take over the grill. The person operating it went on a well-earned break. The grill wasn't any easier to operate than the cash register.

Now consider the same sentences reconfigured into one longer sentence followed by one short one, both of which are constructed differently:

The chaos finally subsided, and, during the sudden lull, the manager asked me to take over the grill so the person operating it could go for a well-earned break. The grill wasn't any easier to operate than the cash register.

The following are examples of different types of sentences:

Simple sentence—one independent clause:

The chaos finally subsided.

Compound sentence—two independent clauses joined by one of the coordinating conjunctions *and, or, nor, for, but, yet,* or *so:*

The chaos finally subsided, and the manager asked me to take over the grill.

Complex sentence—one independent clause joined to one dependent clause by a subordinating conjunction, such as *after, although, as, because, before, during, however, if, since, that, when, where,* and *while:*

When the chaos subsided, the manager asked me to take over the grill.

Compound-complex sentence—a sentence containing at least two independent clauses and one or more dependent clauses:

During a sudden lull, the manager asked me to take over the grill, and the person operating it went for a well-earned break.

Interrogative sentences—these sentences express questions. In essays, questions can be used to set up topics, as in the following example from an essay on bees:

Have you ever wondered whether bees can communicate?

Exclamatory sentences—these sentences express dismay or surprise. When overused, exclamatory sentences can irritate readers, so use them sparingly both in essays and fiction. They are not suitable for reports, which typically have an impersonal, objective tone.

The manager asked me to take over the grill!

Imperative sentences—these sentences indicate commands. They are used most often in process essays, procedures, and instructions.

Turn off the electricity before you install the light fixture.

Using **compound** and **complex sentences**—allows you to combine ideas to add interest to your writing. Examine the blend of compound, complex, and compound-complex sentences in the brief paragraph below:

She had lost the medal, but she retained her dignity. As she crossed the finish line, she did not stagger, fall, cry out, or collapse into the waiting arms of her coach. She held her head high with her shoulders back and paced an extra hundred yards while she resumed her normal breathing.

Using Sentences to Create Style

Varying your sentences, as in the above examples, can improve your writing. Other artful approaches to sentence construction can engage your readers, such as using parallel structure, repetition, the periodic sentence, and sentence fragments.

Using Simple Sentences for Emphasis

Short, simple sentences can be used to make an idea stand out, to create a suspenseful mood, or to provide a dramatic effect. Consider the following examples of simple sentences:

Jonathan thought long and hard about innumerable careers that had crossed his mind at one time or another since he had been a little boy. Should he be a firefighter, a truck driver, or a computer programmer? Jonathan decided that only one career truly captured his longing for adventure. *He would serve his country.*

This simple sentence highlights the importance of Jonathan's decision, making it stand out from the previous sentences.

She bent her knees. Her fingers clutched the metal bar. She inhaled deeply. Perspiration dripped down her forehead. She straightened her back. She hoisted the heavy weight into the air. She held it aloft. *Victory was hers!*

This series of simple sentences emphasizes the dramatic second-by-second effort of weightlifting. Each sentence involves the reader in the painstaking process.

Using Parallel Structure to Create Balance

Parallelism is essential to good writing. When the structure of your writing is parallel, words and sentences are balanced and logical. Notice the difference between these two sentences:

Not parallel:

Derek became top student by listening intently in class, studying for four hours every day, and he gave up his part-time job.

Parallel:

Derek became top student by listening intently in class, studying for four hours every day, and giving up his part-time job.

Parallel structure and repetition can be used very effectively to add poetic rhythm to your writing. Consider the effect of parallel structure and repetition in part of the opening sentence of *A Tale of Two Cities* by Charles Dickens:

It was the best of times, it was the worst of times, it was the age of wisdom, it was the age of foolishness, it was the epoch of belief, it was the epoch of incredulity, it was the season of Light, it was the season of Darkness, it was the spring of hope, it was the winter of despair . . .

The following sentences demonstrate balanced structure: each part of the compound sentences has a parallel form:

I had thirsted for success, but I tasted only failure. I had longed to fulfill my heart's ambition, but I was forced to accept my soul's despair. I had expected to climb to the mountaintop of my profession, but I had stumbled into the valley of enforced labour.

For details about using parallel structure in lists and headings, see Tutorial 23, Chapter 12, on reports.

Using the Periodic Sentence to Create Interest

A periodic sentence is a specialized construction in which the independent clause is placed near the end of the sentence in order to keep the reader's interest and to create suspense. Only when you have read to the end do you have a complete sense of the meaning of the sentence. In the example below, the verb is in italics:

Along neon-lit streets, around busy corners, down narrow, littered alleys, into the dark corner of a neighbourhood park, heart racing as wildly as his feet, the desperate young man *ran*.

Using Sentence Fragments for Effect

Sentence fragments are normally considered a major error in sentence construction because they do not represent a complete thought. However, a capable writer may wish to use a fragment for effect. Fragments may represent half-finished thoughts of a distracted character or a snappy response to a significant question, but more often they are used for emphasis or dramatic effect. Just be certain that you understand why you are using the fragment. Here are some highlighted examples of the use of fragments:

Finally, after many long, dreary months of drifting upon the cold sea, the ship reached the Atlantic coast of Canada. *Home at last*.

He thinks he's going to pin this one on me, make me take the rap for his crime, make me do the time for a deed I never did? *Fat chance*.

Note the colloquial street language of the second example. The fragment works well here because it gives you insight into the personality of the narrator.

Your Turn

- Reread a recent piece of writing you did for English or another subject.
  - Did you use varied sentences? Could you make some sentences more sophisticated or predominant by combining them to create a compound or complex sentence? Would simple, emphatic sentences be more effective?

  - Have you used parallel structure? Can you find a sentence where you could use this construction?

  - Could you add drama, excitement, or emphasis by using a specialized sentence structure such as a periodic sentence or a fragment?

- Reread the first draft of "My First Job." How could the student writer have improved her sentence structure and created variety?

Using the Active Voice

The voice of a verb tells you whether a subject acts or is acted upon. There are two voices: active and passive. In an active sentence, the subject is the actor; in a passive sentence, the subject is acted upon.

Active sentence:

The Allies defeated Germany.

Passive sentence:

Germany was defeated by the Allies.

Active sentences are stronger than passive sentences, but the passive voice is useful if you want to emphasize the receiver of the action. It is the only choice when you do not know the subject, as in the following example:

Asbestos was found in the ceiling of the gymnasium.

When possible, use the active voice in your writing. It is more direct and engaging than the passive voice. Essays, reports, and stories that are written in the passive voice typically make for dull reading.

Choosing the Right Words

Throughout this book we have emphasized that word choice is crucial to a writer's success. Your choice of words should enable your readers to create images in their minds. As you have learned, the most successful images appeal to at least some of the five senses; they are also specific rather than general and precise rather than vague. Reread the two drafts of the student essay, "My First Job." Notice how in the final draft the student uses specific sensory images so that her readers can imagine the scene in the restaurant that she describes. Below is an example from the first and final drafts. Can you find any more?

First draft:

I arrived on time at 6:00 to find the restaurant extremely busy. Some of them were mad because it seemed as if they had been kept waiting for some time.

Final draft:

I arrived at work promptly at 6:00 p.m. to find the restaurant in a state of chaos. Two lines of about 30 people snaked around the tables. I could hardly hear myself think above the screams of a hungry toddler and the loud tones of several angry customers. Six tense-looking staff members were tripping over one another to cope with the customers.

 ## Writing and Revising Subsequent Drafts

Writing can be a messy process, often requiring several drafts before you are satisfied that you have stated things in exactly the right way. You may wish to throw out most of what you wrote in your first draft, or you may wish to remove or add sentences, rearrange paragraphs, add more research evidence, or add a transitional sentence at the conclusion of each paragraph to make the ideas flow better.

Almost no one writes something perfectly the first time. Just as an artist does several sketches before putting paint to canvas, or a filmmaker does many takes of a scene to produce a seamless movie, so a writer must also draft and redraft a piece of writing until it achieves the desired effect with the target audience. Sometimes repositioning a single word, phrase, or punctuation mark can make a big difference. Consider the following variations on a sentence:

Version 1:
The couple reunited after 25 years apart in an airport lounge.

Version 2:
After 25 years apart, the couple reunited in an airport lounge.

When you read the first version, you might think that the couple spent 25 years living in different parts of an airport lounge. However, when you read the second version, you understand that the airport lounge was simply the scene of the couple's reunion after they had spent 25 years apart. Here, the placement of a key phrase at the beginning of the sentence and the addition of a punctuation mark clarifies the idea and aids the reader's understanding.

The revision process consists of three stages:

- **Revising.** This stage refers to large structural changes you make to your paragraphs or essay. It might even include scrapping your essay and starting over.

- **Editing.** This stage refers to changes you make at the sentence level. You may wish to restructure sentences to make their meaning clearer. You may wish to provide greater variety in sentence structure to add impact to ideas and keep your reader's interest, or simply to correct sentence mistakes.

- **Proofreading.** This stage comes at the end of the process when you pore over your work to ensure that every word and punctuation mark is in place. Proofreading is done once you have revised and edited your work.

Although editing and proofreading come at the final stages of the writing process, most people correct errors as they find them, even during the earlier stages of revision.

Your Turn

- Reread your last writing assignment for a subject other than English. Imagine that you are someone who knows nothing about the topic. Is your writing easily understood? Have you defined terms and provided background? Are your ideas clear?

- Now ask one of your family members or someone who knows little about this topic to read your piece of writing and give you an opinion about its clarity.

 Revising Your Work with Writing Partners

You should always write with your purpose and audience in mind. Thus, when you are revising your work, it is particularly helpful to work with one or more writing partners or peer editors. Writing partners provide you with an instant audience to give you feedback on the clarity, correctness, and voice of your writing. Keep the following guidelines in mind when choosing and working with writing partners or peer editors:

- **Choose your partners carefully.** Think about your particular strengths and needs as well as the strengths and needs of your partners. You can complement or complete each other's abilities. For example, you may be a creative person with imagination and many ideas but a terrible speller. Find a partner who may need help with ideas, but who can spot spelling and other errors. Seek out another partner who has just as many ideas as you do but perhaps a different point of view that can inform and strengthen your writing. In a classroom situation, the teacher may sometimes assign peer editors or facilitate this process by providing a block of time for revising and editing conferences.

- **Ask your partners to consider the big picture.** Your partners should first react to the ideas in your writing and to the overall tone. Are the ideas clear? Have you made your case with sufficient proof or illustrations? Is the tone what you want it to be—persuasive, friendly, or matter-of-fact? Or does your tone sound sarcastic, bullying, rude, or even offensive and condescending? Make your partners aware of your specific audience and your need to connect to that audience with both ideas and voice.

- **Do not expect your partners to correct all your errors.** You are responsible for making any necessary corrections, changes, and additions. Ask your writing partners to indicate sentences that seem overly choppy, too long and involved, or unclear. Ask them to underline words that may be misspelled and to circle places where punctuation may be required.

- **Spend time discussing your (and their) work.** Often, through talking, you can clarify and extend your ideas. If discussion time is unavailable, ask each of your partners to write one clear statement about something strong in your writing, and one statement about something that needs to be revised. Do the same for them. These statements allow you to build on your strengths in your future writing and to deal with your problem areas. You might even wish to keep track of your strengths and needs on a Personal Writing Profile recording sheet such as the one on the following page.

The value of writing partners cannot be overstated. One of the most famous writing partnerships was between poets T.S. Eliot and Ezra Pound. When Eliot gave Pound his poem "The Waste Land" to read, Pound recommended that Eliot cut more than a hundred lines from the poem. Eliot trusted and followed Pound's advice, paying tribute to Pound's contribution at the beginning of the poem, alluding to him as "the better craftsman."

PERSONAL WRITING PROFILE—NAME:		
DATE/WRITING ASSIGNMENT	STRENGTH AREAS	AREAS REQUIRING DEVELOPMENT

Your Turn

- Consider the people in your own life who might be good writing partners. What are their strengths? What can they offer you? What strengths can you offer them?

- Ask your writing partners to be tough critics. If they spot the weaknesses in your writing and give you some key feedback, your final product will be all the better.

Making Changes to Your Work

Once you have received feedback and suggestions from your writing partners, you can begin reworking your writing assignment. You will find that the more you write, and the more you discuss writing with other writers, the more you will enjoy the revision process. It is very satisfying to rework a piece of writing until it says just what you want it to say and has just the effect on the reader that you were hoping to achieve. Here are some ideas for how to respond to suggestions from your writing partners:

- **Do not be afraid to throw things out.** Go ahead and eliminate sentences or paragraphs if your writing partners/peer editors feel that they do not work.

Sometimes you may like a sentence so much or have worked so hard to craft it that you do not want to lose it, but it may not work in a particular piece of writing. Add it to your idea book for future reference.

- **Consider meeting with your teacher.** Schedule a conference with the teacher if you are uncertain about where to go next or if your writing assignment seems to be an all-round disaster. The teacher can help, but be prepared to spend the time required to get assistance.

- **Always proofread your work.** When you have finished revising and editing your work, always read it over to check for errors; sometimes your brain works faster than you can write or type and you may omit words, phrases, or sentences. You may also have introduced spelling and punctuation errors during the revision process. Ask one of your writing partners to do a final proofreading of your written work. If you are handwriting your assignment, indicate additions with a caret—an inverted v like this ∧ —with the word written above it (see page 294). Make corrections by putting a single stroke through a word and writing the correct version above it.

Editing for Grammar, Punctuation, and Usage

The final stages in the revision process are editing and proofreading. As mentioned earlier, when you edit and proofread, you focus on sentences, words, and punctuation rather than on ideas and paragraph structure. One way to ensure that your grammar, usage, and punctuation are correct is to consult a handbook when you are editing your work. Handbooks lay out rules for grammar, usage, and punctuation and provide examples of correct form. Some handbooks also show you incorrect examples and common errors. The boxes on pages 308 to 309 contain two checklists for you to use when you are editing your work: the first is a grammar checklist and the second is a punctuation checklist. At the end of this chapter, you will find a Glossary of Usage (pages 316 to 319).

Grammar Checklist

SENTENCES

❏ Do all my sentences have subjects and verbs?

❏ Have I eliminated all fragments (except any I am using for emphasis)?

❏ Have I fixed any run-on sentences?

❏ Have I used subordinate and coordinate phrases and clauses for emphasis and variety?

❏ Have I used pronouns correctly?

❏ Have I put modifiers next to the words they are describing?

❏ Have I avoided dangling modifiers by including the subject in the sentence?

❏ Have I used adverbs and adjectives correctly and effectively?

SUBJECT–VERB AGREEMENT

❏ Have I used singular verbs with singular subjects, and plural verbs with plural subjects?

❏ Do my subjects and verbs agree in the following tricky constructions: with *or;* with *either . . . or, neither . . . nor, not . . . but;* with the word *each;* and with collective nouns such as *team, family,* and *audience?*

VERBS

❏ Have I used correct verb forms?

❏ Have I used the principal parts of irregular verbs correctly?

❏ Have I kept my verb tenses consistent?

❏ Have I used the present tense to write about literature?

❏ Have I chosen active rather than passive verb forms?

❏ Have I used the present perfect tense when expressing general truths?

❏ Have I used the present perfect tense when summarizing an author's views?

❏ Have I used the past perfect tense to express an action already completed at some time in the past?

PRONOUNS

❏ Have I used the correct pronoun form—subject or object?

❏ Have I used pronouns consistently, without mixing up first, second, and third person?

❏ Do my pronouns agree with their antecedents, both in gender and in number?

❏ Have I avoided sexist language by using the third-person plural?

❏ Have I used *who, whom, whoever, whomever, that,* and *which* correctly?

Punctuation Checklist

END PUNCTUATION

❑ Have I used periods and question marks correctly?

❑ Have I been correct but judicious in my use of exclamation marks?

QUOTATION MARKS

❑ Have I used quotation marks to set off dialogue, short passages of quoted material, and titles of short stories, poems, magazine articles, essays, and parts of books?

❑ Have I remembered to always use closing quotation marks?

COMMAS AND DASHES

❑ Have I used commas to separate items in a series?

❑ Have I used commas to separate words, phrases, or clauses that precede an independent clause?

❑ Have I placed commas between two independent clauses joined by *and, but, or, for, yet, so,* and *nor*?

❑ Have I used dashes to set off items I want to emphasize?

SEMICOLONS AND COLONS

❑ Have I used semicolons to replace periods when joining independent clauses that show cause and effect?

❑ Have I used colons after independent clauses when I am introducing an example, a list, or a quotation?

APOSTROPHES

❑ Have I used the correct form of the possessive?

❑ Have I used apostrophes correctly with contractions?

PARENTHESES, BRACKETS, AND ELLIPSES

❑ Have I used parentheses to set off supplementary information, personal digressions, and afterthoughts?

❑ Have I used parentheses to enclose references?

❑ Have I used brackets to enclose words or phrases inserted into a quotation?

❑ Have I used ellipses to indicate missing words in a quotation?

Troubleshooting Guide

This guide explains some of the most common grammar and punctuation errors and contains advice on how to correct them.

Problem 1: Sentence Fragments

A sentence fragment is a group of words that is punctuated like a sentence but is not a complete sentence. A sentence represents a complete thought, whereas a sentence fragment represents only a partial thought. In most cases, sentence fragments lack a verb or a subject. In others, they consist of only a dependent clause.

Problem: Rosie spent hours preparing the food for the party. But accidentally used salt instead of sugar in the lemon mousse. Imagine her horror. When her guests started choking on dessert.

Solution: Rosie spent hours preparing the food for the party, but she accidentally used salt instead of sugar in the lemon mousse. Imagine her horror when her guests started choking on dessert.

TIPS FOR TROUBLESHOOTING FRAGMENTS

- To detect a missing subject, ask yourself who the subject of the sentence is. If the answer is a missing word, your sentence might be a fragment.

- To detect a missing verb, ask yourself what the subject is doing. If you cannot find the answer within the sentence, chances are your sentence is a fragment.

- When you find a fragment, try connecting it to the thought that precedes or follows it.

Problem 2: Run-On Sentences

A run-on sentence is the opposite of a sentence fragment. Where a fragment contains an incomplete thought, a run-on sentence contains too many thoughts. A run-on sentence is missing the punctuation that should separate one thought from another.

Problem: The roads were slippery, Ryan lost control of his car before he knew what was happening he was upside down in the ditch, luckily he was wearing his seatbelt.

Solution 1: The roads were slippery when Ryan lost control of his car. Before he knew what was happening, he was upside down in the ditch. Luckily, he was wearing his seatbelt.

Solution 2: The roads were slippery. Ryan lost control of his car and, before he knew what was happening, was upside down in the ditch; luckily, he was wearing his seatbelt.

> **TIPS FOR TROUBLESHOOTING RUN-ON SENTENCES**
> - Use conjunctions (words such as *and, but, or, yet, because, during, since*) to join two separate thoughts in a complete sentence.
> - Highlight ideas you want to emphasize in short, separate sentences.
> - Use a period or a semicolon to punctuate a run-on sentence. If you connect two complete thoughts with only a semicolon, the sentences must have a clear, logical relationship.

Problem 3: Verb Tense Inconsistencies

In a longer piece of writing such as an essay or a report, it is easy to shift accidentally into another tense. Sometimes, of course, you have to change tenses for meaning, but try to avoid abrupt, unnecessary changes—they can make for awkward reading.

Problem: After he leaves the house, Raj walked to the bus stop.

Solution: After he left the house, Raj walked to the bus stop.

> **TIPS FOR TROUBLESHOOTING VERB TENSE INCONSISTENCIES**
> - Choose one tense in which to write your essay.
> - Do not change tense unless the meaning requires it.
> - Find verb tense inconsistencies by proofreading every verb in every sentence.

Problem 4: Vague Pronoun References

A pronoun is a substitute for a noun. The noun that the pronoun replaces is called an *antecedent*. Readers become confused when they cannot figure out the antecedent that the pronoun replaces.

Problem: Tien saw Jeff in the hallway. He told him he wasn't sure how he had done on the exam. Melanie stopped them outside the school to ask how they had done. They walked home.

Solution: Tien saw Jeff in the hallway, and he told Jeff he wasn't sure how he had done on the exam. Melanie stopped them outside the school to ask how they had done. The three of them walked home.

TIPS FOR TROUBLESHOOTING VAGUE PRONOUN REFERENCES

- Replace the pronoun with the correct noun.

- Rephrase the sentence so that there is no confusion about which noun the pronoun replaces.

Problem 5: Subject–Verb Disagreement—Compound Subjects

A compound subject is made up of two or more nouns or pronouns joined by *or, nor,* or *and*. In sentences that have compound subjects, it may not be clear whether the verb should be plural or singular. See the tips below for clarification.

Problem: The vegetarian casserole and the salmon is unavailable.
Solution: The vegetarian casserole and the salmon are unavailable.

Problem: Either the roast beef or the rack of lamb are delicious.
Solution: Either the roast beef or the rack of lamb is delicious.

Problem: Neither the melon nor the tomatoes is ripe.
Solution: Neither the melon nor the tomatoes are ripe.

TIPS FOR TROUBLESHOOTING SUBJECT-VERB DISAGREEMENT—COMPOUND SUBJECTS

- Do not assume that if your sentence sounds right, the subject and verb agree. For each of your sentences, identify the subject and verb and make sure they agree.

- When editing and proofreading your work, watch for compound subjects and constructions that include *neither . . . nor* and *either . . . or*.

- Remember that when a compound subject is joined by *and*, you always use a plural verb.

- Remember that when a compound subject is joined by *or* or *nor*, the verb must agree with the subject to which it is closest.

Spelling and Usage

Consider the abilities that good spellers have and the strategies they use:

- Good spellers can take a mental photograph of a word and keep it in their heads.

- Good spellers can use the sounds of words to predict which letters are in that word.

- Good spellers do a lot of reading and recognize the correct spelling of unusual words because they see them over and over again when they read.

- Good spellers associate words because of their element of common meaning; for example, *triplets, tricycle, triangle,* and *triad* all refer to things that come in threes or have three parts to them.

- Good spellers associate words by their letter pattern; for example, *eight, freight, weight.*

- Good spellers learn the rules of spelling.

- Good spellers create memory devices for the really tricky words; for example, "The <u>villain</u> enjoyed his *villa in* the hills" or "I say BR in February."

- Good spellers check catalogues, correspondence, directories, or dictionaries to ensure that they have spelled specialized product or business names, or the surnames of company officials correctly.

Consider the Spelling Rules chart on page 314. Do you find any of the words in the example column difficult to spell? If so, try making up a rhyme for the appropriate rule.

Your Turn

- Make a log of spelling errors you have made on writing assignments. You may wish to return to assignments you have done already and add words to your log.

- Analyze the types of errors you are making. Are you making the same errors every time? Are you a phonetic speller, sounding out words, but representing letter combinations differently from the word's true spelling? Can you review some common patterns, homonyms, or rules to help your spelling?

SPELLING RULES	
RULE	EXAMPLES
1. Use *i* before *e*	achieve, believe, relieve, field, shield, yield, pier, piece
• except after *c*	ceiling, receive, deceive, receipt, deceit
• or when sounded like *a* as in *neigbour* or *weigh*	weight, neigh, sleigh, vein, skein
2. *I, y,* and *e* • soften *c* and *g*	cedar, Celsius, civil, cinder, cynic, gerbil, gender, ginger, Regina, gyroscope, gymnast
3. When adding a suffix, change *y* to *i* but never write *ii*.	happy → happiness, cry → cries, beauty → beautiful, try → trying, satisfy → satisfying, cry → crying
4. If the final *e* is not pronounced, drop it when you add a suffix beginning with a vowel.	wave → waving, admire → admiration note → noted (-*ed* was the added ending here)
• Keep the final *e* when you add an ending that begins with a consonant.	awe → awesome, use → useful, safe → safety, nice → nicely
5. When you add a suffix such as -*ed* or -*ing* to a word that ends in a consonant, double the consonant: – if it is a one-syllable word with a short vowel sound – if the final syllable is stressed – if the first syllable is stressed, do not double the final consonant.	tap → tapped, hop → hopping, scar → scarred control → controlled, prefer → preferred focus → focused, travel → traveled, model → modeled
6. To make nouns plural, you generally add -*s* or -*es*.	bank → banks, bench → benches, country → countries
• If a word ends in -*y*, change the *y* to *i* and add *es*	There are exceptions: for example, if the *y* is preceded by a vowel, simply add *s,* as in monkeys, attorneys.
7. Learn to spell irregular plurals through experience and from observing them as you read.	tooth → teeth, woman → women, child → children, ox → oxen

How Can I Improve My Spelling?

1. Decide that spelling is important because it says something about you.

2. Practise some of the strategies of good spellers listed on page 313.

3. Use computerized spell checks and dictionaries.

4. Check the spelling of proper or official names.

5. Learn spelling rules. Seven rules are summarized in the box on page 314.

Publishing Your Written Work

In order to share your writing with an audience of readers, you must publish it in a pleasing, legible format. If you have used a word processing program for your writing, you will find it easy to print a good final draft. You may wish to think about a number of features and formats, depending on your audience:

- Which font style best suits the piece of writing? If you have written a story about times past, you may wish to use a Gothic or Old English font for at least the first capital letter in each paragraph. If you were writing for children, you might want to choose Century Schoolbook or Chalkdust font. If you have written a serious proposal to send to a politician, use a more conservative font such as Times New Roman or Arial.

- Which font size would best suit your audience? If you are writing for senior citizens, use 14- or 16-point size. If you are writing for young children, use 18- or 20-point size. Otherwise, 12-point size is usually a safe bet.

- Computer word processing programs usually allow you to insert symbols, pictures, charts, or graphs. Consider situations where these would be appropriate. You might wish to include diagrams or graphs for a report for science or geography. For details about graphics, see Chapter 10.

- Computer word processing programs also allow you to use bold, italics, underlining, and other features so that you can emphasize certain aspects of your writing. These are particularly useful for reports. See Chapter 12 for more details.

- If you are creating a class newspaper or anthology, work with a group of other students to edit and format your group creation. Use computer publishing software to lay out brochures, flyers, or newspaper columns. Use tables with or without gridlines, or choose column formats to organize and to add interest to your work.

Publishing Class Assignments

If you are publishing an essay, report, procedure, or another piece of writing as an assignment, always find out your teacher's requirements. Otherwise, here are a few general guidelines to follow:

- **Paper.** Print your assignment on plain, white $8\frac{1}{2} \times 11$ (21.5 cm × 28 cm) paper. If you are handwriting your assignment, write neatly on every other line and on one side of the paper only. Number all the pages in your paper, and be sure to keep a copy of your assignment.

- **References.** Include a Works Cited list on a new page at the back of your paper. See pages 171 to 175 for information on how to prepare a Works Cited list.

- **Title.** Attach a separate title page that includes your name, the name of your teacher, the title of your assignment, and the date.

- **Spacing and margins.** Whether you are typing or writing, always double-space your assignment. Leave at least a one-inch (2.5-cm) margin.

Just as your appearance at a job interview should project an image of professionalism, so should your written work. Publishing may be the last stage in the writing process, but it makes the first impression on your reader. So take a little extra time to make that first impression a good one.

Glossary of Usage

Learn to distinguish between words that sound or look alike. Study the examples below to better understand the meaning and use of these pairs of words. Check word meanings in a dictionary if you are still uncertain.

WORD PAIRS	EXAMPLE	MEANING
accept *except*	I accept your proposal. Everyone may attend the assembly except Gerry.	• to agree to • leaving out
adapt *adopt*	The novelist will adapt her work for a movie screenplay. The couple decided to adopt a second child. The committee adopted the motion.	• to change from one form to another • to become parents to a child through legal proceedings • to vote to accept

Continued on next page

WORD PAIRS	EXAMPLE	MEANING
choose	The draw to choose the winner will be held on Friday.	• to make a choice
chose	The coach chose me to be on the volleyball team.	• past tense of the verb *choose*
climatic	The climatic conditions this summer were very poor for growing strawberries.	• referring to the climate, the weather conditions
climactic	The climactic moment in the play occurred when Macduff slew Macbeth.	• referring to the most exciting moment when the action turns; the adjective form of *climax*
coarse	Use coarse salt for making dill pickles.	• larger, less refined
course	The restaurant served a five-course meal to celebrate its opening.	• one plate or serving
	The runner stayed on the course and won the race.	• the path or direction
compliment	It was a great compliment to have my writing praised by a professional editor.	• praise, tribute
complement	The tart raspberry sauce is a perfect complement to the sweet chocolate mousse.	• something that completes or balances another thing
desert	A mother would never desert her children.	• to leave behind
	They came upon an oasis in the desert.	• terrain of sand or arid soil with little vegetation or water
dessert	Did you order the caramel pecan cheesecake for dessert?	• the final course of most meals

Continued on next page

WORD PAIRS	EXAMPLE	MEANING
eminent	She is an eminent scholar of Austen's work, well respected by her colleagues.	• prominent, famous, respected
imminent	The school children were kept indoors for recess because the thunderstorm was imminent.	• about to occur
emigrate	He will emigrate from Canada to Australia later this month.	• leave a country
immigrate	Rajiv's grandparents immigrated to Canada from India 25 years ago.	• arrive in a country
farther	She was able to run two kilometres farther than I could.	• greater distance
further	This decision will require further discussion.	• a greater figurative or imaginary distance
lead	Please use a lead pencil to fill the bubbles on this form.	• an ordinary pencil having a graphite ore
led	She led the children from the flaming building to safety.	• past tense of *to lead* meaning to guide or conduct
loose	The door handle was loose and would not turn.	• not tight
lose	Do not lose the money I gave you for lunch.	• to misplace
passed	I passed my driver's test on the first try.	• verb—to succeed
	She passed that same old house every day of the week.	• verb—to go by
past	For the past six years, I have lived in this small town.	• adjective describing time gone by

Continued on next page

WORD PAIRS	EXAMPLE	MEANING
principal *principle*	The principals in the musical will be named tomorrow morning. Wesley's guiding principle was to do all the good he could.	• main or most important characters, person of authority • rule or standard, especially of good behaviour
site *sight* *cite*	The construction site was surrounded by decoratively painted hoardings. She lost the sight in her right eye in an industrial accident. He could cite poetry for every occasion.	• a particular place or position • ability to see • to quote or state
stationary *stationery*	He rode a stationary bicycle every day for exercise. The manager reordered the company stationery with the new address on the envelopes and paper.	• fixed, not moving • paper and envelopes
than *then*	She is taller than I am. First we went dancing at a nightclub. Then we went home.	• a conjunction used to compare two things. You do not say, "Terry is faster than me," because the verb is implied. Say rather, "Terry is faster than I [am]." • adverb indicating time

Oral Communication Power Tools

Good Oral Communication Skills

The Conference Board of Canada, and other organizations that track the skills required for today's workplace, list communication skills as one of the top four prerequisites employers look for in prospective employees. Use the checklist below to do an inventory of your own oral communication skills, and then compare your skills with those required for (a) university, college, or other postsecondary education, and (b) your planned workplace.

INVENTORY OF ORAL COMMUNICATION SKILLS

		YES	NO
1.	I am comfortable contributing ideas and responding to questions one on one.	☐	☐
2.	I am comfortable contributing ideas and responding to questions in a group.	☐	☐
3.	I can summarize the main points of a discussion after participating in it.	☐	☐
4.	I listen carefully to understand ideas presented and sort them in their order of importance.	☐	☐
5.	I can organize material coherently for oral presentations.	☐	☐
6.	I choose effective examples and lead listeners to logical conclusions in discussions and presentations.	☐	☐
7.	I vary my voice and pacing to engage my listeners during presentations.	☐	☐
8.	I use visual aids and technology such as overheads or PowerPoint to strengthen my presentations and make my message clear.	☐	☐
9.	I allow opportunities for follow-up questions during or after my presentations.	☐	☐
10.	I know and follow accepted protocol for meetings—e.g., waiting my turn, not interrupting other speakers, and directing questions and responses to the chairperson.	☐	☐

Based on your responses to the checklist above, identify areas where you need to improve your communication skills. Read through the sections on Participating in Group Discussions and Oral Presentations to find ideas about how you can improve your oral communication skills.

Speaking and Listening in Groups

Each day you speak with, and listen to, others. At home, you exchange questions and answers with parents, hold conversations with friends, and talk on the telephone to make plans.

In situations beyond home and friends, you must also be an attentive listener or a deliberate speaker. Consider these examples:

- You attend an information session about college and university applications and deadlines.
- You listen to a seminar discussion in history class on the differences between Canada's major political parties.
- You decide to run for student council president and must make an election speech.
- You are a member of a small group in English class that must prepare and present an analysis of a recent poem by a Canadian poet.

These situations require you to demonstrate a variety of speaking and listening skills. Knowing what these skills are and improving them through practice in groups will give you effective communication tools that will benefit you throughout life.

Listening for Main Ideas and Relevant Details

In any conversation or speech, there are ideas that speakers wish to convey or listeners wish to hear. Speakers strive to state positions or facts. Clearly listeners often assess how the speaker's words affect his or her own position. For example, in an information session about college and university applications, a speaker would clearly and thoroughly explain the necessary application procedures, as well as the opportunities for students. A listener would try to determine the relevant details for his or her situation: "What do I need to complete this process? What is the deadline for completing the application?"

Most speakers attempt to provide verbal signals to alert their listeners to main ideas or important details. To hear main ideas and key details, listen actively for signal phrases such as

- My main point is ...
- Take note of ...
- This information is significant.
- Key details to remember are ...
- There are three main points I want to make. First ...
- Do not forget ...
- Let me say again ...

Your Turn

- Listen to an on-air exchange between the host and a caller on a radio talk show. After the conversation, turn down the volume and in your mind create one sentence to sum up the main ideas you heard.

- In the classroom, listen to see if the teacher uses some of the key phrases listed on page 321.

Listen carefully, as speakers often state their main ideas early in their remarks and summarize key points in their conclusions

Clarifying and Extending the Ideas of Others

Communicating ideas between two or more people can be tricky. The speaker intends to express a particular thought, but the listener's reception of those thoughts may be affected by a number of things:

- diction—choice of vocabulary

- background knowledge or experience that is different from the speaker's

- the expectation that the speaker will say something different

- poor listening conditions, making it difficult to hear the speaker

For these reasons, it is important for the listener to clarify any misunderstanding about the speaker's words. Think of the communication process as a continuous loop:

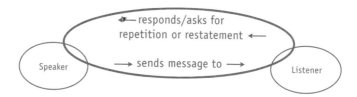

Effective communication requires feedback, an exchange between speaker and listener that indicates that meaning is shared and understood. To clarify the message or ideas of the speaker, the listener may try a number of strategies:

- **Repetition.** If the listener did not hear the speaker, he or she may wish to ask the speaker to repeat the entire message.

- **Clarification.** If the listener did not know some of the words in the message, he or she can ask the speaker, "What do you mean by . . . ?"

- **Interpretation.** If the listener did not understand why the speaker said certain things, because of differences in background or experience, he or she can ask the speaker, "Why did you say that?" or "Why do you think (or feel) that way?"

An active listener will invite the speaker to extend ideas in a conversation in some of the following ways:

- **Asking for more.** You can ask the speaker to provide more details or illustrations. In this case, you can say, "Tell me more," or "Help me understand you better."

- **Restating.** You can get a speaker to extend his or her thoughts simply by restating or paraphrasing parts of his or her last statement. For example, if a friend tells you that she had a big argument with her sister and is very upset, you can paraphrase, "So, you really feel upset about last night."

- **Looking involved.** You can indicate your interest in the speaker's thoughts by leaning forward and looking involved.

- **Disagreeing.** You may wish to extend the thoughts of the speaker by disagreeing. You can say, "Let me tell you why I don't agree" or "I feel differently about this matter."

4) Using Appropriate Language

Using appropriate language in oral communication means that you understand and respect your listener and his or her needs. With friends, your tone can be casual, familiar, and colloquial. You would not, for example, address your friends by saying, "Ladies and gentlemen, we must discuss something." This sentence has a formal tone suitable for the chairperson of a meeting. You might say, "Hey, what's up? Phone me later." This is *colloquial*—common, everyday—language and is appropriate for most casual conversations.

In some situations you will need to use formal or specialized language that is appropriate to the subject of discussion. This will often occur in the classroom, where you must use language suitable to the topic of discussion to demonstrate your familiarity with the subject. For example, in a discussion of poetry you would use the words *metaphor*, *personification*, and *rhythm*. When talking about chemistry, you would use words such as *element*, *compound*, *catalyst*, and *reaction*. Similarly, in a business situation, you may have to learn a particular vocabulary to share a level of understanding and communication with the other employees.

Each workplace has its own terminology. In marketing, for example, words such as *teleconference*, *contact report*, *on-time delivery*, and *point of purchase* are part of everyday language. In the service department of an auto dealership, words such as *torque*, *alignment*, and *suspension* are common.

Participating in Group Work

Knowing how to be an effective group participant will serve you well now and in the future. Group discussions are a fact of life in many businesses and industries. They are used in brainstorming problem situations, planning courses of action, and reaching agreements on goals and procedures. Group dynamics allow people to bring their prior knowledge and points of view to a situation. The result is a broader perspective, multiple ideas, and better-informed decisions.

Group work is also an important feature of your secondary school classes, and of college and university education. You have probably been asked to work through problem-solving exercises in business or mathematics class, analyze poems or stories in English class, give group presentations in law class, or prepare debates for history class. At college or university it is common practice for individual students or small groups to lead seminar discussions on text chapters or to present course topics.

Initial organization within a group is a key to creating a successful group product. A common complaint of committed group members is that they are burdened with the majority of the work while uncommitted members do little. It makes sense to understand and assign group roles when the group first meets. To do this, you need to have a sense of effective group roles and mechanisms for discovering the capabilities of different group members. It is also helpful to have a means of gaining group consensus in case group members disagree about how to proceed or what goals to set.

Your Turn

- The next time you are involved in a telephone discussion with a friend, try to be conscious of the number of times you have to say, "Pardon" or "Could you please repeat that?" Analyze the communication breakdown: Are you listening carefully enough? Is your friend speaking loudly enough? Is there a vocabulary barrier? Is there a difference of background knowledge and experience that makes it difficult for you to understand your friend's situation?

- During small-group work in the classroom, try to get various group members to extend their thoughts by paraphrasing part of the last sentence they said or by saying, "Tell me more."

Assigning Roles for Group Members

Here are some suggestions for assigning roles in a discussion or problem-solving group. These roles should be assumed by different individuals on different days.

- **Administrator.** This person collects items needed by the group to create their final product—for example, chart paper, markers, overheads—and returns any items at the end of the group activity. The administrator also keeps track of the time allocated for the activity, providing reminders of the time remaining, and records task assignments for each group member.

- **Chair.** This person manages the group discussion, making sure that each person has an opportunity to speak, that speakers are heard in turn, and that group members stay on topic. The chair also keeps track of the last significant point made so that if group members do get off track, the chair can provide a reminder of what was said most recently.

- **Researcher.** This person finds background information, looks up terms or specific vocabulary, checks dates, and so forth.

- **Scribe or secretary.** This person makes a summary of the meaningful talk of the group, such as brainstorming, decisions, priorities, or the group report.

- **Reporter.** This person shares the small group's analysis, report, decisions, or priorities with the larger group.

Assigning Tasks and Responsibilities in Groups

If the group work will occur over a period of days or weeks, or the group task involves the compilation of researched information, not just discussion, tasks should be assigned according to the strengths and interests of the group members. It is crucial to the effectiveness of any group presentation that all members complete their tasks to deadline.

- Using the chair and scribe roles described above, brainstorm the topic, its scope, and various aspects with all group members, recording subtopics and relevant details. The chair should ensure that each person truly feels a part of the group and has an opportunity to contribute.

- The chair asks each group member to commit to researching one subtopic and sets a timeline for initial research to be brought back to the group. Anyone expressing no preference is assigned a task.

- Group members take notes of the brainstorming details that are significant to their assigned research.

- The chair schedules another group meeting within a reasonable time to consider the research and set new direction and tasks. Each group member should share researched information so that all members can understand the entire topic and get a sense of how to present it best. For a good group product, each member must fulfill the research responsibilities assigned.

- The chair asks each group member to commit to creating a portion of the presentation or panel discussion based on the research. Group members may choose to work as partners in this task. The chair asks all group members to agree to a reasonable deadline within the time assigned by the teacher.

- The chair calls one more meeting of the group to ensure that each member is ready and understands the sequence of the presentation. Members can rehearse their presentation.

Contributing Information in a Group

Group dynamics can be exciting, as many people have ideas at the same time. But as they build on each other's ideas, every member of a group should have an opportunity to participate. A good group chair will ensure that there is an orderly discussion and that each person gets a chance to contribute opinions and ideas. The chair can accomplish these goals in three ways:

- Wait until the initial energetic discussion subsides, and then invite anyone who has not yet spoken to make a contribution.

- Use a *round robin* approach with each group member having an opportunity to speak.

- Keep a *speaker's list*, writing down the name of each person who indicates he or she would like to speak, and then adding the names of anyone who has not yet had an opportunity.

Reaching Group Decisions

In any group situation where members have different backgrounds, knowledge, and opinions, it is likely that disagreements will arise. These disagreements must be settled quickly, and consensus reached around a course of action, so that the group can accomplish its tasks within the allotted time. Two methods are commonly used to settle disagreements and reach consensus. In a *simple vote*, the majority decision is accepted by all as direction for the group. A better decision builder than the simple vote is the *twice-round vote*. The chair states the decision to be made and then asks group members to agree, disagree, pass, or indicate that they will not block any decision reached by the majority. Each member's decision is recorded. With the exception of those who passed, members then have a brief opportunity to explain their votes. The chair goes around the circle again, asking members to agree, disagree, or state that they will not block a majority decision. No one is allowed to pass this time. The majority decision is accepted.

The advantage of the twice-round vote is that all group members have an opportunity to hear arguments in favour of or against a certain decision and to reconsider their votes. They know that a decision must be made the second time around and that they will have to get off the fence or make up their minds. Once the majority decision is clear, all members must commit themselves to the course of action taken.

Debating in a Group

Group debates are a special kind of group presentation. First, teams of two to four people are selected. Then, a topic is chosen, one team is assigned a point of view about the topic, while the other team is assigned the opposing viewpoint. For example, if the topic is gun control, one team might be assigned the *pro* argument, "Gun control in Canada should be strengthened," while the opposing team might be assigned the *con* argument or counterargument, "Gun control in Canada should not be strengthened."

All the team members participate in the debate. Sometimes, one team member is selected as the debater, while the other members of the team carry out supporting roles such as conducting research and anticipating or rebutting the other team's arguments.

In formal debates, each side is given one or two minutes to present its side of the argument. Then the debaters argue their points back and forth. Finally, each side is given an opportunity for a closing statement. This is usually the way political debates on television are structured.

The principles of debating are the same as the principles of persuasion and argument. We discuss these in detail in Tutorial 28 of Chapter 14 on persuasive essays.

Your Turn

- Think about your own participation in groups. What roles do you typically take? Have you been a scribe, a reporter, a group chair? Are you more comfortable with some roles than with others? What roles would you like to learn to assume?

- How have you resolved disagreements or difficulties in your group? Try one of the methods suggested above—the simple majority vote, or the twice-round vote—to resolve differences the next time you work in a group situation.

- Based on your experience, what suggestions would you make for dealing with people who do not fulfill their task assignments?

Oral Presentations

At school and in your working life, you may be asked to make many different types of oral presentations. In school, you may be required to prepare an individual presentation, a group report, a seminar discussion, or a debate. As part of your job, you may undertake a presentation to clients outlining suggested plans or strategies—for example, how to advertise their product or invest their money. At a meeting, you may be asked to provide a progress report. At a family event such as a wedding you may be called upon to make a toast.

These types of oral presentations all have similar elements:

- You must research appropriate information and distill it into key ideas.

- You must present your information in language appropriate to the topic, purpose, and audience.

- You must refine your information so that it is precise and focused, fits a realistic time frame, and does not become tedious for the audience. In the case of a seminar, you must be aware of meeting the requirements of the assigned task and involving others in discussion about your topic. In a debate, there is a specific format you must follow and timelines will be very precise.

- You must speak clearly and at an even pace, using appropriate expression to emphasize your key points.

- You should guide your audience by using visual support as well as the spoken word. Some people comprehend and learn visually rather than by listening. As a presenter, you need to send your message both visually and orally to ensure that all members of the audience receive it.

Planning a Presentation

Planning an oral presentation, speech, or report is similar to planning a research essay. First, you consider your audience and purpose. Then, you research to find information that is relevant to your topic. Next, you determine a focus for your presentation and organize your ideas for impact, putting the most important ideas near the introduction or conclusion of your remarks. At the same time, you decide what language and information you will use to suit your audience. You begin your speech by giving the listener a verbal road map of where you plan to go with the topic, and you conclude by restating your most significant idea. One technique for planning and delivering a speech focuses on the following three steps:

1. Tell the audience what you are going to say.

2. Say it.

3. Tell them what you have just said.

This technique can work in the following way. Early in the presentation, make a statement such as, "Today I am going to give you one good reason to change, two changes that need to be made, and three ways you can make those changes." In the body of your speech describe these changes and the reasons for them. At the conclusion of the presentation, remind the audience, "You will recall that I gave you one good reason to change, and that was . . . I also outlined two key changes that you need to make in the next month, and those are . . . And finally, I have explained three specific ways in which you can make those changes, namely. . . ." Remember that the majority of your time will be spent on developing the body of your speech.

You should be aware that although there are similarities between preparing a speech and planning an essay, there are also differences. In a speech, you often include less of your researched information than in an essay because of time constraints. Choose the most interesting and important ideas, and organize them clearly. In a speech, use tone of voice, body language, and rhetorical devices such as pauses to emphasize your points. In an essay, rely on language to convey your points. Essays may be supported by graphics, but speeches often rely on visuals to reinforce meaning. This is particularly true of informational speeches.

Coping with Presentation Anxiety

Many people feel nervous about making oral presentations or speeches. When they speak in front of large groups of people, they may experience symptoms such as a dry mouth, or "butterflies" in the stomach.

There are a number of solutions to presentation anxiety:

- Be well prepared so that you can be confident your information will be accurate, relevant, and meaningful to the audience.

- Practise saying your speech aloud several times in front of a mirror and to a friend.

- Use cue cards, overhead slides, or a script typed in large font size so that you will not draw a blank.

- Dress appropriately for the occasion. With family and friends, you can dress in casual clothes. For business or special occasions, you should dress more formally.

- Look for opportunities to make oral presentations. The more practice you get, the easier the task will become. A good way to practise is to answer questions in the classroom, or to choose the role of reporter to present your group's analysis to the class. These types of participation will build your confidence and ease your transition from attentive listening to speaking in front of a group.

Your Turn

- Take inventory of the different kinds of speaking you have done—participation in classroom discussion, group reports, and debates, or more formal speaking at a family or school event.

- Think about your own abilities as a participant in group discussions. What are your strengths? Do you have a clear, audible voice? Do you speak with confidence? What aspects of oral presentation do you need to develop further?

Preparing Visual Supports for a Presentation

Your choice of visual supports for an oral presentation will depend on the location and size of the audience. In a class presentation to 20 people, you may use charts or outline notes on a white board effectively. In a larger room, an overhead projector or screen with overhead slides should be used. You want the audience to be able to see and read the visuals easily. Keep some of the following points in mind:

- Charts should use colour, large print, and simple illustrations or diagrams.

- Overhead slides should be few in number, just sufficient to help the audience follow the key points of your presentation.

- Video clips should be short and to the point—they should not become the show, but should support the speaker's ideas and information.

Detecting Assumptions, Omissions, and Biases

Oral speech can be a powerful tool of persuasion. When you listen to someone speak in a private one-to-one conversation, or when you are a member of a larger audience, try to hear beyond what is being said or the manner in which it is

Technological Tip

Computer presentation software such as PowerPoint can help you create a dynamic, colourful presentation. Ensure that you have the appropriate technology to run this program and that you do not create too many slides. Bring overheads as a backup precaution. Practise using the technology available for your presentation.

said. Use the following questions to analyze the content of the presentation and the manner in which it is presented:

- What are the obvious or explicit messages the speaker wishes to convey? Do you agree with these messages or with the point of view?

- Does the language in the presentation imply an assumption or a bias on the part of the speaker? For example, does the speaker use descriptive words with a negative connotation when discussing a certain group of people in society? Does the speaker's tone of voice imply scorn or outrage when speaking of certain people or situations? Do you feel this attitude can be justified?

- Has the speaker chosen to omit important facts and figures? What difference would these facts and figures make to the ideas the speaker presents?

- Is the speaker's logic reasonable, or has he or she reached a ridiculous conclusion? For example, a speaker might argue: "Smoking is a reckless and stupid activity. Twenty percent of adults smoke. Therefore, those adults are reckless and stupid." Does this logic make sense? Is it truthful based on what you know? For more on the use of logic in a debate, see Tutorial 28 in Chapter 14.

Your Turn

The next time you have an opportunity to watch a speaker make a presentation, live or on television, be conscious of the techniques he or she uses to involve the audience.

- Watch for body language and hand gestures and the use of visual aids or technology. Were they helpful or distracting?

- Listen for pace, voice volume, and expression. Was there variety? Were there appropriate emphases at certain points?

- Analyze the use of anecdotes, jokes, and rhetorical questions. Were they effective?

- Be aware of the organizational patterns of the presentation. Did they help you follow the information? Were the main points repeated at the conclusion so that you could recall them?

- Think about the level of language in the presentation. Was it suitable for the audience? Could they connect easily with the ideas?

- Evaluate the effectiveness of any visual supports. Were they helpful? Why did they work?

When listening to any presentation, you must always be aware of what you know and think about the topic. The speaker may provide you with new information that may change your point of view, but you must assess what you hear based on your previous knowledge and your own experiences. Always take time to reflect on what you have heard before you react.

Requirements of Postsecondary Education and the Workplace

College and university courses require students to listen and speak effectively in order to

- take notes in lectures

- participate in seminar discussions

- make skillful, well-researched presentations individually or in groups

Many employers will tell you that they are looking for employees who have the four Cs: competence, completion, collaboration, and communication:

1. Competence means that you have the knowledge and skills to do the job.

2. Completion means that you can take any assigned tasks to the finish line.

3. Collaboration is the ability to work as part of a team to set priorities, accomplish tasks, and reach goals.

4. Communication is the ability to listen and speak effectively to create a safe, productive work environment.

Of the four Cs, communication is most important. You can understand that communication is very important for the following reasons:

- Listening effectively means hearing information, instructions, or directions accurately the first time. Good listeners can begin their tasks quickly and accomplish them precisely.

- Listening and speaking effectively also contribute to a safe work environment. When information or instructions are precise and employees listen attentively, they can follow proper procedures and avoid injury.

- Speaking effectively allows colleagues to understand your thoughts and ideas so that you can make a significant contribution to the direction of your work.

- Speaking effectively, with respect for your audience and knowledge of their background, allows you to make successful presentations to clients.

If you work to develop competent listening and speaking skills, they will serve you well throughout your education, in the workplace, and in your personal relationships. They are worth the effort.

Media Power Tools

Media Awareness

We live in a culture that is saturated with media. Evidence of this can be found all around us—in our houses, in our cars, on the streets, in stores, on billboards, even on our clothes and accessories. Much of the media we experience is delivered to us electronically, via our television sets, computers, CD players, and telephones.

Electronics have given us the freedom to control the media we consume. We now have the freedom to rewind and replay videos, to fast forward through commercials, and tape our favourite programs for later viewing. But, ironically, although people have this newfound freedom and control, they do not always exercise their right to be critical consumers. How many times have you found yourself looking at a TV program, a commercial, or an advertisement on a bus without thinking about what you were watching? This section of the text gives you some tips on how to improve your media awareness. It also provides insight into marketing, distribution, and production methods used by the media.

Evaluating Media Messages

All media carry underlying messages, whether they are creative media, such as films and CDs, or persuasive media such as advertisements. Many of these messages are presented as symbols or as conventions. When we see a symbol or a convention, our mind automatically makes a connection to something else—to a particular situation, a product, or a television program, for example. In your journal or on a piece of paper, jot down your first responses to the symbols or conventions in the chart on the following page. Then find a partner and compare your responses.

We respond in similar ways to these situations because we have seen them happen the same way over and over again in the media. We expect the man wearing the eye patch and the cowboy hat to be a villain because we have seen him countless times in Western films. We expect the man and the woman in the restaurant to be romantically involved because we have seen this situation before too; we even know the kind of music that is probably playing in the background.

Men and women who work in the media know how people typically respond to messages. They categorize entertainment into different formulas, group people into different consumer audiences, and target particular products or media to these

INVENTORY OF SYMBOL RESPONSES	
SYMBOL OR CONVENTION	YOUR RESPONSE
A shot on the news of bouquets of flowers laid against an iron railing in front of a house	
A shot from a film of a man sporting a black eye patch, wearing a cowboy hat, and carrying a gun	
A scene from a television program of a young man and woman having dinner in the quiet corner of a restaurant, with a candle and bottle of wine on the table	
A woman with a white mustache made from milk	
A beautiful woman wearing sunglasses and driving a sports car around a hairpin turn, her hair and a white scarf flying out behind her	
Five gunmen cornering the hero in the first scene of an action film	

audiences. Television series, for example, are targeted to particular audiences; they are projected to bring in millions of viewers and advertisers; sponsors buy space according to those projections. Not surprisingly, advertisers and sponsors are concerned, first and foremost, with the number of people who watch the programs (and their advertisements). Without advertisers, commercial television would not exist.

Your Turn

Interview a parent or grandparent. Ask them how they experienced media 20, 30, or 40 years ago. Specifically, ask them to tell you about

- their television viewing then compared with now

- how they viewed films then compared with now

- how advertising has changed

- how the way they listen to music has changed

Becoming a Critical Media Consumer

The first step in becoming a critical media consumer is to be aware of how the media manipulate us. If you actively look for underlying messages in a media text, you will find them. (A *media text* refers to any product of the mass media, including advertisements, films, and television.) The more you actively look for messages, the more you will notice the conventions and symbols used by the media. Below is a list of questions to help you become a more critical consumer. For more details on evaluating advertisements critically, see Chapter 15 on advertising.

The media text and the message:

- What is the underlying message?

- Are symbols or conventions used to convey the message?

- If there is a story, does it follow a pattern or formula that you recognize?

- If people are portrayed in the media text, do you detect any stereotypes, or do the people seem realistic?

The audience:

- What is the target audience for the media message?

- How might other audiences—outside the target groups—respond to the media text and message?

- What is your response to the text and the message? Are you a member of the target audience?

The production:

- Who created the media text?

- How do you think the media text was made?

- How is the media text distributed or sold to the public?

- How much do you think the media text cost to make?

- Who will make money from the media text? How will that money be used?

Your Turn

Choose one of your favourite television series. Using the questions above, analyze a program from that series. Did you consider aspects of the program that you had not thought about before? Did your opinion of the series change as you completed this activity?

Media Production Techniques

To become a critical media consumer, you need to become familiar with media production techniques. In this section, we briefly discuss the basics of film production. Some of these techniques can be applied to other media as well. As you read this section, refer to the box on pages 339 to 340, which explains some key film terminology.

Pre-Production

Conceptualization phase. Most films begin with a story idea. During the pre-production phase, screenwriters are hired to write the screenplay, the story is developed, and various components of the film are conceptualized. Typically, the story is visually mapped out on a storyboard, which demonstrates the shot selection, framing, composition, angle, and point of view.

Financing and budgeting. The producer arranges for financing and establishes a budget. Once a budget is established, a crew and actors can be hired and locations can be chosen. Filmmakers on smaller budgets have to be creative in their use of locations and their choice of actors.

Planning details. Before filming can begin, the smallest details must be in place. For example, every shot is mapped out on a breakdown script. The breakdown script ensures that precise details continue from shot to shot: for example, if an actor is wearing a bracelet for one shot, she must have the same bracelet on the same wrist when the action continues the next day. Other items that must be planned and prepared are sets and locations.

Production

Filming. The director of photography or cinematographer interprets the director's vision and works with the camera crew to record the shots, scenes, and sequences from which the film will be constructed. He or she selects the shot, the camera angle, the lens, the focus, the framing, and the lighting of each shot. Some special effects, such as those requiring stunts, are filmed during production; others are added during the post-production phase.

Sound. Only dialogue is recorded during production. Other sounds are added to the film during the post-production phase.

Post-Production

Editing. Without editing, films would be a series of shots filmed in haphazard order. The editor, in consultation with the director of photography and the director, reshapes and reorders the shots, scenes, and sequences filmed by the camera crew.

Dubbing. During sound dubbing, all non-dialogue sound is added to the film, including background sounds. Mixers control the sound effects and blend them into the dialogue. Computerized special effects may also be added at this stage.

Music. Some films have original scores; others have a soundtrack of carefully selected music. The music is added during the post-production phase.

Marketing and Distribution

Marketing. The marketing for a feature film often begins before the post-production phase is complete. Coming-attraction trailers are made, and detailed marketing plans present strategies for appealing to the target market. In the case of blockbuster films such as *The Lion King,* the producers strike deals with numerous companies to make stuffed animals, clothes, and all manner of items that help promote the film.

Sneak previews. The marketing strategies for a film may change after sneak previews are held before a film is released. Invited to these previews are individuals of all ages, sexes, and ethnic backgrounds, as well as a select group of reviewers. Filmmakers use the audience reaction at sneak previews to pinpoint a target market for their film. Then they adapt their marketing plan accordingly.

Distribution. Big-budget feature films are distributed to more than 2000 screens throughout North America. Small-budget films and art films are typically released only to a select number of screens. Depending on the reaction to the film, they may then be released to a larger number of screens.

Classification. All feature films must be classified by provincial film classification boards prior to public screening in Canada. For the classification codes in your province, consult The Media Awareness Network at <www.media-awareness.ca>.

Impact of New Technologies on Production and Distribution

Production. New computer technologies are transforming the way films and other media are made. Filmmakers can now make large parts of their films without setting up a shoot. Special effects have been revolutionized through the use of digital imagery. *Jurassic Park* was one of the first films to exploit the new digital technology—instead of building model dinosaurs, special-effects experts used computers to create digital images of dinosaurs that were then integrated into the film.

Distribution. Converging technologies have affected the business side of filmmaking. Large corporations such as Disney and Warner have built up multimedia empires consisting of film and video companies, television studios, publishing companies, computer companies, and even telephone companies. Executives at these companies foresee a future in which all media will be digitized and information and entertainment will be delivered into our homes via phone lines.

Your Turn

In a group, research production techniques used in either live television or the music industry. How do the production techniques in the industry you chose differ from the process described above?

In a group, research the impact of digital technology and the convergence of media ownership. Prepare a presentation for the class in which you imagine how we will experience media 25 years from now.

Film Terminology

Cut. A cut comes at the end of a shot, and indicates the change from one shot to the next. It may be a gradual fade or dissolve, or a sudden cut.

Scene. A scene is a series of shots all related to one part of the action or an event. For example, one scene may take place in a restaurant, the next out in the parking lot, and the next in the car as it leaves the parking lot.

Sequence. A sequence is a series of scenes all related to one topic or event, with a clear beginning and ending. For example, a typical car chase in an action movie is made up of a series of scenes of the chase.

Shot. A shot is the action recorded in one run by one camera, without interruption or change in point of view. In a conversation between two characters, one shot may show the face of one of the characters; the next shot may show the face of the second character.

Continued on next page

Consider the differences among the following specific types of shots.

- **Close-up (CU):** The camera is very close to the subject; you would see only a character's head and shoulders.

- **High angle:** The camera looks down at the subject.

- **Long shot (LS):** The camera is a long way from the subject; you would see a character—or several characters—and the surrounding scenery.

- **Low angle:** The camera looks up at the subject.

- **Medium shot (MS):** The camera is halfway between a CU and a LS; you would see a character's head and most of the body.

- **Normal or straight angle:** The camera looks straight at the subject.

- **Point of view (POV):** The camera shows what the character would see from his or her point of view. For example, a camera might show only what a character sees as she walks from the room.

- **Tracking or follow shot:** The camera follows the action of the subject. For example, it would follow a character getting up from her seat and walking out of a room.

Evaluating Films, Videos, and Television Dramas

This section offers strategies you can use for evaluating films, videos, and television programs.

Personal Response

When you evaluate a film, video, or television program, always consider your personal response, and do not underestimate your own opinion. Ask yourself why you liked or did not like the film or program. Was it something about the specific program that you did not like? Or, is it simply that you do not typically enjoy this type of program? Think about your favourite and least favourite moments. Did your opinion change when you thought about the program after you had seen it?

In order to respond critically to a film or a television program, you really need to see it at least twice. The first time concentrate on the story, the characters, and the action. The second time look more closely at shot selection, camera angles, cinematography, and editing, and listen carefully to the soundtrack.

Dramatic Quality

When evaluating a film or program's dramatic quality, consider those elements that are common to most dramatic works: theme, plot, mood, and character development. You also need to evaluate it in context. If, for example, you were evaluating an action film like *The Matrix*, you would need to consider how well it compares with other action films. You would not, however, compare it with *Shakespeare in Love* or a television situation comedy. Similarly, if you were assessing an episode of *Friends*, you would need to consider how well it compares with other situation comedies like *Frasier* or *Will and Grace*.

Direction

The director is responsible for the overall quality of the film, video, or television program. A director may have a brilliant cinematographer, but unless he or she can blend all the thematic, visual, and sound elements of the drama together, it will not be a success. Here are some questions to ask when considering the quality of the direction:

- Does the film or program achieve its objectives? If it was meant to be funny, did you find it funny? If it was meant to be sad, were you moved by it?

- Do the cinematography, editing, and sound clarify the theme, establish the mood, enhance the plot, or help to reveal character development?

- Is the film or program original—its shots, camera angles, images, sound, or characters? Or does it strike you as being conventional?

Acting

One of the first things you notice when you watch a film is the actors. The quality of acting is crucial to the success of a film. How can you tell if someone can act? Here are some things to watch for:

- Do the actors speak naturally, as people speak in real life? Are they convincing?

- Do the actors stay in character, or do they occasionally seem to become a different person or to lapse into a different style of acting?

- Do you care about the characters?

- If the actor is speaking with an accent, is the accent realistic or does it sound forced and unnatural?

- Does the actor become the character he or she is portraying? Can you forget that you are watching Kevin Costner or Bruce Willis or Julia Roberts?

- Does the actor have a full or limited range of facial expressions?

- Are the actors able to convey emotion without overacting?

- Are they able to make you feel a certain way—can they make you laugh or feel sad or, perhaps, angry?

Screenplay

The script of a film, video, or television program is usually called a screenplay, and the writer of the script is known as a screenwriter. It is sometimes difficult to distinguish the quality of the acting from the quality of the screenplay. Even great actors have difficulty delivering cliché-ridden or melodramatic lines, or making stereotypic characters come alive. Here are some ways to distinguish the quality of the acting from the quality of the screenplay:

- Is the dialogue itself unrealistic or exaggerated, or is the actor's delivery problematic? Would people in real life use those words? Try to imagine an actor you admire delivering the same lines. How would that actor handle the role?

- Does all the acting in the film seem poor? This often indicates a weak script rather than poor acting.

- Are the characters real, or do you notice any stereotypes among them?

- Do the characters behave in conventional, predictable ways? Are any of them original?

Cinematography

When evaluating the cinematography, consider the composition of the shots and scenes, shot selection, and camera angles. Often we watch films, videos, and television without even considering how the camera is used, even when we are watching something for a second time. If you focus on the shot selection from the very first shot, you will notice things that you usually take for granted. Here are some questions to ask about the cinematography:

- How does the composition of each shot help to convey meaning?

- Why did the cinematographer choose to use that particular shot, from that angle? How does it enhance your understanding of the film—of the plot, of the theme, of the characters?

- Is there variety in the types of shots and camera angles?

- Is there anything that stands out about the shots, angles, scenes, and sequences?

Editing

Editors have to put themselves in the shoes of their audience. They have to ask themselves: Will my audience understand what is happening? Am I giving away too much of the plot? Does this sequence help my audience understand this character's motivation? Here are some things to look for when evaluating the quality of the editing:

- Do the transitions between shots and scenes enable you to follow the action?

- Are the transitions seamless? For example, does a shot of flowers on a table flow seamlessly into the next shot of wildflowers in a field?

- Is there a purpose for sudden, jarring cuts?

- Are images placed side by side or in sequence for a purpose, or does their placement seem accidental? For example, if a violent image suddenly appears after a scene of tranquility, does this say something about the meaning of the film?

- If there is something I do not understand, could this be because the director is holding something back on purpose? There may be abrupt shifts and gaps in the editing to set the scene for an unexpected twist.

- Are there any scenes that seem unnecessary or superfluous to the plot or to character development?

- Is the film an appropriate length? Do you think it should have been shorter or longer?

Design and Lighting

Design in a film, video, or television program includes art direction, scenic composition, set and costume design, and makeup. Lighting is also a very important part of the visual experience of all three media, particularly of film. Ask yourself these questions about design and lighting:

- How do the design elements—the visual aspect of the scenes, the set, the costumes, and the makeup—work together as a whole? Are they unified, or do things seem out of place? How well do the design elements fit with the story and the script?

- How do the design elements contribute to the mood or atmosphere of the film? Do they tell you anything about the characters?

- Are the design elements authentic? For example, in a period piece, are they appropriate to the era?

- How does the lighting contribute to the mood? Are shadows and contrasts used to indicate character development? (Lighting can be particularly important in black-and-white films.)

Sound

Sound includes dialogue, background sounds, sound effects, and music. Sometimes we are so involved with watching a story unfold that we forget to listen to it. Have you ever looked at the credits, only to find there was a song played in the film that you do not remember hearing? If you are watching a film or a television program, try closing your eyes and listening to the sound. See if you can identify the different types of sound in the film. Here are some questions to help you evaluate a film's soundtrack:

- Is sound (and music) used to enhance the drama, or does the film or program rely too much on sound to create drama?

- How effectively is sound (and music) used to establish the mood of a scene, create suspense, or reflect the feelings of a character?

- How effectively is sound (and music) used as a foreshadowing device? (See page 88 in Chapter 7 for more on foreshadowing.)

- Are the different sounds that make up the soundtrack mixed at volumes that can be heard?

- In a television comedy, is a laugh track used or is the laughter real?

- Why do you think the music director chose that particular musical score?

Special Effects

Some films have no special effects; others would be insubstantial without the special effects. If the film you are evaluating has special effects, consider the following questions:

- Are the special effects convincing?

- Are they of even quality?

- What purpose do special effects serve in the scene where they are used? Do the special effects overpower the film?

Your Turn

Choose a film and a television program that both tell a similar story. For example, you might select an episode of a television drama and a film that are both about the police investigation of a murder. Use some of the questions above to evaluate both the film and the program. Note the differences and similarities in the way the two media handle the same subject.

Writing a Film Review

Like other types of writing, the form and content of a film review are determined by audience and purpose. Consider the following key elements before you become a film critic in Your Turn.

- **Audience for the review:** Someone who has not seen the film, but who is considering seeing it.

- **Purpose of the review:** The purpose is to summarize, analyze, and evaluate the film, and to recommend the film, criticize it, or dismiss it entirely. Keep in mind that you should never give away any element of the plot that could spoil your reader's enjoyment of the film. For example, you could say that there is a twist at the end, but you must be sure not to explain the twist.

- **Style and tone:** Film reviews should be written in an informal style. Usually, they are written in a matter-of-fact tone. Occasionally, however, if a film reviewer is highly critical of a film, he or she will use a sarcastic or scathing tone. When discussing the film, always use the present tense.

- **Introductory paragraph:** Identify the name of the film, the director, and the main actors. You could say something about the reputation of the director, and mention any previous films for which he or she is known. If the screenwriter is a notable person, you could also mention his or her name and reputation. You might go on to discuss the purpose of the film: is it an action film, a children's cartoon, a romantic comedy, a murder mystery, or a historic drama? You would then conclude this paragraph with a statement about the film's success or lack of success when considered in light of its purpose.

- **Second paragraph:** You could start this paragraph by providing a brief plot summary and a description of the characters, being careful not to give away the ending. Then you could finish this paragraph with an evaluation of the plot.

- **Third paragraph:** This paragraph could be devoted to the characters and the acting. Are the characters believable? Does the main character (or characters) change during the course of the film? Are the characters rounded or are they flat and lifeless? What is your opinion of the actors' interpretation of the characters? If there are problems with the acting, is it because of the screenplay, the direction, or the actors themselves?

- **Fourth paragraph:** You could discuss and evaluate the technical aspects of the film—the cinematography, editing, design, lighting, and soundtrack. Be sure to mention the film's theme and mood, and how the visuals and soundtrack either support and enhance them or detract from them.

- **Fifth paragraph:** If the book is adapted from a novel or a short story, you could compare the film with the original. Has the director been faithful to the vision of the book? Does the screenplay successfully capture the book's theme, mood, and characters?

- **Sixth paragraph:** Give your overall assessment of the film. How do the various components work together? What are the film's strong and weak points? Support your opinions with examples. You could end your review with a recommendation about whether or not to see the film. (You could also include a star rating, with five stars meaning outstanding and no stars meaning abysmal.)

Your Turn

- Write a film review of a film you have seen at the movie theatre or on video. It is a good idea to see the film twice in order to notice the technical aspects.

- With a group, plan and prepare a short video of no more than two minutes on a subject of your choice. It could be a documentary, a commercial, or a brief skit. Assign group members various roles: one can be the writer and the editor; one the cinematographer and the art director; another the sound technician; and so on. Follow these steps in preparing your video:

  – Plan your video, keeping your audience and purpose in mind.

  – Prepare a screenplay and a storyboard for the video.

  – Consider the composition, shot selection, and camera angle of each shot.

  – Rehearse each scene before you begin filming.

  – Edit the film, and reshoot anything with which you are not happy.

Index

characters and, 66–67
first person, 54, 60–61, 76
limited omniscient, 53, 60–61
narrative, 46–47
in novels, 60–61
objective, 53–54, 60–61
omniscient, 53, 60–61
in poems, 76
in short stories, 46–47, 53–55
third person, 76
Postsecondary education
communication in, 332–33
Pratt, E.J., 74
Preferences vs. judgements, 201
Prefixes, 38, 39
Presentations. *See* Oral presentations
Problem and solution, in essays,
133–34
Procedures
audience of, 149, 150
conclusions in, 147, 150
defined, 140
definitions in, 146
diagrams in, 147, 150, 151
editing of, 151
elements of, 140
materials for, 146, 149–50
purpose of, 149
reading, 141
revising of, 151
role-playing of, 151
safety considerations, 150
steps of, 147, 150
titles of, 146, 149
tone of, 149
unfamiliar terms in, 150
writing, 149–51
Pronouns
editing, 308
references, 311–12
Proofreading, 307
defined, 304
letters of application, 242
narrative essays, 28
Propositions
in editorials, 196, 201, 203–205
in persuasive essays, 206
Protagonists, 46

Publication
date of, 264
of writing, 315–16
Punctuation
editing, 309
of poems, 80
Puns, 78
Purpose
of debates, 216
of editorials, 203–204
of film reviews, 345
of graphics, 158
of literary essays, 57
of narrative essays, 25
of procedures, 149
of reports, 188
of writing, 281–84

Quotation marks, 309
Quotations, in essays, 84

Reader Response Journals, 56–57,
277
Reading. *See also* Rereading
advertisements, 221
for appreciation, 251
biography, 31
comprehension, monitoring of,
255–56
descriptive essays, 5
drama, 88–89, 261
editorials, 197
for enjoyment, 250–51
fiction, 260
genres, 260–61
graphics, 153
for information, 251–52
informational essays, 123
letters of application, 232–33
longer works, 265–70
narration, 261
narrative essays, 14–15
non-fiction, 260, 261, 268–70
note taking and, 160, 161
novels, 61, 266–68
pace of, 252–56
persuasive essays, 207
poems, 73, 261, 266–68

predicting content, 256–60
prior knowledge in, 257
procedures, 141
purpose for, 250–52
reports, 177
short stories, 47, 56
textbooks, 260, 261–62
Refutations, 213
Repairing Lamps, 155
Repetitive arguments, 217–18
Reports, 121
audience of, 188
defined, 176
drafts of, 189–91
elements of, 176–77
graphics in, 189
group research plan, 191
headings in, 189
order of ideas, 189
outline of, 188–89
purpose of, 188
reading, 177
types of, 188
visual clues in, 185–87
writing, 188–91
Rereading, 255–56
Research
note taking and, 161, 169–75
plans, 288
Resolution, in drama, 88
Revising
defined, 304
descriptive passages, 8–9
first drafts, 26–27
graphics, 159
letters of application, 235–38
narrative essays, 24–29
procedures, 151
sentences, 28
words, 28
writing, 303–15
Rhyme, 79
Rhythm, 79
Richler, Mordechai, 62
Ringwood, Gwen Pharis, 90
Rising action, 46, 88
Roots, of words, 38, 39
Run-on sentences, 310–11

ACKNOWLEDGEMENTS

Text

pp. 6-7 Dorey, Nancy. "The Skier." <u>Contest: Essays for Canadian Students</u>. 3rd ed. Toronto: Harcourt, 1998: 27-28. pp. 16-21 Geddes, Carol. "Growing Up Native." Copyright © 1990 by Carol Geddes. Reprinted by permission of the author. pp. 32-36 Gildiner, Catherine. "Roy." <u>Too Close to the Falls</u>. Toronto: ECW, 1999. pp. 43-45 Trudeau, Justin. "Eulogy for Pierre Trudeau." <u>National Post</u>. 4 Oct. 2000: B5. Reprinted by permission of Justin Trudeau. pp. 48-52 Buckler, Ernest. "Long, Long After School." <u>The Rebellion of Young David and Other Stories</u>. Toronto: McClelland & Stewart, 1975. pp. 62-65 Richler, Mordecai. <u>The Apprenticeship of Duddy Kravitz</u>. Toronto: McClelland & Stewart, 1989. Used by permission. p. 72 <u>Canadian Oxford Paperback Dictionary</u>. p. 74 Pratt, E.J. "A November Landscape." Reprinted by permission of University of Toronto Press. p. 75 Livesay, Dorothy. "Winter." p. 78 Cloutier, Cécile. "Birth." <u>The Poetry of Modern Quebec</u>. Ed. Fred Cogswell. Montreal: Harvest House Ltd., 1976. p. 78 Perrine, Laurence. "Two Brothers Devised What at Sight." <u>A Limerick's Always a Verse: 200 Original Limericks</u>. Copyright © 1990 by Harcourt Inc. Reprinted by permission. pp. 90-107 Ringwood, Gwen Pharis. "Still Stands the House." <u>The Collected Plays of Gwen Pharis Ringwood</u>. Ed. Enid Delgatty Rutland. Ottawa: Borealis Press, 1982. p. 112 Frost, Robert. "Stopping by Woods on a Snowy Evening." <u>The Poetry of Robert Frost</u>. Ed. Edward Connery Lathem. Copyright © Robert Frost. Reprinted by permission of Henry Holt & Co. p. 113 Browning, Robert. "Meeting at Night." p. 113 Lowell, Amy. "The Taxi." <u>The Complete Poetical Works of Amy Lowell</u>. Copyright © 1955 by Houghton Mifflin Company. Copyright © renewed 1983 by Houghton Mifflin Company, Brinton P. Roberts, and G. D'Andelot Belin, Esquire. Reprinted by permission of Houghton Mifflin Company. All rights reserved. p. 114 Oodgeroo of the Tribe Noonuccal. "We Are Going." <u>My People</u>. 3rd ed. Copyright © The Jacaranda Press, 1990. Reproduced by permission of John Wiley & Sons, Australia. p. 115 Angelou, Maya. "Africa." <u>Oh Pray My Wings Are Gonna Fit Me Well</u>. New York: Randon House Inc., 1975. Used by permission of Random House, Inc. pp. 116-120 Achebe, Chinua. "Marriage Is a Private Affair." <u>Girls at War and Other Stories</u>. Copyright © 1972, 1973 by Chinua Achebe. Reprinted by permission of Heinemann Educational Books. p. 124-130 Shulman, Polly. "Blowing the Whistle on Concussions." <u>Scientific American Presents</u>. 11.3 (2000): 44-51. p. 132 Middleton, Don. "American Black Bears." 1997. <u>The Bear Den</u>. 3 Nov. 2000. <http://nature-net.com/bears/black.html> pp. 147-148 Gookin, Dan. "Boxing in Small Bits of Text or Paragraphs." <u>Word 2000 for Windows for Dummies</u>. Foster City, CA: Hungry Minds Inc., 2000: 232-233. p. 154 Watkins, John. "Deaf Rock Star." Home Page. July 2000. 26 Nov. 2000. <http://dreamwater.net.deafrockstar/>. p. 154 "Loud Music." <u>Biology in Action</u>. Harcourt, 1992: 318-319. p. 155 "Repairing Lamps." <u>Basic Wiring</u>. Menlo Park, CA: Sunset Books, 1995: 34-35. pp. 162-165 Krueger, Ralph, Ray Corder, and John Koegler. <u>This Land of Ours: A New Geography of Canada</u>. Ed. Ralph Krueger, Ray Corder, and John Koegler. Toronto: Harcourt (HBJ), 1991: 242-244, 365. pp. 192-194 Uniya, Miki. "The Cellular Phone Virus in Japan." <u>Contest</u>. 3rd ed. Ed. McArthur. Toronto: Harcourt, 1998: 126-128. pp. 198-200 Wente, Margaret. "Medical Care That's Not Even Fit for a Horse." <u>The Globe and Mail Web Centre</u>. 14 Oct. 2000. 18 Oct. 2000. <http://archives.theglobeandmail.com/s97i...ts%26ResultStart%3DI% 26ResultCount%3D10&> Reprinted with permission from The Globe and Mail. pp. 222-223 Reproduced by permission of Audi America, Inc. pp. 244-246 Fontaine, Phil. "For Canada and First Nations." <u>The Globe and Mail</u>. 9 June 1997. Reprinted by permission of the author. pp. 246-247 Baird, Vanessa. "Spiked! News from Developing Nations." <u>Mass Media and Popular Culture</u>. Ed. Duncan et al. Harcourt, 1998.

Photographs

p. 33 ECW Press; p. 49 Paul Hoeffler; p. 65 Canadian Press/Moe Doiron; p. 125 Ezra Shaw/Allsport Photo; p. 176 Bruce Ayres/Stone; p. 220 British Columbia Lung Association; p. 222-223 Reproduced with permission by Audi America Inc.

Illustrations

Nathalie Dion: p. 7; Carey Sookocheff: p. 17; Mélanie Baillairgé: p. 75; Isabelle Cardinal: p. 91; Jock MacRae: pp. 145, 155; Kathryn Adams: p. 168.

Cover Illustration and Icons

Lyse-Anne Roy